TRANSFORMATIONS IN SELF PSYCHOLOGY

PROGRESS IN SELF PSYCHOLOGY
VOLUME 20

PROGRESS IN SELF PSYCHOLOGY
EDITOR, WILLIAM J. COBURN, PH.D., PSY.D.

Contributors: Please submit your original manuscript (double-spaced, including references, footnotes, quoted passages, and dialogue) via e-mail as an attached file in MS Word, WordPerfect, or RTF format to Progress@psychologyoftheself.com. The manuscript style and format should conform to The Analytic Press guidelines (found in the *Progress in Self Psychology* section of the Psychology of the Self website at www.psychologyoftheself.com).

TRANSFORMATIONS IN SELF PSYCHOLOGY

PROGRESS IN SELF PSYCHOLOGY
VOLUME 20

WILLIAM J. COBURN
EDITOR

THE ANALYTIC PRESS

2004   Hillsdale, NJ   London

© 2004 by The Analytic Press
101 West Street
Hillsdale, NJ 07642

ISBN 0-88163-374-7
ISSN 0893-5483

Printed in the United States of America
10 9 8 7 6 5 4 3 2 1

This volume of *Progress in Self Psychology*
is dedicated in loving memory to
John Lindon, M.D.
(March 11, 1924–January 31, 2004)

CONTENTS

CONTRIBUTORS

Peter Buirski, Ph.D. is Dean of the Graduate School of Professional Psychology at the University of Denver.

Melanie L. Burke, L.C.S.W., Psy.D. is Member, Institute of Contemporary Psychoanalysis, Los Angeles.

Michael D. Clifford, M.Div., C.S.W. is Faculty and Supervisor, National Institute for the Psychotherapies, New York City; Co-Founding former Director, Program in Child and Adolescent Psychoanalysis, NIP.

Margaret Crastnopol, Ph.D. is Faculty and Supervisor of Psychotherapy, William Alanson White Institute, New York City; Faculty, Northwest Center for Psychoanalysis.

Stan T. Dudley, Ph.D. is Educational Director, Cincinnati Center for Self Psychology.

James L. Fosshage, Ph.D. is President, International Council for Psychoanalytic Self Psychology and Founding Faculty Member, Institute for the Psychoanalytic Study of Subjectivity, New York City.

Paula B. Fuqua, M.D. is Faculty, Institute for Psychoanalysis, Chicago and Associate Editor, *Progress in Self Psychology*.

Virginia Goldner, Ph.D. is Associate Clinical Professor of Psychology, New York University Postdoctoral Program in Psychotherapy and Psychoanalysis; and Founding Editor, *Studies in Gender and Sexuality*.

Hans-Peter Hartmann, M.D., Ph.D. is Member, Institute of Psychoanalysis and Psychotherapy, Giessen, Germany; Lecturer for Psychoanalytic Psychology at the University of Giessen; and Member, International Council on the Psychology of the Self.

Sally A. Howard, Ph.D., Psy.D. is Vice President, Faculty, and Training and Supervising Analyst, Institute of Contemporary Psychoanalysis, Los Angeles.

Jennifer Leighton, C.S.W. is Supervisor and Training Analyst, Harlem Family Institute; formerly Faculty, Supervisor, and Training Analyst, Training Institute for Mental Health; and Member of EMDRIA SIG, New York City.

Arthur Malin, M.D. is Clinical Professor of Psychiatry, UCLA School of Medicine; Training and Supervising Analyst, Southern California Psychoanalytic Institute and Los Angeles Psychoanalytic Society and Institute.

Carol A. Munschauer, Ph.D. is President, Psychoanalytic Society of Upstate New York and Clinical Assistant Professor, Department of Psychiatry, State University of New York, Buffalo School of Medicine.

Stuart D. Perlman, Ph.D. is a training analyst and member of the Board of Directors at the Institute of Contemporary Psychoanalysis in Los Angeles.

Lynn Preston, M.A., M.S. is Faculty, Institute for Contemporary Psychotherapy and the Training and Research Institute for Self Psychology, New York City.

Luis A. Rubalcava, Ph.D. is Associate Professor, Department of Educational Psychology and Counseling, California State University, Northridge.

Ellen Shumsky, C.S.W. is Faculty and Supervisor, Institute for Contemporary Psychotherapy and the Training and Research Institute for Self Psychology, New York City.

Steven Stern, Psy.D. is faculty member at the Chicago Institute for Psychoanalysis.

Jeffrey L. Trop, M.D. is Training and Supervising Analyst; Faculty, Institute of Contemporary Psychoanalysis, Los Angeles; and Assistant Professor of Psychiatry, UCLA School of Medicine.

Nancy VanDerHeide, Psy.D. is Faculty, Institute of Contemporary Psychoanalysis, Los Angeles.

Kenneth Waldman, Ph.D. is adjunct instructor, Antioch University and Union Institute, Los Angeles.

Todd F. Walker, Psy.D. is Adjunct Professor, School of Professional Psychology, Wright State University, Dayton, Ohio.

Joye Weisel-Barth, Ph.D., Psy.D. is Member and Faculty, Institute of Contemporary Psychoanalysis, Los Angeles.

INTRODUCTION

WILLIAM J. COBURN

*T*his introduction has as its point of departure the rich, complex, and controversial history of psychoanalysis and in particular the continuing evolution of psychoanalytic self psychology. The previous 19 volumes of *Progress in Self Psychology* embody much of this history. Controversial partly because Heinz Kohut had the courage to be himself in challenging the doctrinaire traditional drive/structure models so prevalent in the first half of the twentieth century. Controversial because many of his ideas threatened his colleagues' sense of what they felt to be subjectively true and real. And controversial because ideas, once spoken or written, are subject(ed) to interpretation. As we witness the strong presence of creative theorizing within the pages of past volumes of *Progress in Self Psychology*, we are treated also to a great deal of argument—argument mostly born out of a passion for ideas and for transformative dialogue.

A continuing series of revolutions within a revolution, contemporary psychoanalytic self psychology has great theoretical breadth. I was reminded of this as I read and reread the evocative contributions that comprise this recent offering, the twentieth volume of *Progress*. In these pages, we witness not just the elaboration and, at times, the syncretism of several essential themes, such as enactment, trauma, multiculturalism, countertransference, relationality, shame, contextualism, and listening perspectives, but also the human struggles that bring these themes to life in the context of working with patients under challenging circumstances. We witness the rich pluralism in psychoanalysis that enlivens as well as perplexes. But in addition, this theoretical breadth now encompasses ideas about emotional experience, human development, and therapeutic action not originally accessible to traditional self psychology, ideas informed by the contemporary stretching of other disciplines such as infant research, attachment theory, relational theory, complexity theory, and neuroscience. For illumination or for bemusement, these added narratives have infiltrated psychoanalytic self psychology, inexorably transforming the way we think and the languages we embody.

In the context of the greater psychoanalytic community, Heinz Kohut underscored and elaborated, among other things, a theory (and a practice) of personal lived experience. For some, he provided someone to follow, to learn from, to emulate; for others, someone to question, and at times to oppose, as one means of developing new ideas. I like Phillips's (2001) comment, in considering the relationship between literature and psychoanalysis, that "people who love psychoanalysis can teach it, write it, read it, *and* practice it." Because we can *practice* what a psychoanalyst writes about, he wonders "by the same token, what it would be to practice Henry James or Shakespeare" (p. 366). Kohut's implicit focus, because of his emphasis on the uniqueness of an individual's lived emotional experience, is what it would be to *practice oneself*. In other words, out of all the ideas today that infiltrate, at times subvert, the self psychology of Heinz Kohut *and* those that in reverse fashion are profoundly influenced *by* his thinking, I am continually drawn to those that do not emphasize solely the establishment and elaboration of the patient's sense of personal freedom, but those that underscore that of the analyst as well. That is, psychoanalytic practice means to practice one's (clinical) self, to be oneself, in the context of living within psychoanalytic relationships. Practicing ourselves, as clinicians with individual sensibilities (and responsibilities), emerges not out of thoughtless adherence to something cherished, nor from mindless devaluation of something opposed, but out of a concerted and playful contemplation of the rich variety of perspectives increasingly available to us. As Kohut (1984) made explicit, "what is required is the testing, with the aid of detailed clinical observations, of the various claims that I have made" (p. 100). In doing so, we benefit—as we would in any context in which ideologies and personal loyalties comprise a portion of the landscape—from questioning at which point the vitality of playful opposition, and the occasional needed subversion, slide into simple rancor and plain rebellion for rebellion's sake. And at which point does respect and admiration for the utility of a pioneer's ideas descend into simple loyalism or into a blind adherence to the dictates of a theory? Of course answers to these questions are as unique as the individuals who ask them.

This *Progress* volume implicitly explores the bidirectionality of influences between our core self-psychological theorizing and other paradigms that offer equally compelling narratives about human experiencing and the relationships that give rise to it. I say *implicitly* because this theme was not one of design but rather emerged from the independent, though now combined efforts of the contributing authors, many of whom are clearly influenced by the bidirectional impact of competing theoretical forces to which we are increasingly exposed.

A striking example, Stern attempts to confront the potential syncretism in psychoanalytic self psychology and relational theory in his examination of how they conceptualize transference–countertransference enactments. Here Stern proposes two theoretical bridges, one based on contrasting conceptualizations of the unconscious—what he refers to as the "yin and yang of unconscious experience." The other theoretical bridge involves the expansion of our current understanding of self and interactional regulation. His chapter indeed helps to bridge this conceptual gap, highlighting one of our more demanding controversies.

In a similar vein, one particularly evocative exchange (by Fosshage and Munschauer, Fuqua, Trop and Burke, Crastnopol, and then Fosshage and Munschauer in response) centers on several pivotal concepts in contemporary self psychology, not the least of which is the meaning and role of what is often referred to as *enactment*. This term has increasingly insinuated itself into our self psychology lexicon, despite the fact that many of its original meanings are in some ways antithetical to a self psychological sensibility (though Kohut himself used the term vis-à-vis resistance). *Enactment* is seldom considered a value-neutral concept (though I think it should be), sometimes understood as clinical or self-selfobject phenomena to be avoided or repaired via the restitution of a selfobject tie, and in other instances conceptualized as the centerpiece of the (therapeutic) action. Alongside *enactment*, we witness the palpable tension between perspectives centered on the empathy/authenticity dichotomy, which tension is resolved by some (see Orange, 2002) who hold that the dichotomy itself is illusory. Each of these authors courageously tackles these issues in the context of challenging clinical circumstances.

This volume also underscores our increasing interest in and redefining of gender and sexuality (the topic of the 2002 International Conference on The Psychology of The Self). These themes, along with the invariable countertransference reflections and (sometimes) explicit disclosures that accompany them in the consultation room, thread their way through a variety of chapters, I think most explicitly found in the exchanges between Clifford and Goldner and between VanDerHeide and Hartmann. Goldner's chapter, in particular, explores "the intersubjective act of naming and being named a gender [that] is a fraught dialectic. . . . From this social, intersubjective perspective, the question shifts from what gender 'is' to how it is 'used.'"

In each of these clinical instances, we witness the intensity with which we humans at times hold tenaciously (or at least aggressively *try* to hold) onto what we feel to be subjectively true and real, along with the expectation or demand that others too hold fast to *our* view of truth and reality. In contrast, we also witness the at times profound difficulty individuals experience in even *having* a felt sense of subjective truth and reality—this seen particularly in the chapters by Perlman and by Walker and Dudley, in which they witness and explore the sequelae of severe trauma, including individuals' perpetual search for safety.

The spirit of Clifford's patient's question, "Am I safe enough to go out?" reverberates throughout many of the experiences and contexts of both patients and analysts in this volume. This question encapsulates the quintessentially human conundrum that is fulcrumed between the potential expansiveness of forward edge tendrils (Tolpin, 2002) and the anticipated dread to repeat (A. Ornstein, 1974). Many of the chapters address one variation or another of this ubiquitous conundrum. Am I safe enough (and able) to allow the emergence of a broader range of affect (Walker and Dudley), safe enough to connect with another person under traumatizing circumstances (Perlman), safe enough to be courageously reflective and more vulnerable with my patient (Leighton, and Preston and Shumsky)? Indeed these authors exemplify strong personal and clinical courage in their unremitting willingness to focus not only on the vicissitudes and idiosyncrasies of their patients' experiential worlds but upon their own subjective worlds and the impact they invariably have on their patients. And one chapter in particular (Walker and Dudley) reminds us of the continuing impact of traumatic experience over time, in this instance the ongoing and potent reverberations of the horrific events of September 11.

Another pivotal theme brought to light in this volume is the increasing emphasis on a more explicit form of contextualism, a deepening appreciation that emotional experience always emerges within a self-selfobject matrix, a context in which the ebbing and flowing of human relating is unremitting and seamless. A broad contextualist sensibility implicitly expands the greater contexts we envision in attempting to account for the way we organize experiences and their emotional meanings—for instance, we attempt to consider, among other sources of experience, the cultural milieu in which individuals' emotional lives coalesce. This is the spirit of the chapters by Rubalcava and Waldman and by Howard. Rubalcava and Waldman integrate "contemporary psychoanalytic perspectives with interpretive anthropology to offer a coherent approach to working with intercultural couples." They draw from self psychology and intersubjectivity theory to address marital partners' organizing themes that are grounded in apparently divergent cultures. From a contrasting perspective, Howard demonstrates a contextualist sensibility in the treatment of a multicultural couple, doing so via an attachment systems perspective. Each of these authors expresses an appreciation for the uniqueness and co-constitutive nature of the specific "culture" two or more individuals come to establish for themselves through reflective dialogue.

And speaking of context, this year's volume includes a "personal reflections" chapter, in which Malin contextualizes the last fifty years of psychoanalysis through the multifaceted lens of his own personal, historical experience. This offering was originally delivered orally as the 2001 Kohut Memorial Lecture.

Perspicacious readers will notice also the addition of a Book Review section in this year's volume. Weisel-Barth and Buirski independently explore the evocative worlds of psychoanalytic writing as they focus on the work of Frank Lachmann and of Robert Stolorow, respectively. Contemporary psychoanalytic self psychology has become increasingly understood as a collaborative process, and similarly these authors explore the experience of collaboration in the context of the creative writing process.

And finally, a few words about *Progress*. This publication remains dedicated to the continued exploration and expansion of contemporary, psychoanalytic self psychology. The work of Heinz Kohut and his colleagues provided the basis of what has become one of the most prominent and burgeoning sectors of the international psychoanalytic community. This spirit needs to be celebrated, not only through the interpretation and reinterpretation of the essence of self psychology, but also through a sensitivity toward its continued expansion. Expansion here refers not only to the contemporary elucidation and elaboration of self psychological thought, some of which has blossomed out of the influences of other contemporary paradigms, but also to our increasing awareness of the impact that psychoanalytic self psychology has on the very paradigms that are considered "outside" the immediate self psychology community. I am reminded by Arnold Goldberg's editorial preface in *Progress* (1985) that this was the essential spirit on which *Progress* was founded and that "much awaits us in exploring the psychology of the self, as there is no finished business in psychoanalysis" (p. viii). As the incoming Editor of *Progress*, I aim to maintain and enhance this spirit through the continuation and expansion of *Progress* itself.

Thus, it is my privilege to invite you into the sense of passion and adventure that is palpable in the pages to follow. I wish to extend my deepest gratitude to my more recent predecessor, Mark Gehrie, for his warm support during this past year of Volume 20 preparation, and to Estelle Shane, James Fosshage, Paul Ornstein, and Robert Stolorow for their continued support and encouragement. I also want to underscore that this volume would not have come to fruition without the passion and dedicated work of the Associate Editors, in particular Gary Rodin, Paula Fuqua, Peter Buirski, Gianni Nebbiosi, Hans-Peter Hartmann, Wolfgang Milch, Joye Weisel-Barth, Lester Lenoff, and Ellie Pynes, on whom I rely on a weekly if not a daily basis. And I wish to thank Paul Stepansky and Meredith Freedman of The Analytic Press for extending their ever-present warmth, guidance, flexibility, and support.

REFERENCES

Goldberg, A. (1985), Preface. *Progress in Self Psychology*, Vol. 1., ed. A. Goldberg. Hillsdale, NJ: The Analytic Press.

Kohut, H. (1984), *How Does Analysis Cure?* ed. A. Goldberg & P. Stepansky. Chicago: The University of Chicago Press.

Orange, D. (2002), There is no outside: Empathy and authenticity in psychoanalytic process. *Psychoanal. Psychol.*, 19:686–700.

Ornstein, A. (1974), The dread to repeat and the new beginning: A contribution to the psychoanalysis of the narcissistic personality disorders. *The Annual of Psychoanalysis*, 2:231–248. New York: International Universities Press.

Phillips, A. (2001), *Promises, Promises*. New York: Basic Books.

Tolpin, M. (2002), Doing psychoanalysis of normal development: Forward edge transferences. In: *Postmodern Self Psychology: Progress in Self Psychology, Vol. 18*, ed. A. Goldberg. Hillsdale, NJ: The Analytic Press, pp. 167–190.

TRANSFORMATIONS IN SELF PSYCHOLOGY

PROGRESS IN SELF PSYCHOLOGY
VOLUME 20

Part One

INTEGRATION AND SYNCRETISM

One

THE *YIN* AND *YANG* OF
INTERSUBJECTIVITY
INTEGRATING SELF-PSYCHOLOGICAL
AND RELATIONAL THINKING

STEVEN STERN

A patient has a dream that she is with her Buddhist husband on one of his retreats. She is not participating very much, but instead is using the time for biking and other nonmeditative activities. Then, she is in her living quarters when the teacher comes in and speaks to her. He says he is disappointed that she is not putting more of herself into the retreat, and that she needs to take her meditation more seriously. She knows he is right, and she feels bad. Among her associations to the dream are her bad feelings that she is never able to follow through on any of her self-improvement programs such as yoga, exercise, or improving her diet. She is overweight, which is one of the symptoms that brought her to therapy this time. One of my associations is that she has been having difficulty making both of her weekly sessions ever since she increased from once to twice a week, at my urging. She always has seemingly good excuses due to her successful and extremely busy academic career, and she has had to make changes in her prior commitments in order to fit the new session in.

In the following week she is late to one of her sessions and feels this is indicative of how out of control her life feels. In the week after that she calls the night before a session saying she has food poisoning and won't make her appointment the next afternoon. I am aware of feeling irritated when I get this message. I think: how does she know

3

how she is going to be feeling by tomorrow afternoon? I wonder if I should, or will, charge her for this cancellation. I do not doubt her fundamental commitment to the treatment, and have believed her when she has said, recently, that she has started to look forward to coming, though she does not know why. But I feel frustrated that her cancellations seem to prevent us from getting any sense of consistency going.

In her next session she begins by saying she had lots of things she wanted to talk about, but now she has either forgotten them or they seem less important. Almost immediately, she reports feeling tired, like she could fall asleep. I am aware of feeling distant and vaguely angry with her—not my usual receptive self—and am not sure what to do with these feelings. She is feeling at a loss as to what to talk about. I suggest she talk about what she is feeling. She says she is feeling reluctant to talk because she is thinking that I am irritated with her. Instead of my absorbing things like a "sponge," I seem "slicker" today, as if her words are just bouncing off of me. She thinks I am irritated because of her missed session. At this point I hesitate briefly, but then reluctantly admit that there is truth to her experience: I *am* irritated with her. I do not doubt that her excuse was sincere when she called, but I feel there have been enough late arrivals and missed appointments since she increased her sessions that it feels more than coincidental. At this point I remember her dream and say I feel like the Zen teacher in the dream. She is quiet for a minute, obviously affected, though I am not sure how. Then she says that, although she felt angry and defensive at being criticized, she senses that I am right. She also says she is wide awake now and much more engaged than when she came in. We then go on to have an intense session in which she talks about her difficulty trusting me. She does not trust that I will not make the therapy more about my needs than hers; that I will not need her to come to sessions and participate, making her feel burdened. This anxiety relates to her mother, who, we have come to understand, subtly makes all interactions with the patient more about the mother's needs than the patient's.

In the weeks following this session the patient, for the first time, settles into our twice-weekly schedule. She also begins to bring forward, in a more determined and sustained way than previously, what I feel is truly her central and most painful concern: her feelings about her eating and her weight.

What is the most useful way to understand these interactions? This question goes to the heart of recent dialogue between relationally and self-psychologically oriented analysts. Relational analysts tend to view such interactions as repetitions or reenactments of something from the patient's past, something externalized from the patient's internal object world through the process of projective identification (Mitchell, 1988; Davies and Frawley, 1991; Ogden, 1994). Most self psychologists repudiate this kind of understanding on both theoretical and clinical grounds. Stolorow and his associates have been explicit about this repudiation. Theoretically, they argue that projective identification implies a "unidirectional influence system" that fails to recognize the mutually constituted nature of all transference–countertransference phenomena (Stolorow, 1994; Stolorow, Orange, and Atwood, 1998). Clinically, they feel the concept fails to take into account the analyst's own subjectivity, the analyst's "organizing principles," as significant contributors to the analyst's countertransference reactions. They also feel it predisposes the analyst not to focus empathically on the patient's current experience of the analyst that might be leading him or her to act in the defensive or provocative ways to which the analyst is responding (e.g., Brandchaft, 2002). Relationalists might, in turn, reply that they do take into account the analyst's contribution to cocreated enactments but that the co-creation process is often asymmetrical (privileging the patient's subjectivity) and thus provides an important window into the patient's unconscious relational world (Stern, 2002b).

Although it might not be apparent from this hypothetical argument, the gap between these two perspectives has actually been narrowing (Fosshage, 2003). In both the relational and self-psychological versions of intersubjectivity, the domain of interest is now defined as the fluid, context-sensitive, mutually constituting relationship between subjectivity and intersubjectivity, both in development and in the analytic process (Mitchell, 1988; Benjamin, 1990; Stolorow and Atwood, 1992; Ogden, 1994; Stolorow, 1997; Beebe and Lachmann, 2002). Yet differences do remain. One difference is that relationalists, reflecting their postmodern sensibilities, tend to resolve tensions among different frames of reference dialectically, while

self psychologists, including self-psychological intersubjectivists, seem
to be stuck in a more binary, categorical referencing system. Thus,
where Stolorow and his collaborators (Stolorow and Atwood, 1992;
Stolorow, Orange, and Atwood, 1998) eschew the concept of
projective identification as a metapsychological demon, signaling
doctrinal and linguistic adherence to an archaic one-person
epistemology (i.e., a binary of bad old theory vs. good new theory),
relationalists such as Ogden (1994), Hoffman (1998), and Pizer (1998)
point toward paradoxical and dialectical solutions wherein such
concepts are recontextualized within a contemporary intersubjective
language and theoretical framework.

In sympathy with this latter view, I would say of the clinical
sequence with which I began the paper that there is no question that
my patient's ambivalent engagement with me is activating some of my
own vulnerabilities and organizing principles. And it is certainly true
that my openness to her experience of me as potentially narcissistic
and untrustworthy is a crucial element in our deepening analytic
project. But to stop there, and not be interested in how, exactly, I
came to feel like a character in *her* dream, or in the impact of my
acknowledging my irritation as an aspect of therapeutic action is, I
believe, to seriously limit the analytic, *intersubjective*, exploration and
potential transformation of our complex relational engagement.

Like a number of other psychoanalytic authors who, because of
their identifications with both the relational and self-psychological
perspectives, have been working to construct conceptual bridges
between them (e.g., Sands, 1997; Ringstrom, 1998; Teicholz, 1999;
and Fosshage, 2003), I have been working on my own synthesis (Stern,
1994, 2002a, b, c, 2003). In the present paper I pursue this project
further by way of two theoretical strategies. The first is to make explicit
the conceptions of the unconscious implicit in the two models. This
is useful because theories of therapeutic action are so closely tied to
theories of the unconscious, and any integration of the former must
ultimately be grounded in an integration of the latter. The second
strategy is to import the concepts of mutual and self-regulation from
contemporary psychoanalytic infancy research (Beebe and Lachmann,
2002)—concepts that have been adapted to adult treatment by both
relational and self-psychological authors—and demonstrate how these
concepts might be used to form a bridge between relational and self-
psychological thinking.

STRATEGY 1: CONCEPTIONS OF THE UNCONSCIOUS

One of the fundamental differences between relational and self-psychological understandings of intersubjectivity is their different conceptualizations of the unconscious. The relational unconscious is an active, intrusive, controlling unconscious, whose power to evoke concordant and complementary identifications, and to thereby subject the analyst to cocreated versions of the patient's internal world, cannot be evaded (e.g., Bollas, 1987; Mitchell, 1988, 1997; Davies and Frawley, 1991; Ogden, 1994). Summarizing relational conceptions of the unconscious, Hirsch and Roth (1995) wrote: "the [relational] unconscious is lived out, negotiated and constructed within the transference–countertransference matrix" (p. 268). By contrast, the contemporary self-psychological unconscious is more self-contained: it consists of organizing principles (Stolorow and Atwood, 1992), disowned affects, negative selfobject representations (Gehrie, 1993), accommodations (Brandchaft, 2002), and selfobject longings, transferences, and fantasies (Bacal, 1990; Goldberg, 1995), all of which control the *patient's* subjective experience but do not necessarily compel or enable him or her to control the experience of the analyst. Within this model transference is *experienced*, but does not aggressively evoke complementary countertransference in the analyst. The core theories of therapeutic action differ accordingly. The self psychologist's empathic-introspective listening stance, and the interpretations and responses that derive from it, are sufficient to grasp, provide a new experience for, and transform the patient's more self-contained unconscious "world" (Stolorow, Orange, and Atwood, 2001), whereas the relationalist is always having to work her or his way out of co-created enactments, mutual projections, and cross-identifications to provide the transforming, needed new experience.[1]

---

[1] I would anticipate objections at this point from subscribers to the "intersubjective systems" model elaborated by Stolorow and his collaborators, as they have taken pains to differentiate their perspective from self psychology (Stolorow and Atwood, 1992; Trop, 1994). I understand and agree with many of the bases for this differentiation, but I would argue that, in their conception of the unconscious (Stolorow and Atwood, 1992; Stolorow, Orange, and Atwood, 2001), there is still an essential continuity with self psychology—one that differentiates both groups from relational theorists. The relational unconscious is not only a center of restricted awareness (restricted "horizons"), unformulated experience, and implicit relational

My own view is that both of these understandings have validity. Although ostensibly irreconcilable, they in fact represent a kind of *yin* and *yang* of intersubjectivity. Relational theory is the *yang* principle, portraying the unconscious as more aggressive, probing, and controlling. Self psychology is the more *yin*, characterizing the unconscious as self-contained and receptive. My experience is that both qualities are present in complex tension with one another, and that both our analytic listening stance and our model of therapeutic action need to take this complexity into account. Our listening stance must be able to hold in tension both a disciplined effort to empathically explore and grasp the patient's psychic reality and, at the same time, an equally empathic ongoing recognition of our own responses as we are affected by the patient.[2] Similarly, our model of therapeutic action needs to hold in balance more empathic and interpretive interventions that seek to convey our understanding of the patient's subjectivity, *and* more expressive interventions necessary to assert or reclaim our own subjectivity in the midst of reenactments.

Even as I advocate for integrating these two principles, I am aware that dichotomizing them in this way is a vast oversimplification. Attending to our own responses to the patient, for example, is always ultimately in the service of understanding the patient (Bollas, 1987). Attempting an empathic intervention is always, simultaneously, one

---

knowledge, but also of *procedural operations* gleaned from early relationships that are continually acting upon the dyadic partner (Bollas, 1987; Mitchell, 1988; Ogden, 1994). The unconscious "world" that Stolorow and his collaborators describe is a center of awareness (and restricted awareness) but not (at least not in any way that they make explicit) of procedural activity that operates on the other at all times.

[2] Fosshage (2003, and elsewhere) makes a very similar point in his recognition and delineation of the "other-centered" listening position in addition to the "empathic" listening stance. The difference between Fosshage's model and the one I am proposing is that, for me, and I think for many relationalists, recognizing the patient's effect on the analyst's current subjectivity is not exactly an "other-centered" position since the analyst's countertransference is understood to be in part *shaped* by the patient's transference engagement—that is, it is in part a co-creation of an aspect of the patient's unconscious intersubjective world. This unconscious shaping process is perhaps most explicit in Bollas's (1987) "expressive use of the countertransference" and in Ogden's (1994) concept of the intersubjective "analytic third," but is implicit in most relational theorizing. It is a sensibility that comes to relational psychoanalysis from object relations theories, especially the concept of projective identification.

form of expressing our own subjectivity. And choosing to express one's own subjectivity often has the unintended effect of making the patient feel recognized in a new way (Ehrenberg, 1996). The process is infinitely complex. Nevertheless, I think it is useful to recognize these two principles even though, like *yin* and *yang*, they are continuously and inextricably embedded in one another.

Relationalists such as Mitchell (1997) and Bromberg (1989) have been critical of self psychology for advocating adherence to a pre-ordained empathic stance and failing to recognize the degree to which the analyst's subjectivity, including the capacity for empathy, is constantly subject to the shaping influence of the intersubjective context. One of my favorite metaphors for the relational listening perspective was offered by Black (2001) when she compared the relational analyst's receptivity to the patient to "warm and malleable clay": the analyst expects to be shaped by the patient's unique unconscious patterns of interacting and repeating. I resonate to this analogy, and I agree with the relationalists that we are always being affected by the patient's unconscious engagement with us. At the same time, what makes our participation analytic is that we are constantly, even in the midst of enactive pressures of all kinds, trying to stay sufficiently afloat or intact to be able to work toward empathic recognition of, and responsiveness to, the patient's subjectivity. The patient counts on our commitment to this process of progressive recognition, and, as Hoffman (1992) has argued, this commitment provides the necessary backdrop for the analyst's more expressive participation.

STRATEGY 2: THE CONCEPTS OF MUTUAL AND SELF-REGULATION AS A BRIDGE

Relationalists, reflecting the Kleinian influence in relational theory, have tended to view the patient's unconscious, active, procedural engagements with the analyst as forms of projective identification or some similar process that goes unnamed but is responsible for the co-created reenactments of the patient's early relational scenarios. I suggest that many such enactments might usefully be reconceptualized as the patient's introduction into the analytic relationship of patterns of pathological interactive and self-regulation that were learned in his or her earliest relationships.

Beebe and Lachmann (2002), based on their own and others' developmental research (e.g., Stern, 1985; Sander, 1995; Tronick, 1998), and their creative application of these research findings to adult psychoanalytic treatment, have proposed a model of interaction and therapeutic action wherein the change process is understood to be mediated by a progressive coordination between patient and analyst in the movement toward more effective interactive and self-regulation of the patient's mental states. Both their theory and their clinical examples point toward a therapeutic model in which the therapist, based on an empathic reading of the patient's various regulatory strategies, seeks largely non-verbal ways of "entering" the patient's regulatory system and coordinating with the patient so as to facilitate a gradual revision of the patient's implicit relational expectations and regulatory competence.

Beebe and Lachmann (2002) state that in their "co-construction model, each partner's subjective experience is an emergent process, continually affected by the interaction as well as by the person's own self-regulation" (p. 212). It is clear from their clinical examples that they believe the analyst is *consciously* affected by, and often must attempt to match, the patient's regulatory patterns. It is not clear to me that they would extend this to say that the analyst participates *unconsciously* in the patient's pathological regulatory patterns. I suggest that the full realization of this model would recognize the possibility, if not inevitability, that patients will sometimes draw the analyst into their pathological regulatory patterns and that the movement toward increasingly competent interactive and self-regulation would therefore necessarily entail a transformation of these dysfunctional patterns from "the inside out" (Bromberg, 1991). Such an expansion of this model (if, indeed, it is an expansion) would cover approximately the same territory as the relational and contemporary Kleinian theories of transformation via projective identification and thus, perhaps finally, offer a credible bridge between the self-psychological and relational paradigms.

To take this idea one step further, it often seems that pathological regulatory patterns are the result of early caregiving systems that are organized primarily around regulating the *parent's* rather than the child's mental states. This may take any number of forms. For example, the parent may use the child in some way for purposes of self-regulation or, alternatively, the parent may be so preoccupied with self-regulation that she or he in effect disengages from the child, leaving the child to develop compensatory self-regulatory strategies (Tronick, 1989). The possibilities are endless given that patterns of interactive and self-regulation are embedded in the multiple, complex, ever-shifting intersubjective realities and meaning systems of family life. Moreover, the form the patient's pathological regulatory strategies ultimately take, and how he or she seeks unconsciously or implicitly to implement them in a given relationship, such as a romantic relationship or the analytic relationship, undoubtedly depends on a multiplicity of factors.[3] But, however the patient's regulatory strategies play out in the analytic relationship, I think it likely that the analyst will be "given a taste" of what it was like to be part of the patient's early regulatory systems (either in the role of the patient, or of the pathologically-regulating other, or both) and that this experience will often be the necessary starting point for the transformation to more effective interactive regulation and self-regulation.

THE STRATEGIES APPLIED: THE CASE OF JILLIAN

With these various integrating strategies in mind, let us now return to my patient, whom I will call "Jillian," and me. I will begin by contextualizing our interaction so that you have a better sense of both of our subjectivities at that point in the treatment.

When Jillian entered therapy about a year prior to the interaction in question, she was happily married, her career was taking off, she had a wide circle of good friends, and in general felt her life was going extremely well. The problem was that the better things got, the more intensely and pervasively she was experiencing three persistent problems: anxiety attacks that seemed to come out of nowhere; psychosomatic symptoms and preoccupations that never amounted to serious medical problems but worried her intensely nonetheless; and bad feelings about her weight. She was overweight and struggled

---

[3] Here the theory of interactive and self-regulation might usefully be coordinated with attachment theory. Thus, for example, whether the patient insistently seeks to enlist the analyst in regulatory interactions or remains excessively reliant on self-regulation while defending against interactive reliance on the analyst, may depend on the patient's characteristic attachment style (in this instance, ambivalent versus avoidant).

with her eating. Although she was not manifestly depressed, she felt helpless and hopeless about ever changing these three problems, and expressed extreme doubt that therapy could help her with them. There was a sense of her being locked in a kind of prison, and no one would be able to reach her or help her in any meaningful way. I would add to these problems a fourth that became more articulated during the first year of therapy. There was a general sense of feeling out of control in her life. She had a hard time saying no to friends' requests of all kinds, and to the many professional opportunities that were always presenting themselves. Consequently her life was overfull. She recognized that in a way she preferred this constant activity to having much down time, but it also made her feel out of control, and often had the consequence of causing her to short-change her commitments. She tried various strategies for taking better hold of her life, yoga being the main one, but she could never stick with them for very long.

Over the year of treatment leading up to the interaction I described, Jillian and I had begun to construct a genetic understanding of some of her mental states and struggles. Much of this focused around her relationship with her mother who, like Jillian, is highly intelligent, high-powered, and successful in an academic career. She was very involved with Jillian growing up, and Jillian idealized her in many ways, crediting her with cultivating many of the talents and strengths that have made her life so rich and successful. At the same time Jillian had always found interacting with her mother inexplicably tiring, anxiety provoking, and at times enraging. There were disturbing thoughts that she wouldn't mind if her mother died—that this would be a profound relief in some way. As we explored their relationship in a more fine-grained way, it emerged more and more clearly that the mother was often if not always subtly violating Jillian's psychic boundaries, infusing her with anxiety, and exerting a kind of relentless control through a mixture of charm and hysteria that made all of their interactions more about meeting the mother's needs than the daughter's. What made matters more complex was that the mother was consciously well-intentioned, was almost self-aware enough to know that she was too self-focused, and was very concerned that she be seen as a good mother. These qualities contributed to Jillian's complex feelings about her mother and supported the complex combination of accommodation and attempted differentiation that characterized her unconscious relationship to her mother.

I will give two examples of the mother's toxic effect. Jillian idealized her childhood up to the age of about 11, feeling everything was just about perfect and that she could do no wrong in her mother's eyes. Then, around age 11 or 12, the mother began to become extremely worried about, and over-involved with, Jillian's weight and eating. Jillian feels clear that the mother's anxiety about this long-preceded her developing any significant weight problem; that the mother was grossly overreacting to what must have been only minor or normal body changes. Yet the mother became preoccupied with Jillian's weight, constantly monitored her eating, and was always challenging her to diet and exercise. A second example is the mother's handling of Jillian's birthdays. The mother always likes to make a big deal of her daughter's birthdays, but in such a way as to subtly focus attention on herself. If they go out to eat, it somehow ends up being to a restaurant of the mother's choice. If there is a party, it ends up being larger than Jillian would really like it to be. And the gifts, while often creative and unusual, are usually the kinds of things the mother likes. Yet it is important to the mother to hear how much Jillian likes them. Thus Jillian has always felt a sickening mixture of gratitude and resentment, but has never quite been able to put her finger on why she feels bad; as a result, she blames herself for not just feeling loving and appreciative.

These are only dramatic examples. Based on the patient's vivid reports, the mother does the same kind of thing in microcosm in all of their interactions. Thus it seemed to me, and I began to interpret to Jillian, that the mother had enlisted her in a kind of psychic fusion, the purpose of which was to regulate the mother's anxiety and narcissistic needs. The mother did not and could not recognize her as her own person with her own needs, and had constantly undermined Jillian's differentiation process. Jillian's typical response to these interpretations was an emphatic "Yes!" conveying that something important was being recognized and named for the first time.

Let us add here that the father had his own forms of toxicity that, in a way, felt even more difficult for Jillian. He was also very intelligent and resourceful—he could build her a tree house, or now, in adulthood, help her with the computer. But he was painfully remote and inhibited, and a lifelong, unrecovered alcoholic. The worst part of being with him, however, is her feelings of extreme self-consciousness, awkwardness, and "creepiness" when they are alone together. She cannot stand any expression of intimacy or emotion with him and, as with her mother, has thoughts that it would be better if he died. At this point in her life she does not see him very often, and dreads all encounters with him.

To get into the analytic transference and countertransference in the sequence I described I will now invoke the metaphor of self- and interactive regulation. It seems to me that both of Jillian's parents have extreme difficulty with self-regulation, causing both of them to rely on addictive solutions. The father uses alcohol and the mother uses her symbiotic tie with Jillian. Because of these difficulties, neither parent could provide the kinds of mutual regulatory interchanges that would lead to Jillian's developing effective self-regulatory capacities. In fact they had the opposite effect: increasing her anxiety to intolerable levels. This understanding helps account for all of her presenting symptoms. Her sense of feeling out of control, her dissociated anxiety states, her somatic preoccupations, and her overeating all speak to faulty self-regulation. At the same time, the failures in mutual regulation have led her to be, in another sense, excessively self-regulating, as the infancy research would predict (Tronick, 1989; Beebe and Lachman, 2002). Her tendency to overcommit, her tendency to dissociate her anxiety from its source, her limiting the level of intimacy and dependency she will allow in any caregiving relationship, and her overeating all represent ways she has developed for regulating her tension levels as well as her emotional connection to herself and to others.

From the beginning, questions of self- and mutual regulation have been implicit in Jillian's concerns and in our interactions. In the first consultation session, she had made it clear she was shopping around, and that it was important to her, among other things, to choose a therapist who was not too anxious, and whom she would not make anxious. Yet I found myself feeling anxious in her presence. I decided, on a gut feeling, to share this with her, saying I wasn't sure why I was feeling this way, but it seemed significant. She was taken aback, but also seemed relieved. I think this interchange was decisive in her choosing to continue with me.

Virtually from the beginning Jillian experienced a sense of not knowing what to talk about in sessions. There always seemed to be many possibilities, multiple strands of her experience representing multiple, somewhat dissociated, self-states. And there was her feeling that no matter what she chose to pursue, it would not lead to any tangible therapeutic results. It all seemed so arbitrary. How could she be confident that I would lead her toward understandings that were truly helpful? How could she trust that I would not be primarily in it for my own narcissistic gratification? Here, in contrast to the anxiety contagion of the first session, I felt relatively non-defensive and calm. While not dismissing her concerns, I would convey that I believed our openness to her associations and feelings, beginning with the feeling of not knowing what to pursue, would ultimately lead us to meaningful and useful understandings. This apparently reassured her (effective interactive regulation) because she would usually end up diving into some area of vivid importance to her, and there was a sense of our beginning to understand her better.

Yet I felt that, at one session a week, we were barely scratching the surface. There was so much to talk about and so little time. I began to feel that the therapy structure was enacting her core problem. On the one hand, there was a sense of her feeling overwhelmed by all there was to talk about, and feeling increasingly hungry for our interactions. On the other hand, she needed to regulate our involvement because of not quite trusting that a caregiver could actually sense her needs and help her to meet them. I began to feel as imprisoned as she did, constrained from becoming involved enough with her to provide the kind of help that would begin to make a difference. So I began to push for us to meet more often. When I had tried this once several months earlier she had said she was not sure what her finances would allow, and she would get back to me about it; but she never did. This time, surprisingly, I did not get much apparent resistance. She said she needed to work out the finances, which was not so easy given that money was another area of her life that felt out of control. But within a few weeks she reported that she had worked it out, and we quickly set up our new schedule. Virtually from the beginning of the change, three things happened. First, it was immediately clear to both of us that twice a week was better than once: there was finally the sense of having sufficient time to go into more things in more depth. Second, Jillian began looking forward to her sessions more, and missing them more when there were scheduled breaks (though she was reluctant to share this with me because I might be too gratified by it). And third, there was also an increase in her arriving late or canceling sessions due to poor planning or her overcrowded schedule. At least half the time, it seemed, we were still meeting once a week!

This, then, was the backdrop for the sequence I reported when I expressed my irritation with Jillian for missing sessions. I want to argue, and hope now to demonstrate, that the integrative model I have proposed is helpful in grasping the intersubjective complexity of this interaction. I think the best way to capture this complexity is with a series of questions or, if you will, *koans*. Indeed, both the relational approach and my integrated approach are, by their nature, so grounded in uncertainty about the meaning of interactions, and in the ongoing struggle between ambiguity and conviction, that an ongoing series of questions, one leading into another, seems the best way to capture the spirit of this approach.

As an arbitrary entry point, I might ask: Was I wrong to push Jillian to increase her sessions? I worry about that because of the potential for repetitive meanings. She might experience me as pushing her to do something, as her mother pushed her to diet. That would certainly be a recipe for resistance. Or it might feel like asking her to spend more time alone with her creepy father, with the implicit expectation of becoming more intimate and emotionally expressive, which we know is highly aversive to her. On the other hand, if she is locked inside a prison of self-protective and ineffective self-regulation, and I am sitting in our once-a-week sessions feeling helpless about connecting enough with her to make a difference and feeling pretty confident that meeting twice a week *would* begin to make a difference, is it not my responsibility to initiate what I feel are the necessary conditions for the changes she is hoping to make? Might not that be the necessary beginning of positive interactive regulation in this case? Yet there is the nagging question, whose tension am I regulating anyway? *She* is not pushing for more sessions. Maybe it is I who is feeling tense and impatient sitting with her characterological solutions, which I should expect would manifest themselves in our relationship in this very way. Maybe true mutual regulation would begin with my learning to sit calmly with her characterological self-imprisonment until *she* initiates greater involvement. That, in turn, raises the question, where is my impatience coming from? Is it primarily coming from my own selfish, or personal, or theoretical motives? Am I just imposing my own preconception of the necessary conditions for a minimal analytic treatment? Do I just want to spend more time with

Jillian? Am I competing to be more of a priority in her crowded life, to be more than just one half-hearted commitment among many? I would honestly have to say the answer is "yes" to all of these! But is that all there is to it? Is it just about my organizing principles? My gut feeling, which often is all we have to go on, is no: I think there is something about Jillian's engagement with me, something about the way her unconscious is actively reaching out to mine, that is saying, in effect: "I want you to know I need you, but I cannot imagine your being of any real help to me. So I am limiting our involvement: what are you going to do about that?" And the problem, for which there may be no "clean" solution—that is, no solution that does not involve some element of repetition—is how to respond to the mixed message. I err in the direction of nudging her toward greater involvement, feeling pretty clear that I am doing so mainly for her benefit, but knowing that she will almost certainly experience it as, in part, a repetition. I am feeling prepared to take the heat, which may be, in this instance, an element of mutual regulation. But then, if I was so prepared to take the heat, why did I become irritated when she, predictably, continued to enact her strategies of self-regulation by missing sessions? Is this not exactly what she does not need: another mother figure burdening her with obligations and with disappointment when she fails to meet them? Maybe, but maybe not. Maybe there is no getting around the messiness and awkwardness of joining our two subjectivities into what we both hope, at some level, will become a functioning mutual-regulatory system. So my irritation, while perhaps not exactly optimal, is not exactly unexpected either. I have, after all, become like the Zen teacher in *her* dream. Maybe what is crucial for mutual regulation is not the avoidance of my reactive affectivity, but my capacity to acknowledge it when I sense it would serve our purposes to do so, and to use it in the service of understanding her intersubjective world, and our intersubjective system, better. That, at least, seemed to further our process in the vignette I reported.

CONCLUSION

In the evolving, mostly warming relationship between self psychology and relational psychoanalysis the latter's continuing use of the concept of projective identification, in any of its various forms, remains a lightning rod for contentiousness and misunderstanding between exponents of the two theories—what Tolpin (2002) might call the "trailing edge" of this otherwise fruitful theoretical dialogue. In this chapter I have proposed what I hope are two useful strategies for facilitating more constructive dialogue regarding analytic interactions in which the analyst seems to become caught in the patient's relational web. The first strategy involves delineating, and then integrating, both theories' implicit assumptions about the unconscious: the *yin* and *yang* of intersubjectivity. The second strategy involves enlarging the concepts of mutual and self-regulation to account for and even deepen our understanding of at least some of the phenomena referred to by the term projective identification. While my aim has been, in part, to foster communication between the two perspectives, I am aware that my particular integration is leaning in the relational direction. That is, I find myself increasingly embracing the dialectical and paradoxical tensions that are at the heart of the relational approach.

I have tried to dramatize this dialectical tension in the presentation of my early work with Jillian. One sense I have of this work is that Jillian and I were traversing the territory between her mother's legacy of pathological regulation—interactions whose primary agenda was regulating the mother's anxiety and need states—and new interactive regulations that have as their guiding aim the successful regulation of Jillian's anxiety and need states. While my own tension states, and associated regulatory strategies, are activated, these elements of my subjective world are selectively evoked and reconfigured by our asymmetrical "attraction" to the problematic aspects of Jillian's subjective world, to which we are both attending and which we are both working to recognize and transform.

REFERENCES

Bacal, H. A. (1990), The elements of a corrective selfobject experience. *Psychoanal. Inq.*, 10:347–372.

Beebe, B. & Lachmann, F. M. (2002), *Infant Research and Adult Treatment: Co-constructing Interactions.* Hillsdale, NJ: The Analytic Press.

Benjamin, J. (1990), Recognition and destruction: An outline of intersubjectivity. Reprinted with Afterword in *Relational Psychoanalysis: The Emergence of a Tradition*, ed S. A. Mitchell & L. Aron. Hillsdale, NJ: The Analytic Press, 1999, pp. 181–210.

Black, M. J. (2001), Discussion of case presentation by Judith Pickles. Presented at the 24th Annual International Conference on the Psychology of the Self, November 8–11, San Francisco.

Bollas, C. (1987), *The Shadow of the Object: Psychoanalysis and the Unthought Known.* London: Free Association Books.

Brandchaft, B. (2002), Reflections on the intersubjective foundations of the sense of self: Commentary on paper by Steven Stern. *Psychoanal. Dial.*, 12:727–745.

Bromberg, P. M. (1989), Interpersonal psychoanalysis and self psychology: A clinical comparison. In: *Self Psychology: Comparisons and Contrasts*, ed. D. W. Detrick & S. P. Detrick. Hillsdale, NJ: The Analytic Press, pp. 275–291.

————— (1991), On knowing one's patient inside out: The aesthetics of unconscious communication. *Psychoanal. Dial.*, 1:399–422.

Davies, J. M. & Frawley, M. G. (1991), Dissociative processes and transference-countertransference paradigms in the psychoanalytically oriented treatment of adult survivors of childhood sexual abuse. *Psychoanal. Dial.*, 2:5–36.

Ehrenberg, D. B. (1996), On the analyst's emotional availability and vulnerability. *Contemp. Psychoanal.*, 32:275–286.

Fosshage, J. L. (2003), Contextualizing self psychology and relational psychoanalysis: Bi-directional influence and proposed syntheses. *Contemp. Psychoanal.*, 39:411–448.

Gehrie, M. (1993), Empathy in broader perspective: A technical approach to the consequences of the negative selfobject in early character formation. In: *Basic Ideas Reconsidered: Progress in Self Psychology, Vol. 12*, ed. A. Goldberg. Hillsdale, NJ: The Analytic Press, pp. 159–179.

Goldberg, A. (1995), *The Problem of Perversion: The View from Self Psychology.* New Haven, CT: Yale University Press.

Hirsch, I. & Roth, J. (1995), Changing conceptions of the unconscious. *Contemp. Psychoanal.*, 31:263–276.

Hoffman, I. Z. (1992), Expressive participation and psychoanalytic discipline. *Contemp. Psychoanal.*, 28:1–15.

————— (1998), *Ritual and Spontaneity in the Psychoanalytic Process: A Dialectical-Constructivist View.* Hillsdale, NJ: The Analytic Press.

Mitchell, S. A. (1988), *Relational Concepts in Psychoanalysis: An Integration.* Harvard University Press.

————— (1997), *Influence and Autonomy in Psychoanalysis.* Hillsdale, NJ: The Analytic Press.

Ogden, T. (1994), *Subjects of Analysis.* Northvale, NJ: Aronson.

Pizer, S. (1998), *Building Bridges: The Negotiation of Paradox in Psychoanalysis.* Hillsdale, NJ: The Analytic Press.

Ringstrom, P. (1998), Therapeutic impasses in contemporary psychoanalytic treatment: Revisiting the double bind hypothesis. *Psychoanal. Dial.*, 8:297–316.

Sander, L. (1995), Identity and the experience of specificity in a process of recognition: Commentary on Seligman and Shanok. *Psychoanal. Dial.*, 5:579–593.

Sands, S. (1997), Self psychology and projective identification—Whither shall they meet? A reply to the editors (1995). *Psychoanal. Dial.*, 7:651–668.

Stern, D. (1985), *The Interpersonal World of the Infant.* New York: Basic Books.

Stern, S. (1994), Needed relationships and repeated relationships: An integrated relational perspective. *Psychoanal. Dial.*, 4:317-346.

——— (2002a), The self as a relational structure: A dialogue with multiple self theory. *Psychoanal. Dial.*, 12:693-714.

——— (2002b), Reply to commentaries. *Psychoanal. Dial.*, 12:747-762.

——— (2002c), Identification, repetition, and psychological growth: An expansion of relational theory. *Psychoanal. Psychol.*, 19:722-738.

——— (2003), Models of the unconscious: Implications for therapeutic action. *Self Psychology News*, Vol. 1, No. 1. Available: www.psychologyoftheself.org.

Stolorow, R. D. (1994), More integrative than thou: Commentary on Steven Stern's "Needed Relationships." *Psychoanal. Dial.*, 4:353-356.

——— (1997), Dynamic, dyadic, intersubjective systems: An evolving paradigm for psychoanalysis. *Psychoanal. Psychol.*, 14:337-346.

——— & Atwood, G. E. (1992), *Contexts of Being: The Intersubjective Foundations of Psychological Life.* Hillsdale, NJ: The Analytic Press.

——— ——— & Brandchaft, B. (1994), *The Intersubjective Perspective.* Northvale, NJ: Aronson.

——— Orange, D. M. & Atwood, G. E. (1998), Projective identification begone! Commentary on paper by Susan H. Sands. *Psychoanal. Dial.*, 8:719–725.

——— ——— & ——— (2001), World horizons: A post-Cartesian alternative to the Freudian unconscious. *Contemp. Psychoanal.*, 37:43–62.

Teicholz, J. G. (1999), *Kohut, Loewald, and the Postmoderns: A Comparative Study of Self and Relationship.* Hillsdale, NJ: The Analytic Press.

Tolpin, M. (2002), Doing psychoanalysis of normal development: Forward edge transferences. In: *Postmodern Self Psychology: Progress in Self Psychology, Vol. 18,* ed. A. Goldberg. Hillsdale, NJ: The Analytic Press, pp. 167–190.

Tronick, E. (1989), Emotions and emotional communication in infants. *Amer. Psychol.*, 44:112–119.

——— (1998), Dyadically expanded states of consciousness and the process of therapeutic change. *Infant Mental Health J.*, 19:290–299.

Trop, J. L. (1994), Self psychology and intersubjectivity theory. In: *The Intersubjective Perspective*, ed. R. D. Stolorow, G. E. Atwood & B. Brandchaft. Northvale, NJ: Aronson, pp. 77–91.

TWO

FACILITATIVE ANALYTIC INTERACTION IN A CASE OF EXTREME NIHILISM AND AVERSIVENESS

JAMES L. FOSSHAGE
CAROL A. MUNSCHAUER

*W*ith new theoretical understandings and expansion of technical guidelines, psychoanalysis has, over the past three decades, become a therapeutic modality applicable to the entire range of human psychopathology. Essential to these new understandings is recognizing the variable co-contribution of analyst and patient to the analytic encounter (Stolorow, Brandchaft, and Atwood, 1987; Mitchell, 1988). This recognition emerges out of two ongoing paradigmatic shifts within psychoanalysis—the shift from positivistic to relativistic science and, for some, to hermeneutics, and the shift from intrapsychic to relational field or systems theory. Hence, our understandings of psychoanalytic treatment, involving the participation of the analyst as well as the patient, have become far more complex, requiring a substantial reformulation of theory and treatment guidelines.

The treatment to follow (C.A.M. was the analyst and J.L.F. was the consultant) concerns a man of deeply intractable nihilism and aversiveness (Lichtenberg, 1989; Lichtenberg, Lachmann, and Fosshage, 1992, 1996) and serves as an example of a person for whom, without new understandings and reformulation and expansion of traditional analytic technique, psychoanalytic treatment would not have been possible. Difficult treatments such as this often require extraordinary measures to facilitate treatment, and even to make treatment possible. These extraordinary measures, on occasion, may require, as this treatment did, a reconsideration and an individual re-framing of needed actions that traditionally are lumped together as boundary violations (an example is the recent reassessment of physical touch as a form of communication in psychoanalysis—see *Psychoanalytic Inquiry*, 2000). Unusual treatment situations need to be included in our literature to remind us of how intrinsically creative the psychoanalytic encounter is, requiring us to remain flexible and open to a range of possibilities not previously thought acceptable to facilitate the analytic process.

Patients of extreme nihilism and aversiveness are most difficult for all analysts, for they relentlessly devalue and denigrate the analyst and analysis (see Lachmann, 2000; Lichtenberg, Lachmann, and Fosshage, 2003). Not only do these treatment situations require an analyst's survival (Winnicott, 1949, 1958), but they also require an analyst to find a way to engage the patient to reflect on, understand, and gradually transcend the chronic nihilism and aversiveness. The treatment to follow illustrates the need for the analyst both to survive and to remain available to participate in and create with the patient an analytic healing process. Often in these most difficult treatment cases a consultant is required to steady ("to hold" or to shore up) the analyst who, in the face of the patient's intense devaluation, can easily feel undermined, discouraged, and potentially retaliatory in an effort to self-regulate. In this instance, we understood the patient's nihilism to reflect a profound hopelessness and despair about obtaining the necessary relational nutrients of life, based on a history of extreme emotional deprivation. We also understood that the patient's unrelenting nihilism and aversiveness provided an impenetrable protection against hope, relational engagement, and expected painful failure in others' responsiveness. Finally, we understood that the patient had developed a characteristic aversive style that enabled him to disavow feelings of relational need and associated feelings of weakness and to bolster as well a sense of self-sufficiency and strength. While our understanding of the patient's nihilism and aversiveness corresponds with Sullivan's (1953) description of what he called "malevolent transformation" (pp. 213–216) and its developmental origins, our treatment approach, as will be delineated, is quite different.

In an attempt to delineate the facilitating analytic interaction (Bacal, 1985, 1998; Fosshage, 1997), we will focus specifically on the shifting needs of the patient as expressed in different forms of relatedness. We will describe the analyst's listening/experiencing perspectives and the variable requisite disclosure of the analyst's own experience. We will also briefly address the term "enactment."

As an organizing concept, we view attachment needs and forms of relatedness as ranging along a continuum (Shane and Shane, 1996; Fosshage, 1997; Shane, Shane and Gales, 1997; Lichtenberg, Lachmann and Fosshage, 2003). At one end, self-needs and selfobject relatedness are in the forefront of experience. This is the area of Kohut's (1971, 1977, 1984) mirroring and idealizing selfobject needs and connections. Then there are needs for or concerns about self-with-other that Stern (1985) and Benjamin (1988, 1995) have called intersubjective relatedness (what Shane, Shane, and Gales, 1997, refer to as self with interpersonal-sharing other). And lastly, there are what we call needs to focus on or show concern for the other, a "caretaking" relatedness—for example, a parent with children, a teacher with students, an analyst with patients. All forms of relatedness can generate vitalizing or selfobject experience. Most analytic work, as the following analytic material illustrates, will demonstrate a shifting priority of needs and forms of relatedness that have to be examined from the perspective of each participant in the analytic encounter. To facilitate analytic interaction, self-needs in the foreground for the patient optimally require the analyst's reciprocal concern for the other, or caretaking relatedness. A patient's need for intersubjective relatedness requires reciprocal intersubjective relatedness from the analyst. And when a patient demonstrates concern for the analyst, the analyst needs to be reciprocally comfortable with his or her selfobject needs coming to the fore and with receiving a patient's caretaking. These shifts in forms of relatedness for patient and analyst are often quite seamless in a foreground/background configuration.

When a patient's selfobject needs are in the forefront of experience, the analyst makes use of the empathic listening/experiencing stance (Kohut, 1959, 1982), that is, we listen and experience, as best we can, from within the patient's perspective: this facilitates the analytic interaction. When a patient shifts into intersubjective relatedness, the patient, for example, may inquire about our reactions to the patient generally or during a particular interaction.

In addition to the empathic perspective, the analyst must also have data gathered from the other-centered listening/experiencing perspective, that is, to listen and experience as the other in a relationship with the patient (Fosshage, 1995a, 1997), to respond to the patient and facilitate analytic interaction. Moments when any of these three forms of relatedness is in the forefront may require a third perspective, the analyst's self-perspective (Fosshage, 2003). An analyst's own perspective that, rather than emanating out of an empathic or other-centered patient focus, reflects the analyst's self-experience, not patient-centered, but as a separate person. An analyst may use his self-perspective internally or share directly his perspective in a variety of clinical situations. For example, in attempting to understand who is contributing what to a patient/analyst interaction, an analyst must independently assess, as best he can, his subjective experience during the interaction.

Sullivan's (1953) interpersonal approach and that of those American Relational authors (Mitchell, 1988; Bromberg, 1998) who integrate the interpersonal within their relational approach lean toward utilizing the other-centered perspective directly and confronting a patient with what he "is doing" to the analyst and others in his life (Fosshage, 2003). In contrast, self psychologists traditionally have emphasized the unwavering use of the empathic perspective in efforts to explore the patient's experience. We, on the other hand, are proposing the important usage and integration of the empathic, other-centered, and self listening/experiencing perspectives to enhance recognition of and facilitative responsiveness to the patient's shifting attachment needs and forms of relatedness.

Emanating from an intrapsychic model, self-disclosure refers to the revelation of the analyst's subjectivity. From relational field theory or an interaction systems model (Mitchell, 1988; Lichtenberg, 1989; Beebe, Jaffee, and Lachmann, 1992; Lichtenberg, Lachmann, and Fosshage, 1992, 2003; Fosshage, 1995b; Stolorow, 1997; Beebe and Lachmann, 1998), an analyst is always, verbally and nonverbally, self-disclosing. For example, an analyst's inquiry discloses the analyst's interest; an interpretation discloses the analyst's particular organization of the data. Thus, we view disclosure along a continuum, ranging from an "uh-huh" to "I experienced you as aversive." Conscious disclosures differ according to the prominent listening/experiencing perspective and must be coordinated with the patient's shifting attachment (and other) needs.

Traditionally *enactment* addressed unconscious action (initiated by a patient's transference or an analyst's countertransference) in contrast to verbalization, a differentiation that is rendered obsolete when it is recognized that verbal exchange is also an interaction (Gill, 1994; Fosshage, 1995b). Silence, of course, is also an action (Gill, 1994). We assume that unconscious and conscious elements variably participate in all actions, not just in what has traditionally been labeled enactment. Over the years, psychoanalysts have expanded the term enactment to include repetitive transference/countertransference interactions (for example, analysts are drawn into patients' repetitive transferences) and growth-producing interactions (for example, analysts are pulled into patients' selfobject strivings, cocreating a new selfobject or relational experience) (Stolorow, Brandchaft, and Atwood, 1987; Fosshage, 1994). In Stern's (1994) felicitous phrase, patient and analyst cocreate "needed and repeated relationships." In light of these considerations we redefine enactment to refer to an affectively poignant (powerful) and meaningful interaction that either can be facilitating of new growth-promoting relational experience or replicating of traumatic past experience (Fosshage, 1995b).

Case Illustration: Presenting Complaint and Background

Jack is a 50-year-old Canadian who first consulted me (C.A.M.) because he was struggling with two losses: his wife's unexpected ending their marriage of three years and a physically violent rift with his father involving Jack's purchase of an extremely successful family business, located on the outskirts of Toronto, where he lived.

In addition, Jack complained, "I always find people boring. I find everything boring. I have to go from one exciting thing to another." He had a "been there, done that" attitude towards life. He felt that "there is no thrill in anything. . . . I've never been able to have any fun."

At the time of our first contact, I saw Jack only twice. His reaching out for help was quite tenuous, for he quickly became aversive to treatment. He stated that he had "no respect for people who could not do things on their own" and disparaged anyone who needed to "rely on others." He said, "I don't want anybody; I don't need anybody." He was emphatic about how he did not want to change the way he was, and that, if he did, he could do it himself. He added that he had no interest in giving up any of his angry feelings because, "anger gives me an edge." Very consciously not using the word "need," I suggested to him that it might help to at least talk through some feelings about his broken marriage; however, it was abundantly clear that he was pushing me away, repelling any idea of treatment at that time. I chose not to debate him on his justifications for rejecting treatment, feeling that to do so would exacerbate his aversiveness, but simply left the door open for him to return should he change his mind.

A year and a half later, Jack returned to me explaining that his "rage has become intolerable" and he wanted to understand why it took on such large proportions. He expressed his belief that he could actually hurt somebody and described an "intrigue about killing someone." His life situation had changed in that he had just retired from active management of his company and had become engaged to a woman. His fiancée was expressing that she did not feel emotionally connected to him and complained about his resentment of her desires for friends and for a social life with him.

At the very start, Jack took the reins about structuring our contact. He made it clear to me that, despite his open schedule and his considerable wealth, he could only come once a week. He also asserted that one hour "was not enough," and that I must offer him a double session or he would not get involved in treatment. Although this was not the format I would have chosen, I acceded to his request, feeling his proposal to be an expression of his ambivalence and an assertion of what he needed in order to get treatment started. Jack's taking the reins also enabled him to retain a sense of control and self-sufficiency. Under these circumstances, I extended myself and modified my schedule with the hopes of creating a viable treatment situation.

FAMILY HISTORY

Jack was an only child who came from a well-to-do family. His parents separated when he was three and he saw his father only on weekends. Jack spent his time as a child mastering all sorts of activities that vitalized him (what Lichtenberg calls exploratory–assertive activity [Lichtenberg, 1989; Lichtenberg, Lachmann, and Fosshage, 1992, 1996]) and helped him to fortify a sense of self-sufficiency. In his own words he said, "I am a classic type-A with a genius IQ, and I can do anything with my hands and eyes."

Jack described his father as a short but very handsome man, who was extremely seductive to women. He had a "Napoleonic complex and was preoccupied with money, big tits and blond hair." Before adolescence Jack had enjoyed going on business trips with his father and playing golf. However, when he physically outgrew his father and his game became competitive, his father turned on him and became critical, mocking, and ridiculing. His father, an alcoholic, sadistically denigrated Jack and embarrassed him in both social and business situations. He said, "I couldn't win—if I did poorly, I was a 'loser', and if I did well, he would mock and attack me." Jack, however, was in touch with and expressed directly in the analysis his rage at his father. In his daily life, Jack tended to compartmentalize this struggle. In fact, he and his father had not spoken in years, subsequent to a vicious fight in which his father had brandished a knife at him.

His descriptions of his mother portrayed her as a much less defined person. Jack described her as "always there" and observed that "she never laughed much." According to Jack, his mother, out of guilt over her divorce, subjugated herself to her son. She lavished gifts and indulgences upon him, which Jack understood were intended to compensate for her guilt and the psychological abuse he experienced at the hands of his father. Although he felt catered to, he despised her caving into what she felt were his expectations of her, consistently subjugating her subjectivity to his. For example, she would ask him what he wanted for Christmas, and he would make a list. He said that it was boring because he knew exactly what would be in every package, for he received every item from his list. From his perspective, he felt that he had "never learned to share" or to negotiate disappointments as a result of these indulgences.

Jack amused himself by playing alone, rejecting the company of other children. Many times he refers to a model scene (Lichtenberg, Lachmann, and Fosshage, 1992) that he was told about, and seemed to remember, of shrieking and protesting if another child was put in (or near) his baby carriage.[1] As a child, whenever he expressed his aversion to being with other children, his mother backed off and never explored or challenged his reluctance. His aversion to people has

---

[1] Joseph Lichtenberg (personal communication) noted that there is a diagnosis of tactile hypersensitivity and secondary aversiveness referring to individuals who, from birth, have a hyper-reactivity to tactile stimuli that is experienced as irritating.

consistently emerged with his girlfriends who have wanted to include him in their social world. Thus, there most likely were genetically-based contributions to Jack's temperamental problems. The experience of stimuli as irritating and the consequent aversiveness became a repetitive relational scenario (making this early experience a model scene) for Jack.

PSYCHOANALYTIC PROCESS

Jack is a tall, stately, impeccably dressed, disarmingly articulate, lean and graceful-looking man. His interpersonal style with me was wearingly provocative and challenging from the start. Although he came faithfully to his sessions, he was always oppositional and frequently challenged me with confrontations such as, "So, what are you gonna do to help me?"

The beginning of our work centered on a litany of Jack's massive devaluations. They included various ethnic groups whom he considered "pond scum," people who were lacking in excellence in their jobs, people who used poor grammar, people who went to football games, people who wore blue jeans, and people who lived in middle-class housing. A particular focus for his rage was anyone whom he construed to be "rude and inconsiderate." Examples were people who had poor table manners, were loud, or "gawked" at him as he drove down the street in one of his expensive cars. Extraordinarily wealthy, Jack owns many cars and other items that catch people's eyes. He, in turn, had disdain for their looking at him either in awe or in any way he might perceive as mocking. Jack had no friends, never socialized, and rarely left the confines of his house. His energies were focused on renovating this mansion spending, to my ears, staggering amounts, such as $5000 for "the perfect doorknob."

Jack's central complaint continued to be boredom. He amassed things and experiences that gave him an "adrenaline charge"—bigger houses, splashier vacations, more expensive cars, and sexual variety, including the persistent fantasy of sexual "threesomes" (involving himself with two women). He described himself as having "affluenza," a "behavioral disorder of the wealthy where one has everything one could want, has done everything he wants to do, and where there remains no joy and nothing to look forward to."

During our inquiry we were soon able to link his need for an adrenaline charge with his effort to enliven himself and to overcome deeply embedded negative views of himself and of others. I said to him, "Because of your father's attacks, you never felt that you, yourself, had any intrinsic value." He confirmed my interpretation by saying, "That's right, my value to a person is what I can do for them, what I can pay for them, I feel like I have nothing to offer and that they have nothing to offer." Yet, my comments appeared only to frustrate him. When I ventured to interpret his primary feeling of being unlovable, his attitude was a dismissive, "So what?"

Jack remained unrelentingly nihilistic and aggressively aversive for the first two years of our work together. I found sitting through the long and intense period of Jack's nihilism and contemptuous remarks to be highly stressful and found myself reacting at times with repugnance. I often found myself dreading anticipated sessions. He ridiculed people who put any value on human life and bragged that he would be able to shoot someone with no compunction or guilt. He expressed contempt for strangers and described fantasies of going into a bar with a rifle, shooting and killing them with no feelings at all.

In attempting to understand his nihilism and aggression, I struggled with the tension between my own undoubtedly harsh judgment of his pathology emanating from my experience as an other in a relationship with Jack (that is, from the other-centered perspective) and my attempts to remain open to his experience of the world from within his vantage point (that is, from the empathic perspective). He doggedly insisted that there was no value to his life, no value to human life and, looking at me with steely blue eyes, he suggested that he might need to illustrate how strongly he felt by going out and shooting somebody, "then you'll believe I really feel this." In addition, the threat of suicide always remained in the background. "As long as I can go out on my tractor, I can be happy. I don't have to worry about anything on my tractor until the fall comes, and the sun goes down, and then I'll probably kill myself." His self- and other-directed aggression appeared to be an expression of rage toward those who failed him and toward himself for failing and a protection against anticipated self and other failures.

I listened to hours and hours where he described the many human events, such as his father's heart attack and his mother's various illnesses, which did not touch him at all emotionally. He was contemptuous of any sentimentality he sensed in me or any grief at loss. On the other hand, he could not bear the scene in the movie *Dances with Wolves* where the wolf was shot. For several years, this was the only expression of more tender feelings. Any subtle or explicit suggestion, emanating from my own subjectivity, that life does have value (self perspective) was met inevitably with sarcasm and ridicule. Any attempt I made to (try to) empathize with his dark and nihilistic state of mind was met with scorn. He always experienced my more empathic, tender attitudes as a mark of weakness.

Jack rejected my empathically based reflections on his nihilism and any attempt to illuminate its origins (Lachmann, 2000, has described similar experiences with chronically aversive patients). He exhibited a "catastrophic response " (Munschauer, 1987) to a purely empathic connection. "I'm tired of going back to the same old shit. When you see a snake, you should kill it. I didn't want to go over the same old turf over and over. Is there a way to fix it? Let's fix it . . . I don't want to talk about it. I don't want to go back and talk about why fifteen times." Talking about "why" made him feel like "something even more is wrong with me. Let's not talk about it, let's do something, take some proactive steps. It's counterproductive to talk about it over and over, I want to move forward." He scoffed at me anytime my own hopes about his being able to value himself emerged. He fully believed that he could have anything in the world—anything except a relationship. Jack was keenly aware of having no friends, and referred to himself as an "isolated social retard," and "unfit for human companionship."[2]

Early in the treatment, Jack extended an invitation to my husband and me to his large, formal annual office Christmas party. (My husband's law firm had briefly provided legal service to Jack's

---

[2] Wolf's (1988) description of this developmental scenario is quite fitting: "It is as if a child were clothed in a suit of protective armor whose heaviness forced him to grow into grotesque shapes and drained him of energy. Worse yet, after wearing the armor for some years, the growing body becomes so structurally distorted that the armor can no longer be taken off, even though the dangers against it which it protected have passed. For all practical purposes, it is as if the armor has become part of the skin, and keeps away not only the archaic dangers but also the always needed and longed for soft, warm human touches. The psychological makeup imposed on a child remains in adulthood indeed, throughout life" (p. 44).

company prior to the analysis.) At this point, I took the traditional stance and told him that it was not appropriate for me to mix professional and personal relations, and declined the invitation. My action affirmed for Jack that I was "a despicable weakling." For Jack, my traditional stance meant that I was bound by rules, unable to think independently, and unwilling to act like a real person. At this point, he coined his nickname for me, "Pussy Faggot." Since Jack disavowed any need for tenderness and affection, he roundly rejected anyone whom he considered soft or whose subjectivity was dominated by the subjectivity of another (like his mother). I learned, however, that Jack's protest that I was a "pussy faggot," not tough enough, not confrontational toward him, and too influenced by the "rules of my profession," was Jack's "distressed point of entry" (Joseph Lichtenberg, personal communication). I had to learn that his nihilism and devaluation of human life was "ego syntonic"—that was not his point of pain (despite my subjective sense that on some level it "must be").

Although Jack went to work and interacted with people on a professional and business level, he had resigned himself to a reclusive life of self-sufficiency in his mansion, similar to the life of Howard Hughes. Jack disavowed relational needs. He told me that, if he went on a cruise through the most beautiful islands of the world, he would not be talking to people or looking at the scenery, but would be down in the basement figuring out how the boiler worked. When I became involved with Jack, his only real relationship was with his banker, who had become his fiancée, and was a part of the business world he controlled and experienced as safe. Although he had been involved with many women, including a wife, according to Jack, they all had dropped him because they could not tolerate his intensity, his hardness, his possessiveness, his nihilism, and his isolation. Jack consistently denied that these losses affected him. Although Jack openly acknowledged that his relationships with women were troubled and that it was odd that he had no friends, he persisted in vehemently denying a need for anyone. He attributed his callousness to biological and genetic causes, saying,

> The part of my brain that should receive emotion just didn't get enough oxygen. I didn't have the lessons I needed from my parents to be able to have relationships. . . . There's no way you can teach me anything to make me feel like I'm

> acceptable in a relationship. I didn't learn these skills back
> then, how to socially interact, and I'm tired of going through
> all this with you. It's a big waste of time—you're not gonna
> do anything to help me. I think in terms of odds . . . if
> I've never had these relationships before, the odds are that
> I won't, and why should I try? I don't view human beings as
> having any intrinsic value, so why would I want to connect
> with any human being?

I felt that I was always bucking Jack's conviction that things I valued,
the field of psychoanalysis, relationships, and life itself, had nothing
to offer him. His stance with me was always one of provocation and
he staunchly maintained that his intolerance for human life was
"genetic," and that certainly, I would be unable to have any impact
on that idea. Meanwhile, he would lie on his bed in his mansion fiddling
with guns and bullets.

Jack described his life "like being on a big ladder, going up and
up. You can climb to the last rung and then that last rung breaks for
me—I can never get what I really want, because the last rung depends
on someone else. When you have to reach out, and rely on someone
else, it all comes apart." He felt that relationships would last a
maximum of three years, akin to his father's leaving their house when
he was three years old.

It became clear during this first phase of the analysis that any
attempt to break through Jack's nihilism (at times motivated by my
own survival needs) failed and typically provoked increased
antagonism. I readily experienced (from the other-centered listening/
experiencing stance) how Jack could make a woman feel depressed,
defeated, unable to help him, unable to make him happy, and unable
to affect his nihilism, especially since any feelings of being given to
were met with aversiveness. I, in turn, took my frustration, anger and
discomfort to my consultant where the opportunity to express and
explore my feelings helped to restore my battered self and enabled us
to regenerate an effort to find an avenue of access to this man. I had
to find a way, I learned, of staying "in there" with him, meeting,
perhaps, a fundamental need for a sustainable human presence. In
other words, I tried to immerse myself empathically in his subjective
world, so that he could feel understood (what Kohut, 1977, referred

to as a sustained understanding phase) without becoming threatened by or countering his nihilism and aggressiveness.

This empathic immersion appeared for some time to facilitate his articulating his world. Jack, however, gradually began to pressure me more and more. He did not want to be "just understood." He wanted me to actually tell him what was "wrong" with him, to "bump up against him," to "go head on" with him. He said to me, "Don't be passive and just listen—piss me off, don't just sit there. People have listened to me for a long time and they just told me to go do whatever I wanted to do. You've gotta have balls—I want you to have balls!" Jack was clearly experiencing my empathic immersion and responses as too concealing of my subjectivity and replicating for him the traumatic experience of his mother's insufficient and permissive presence. Gradually I took up Jack's prompting (empathic perspective) and I learned to "thump him" offering more of my perspective and reactions (self-perspective), including at times my experience as the other in a relationship with him (the other-centered perspective). I challenged and nudged him more and more, taking a position that vigorously bumped up against his subjectivity. Although this was not my usual style and it felt inordinately pugnacious to do in a therapy hour, when I was able to do so, Jack became increasingly invigorated and engaged. At first I thumped him gently, pressing him on the number of visits per week, saying, "Try it, you might like it." In this case, he burst out laughing, and called me a day later, leaving a message on my answering machine in a sweet, little boy voice, tenderly saying, "I've been thinking about what you suggested, and I think I'd like to try it." I felt very encouraged at this point, because he was opening up, reaching out, and implicitly acknowledging that we had a connection.

A few years into the therapy a major turn occurred when Jack demanded a "progress report" about what was "wrong" with him, what was "broken and needed fixing." He told me I had one week to think about this—that the other things we had talked about were "interesting but hadn't helped anything," and that he would quit unless I could come forth with what he demanded. With regard to his intensified demand for a progress report, I felt that he was feeling more desperate and needed me to go to the mat with him as a real person and someone who would share with him fully my views of him and of his treatment.

Instead of my more usual spirit of inquiry and investigation as to why he was asking for such a thing and what it would mean to him, I felt that he needed me to share directly my subjective views with him. His father had been a devaluing and humiliating adversary, sadistically clobbering him, both physically and psychologically. His mother, in stark contrast, collapsed at his every request and quickly surrendered her own subjective position. I thought that Jack, now feeling safer with me, longed for a relationship with a separate, "real" person (intersubjective relatedness) who could push back at him without his father's sadism.

Feeling considerable anxiety that somehow I was "breaking the rules," I summoned up my courage, bolstered by my consultant, and de-centered from my natural style of responding and the tone of my past training, and I forcefully took him on. Enjoying my aggressively tinged assertiveness, I told him, "Your boredom and your need to stimulate yourself with more and more material assets, or sexual experiences, is of great concern to me. You're in danger of mid-life depression, and even suicide, since you've nearly exhausted all the experiences that provide kicks for you in your life. And furthermore, I know you don't feel it, but I feel very involved with you, and like I'm not just sitting here listening, but that I am being very engaged and interactive." (I left out the expletive "you schmuck!") I followed up by expressing my curiosity and shock about why he experienced our interactions so differently. Even though I had felt I had been very confrontational, Jack claimed he didn't "feel anything," in fact, he "didn't feel a lot of things," and that he thought his "skin was dead." He followed up by some ridiculing comments about all the other "pussy faggots" I must be treating who might be disrupted by such an intervention. So, we continued our wrestling match . . . [3]

Jack clearly enjoyed my taking an oppositional or adversarial position in sort of a manageable punch and counter-punch interaction. Although it did not come naturally, I did it in several ways. I made it overtly clear to him that I wasn't going to leave him at the last rung of the ladder, even though I thought he was "a tough cookie." "You're not gonna relegate this to another one of those three-year

---

[3] This is an example of an adversarial selfobject relationship that can be self-delineating and self-enhancing (Wolf, 1980, 1988; Lachmann, 1986).

relationships," I said. At times, I showed my reaction by making grimaces of frustration and confirming that "Yes, you can be a pain" (other-centered information directly revealed).

This "mutually defined pattern of interaction" (Tansey and Burke, 1995; Beebe and Lachmann, 1998) created a new relational experience that fostered his feeling like a "someone" (and a mutual feeling of being "someone" with each other). It contrasted with his father's crashing down on him and humiliating him, making him feel like a nobody, and his mother's collapsing in the face of his subjectivity, which engendered contempt.

At one point, well into the treatment, Jack invited me to Canada to visit his mansion to see the architecture, the grounds, and the antiques he had assembled to create an authentic reproduction of a historic landmark. He carefully framed this as a "field trip," hoping to ameliorate anxiety I might have about the "rules" of my profession. This time, I and my consultant felt that his offer for me to come to his home represented an important reaching out to me (what Tolpin, 2000, has described as the emergence of a "tendril of his self") since his house and inanimate objects were among his most vital connections. This time, rather than "bumping," he wanted me to understand and affectively resonate with his connections to these inanimate objects. I also realized that, because this was such a locus for vital engagement, it also was an area of keen vulnerability. Since I knew I could be genuinely appreciative of his creative endeavor and elegant possessions, I agreed to accept the proposal. I also thought that the meaning for him would be profound, if I cared enough about him to "break the mold" and deviate from the standard procedure.[4]

When I arrived at the tightly gated mansion, he greeted me. After his butler served us coffee, Jack gave me an extensive tour of the grounds, the art work, the paintings, the beautiful tapestries imported from Europe, and the expensive cars, which were all very easy for me to admire. He proudly showed me the large flawless

---

[6] The analyst's agreement to see the patient's home can be construed as "throwing the book away" (Hoffman, 1998), an instance in which the patient is able to impact the analyst, to get the analyst to spontaneously break out of the ritual rules of analysis, and to become a real person, one example of what Stern et al. (1998) refer to as a "moment of meeting" (see also chapter 4 in Lichtenberg, Lachmann, and Fosshage, 2003).

diamond he had bought for his fiancée and the exquisite diamond necklace he had given to her. I was spontaneously appreciative of their beauty. I also noticed that he had photographs of cars and other possessions displayed; yet, there was not a single photograph of a person in the whole mansion. The most interesting part of the "field trip" was that I observed, for the first time, Jack being truly affectionate as he talked, with the tenderness of a loving parent, about his cars and tractors, all of which he had given pet names. In his element, surrounded by his "things," a softer side of Jack emerged that I had never witnessed before. After this field trip, he began to talk to me in a softer and more childlike way, even commenting on the "cute" figurines in my office. A far warmer atmosphere emerged between us.

Still, the content of our therapy hours continued to be a struggle about whether I had anything to offer him:

"There is nothing you can do for me. I don't think you have ever done anything for me. Nothing has changed; my attitude isn't any different. My feelings aren't any different.

"Other doctors, like my M.D., can give me an antibiotic and fix what is wrong with me! I guess I resign myself to not getting anything here. I have lowered my expectations. So I am less overtly angry . . . I just figure nothing is worth it. I don't see any reason to come here. I thought maybe you would find some key to unlock the problem . . . but my attitude is the same as it was two years ago. I have decided that, when it comes to any relationship where people are involved, whether it be in my work, or any contribution my analyst might try to make to me, or my attorney, whenever people enter the equation with me, I should not expect much. No matter what I do, no matter what I contribute, it will not have any impact on what I receive, and that is how I see everything. You can't control other people. All I can do is lower my expectations."

Trying a verbal interpretation, I said to him, "Yes, it is your template; no matter what you do, you're not going to get squat back." His reply was:

"With people, all you can try for is the absence of negative. I don't care to ask for anything anymore. I don't expect anything, I don't want to be disappointed. Nothing is going to change. I don't want to be on this roller coaster again. The only thing I want to do is go out there and ride my golf cart or my tractor. You're setting me up to hope, and I don't want to be hurt, so I have just 'turned off.'"

Having shown a more open, softer side of himself, his aversiveness intensified. Jack unilaterally discontinued his treatment with me shortly thereafter, saying that he had decided to "get used to the way things are in this world, and make the best of it." After this period, we exchanged several written correspondences in which we wrestled with the concept of whether change is possible or whether personality characteristics are "genetic."

Jack called me several months later and said that he "felt better" because he was not coming to see me anymore and, "could forget about things, grow up, and think about the rest of my life." He invited my husband and me to come to his mansion for a formal dinner (with him and his fiancée) to be served by his butler.

I accepted his invitation to my husband and me for dinner at his home with the appreciation that, since he was extremely reclusive and never had a guest come to his house, he really needed me to respond to this gesture of reaching out toward me. Although he had expressed disdain for a therapeutic relationship and contempt that I could "do nothing for him," I sensed that he desperately longed to stay connected with me. I accepted the invitation, but again with a certain amount of anxiety—thinking of the "ethical guidelines" and "dual relationship" admonitions.[5] I felt, however, that the enactment itself in its affirmation would be facilitative and possibly provide an avenue for re-engaging him in the analytic work. I knew it would be a lavish, extremely formal dinner, served by a butler, and I was confident that I could both feel comfortable in such a setting and genuinely appreciate its grace and elegance. I also knew that the high formality would help to keep the experience sufficiently structured.

In fact, the dinner was the height of elegance, and the conversation playful, as Jack clearly enjoyed jousting with me, in light banter, about themes from our sessions. They included whether anybody "had to be happy," whether it was "normal" not to feel guilty about rageful and murderous feelings, and whether emotions were

---

[5] Hedges (1997) addresses this issue: "The faulty shift of ethical focus from 'damaging exploitation' to 'dual relationships' has led to widespread misunderstanding and incessant, naïve moralizing, which has undermined the spontaneous, creative, and unique aspects of the personal relationship that is essential to the psychotherapeutic process" (p. 221). Also see Lazarus and Zur (2002) on a careful reassessment of dual relationships in psychotherapy.

"genetic" and, therefore, ultimately unalterable. My position with him during the dinner was to "keep it light" and "playfully polite" and delicately to invite him to return to discuss these loaded issues in my office. Although he said, genuinely, that he would like for the four of us to get together, and "play" again, I did not hear from him for almost one year. My hypothesis at the time was that he was struggling against the softening that had come with having had me in his home and having his guard down.

Then, to my surprise, almost a year later, Jack consulted me when his fiancée broke their engagement and suddenly moved out of his mansion. His words were that he "wanted to come to talk" to me and "needed to continue the analysis" and "to get some medication." Immediately, he became very involved in trying to diagnose the quality of his deepening depression, and was ready to fly anywhere for a medication consultation. Since I had not seen him in treatment for almost a year, it was difficult in terms of my schedule initially to reinstate the double session required. I was acutely aware of how difficult it must have been for him to turn to me in need. I also remembered one of his model scenes—"the last rung of a ladder where you reach for help and there is no one there." I, therefore, felt that I needed visibly to reach out in his direction. For this reason, when he was extremely upset and I happened to be in his town, I agreed to make a two-hour "house call" to his mansion. We enjoyed a formal butler-served lunch and then had a therapy session in his library, where he dragged out a dusty old box with photos, all in disarray, and pulled out some of his mother to show me and to talk about.

Shortly thereafter, we were able to resume our double sessions. At the first office visit he greeted me in the waiting room and said, "Carol, help me! Help, I need a hug." I made myself available for a brief shoulder-to-shoulder hug and he came into my office and poured out how terrible he felt and how desperately he hoped that this problem was "biological" and that medication would hold the key to his relief. I told him that in his asking for help from a psychopharmacologist (after having denigrated the field of psychology for years) he was now opening himself up to needing something from me, too—a state of self which he had assiduously avoided, always maintaining that he did not need anybody and that nobody had anything to offer him. I was clear about letting him know both what progress I felt this reaching out was for him and how risky it must feel. I intended to pick up on the leading or forward edge (Miller, 1985; Tolpin, 2000), the developmental striving, implicitly to affirm him for reaching out, and to focus on underlying fears that needed to be closely tracked.

Jack became fixated on finding a DSM diagnosis for himself to account for his "genetic problem" and to serve as the basis for pursuing medication as a treatment. He made it his mission to consult with the best psychopharmacologists in different cities and found people who were willing to micromanage his medication daily by phone. It became clear that Jack lacked self-soothing capacities, so that the world was often experienced as painfully overstimulating and, even more, hostile and dangerous. He suffered greatly with somatic hyperirritability, migraines, insomnia, food dislikes, dislike of noise, light aversion, and extreme sensitivity to dark weather, to alcohol, and to any dose of medication.

Despite many attempts to find an effective medication, it became clear fairly quickly that none of the psychiatric medications helped Jack at all, and they all gave him powerful, idiosyncratic side effects. When he was frustrated at being unable to find a genuine DSM diagnosis for himself and, at the same time, he and I had developed a warm and congenial relationship in the analysis, I was able to tease him a little about this. I said to him, "So, you've been to all the best psychopharmacologists in the big cities, you've flown everywhere seeking out the best diagnostic opinion, but here it was, your own little analyst, who had the right diagnosis all along." Glued to what I was saying, he asked what diagnosis was that, and I could feel the tension as he awaited my response. I said to him, "You are a Closet Sweetie Pie . . . been in the closet most of your life!" He laughed and responded with delight to my appreciative affirmation of the hidden tender part of himself that had been sequestered since it had been linked with fear, vulnerability, and disdain for his "weak mother." Subsequent to this intervention, the term Closet Sweetie Pie (CSP) became a nickname we used frequently to highlight these emergent tender parts of himself. He referred to himself as "SP" (Sweetie Pie) when he was "out of the closet" and in touch with his tenderness and need for relatedness, and we called him "CSP" (Closet Sweetie Pie) when he was locked in his closed-off aversive state and was hard and unreachable.

In parallel, as I have indicated before, Jack's nickname for me was "PF." He called me this quite consistently and affectionately. It was an abbreviation for "Pussy Faggot," and we both understood that it represented three things: his experience of my weakness, his experience of the weakness of his mother, and his disavowal of his own tenderness or weakness. In one phrase he denigrated what he saw as the weakness in a woman and a man. It is important to remember how much he needed "thumping" or "bumping" in the middle stages of treatment (and how I had to be shaped to respond in that way [Slavin and Kriegman, 1998]). In contrast, when he experienced me as acting on my own authentic initiative (outside of the rulebook) he affirmingly called me "PPF" (Previous Pussy Faggot). I subsequently explained to him (and he agreed) that maybe what had happened between us in the therapy was that I had become tougher than I was before, and he had become more tender than he was before.

Sessions continued, and we were able to further illuminate his expectation that no one could be counted on to give him a hand or to go out of their way for him. Increasingly, I saw less and less of the aversiveness I had experienced in the earlier phases. The tenor became more congenial, playful, and warm, and not at all confrontational. He seemed to be experiencing with me "a novel interpersonal reality." (Hedges, 1997). I always had in my mind the precarious position he must have felt that he was in in allowing himself to turn his "magnet" toward other people, instead of in the repellant position.

In his life, Jack "opened the gates" and began to try to meet women, especially through creative adventures on the Internet. Sometimes, he flew to meet the woman in person. Eventually, quite by happenstance, he reconnected with a childhood love, who lived in California but was visiting her family's farm in Canada. They courted by e-mail and telephone. They fell in love once again, and he was able to induce her to leave her husband in California and "come home" to move in with him. Because of his growing confidence in me and residual distrust in other analysts, he asked me to begin telephone therapy with her. Under these circumstances, I felt it was particularly important to him that I was professionally available for his girlfriend and that I not be confined by the "rules" with its meaning of being the subjugated mother.

His girlfriend was having trouble keeping in touch with her own needs and her own desires. She had been living in an unhappy marriage for more than twenty years; her husband had had multiple affairs. The totality of her days were dedicated to meeting the needs of others.

She had been unable to take any stand on her own behalf. Her pattern had been one of pathological accommodation (Brandchaft, 1994)—taking care of her husband, her children, and other members of her husband's extended family at the expense of her desires and needs. Having reconnected with Jack, an opportunity opened up to her to meet deep needs of her own for love and validation and to give up her prior pattern of defining herself exclusively through the caretaking of others. Yet, Jack also made demands that created intense conflict for her, for which she was seeking my help. For example, one focus of treatment became whether or not she was willing to undergo procedures that would make her more blonde and buxom.

Jack and I continued our analytic work for a while, but it soon became clear that he was "blissfully happy." He told me, "It doesn't get any better than this!" We discontinued our sessions with the understanding that he could resume as needed. Interestingly, it was important to him that I continue treating his now new wife. Currently, she still comes to see me regularly, and there continues a warm relationship between Jack and me, sort of by proxy now. The relationship with his new wife is extremely important to him, and I feel deeply honored and trusted that he has dropped his adversarial position and allowed me, "a stranger," into his baby carriage.

Two years later, Jack surprised me by appearing by himself at his wife's appointment time. He told me that he wanted to rid himself of some of his possessions and have a smaller house and fewer servants, so that he could enjoy more private time with his wife (the first woman, besides me, who had stuck with him for more than three years) and not be so burdened with the upkeep of material things. He said, "You know why I used to need to have those things, but I don't need that anymore since I have my home life with her." He told me, "I love my life!" and because of this state, he talked about a new-found faith in the transcendent and a sense that "someone good was watching over him." Once again, he invited my husband and me to take a drive to his mansion for dinner. This time, and with far less anxiety, I accepted. My patient and his wife were both casually dressed, and the servants had been dismissed. Jack cooked us a cheeseburger on his grill overlooking the beautiful and magnificently lit swimming pool and grounds, while his wife boiled noodles in their Better Homes and Gardens kitchen. He showed me the ping-pong room where he and his wife ritualistically enjoyed "thumping" each other with a lively game every night after dinner. Again, we toured the mansion. This time I was struck by all the photographs of people that were displayed— photos of Jack and his wife, of him hugging their new dog, and of him with various prominent film makers and socialite friends with whom he had developed "family" relations. Much of the conversation centered on his wish to relocate to California, where he saw people "enjoying being alive." Tears came to my eyes as I saw a little stone sculpture on his desk, which said, "Success is getting what you want; happiness is wanting what you get."

DISCUSSION

To reiterate, we understood Jack's nihilism to reflect a profound hopelessness and despair about obtaining the necessary relational nutrients of life, based on a history of extreme emotional deprivation. We also understood that Jack's profound nihilism and aversiveness provided an impenetrable protection against hope and relational engagement (illustrated by his extreme difficulty in beginning treatment) and that he expected a painful failure in others' responsiveness. Early in life Jack, influenced by his familial environment and perhaps by a genetic predisposition for tactile hypersensitivity, found human relations to be inimical. Feeling unloved and unlovable, Jack had developed a characteristic aversive style that enabled him to disavow feelings of relational need, together with associated feelings of weakness, and to bolster a sense of self-sufficiency and strength. He became easily enraged and devaluing of people, often taking a superior position, which was fortified by his keen intelligence. Jack substantially withdrew from people and turned instead to an inanimate world for vitalizing attachment and exploratory-assertive experiences (Lichtenberg, 1989; Lichtenberg, Lachmann, and Fosshage, 1992, 1996, 2003). Jack had been able to survive through attaching to inanimate objects and accentuating exploratory-assertive activities, evident in his focus on and mastery of his inanimate environment and culminating in his extremely successful business pursuits.

During the initial phases of psychoanalytic treatment, the analyst attempted to listen to and experience Jack from an empathic perspective. Jack's nihilism and aversiveness dominated the scene. Under these conditions, the analyst understandably had considerable difficulty in establishing traction for analytic inquiry. When inquiry and interpretations emanating from an empathic perspective focused on his articulated experience of negative self feelings, negative expectations, and their origins, Jack repudiated them. Jack appeared to experience this line of inquiry and interpretive foray as critical and/ or as potentially exposing him to relational selfobject needs that he desperately needed to disavow. Thus, he responded with intensified aversiveness. Moreover, when the analyst's interpretations implicitly challenged Jack's nihilism (emerging, at times, out of the analyst's effort to survive), Jack averted the analyst's challenge through fortifying his nihilistic fortress.

Shifting somewhat, but still using the empathic stance, the analyst attempted to be more of an understanding presence (Kohut's, 1977, phase of understanding), immersing herself within Jack's subjective world without becoming threatened or taken over by it. Explanations (interpretations) were minimized. During this period, Jack's unarticulated need to be listened to, to be heard, and implicitly to be acknowledged—mirroring selfobject relatedness—was in the foreground. Gradually Jack appeared to feel safer. He and the analyst were able to forge a connection. Feeling fortified, Jack began to push for a fuller interactional experience. He did so especially because he began to experience the analyst as too concealed, potentially replicating his experience of his mother's subjugation of her personhood. Because Jack was assimilating the analyst's particular analytic stance into the thematic relational configuration of his subjugated mother, it was necessary for the analyst to alter her stance to prevent further replication of this traumatic experience. He wanted to experience the analyst as a separate, "real" person. Intersubjective relatedness had moved into the foreground. The empathic, other-centered, and self listening/experiencing perspectives were all needed in order for the analyst to understand and to respond more fully as a separate person—to take him on, to "thump" him. To have remained exclusively anchored within the empathic mode would, in our view, have limited the analyst and prevented her from sharing sufficiently her subjectivity. For example, the analyst now could share with him in the face of his nihilistic and aversive pronouncements her experience of him as pushing her away and, in the vernacular, how she could experience him as a "real pain." Another example is the analyst's willingness to respond to Jack's request "to wrestle" with him that enabled them to cocreate a self-enhancing adversarial experience, unlike his experiences with his subjugated mother and attacking father. In contrast, if the analyst had used other-centered data too early in treatment, Jack could easily have felt criticized, especially in light of his denigrating father, all of which would have prompted further aversiveness. The analyst had to be relentlessly persistent in her inquiry and responses, determined not to leave him alone or withdrawn in his aversive position, and to demonstrate that she would not be pushed away by his aversiveness—that she would be "there." The analyst, thus, was able to interact with Jack more openly, replicating neither the subjugated mother, nor the sadistically critical father, cocreating new more vitalizing relational experience.

The analyst had to have a place, cocreated with her consultant, to reassess, to reframe, and ultimately to break with the rules of more traditional analytic practice. The lunch and tour, the formal dinner, the two-hour session at his home, the last dinner with Jack and his wife, and the analyst's willingness to work with the woman who became his wife were all poignant interactions or enactments that, in our view, profoundly facilitated the analytic engagement. Jack experienced the analyst as willing to engage with him fully as an interested, caring person—a deeply affirming experience. These enactments also meant to Jack that the analyst, unlike his mother, was able to think and act independently, thus enabling him to form a needed idealized selfobject connection. Based on these new experiences, Jack was able to respect and engage a woman, rather than disparage her (like his subjugated mother). In addition, the dinners, perhaps especially the last dinner, enabled Jack to be "caretaking" of the analyst. The analyst's relative ease in accepting his caretaking without subjugation also provided a valuable new model of a caretaking interaction. Willing to engage in these unusual forums, the analyst, while spontaneously and authentically present, was able to maintain a sufficiently asymmetrical engagement so that the interactions did not "deteriorate" into a social relationship, but were focused and contained in order to facilitate the analytic process.

To reiterate, we feel that a patient's attachment needs and forms of relatedness can be conceptualized as ranging along a continuum. These shifting needs, as they are expressed in different forms of relatedness, need to be closely tracked in order to facilitate the analytic interaction. When a patient's selfobject needs for mirroring and idealization are in the foreground of experience, the analyst's use of the empathic perspective for inquiry and responding is most facilitative. When a patient moves from a selfobject to intersubjective relatedness and to caretaking relatedness, the analyst needs to have available additional data obtained from other-centered and self-listening/ experiencing perspectives to facilitate the analytic interaction through the use and disclosure of a fuller range of the analyst's experience.

REFERENCES

Bacal, H. (1985), Optimal responsiveness and the therapeutic process. In: *Progress in Self Psychology*, Vol. 1, ed. A. Goldberg. Hillsdale, NJ: The Analytic Press, pp. 202–227.

———— ed. (1998), *How Therapists Heal Their Patients: Optimal Responsiveness*. Northvale, NJ: Aronson.

Beebe, B., Jaffe, J. & Lachmann, F. (1992), A dyadic systems view of communication. In: *Relational Perspectives*, ed. N. Skolnick & S. Warshaw. Hillsdale, NJ: The Analytic Press. pp. 61–81.

———— & Lachmann, F. (1998), Co-constructing inner and relational processes: Self- and mutual regulation in infant research and adult treatment. *Psychoanal. Psychol.*, 15:480–516.

Benjamin, J. (1988), *The Bonds of Love*. New York: Pantheon Press.

———— (1995), *Like Subjects, Love Objects*. New Haven, CT: Yale University Press.

Brandchaft, B. (1994), To free the spirit from its cell. In: *The Widening Scope of Self Psychology: Progress in Self Psychology*, Vol. 9, ed. A. Goldberg. Hillsdale, NJ: The Analytic Press, pp. 209–230.

Bromberg, P. (1998), *Standing in the Spaces: Essays on Clinical Process, Trauma, and Dissociation*. Hillsdale, NJ: The Analytic Press.

Fosshage, J. (1994), Toward reconceptualizing transference: Theoretical and clinical considerations. *Internat. J. Psycho-Anal.*, 75:265-280.

———— (1995a), Countertransference as the analyst's experience of the analysand: Influence of listening perspectives. *Psychoanal. Psychol.*, 12:375–391.

———— (1995b), Interaction in psychoanalysis: A broadening horizon. *Psychoanal. Dial.*, 5:459–478.

———— (1997), Listening/experiencing perspectives and the quest for a facilitative responsiveness. In: *Conversations in Self Psychology: Progress in Self Psychology*, Vol. 13, ed. A. Goldberg. Hillsdale, NJ: The Analytic Press, pp. 33–35.

———— (2003), Contextualizing self psychology and relational psychoanalysis: Bi-directional influence and proposed syntheses. *Contemp. Psychoanal.*, 39:411–448.

Gill, M. (1994), *Transitions in Psychoanalysis*. Hillsdale, NJ: The Analytic Press.

Hedges, L. (1997), In praise of the dual relationship. In: *Therapists at Risk: Perils of the Intimacy of the Therapeutic Relationship*, ed. L. Hedges, R. Hilton, V. Hilton & B. Caudill. Northvale, NJ: Aronson, pp. 221–250.

Hoffman, I. Z. (1998), *Ritual and Spontaneity in the Psychoanalytic Process: A Dialectical-Constructivist View.* Hillsdale, NJ: The Analytic Press.

Kohut, H. (1959), Introspection, empathy and psychoanalysis. *J. Amer. Psychoanal. Assn.,* 7:459–483.

────── (1971), *The Analysis of the Self.* New York: International Universities Press.

────── (1977), *The Restoration of the Self.* New York: International Universities Press.

────── (1984). *How Does Analysis Cure?* ed. A. Goldberg & P. Stepansky. Chicago: University of Chicago Press.

────── (1982), Introspection, empathy and the semicircle of mental health. *Internat. J. Psycho-Anal.,* 63:395–408.

Lachmann, F. (1986), Interpretation of psychic conflict and adversarial relationships: A self-psychoanalytic perspective. *Psychoanal. Psychol.,* 3:341–355.

────── (2000), *Transforming Aggression.* Northvale, NJ: Aronson.

Lazarus, A. & Zur, O. (2002), *Dual Relationships and Psychotherapy.* New York: Springer.

Lichtenberg, J. (1989), *Psychoanalysis and Motivation.* Hillsdale, NJ: The Analytic Press.

────── Lachmann, F. & Fosshage, J. (1992), *Self and Motivational Systems: Toward a Theory of Technique.* Hillsdale, NJ: The Analytic Press.

────── ────── ────── (1996), *The Clinical Exchange: Techniques Derived from Self and Motivational Systems.* Hillsdale, NJ: The Analytic Press.

────── ────── & ────── (2003), *A Spirit of Inquiry: Communication in Psychoanalysis.* Hillsdale, NJ: The Analytic Press.

Miller, J. (1985), How Kohut actually worked. In: *Progress in Self Psychology, Vol. 1,* ed. A. Goldberg. New York: Guilford, pp. 13–32.

Mitchell, S. (1988), *Relational Concepts in Psychoanalysis.* Cambridge, MA: Harvard University Press.

Munschauer, C. (1987), The patient chase: A bridge between the theories of Kernberg and Kohut. *Psychoanal. Inq.,* 7:99–120.

Shane, M. & Shane, E. (1996), Self psychology in search of the optimal: A consideration of optimal responsiveness, optimal provision, optimal gratification and optimal restraint in clinical situation. *Basic Ideas Reconsidered: Progress in Self Psychology, Vol. 12,* ed. A. Goldberg. Hillsdale, NJ: The Analytic Press, pp. 37–54.

────── ────── & Gales, M. (1997), *Intimate Attachments: Toward a New Self Psychology.* New York: Guilford.

Slavin, M. & Kriegman, D. (1998), Why the analyst needs to change: Toward a theory of conflict, negotiation, and mutual influence in the therapeutic process. *Psychoanal. Dial.,* 8:247–284.

Stern, D. (1985), *The Interpersonal World of the Infant.* New York: Basic Books.

────── Sander, L., Nahum, J., Harrison, A., Lyons-Ruth, K., Morgan, A., Bruschweiler-Stern, N. & Tronick, E. (1998), Noninterpretive mechanisms in psychoanalytic therapy: The "something more" than interpretation. *Internat. J. Psycho-Anal.,* 79:903–921.

Stern, S. (1994), Needed relationships and repeated relationships. *Psychoanal. Dial.,* 4:317–345.

Stolorow, R. (1997), Dynamic, dyadic, intersubjective systems: An evolving paradigm for psychoanalysis. *Psychoanal. Psychol.*, 14:337–346.

———— Brandchaft, B. & Atwood, G. E. (1987), *Psychoanalytic Treatment: An Intersubjective Approach*. Hillsdale, NJ: The Analytic Press.

Sullivan, H. S. (1953), *The Interpersonal Theory of Psychiatry*. New York: Norton.

Tansey, M. & Burke, W. (1995), *Understanding Countertransference: From Projective Identification to Empathy*. Hillsdale, NJ: The Analytic Press.

Tolpin, M. (2000), Forward and trailing edge transferences: Crucial developmental distinctions. Presented at 23rd Annual International Conference on the Psychology of the Self, Panel I, November 10, Chicago.

Winnicott, D. (1949), Hate in the countertransference. In: *Collected Papers*. New York: Basic Books.

———— (1958), *Through Paediatrics to Psychoanalysis*. London: Hogarth.

Wolf, E. (1980), On the developmental line of selfobject relations. In: *Advances in Self Psychology*, ed. A. Goldberg. New York: International Universities Press, pp. 117–130.

———— (1988), *Treating the Self*. New York: Guilford.

Three

A SELF-PSYCHOLOGICAL VIEWPOINT
A DISCUSSION OF FOSSHAGE AND MUNSCHAUER'S CLINICAL CASE

PAULA B. FUQUA

*I*t is a pleasure to discuss this inspiring, instructive chapter. In the context of a very difficult case, Fosshage and Munschauer have delineated three listening/experiencing perspectives an analyst may take. They have shown how the analyst used herself creatively in all three modes in the therapy of a man who suffered from rage, could not maintain a relationship with a woman, and was controlling and resistant to treatment from the beginning.

The three types of relating the authors have described are (1) the selfobject type, in which the analyst listens and interacts in a primarily empathic way, (2) the self-with-other or intersubjective type, in which the listening/experiencing stance of the analyst is more other-centered, and (3) a caretaking mode, in which the selfobject needs of the analyst become the focus of a caretaking analysand. An overarching principle is that the analyst must be prepared to adjust to what the patient needs for psychological growth at any given time and that the patient's needs can change more than once in the course of treatment.

The authors also redefine the time-worn term *enactment* as "an affectively poignant (powerful) and meaningful interaction that can either be facilitating of new growth-promoting relational experience or replicating of traumatic past experience."

In my discussion, I will try to show that the three types of listening/experiencing, so appealingly neat and seemingly clear-cut, are not so clear, and that all three modes of relating are still guided by empathy. I maintain that empathy is not one of three stances, but the supraordinate principle determining whatever stance the analyst may take. In each stance, the therapist's subjectivity is also important. When enactments are involved, the differentiation of growth-promoting enactments from boundary violations depends on both the empathy and character of the therapist.

First, let us review some of the salient features of this remarkable case. Jack was rich, isolated, bored, and sometimes suicidal. From the beginning, he devalued Munschauer and insisted on special treatment at the same time. She was able to give him the double length, once-a-week sessions he demanded as she flexibly adapted to see if she could make treatment possible. One can imagine the pressure one might have felt if one were in Munschauer's shoes when Jack challenged her to "do something," yet spurned her interventions, contemptuous of her affective availability. At that point, many of us would have given up on this difficult man, but Dr. M showed remarkable patience and persistence. Early in the treatment she recognized his need for her to listen attentively and see things from his vantage point without intruding her own more hopeful view. Later, Jack wanted and needed her to be a firm presence against whom he could bump up, unlike his milquetoast mother. Despite Munschauer's usually gentle demeanor, she found it within herself to respond with spunk. When Jack demanded to know "what was wrong with him," she provided a frank and realistic view. Her caring vitality came through as a new experience for Jack.

When Jack asked Dr. M to see his architecturally significant house, she recognized that he was beginning to need a different kind of selfobject relatedness that represented a new and vulnerable structure in Jack's personality. Buttressed by the support of her consultant, Dr. M made a "house call" and Jack warmed up, but still cycled back to negativism and soon discontinued treatment. Somewhat later still, Jack invited Dr. M and her husband to dinner. Recognizing another moment in which Jack was reaching out, she accepted. Throughout the dinner, she kept in mind the importance of providing a growth-promoting experience in a new form. Fosshage and Munschauer identify these visits as enactments and redefine the term as affectively powerful interactions that may either replicate old traumas or provide a new, mutative experience.

After Dr. M's second visit to Jack's mansion, there was a long hiatus in the treatment. Then Jack broke up with his fiancée and issued a cry for help. Dr. M recognized his desperation and made another "house call." Treatment resumed. After a period in which Jack fruitlessly sought a psychopharmacologic solution to his unhappiness, a playful tenderness and affection blossomed. He nicknamed her his "pussy faggot" and she called him a CSP— Closet Sweetie Pie. Jack opened up more and more to his need for relationships.

In another somewhat unorthodox move, Dr. M agreed to see Jack's new fiancée while Jack was still in treatment. Jack himself was finally happy and soon discontinued his therapy. Two years later, Jack again invited Dr. M and her husband to dinner. In contrast to the butler-served extravaganzas of the past, Jack grilled cheeseburgers. He enjoyed being able to personally provide something for his guests, and Dr. M warmly accepted his caretaking.

In Fosshage and Munschauer's interpretation of what happened in this heroic treatment, Jack first needed an empathic response from his therapist. Later he needed a firmer interaction with a cohesive and well defined other. This was the "bumping up against each other" relationship. Finally, things evolved and a mature Jack needed to give something to Dr. M. The fact that she was able to take it in, allowing her own needs to be gratified, seemed to be a third therapeutically important type of relationship for Jack.

There are many clinical pearls in this paper. Some of these are familiar, but still worth dwelling on. First, the authors remind us in action of how important a consultant can be. The consultant offered selfobject support for the therapist in a situation that was demeaning, discouraging, affectively depriving, and perhaps frightening, too, considering Jack's suicidality. Kohut (1971, p. 270) pointed out long ago that the therapist has selfobject needs. These must be legitimized, understood, and provided for one way or another for any treatment to succeed. As therapists, it is our responsibility to seek support outside the treatment when the situation within is undermining our own narcissistic balance. Naturally, we also must use our reactions in the treatment to understand what is going on.

The consultant also gave the therapist an additional perspective that affirmed the safety of the enactments and their likelihood of promoting growth rather than traumatic repetition. I may be reading something into what the authors described, but it appears to me that the consultant felt that Munschauer's visits would be constructive for Jack. When we are doing anything "outside the box," we feel better with a second opinion.

Another point worth dwelling on is that this treatment took place over a very long time, with several comings and goings. It serves to remind us that interruptions do not necessarily mean endings. We need to see them as Dr. M did, as one moment in what may be an ongoing process. Any termination could actually turn out to be an interruption and any apparent interruption could actually represent a termination. We do not always know the meaning or outcome when there is an interruption/termination, but it is appropriate to behave in a way that allows for a later resumption. In "happy endings," we balance our allowance for a possible resumption with a joyful acknowledgment of what has been achieved.

Dr. M balanced skillfully between Jack's need for a response that was not rule-bound and the pitfall of a boundary violation. She kept his best interest paramount, even while she was working in a nonstandard way. In exploring and understanding this, I would like to know more about Dr. M's reactions to Jack. She was irritated at his negativism and tempted to despair of his treatment. Is there more? Jack was rich, powerful, and attractive. How seductive might that have been? Could that have been a factor in their aggressive-submissive enactment?[1] If so, in other hands the enactment might have led to a boundary violation, but this did not happen. Clearly, Dr. M avoided that temptation, which leads one to ask, how did she—or the consultant—know what was appropriate? What can we learn that is applicable to our own practice? I do not think the authors have answered this question, although one cannot take them too much to task for it, because all the great minds in the field have not as yet provided a blueprint for dealing with this type of question. I, myself, would simply add that Dr. M's behavior must have been guided not only by empathy for Jack, but also by her firm sense of morality. This I would place within the intersubjective realm, as a contribution from

---

[1] Thanks to Steven Stern, Salee Jenkins, and Jill Gardner for drawing my attention to this point.

her particularity. In treatment a great deal does hinge on who we are.[2] What we do as therapists is guided by empathy, but also depends on our maturity, morality, and inner commitment to the growth of our patients. This may be buttressed by consultation, but really cannot be taught or mandated, since it is the condensation of all that makes us ourselves at any given moment.

In my introduction, I questioned the authors' categorization of therapist–patient relationships into three types: empathic, self–other, and caretaking. I believe that one cannot discount the significance of empathy as the most important factor in all three types. In the first type, empathy is important by definition. It also guides the interpersonal—or intersubjective—"bumping up against each other" of the second type. How could Dr. M have known the proper course to take without the prior exercise of empathy? Her realization that Jack's nihilism "was not his point of pain" illustrates the guidance provided by her attunement and understanding once she transcended some stereotypical assumptions about Jack's condition.

I argue the same in regard to the third type of relatedness Fosshage and Munschauer delineate. Even though Dr. M allowed herself to enjoy Jack's caretaking, her participation was also guided by empathy. She chose, out of the extensive repertoire of her feelings and behavior, what was most needed by Jack. Here too, it seems that empathy is not one of three types of relating, but an overarching guide to all relating. It also seems that, as a guiding stance, empathy is about listening in all three modes.

An underlying assumption in the background of Fosshage and Munschauer's paper is that attachment needs are primary and remain the wellspring of health and growth. In this I am in total agreement and regard empathy as one epiphenomenal manifestation of that underlying principle.

So the three stances are not about listening in different ways because, as therapists, we are always listening in an empathic way, no

---

[2] Kohut famously noted that in cases of addiction, who the parents of the patient are is more important than what they do. He clarified later that this dictum was not meant to apply to analysts because empathy is teachable (Ornstein, 1991, p. 641). That may be true, but the complexity of an analyst's character and morality, while maybe modifiable, is slow to change and very much a manifestation of who the analyst is, at any given moment, in my view.

matter how we choose to interact. I do not think the three stances are about experiencing either. The analyst's specific experience is ongoing and provides a matrix (intersubjectively determined) out of which the analyst chooses certain actions rather than others. Metaphorically, one of our ears is (at)tuned to the "other" and another is (at)tuned subjectively. This self–other structure is ongoingly entwined with the "we-ness" of mutual understanding in every moment in time.

Nevertheless, we still have three particular types of interaction the analyst can take with an analysand, that of listening in a way that is affectively present but not intruding or adding much, that of telling the patient what the analyst thinks and feels in contrast to what the patient feels, and that of allowing oneself to enjoy and conveying to the patient our enjoyment of what the patient has to give.

One may then ask, does the delineation of the three types of interaction advance clinical practice? There I believe the answer is yes, based on my own clinical experience. Patients do need us to listen quietly sometimes, to "bump up" against them with our own views and reactions sometimes, and to joyfully accept their kindness and gifts. Having the three types of interacting in mind allows therapists to choose more consciously which approach to take and to clarify why they are taking it. This is the true contribution of Fosshage and Munschauer.

REFERENCES

Kohut, H. (1971), *The Analysis of the Self.* New York: International Universities Press.

Ornstein, P., ed. (1991), *The Search for the Self: Selected Writings of Heinz Kohut: 1978–1981.* Madison, CT: International Universities Press.

Four

A DYNAMIC SYSTEMS VIEWPOINT
A DISCUSSION OF FOSSHAGE AND MUNSCHAUER'S CLINICAL CASE

JEFFREY L. TROP
MELANIE L. BURKE

*O*ur intent in this discussion is to describe how we use the concept of nonlinear open systems theory as a frame for understanding the psychoanalytic process, as patient and therapist in context constitute a dynamic system.

Nonlinear system principles were originally employed in chemistry, physics, and mathematics. Developmental biologists Thelen and Smith (1994) apply these principles to human development in an attempt to elucidate the environmental factors in complex systems that stimulate change. It is our intent to offer our viewpoint on the application of these ideas to approaches in facilitating change by using the case history described by Fosshage and Munschauer.

Thelen and Smith (1994) summarize the logic of dynamic systems as follows:

> Although behavior and development appear structured, there are no structures. Although behavior and development appear rule-driven, there are no rules. There is complexity. There is a multiple, parallel, and continuously dynamic interplay of perception and action, and a system that seeks certain stable solutions. These solutions emerge from relation, not from design [p. xix].

Dynamic systems theory is not designed as a specific protocol for the psychoanalytic treatment situation, but its underlying emphasis on contextualism makes it a rich source of generalized ideas for integration into psychoanalytic theory and technique. As we stated in a previous work summarizing dynamic systems theory,

> order emerges from the self-organization of a system within time-locked contexts. Development unfolds in a spontaneous, nonlinear fashion, and it is this 'messy' character of development that is captured by a dynamic approach. Mind is conceived as process and not as a warehouse of structures [1999, pp. 205–206].

One of the most basic and fundamental elements of dynamic systems is the repetition of behavioral, cognitive, and physiological patterns. A person is faced with a context or set of contexts that provide him or her with specific tasks and incline him or her toward certain actions. In the process of performing these tasks, learning takes place. The person learns that certain behavioral patterns, certain cognitive attitudes and ways of thinking, are associated with or appropriate to certain contexts. Through the repetition of behavioral and cognitive responses within these contexts, the person develops preferred patterns, both conscious and unconscious, that emerge because of the coordinated history between internal and external contexts.

The patients who come to see us are motivated to understand and change the patterns that organize and structure their lives. These patterns, which are often unconscious, developed as an adaptation to the context in which they were raised as children. These patterns are often entrenched precisely because they functioned as efficient adaptations to environments which were flawed in their capacity to respond to the potential diversity of affective cues of the individual.

NOVELTY AND PERTURBATION

Providing an explanatory mechanism for the development of mental states and patterns is an important goal of a dynamic systems theory of psychoanalysis; however, the most relevant aspect of the theory as it relates to psychoanalytic practice is the centrality of novelty and the possibility of change. As a person develops, she or he may exhibit pathological patterns of thinking, feeling, and behaving. The repetition of these patterns often pull a person to process experience or act in accordance with his or her prior patterning activity. The goal of psychoanalysis is to develop an awareness of the patterning of experience that is unique to each patient. Analytic therapy provides opportunities to disrupt the pull of these unhealthy or pathological patterns and instigate the development of new "healthy" patterns.

In order to accomplish this, dynamic systems theory offers a potential methodology of perturbation through the introduction of novelty into a system of pathological patterns. As Thelen and Smith (1994) state, there exist "attractors of such strength and stability that only the most severe perturbations can disrupt them" (p. 61). They emphasize that "developing systems must be in [an] unstable or quasi-stable mode to explore new cooperative patterns (or strategies) and select those that provide a functional match" (p. 65). A system must be unstable in order to pave the way for the development of novel patterns, and cocreating the experience of instability and perturbation is the analyst's most important function.

As we previously stated (Trop, Burke, and Trop, 1999):

> Perturbing the system is not, however, tantamount to producing a shock effect; . . . *understanding* the patient is often one of the factors that alters a patient's subjective world and disrupts the emergence of pathological patterns. After all, for some patients, being understood may represent a form of novelty, and introducing a certain empathic listening stance into therapeutic sessions may procure precisely that perturbation of the system needed to alter a dynamically stable and pathological attractor state [p. 219].

It may be necessary, however, to introduce analytic observations that create considerable anxiety and disruption. Changing a patient's pathological patterns is therefore a matter of cocreating a context in which novelty can occur. In order to accomplish this, analyst and patient both need to have the capacity to tolerate the anxieties and disruptions associated with change.

Interpretation functions in a dynamic system not only as insight but more specifically as it enters into the attempt to "perturb" and form new, dynamically stable patterns of experience. The value of explanation lies primarily in the power to provide narratives that facilitate the patient's capacity to tolerate the affective experience of change. An explanatory narrative is helpful in providing inspiration for change.

DISCUSSION

We are in agreement with Fosshage and Munschauer that psychoanalytic theory and new treatment perspectives have considerably enhanced the possibility for working with patients who present with significant depression, cynicism, and negativity. In addition, their emphasis on the use of a consultant to provide support and input to the therapist is an important detail. Therapists who treat patients who are withdrawn and often denigrating are challenged in efforts to sustain their own sense of well-being and validity. An extended support system, including a consultant, provides a needed buffer to the therapist–patient system. We respect the courage of the authors in describing the specific philosophy and nuances of their therapy. The thrust of their vantage point demonstrates an advocacy of repetitive and extreme enactments as providing the essential and necessary conditions for growth and development in this case. We are centrally opposed to this viewpoint and hope to illuminate our differences.

Jack entered treatment with a sense of boredom and emptiness. He described himself as devitalized. He was seen initially for only two sessions. It appeared that depending upon the therapist for assistance was in conflict with his ideal of himself as fiercely independent and self-reliant. Clearly, one problem that plagued Jack from the beginning of his life was his difficulty in evolving a model of healthy dependence in relationships. Being dependent on someone else was accompanied by a feeling of disgust with himself.

Returning in a year and a half, he presented with concern about his intense rage. He stated that he felt so violent that he might actually kill someone. In addition, he was engaged to a woman who complained of his resentment of her wish to be with friends and have a social life involving him.

Jack's background was complex. His parents divorced when he was three. He had limited contact with his father who ended up in Jack's adolescence being demeaning, competitive, and undermining. His father was a seductive man preoccupied with "money, big tits, and blond hair." His mother, apparently in attempts to compensate for Jack's trauma, gave him every present he wanted. Her dedication to him was overwhelming, and it appeared she was willing to sacrifice her own needs for his. Jack insightfully communicated early in therapy that he had "never learned to share" or to negotiate disappointments.

His mother would be totally intimidated by Jack when he refused to play with other children. Her inability to tolerate his anger was a central theme.

Jack described early in treatment how all people would disappoint him and he needed to lower his expectations. The therapist's interpretation at this time was "Yes, it is your template; no matter what you do, you're not going to get squat back." Jack subsequently quit treatment.

We would see this material differently. Jack conceptualizes the problem as outside of him—people will disappoint him. His disappointment is centrally seen as a limitation of people around him and he does not recognize his contribution to this. We would have taken the opportunity to inquire with Jack what were his own contributions to his disappointments. For example, what are the details of Jack's opposition to his fiancée's wish for a social life? Does Jack feel threatened by her independent needs? Does it make him feel bad about himself that she chooses other friends who are interesting?

We feel that Jack is caught by the patterning of organization that emerged repetitively with his mother and remains an embedded expectation as part of being loved. Even though he had disdain for his mother, his model of maternal capitulation to his needs is activated in his relationship with his girlfriend. Deviations from this mode of relating are jarring and unfamiliar and cause reactive withdrawal and isolation. It is very difficult for Jack to feel a sense of pleasure by giving to others and compromising his needs. Underneath his reactive withdrawal potentially resides a feeling of invalidity and defectiveness as a residue of his relationship with his father. This feeling of uneasiness about his own value and validity is covered over by his defensive grandiosity and belittling of other people. The irony of his defensive activities, such as looking at ethnic groups as "pond scum," is that it is very similar to his father's belittling interactions with him.

We think that Jack could benefit from an awareness of these repetitive contextual pulls. His relationship with his mother has left him without opportunities to feel joy and vitality through healthy accommodation and reciprocity to the needs of others. His model for feeling loved and cared about is the relinquishment and surrendering of the other's needs to him.

In addition, he seems to remain at some deeper level undermined in his self-esteem and value by his relationship with his father. In an unconscious attempt to shore himself up, his reactive grandiosity and belittling of others are very similar to those of the father he despises.

To summarize, at the beginning of treatment, the therapist clarifies Jack's cynicism about the world by commenting that he anticipates he will get nothing back no matter what he does. Jack then unilaterally quits treatment "to get used to the ways things are in the world, and make the best of it." We believe that Jack could benefit from an increased awareness of the co-determining nature of the outcome of his disappointment in the world.

The painful trauma of his childhood has left him without a relational model of healthy dependency and with the presence of a defensive and haughty sense of independence. His mother was unable to assist him in dealing with his anxiety about being with other children. As a result, he was a lonely and isolated child. This left him feeling uneasy and ill-equipped in social situations. His sense of superiority acts to cover over these deeper vulnerabilities.

Jack terminated his therapy feeling hopeless; yet, a critical moment unfolds several months later. He called to invite the therapist and her husband to dinner with him and his girlfriend. In considering her decision, the therapist points to Jack's reclusiveness saying that "he really needed me to respond to his gesture of reaching out to me." This was the first of several enactments that were deemed necessary for the treatment. We see these enactments differently. The difficult therapeutic task here would reside in exploring his motivation for the invitation. We would have tried to elucidate his state of mind in tolerating the disappointment of the therapist's not coming to dinner and the affects stimulated in not getting what he wanted from the therapist. Would Jack organize this experience as a rejection of him? Could he understand the therapist's need to maintain her own ideal of herself? Could Jack come to understand and support another person's sense of herself even if it meant feeling rejected? It is a difficult developmental task, but it seems essential for Jack to develop a capacity to regulate and manage disappointment and maintain a relational bond. The experience of saying no and the limits of the therapeutic relationship could have provided him with a novel experience that he never had with his mother, who had surrendered herself to him. This novelty could still be presented with caring and concern to help him avert a feeling of humiliation. It could be valuable to experience in the transference the assimilated meanings that Jack might feel around a sense of impingement and loss of control. Jack needs to acquire the potential to see the value of compromising his needs in a relationship. It is precisely the moments in which Jack is requesting enactments that provide Jack with the opportunity for novelty, the perturbation of compromise, and integration of conflicting subjectivities as a new relational model. These enactments cover over the opportunity for destabilizing his entrenched patterns of isolation and reactive grandiosity. Jack's multiple requests for deviations from the therapeutic stance all provide opportunities for this deeper exploration of these issues, including his need for a confirmation of his own specialness and uniqueness. It is our belief that the details of self-experience that could emerge in these episodes would provide an opportunity to consolidate a sense of new relational perspectives.

These opportunities are lost, as the therapist continues the process of reenacting maternal compliance when Jack asks her to counsel his girlfriend through telephone therapy. The therapist uses the rationale that Jack has a residual distrust in other analysts.

The therapist states that it was important "to be professionally available to the girlfriend and not be confined by the 'rules' with its meaning of being the subjugated mother." We have several problems with this. As stated above, we actually feel she is reenacting the behavior of the subjugated mother by not saying "no." In addition, because Jack has terminated therapy, we are concerned about his distrust of other analysts as representing a lack of flexibility needing further resolution. His distrust needs deeper understanding and elucidation. Jack does not get the opportunity to feel his disappointment and to exercise a capacity to self-regulate while still maintaining a tie with his analyst. The therapist then notes that in Jack's girlfriend's work: "Jack also made demands that created intense conflict for her for which she was seeking my help. For example, one focus of treatment became whether or not she was willing to undergo procedures that would make her more blond and buxom." The therapist has put herself in a very difficult situation, as it might be most appropriate to vigorously help her patient extricate herself from a man who finds her centrally unacceptable as she is. We question whether it is actually possible in this context for the therapist to decenter from Jack's desires and to be available to his girlfriend in a therapeutic setting.

Another important aspect of Jack's needs emerges here. In the beginning of treatment, Jack spoke disdainfully about his father's superficiality in wanting women with "big tits and blond hair." After terminating treatment, Jack is determined to persuade his girlfriend to change her appearance in exactly the same way. It raises questions for us regarding Jack's transformation and his need to alter his girlfriend's physical appearance to enhance his feeling of connection with her. We feel that the appropriate stance at this moment would be to attempt to reestablish Jack's therapy. Jack does not seem to have integrated two widely divergent attitudes towards his father and remains unconscious of the tension between them. He has previously commented negatively about the father's superficiality regarding women. However, it appears that he has an unconscious identification with his father's need for "blond hair and big tits" and acts to maintain a tie with his father by adopting the same requirements for a woman. It is not clear whether these conflicts are ever explored. In addition, if the therapist had refused to see his girlfriend and reinstated treatment with Jack, the issues of adapting to a woman's needs and notions of reciprocality could have been addressed in the transference reactions with his therapist.

In summary, we view each enactment in the treatment as a missed opportunity for exploring the painful underlying affective states of disappointment and loss of control. These were all potential entry points to help the patient experience and consolidate compromise and healthy accommodation to the standards and requirements of another person. It is precisely these moments of intense perturbation that could offer the chance to destabilize entrenched patterns of reactive isolation, defensive grandiosity, and fear of submission.

Despite our disagreements, we remain very admiring of the authors' willingness to self-disclose. We believe that disagreement and differing subjectivities offering multiple perspectives can only enhance and strengthen opportunities for understanding the process of change.

REFERENCES

Thelen, E. & Smith, L. (1994), *A Dynamic Systems Approach to the Development of Cognition and Action*. Cambridge, MA: MIT Press.

Trop, G., Burke, M. & Trop, J. (1999), Contextualism and dynamic systems in psychoanalysis: Rethinking intersubjectivity theory. *Constructionism in the Human Sciences*, 4:202–223.

Five

A RELATIONAL VIEWPOINT
A DISCUSSION OF FOSSHAGE AND MUNSCHAUER'S CLINICAL CASE

MARGARET CRASTNOPOL

osshage and Munschauer have done us an important service in tackling the demanding and possibly sometimes aversive task of writing about such a demanding and sometimes aversive patient. The "deeply intractable nihilism" of someone like Jack tends to work its way into the analyst's unconscious willy-nilly, leaving him or her in need of a reliable, thoughtful vantage point (through obtaining consultation, or via reading a paper such as this) to help put the experience in perspective—to detoxify it, as it were. The authors have provided a very experience-near and bold account of the twists and turns of a difficult treatment, one that allows the reader to "feel the pain" of both therapist and patient over the course of a rough therapeutic road. In introducing their contribution, Fosshage and Munschauer call for more discussion in our literature of unusual treatment situations that challenge our accepted notions of the proper conduct of an analytically oriented treatment. The authors themselves offer such material with the requisite candor, honesty, and detail to foster our careful scrutiny and consideration.

The chapter is written from a theoretical position based in self-psychological thinking, but incorporates a close appreciation of the analyst's co-participation and subjectivity. Among the thought-provoking concepts emanating from the authors' viewpoint is the notion of a continuum of relational needs from self and selfobject needs to concerns about self-with-the-other (or "intersubjectivity"), to concerns for the other (or "caretaking"). The authors maintain that facilitative interaction requires that the analyst respond in reciprocal fashion. The analyst should be able to meet a patient's self needs with an analytic attitude of caretaking, or respond to the patient's need to caretake with a receptivity to having the self cared for, and so on. Perhaps such reciprocity does indeed facilitate analytic relatedness in general, though there might be times when the absence of reciprocity is valuable to the analytic exchange. If reciprocity in needs for relatedness is indeed important, then we can see how individual differences in personality structure with respect to such needs could make or break the fittedness between a particular patient and a particular analyst. With this line of thought, the authors certainly offer us a direction for empirical study.

A related and equally valuable observation is how the therapist's comments may shift from the *empathic listening/experiencing stance*, to an *other-centered listening/experiencing perspective*, to the analyst's *self perspective*. A simple statement perhaps, but parsimonious and very useful in the way it sharpens and demonstrates the complementarity of self-psychological and various types of intersubjective thought.

The clarity and comprehensiveness of this clinical presentation makes it possible to consider other possible analytic routes if the analyst were a different person with a different character structure and theoretical orientation. It is likely that, with an analyst of another stripe, there would have been differences in: (a) the clinician's experience of his/her subjectivity, including the countertransference; (b) the technical use of the clinician's subjectivity; (c) the nature and use of the "real relationship" (including the working alliance and the personal aspects of the analytic bond); (d) the nature and use of transference/countertransference scenarios; and (e) the degree to which the patient's bids for direct gratification and the analyst's direct provision of emotional supplies were played out (please note that I consider this *playing out* rather than *enacting,* a term I prefer to reserve for actions expressing unconscious motives rather than conscious choices).

I would like to revisit Jack's treatment process with special attention to some of these features from my own particular vantage point as an analyst identified with the relational orientation. For the sake of argument and clarity of exposition, I highlight areas where an alternate conceptualization might have yielded certain advantages. But let us keep in mind that, whatever clinical approach one takes has its drawbacks, and that my own tack would undoubtedly involve a trade-off of potential gains with real sacrifices relative to the tack that was actually taken by this analyst/patient dyad.

Jack first arrives for a consultation in a state of considerable need but with great resistance to acknowledging his psychic pain, weakness, and dependency. Munschauer listens carefully and does not "debate" his resistance. Her rationale is that challenge would feed his oppositionalism, but I wonder whether the patient could have read her mildness as an absence of self-conviction or as reflecting passivity, in accordance with the analyst's own later formulation along similar lines. Would a more insistent, authoritative posture have facilitated Jack's early surrender (Ghent, 1990) to a much-needed treatment? Possibly so.

Jack returns when his boredom, rage, emotional isolation, and emotional insufficiency vis-à-vis his fiancée have become more problematic. His self-diagnosis of "affluenza" is thoroughly apt. Jack demands a double session once a week, to which the analyst accedes, a concession that seems constructive and yields few complications for the transference–countertransference at this point. The beginning phase of the work is characterized by Jack's rampant devaluation of others, narcissistic self-aggrandizement, aggression, and of course, nihilism. We learn that he persistently imagines having a sexual threesome with two women, a fantasy that by its very nature undermines or subverts the deeply mutual relating of dyadic intimacy. This fantasy is enacted figuratively in various permutations throughout the treatment. Fantasied and sometimes actual interactions take place among the patient, analyst, and patient's butler; patient, analyst, and analyst's other patients; patient, analyst, and analyst's discipline; patient, analyst, and analyst's husband; patient, analyst, and patient's girlfriend; and even in a sense among the patient, analyst, and analyst's consultant.

As with any type of gratifying provision, the playing out or enactment of a particular triadic arrangement is not *necessarily* a problem for the analytic dyad (though in some of these instances, it may have been). It depends on what each manifestation means to the patient unconsciously and whether that meaning is optimally utilized for therapeutic purposes. To me, ensuring optimal utility usually involves subjecting it to mutual analytic interpretation, an approach Fosshage and Munschauer seem to emphasize less than I would.

No doubt each of the particular threesomes Jack imagines or tries to play out has its own specific psychic referent. The ménage a trois fantasy itself may have embodied Jack's effort to master conflicted feelings about the quasi-oedipal victory involved in the early parental breakup. If nothing else, he is certainly outdoing his short Napoleonic father if he can handle two women at once. But this is speculation, and I doubt that Jack could have made serious use of any such interpretation, given his limited capacity (and obvious scorn) for psychic mentalization (Fonagy and Target, 1996).

To return to the analytic relationship, Jack in this early phase must be benefiting from aspects of the analyst's accepting, patient stance toward him, much as he disavows it. We can imagine that Munschauer's effort to understand his experience from the inside-out presents him with the possibility of a positive transference to a nurturing other, a developmental experience he certainly lacked with either actual parent.

But now the picture becomes complicated (constructively, in my view) with the analyst's dawning recognition of her own dread of and repugnance toward her patient. We learn of her struggles to balance her felt need to remain empathic with unbidden judgmental reactions to his contempt and murderous impulses. She is frustrated by his denigration of her interpretations, his attempted destruction of her more life-affirming values and attitudes.

And so to the first direct test of the analyst, in which Jack asks Munschauer and her husband to join him extratherapeutically at a social event. Her automatic, categorical refusal frustrates him and also gratifies his wish/need to vilify her. She is now seen as a "despicable weakling," akin to the inadequate maternal imago. In this variant of the triad, Jack is clearly vying for primacy in his analyst's affections, pitting his desires for the analyst/parent against the analyst's bond with her professional discipline, with her personal set of principles, and with her husband.

As with any oedipal triangle, this is a contest in which winning in one sense means losing in others. Here of course Jack loses—loses, that is, vis-à-vis his conscious desire to be directly admired, to have sway over and be special to his analyst. The analyst now begins to question the therapeutic value of her decision. (She will of course reverse it in the next and most future iterations of the same request.) It seems she now wonders whether her refusal to be a real-world reparative figure (a paid friend of sorts) at this juncture was truly damaging to the therapeutic goal of shoring up his internal world via direct provision. And it is hard to say. Perhaps hewing to her analytic role does just what it is meant to do —bring forth enough semi-conscious and unconscious negative transferential material to deepen the analytic process significantly. The data presented in the paper lead me to the second conclusion, though it seems the authors opt for the first.

Jack now dubs his analyst a "Pussy Faggot," a moniker that interestingly conflates the female genitalia with a homosexual (male) designation. Jack's choice of the term indicates that he wants and probably needs a masculine element in his analyst, but also that he cannot reconcile masculinity with a capacity for warm relatedness or tenderness with strength. The patient's anxieties with respect to his gender and sex-role pervade the treatment. I wonder whether his preoccupation with biological/genetic versus environmental causation vis-à-vis his psychopathology extends in his fantasy to his gender anxieties and confusion. I can imagine him believing that gender and therefore, sex roles are inscribed constitutionally, leaving open only two polarized, mutually exclusive possibilities. As a male he should be masculine, and the masculine prohibits tenderness, weakness, or interdependence (see Harris, 1991). In that respect he is implicitly superior to his "Pussy Faggot" analyst, again a conscious gain and an unconscious loss.

With Jack's excoriation and name calling, the analyst's negative countertransference naturally mounts further. I imagine sitting in Munschauer's chair and am relieved that sustaining an empathic posture is not as central to my view of the optimal therapeutic environment as it is to hers, since my sympathy, not to mention empathy, would now have been sorely challenged. Experiencing the weight of the patient's superciliousness, arrogance, and greed, I would be getting very angry, even antipathetic. However, I would feel less worried about and guilty over my anger than curious and eager to glean as much as I could from it (see Mitchell's, 2000, instructive handling of his own exasperation and hatred toward a provocative patient in the last chapter of *Relationality*). Munschauer also takes stock of her reaction and begins to revise her view of the impact of her stance of "empathic immersion." She now comes to realize that its unintentional side effect has been the arousal of the patient's hostility toward the passive/submissive, overly permissive, internalized mother. As much as the empathic immersion was providing a new positive, caring maternal experience in the real therapeutic relationship, its virtues were being seriously challenged by its limitations. Listening carefully to her patient, Munschauer is now able to hear her patient cry, "I want you to have balls!"

Where the authors hear in this an unmet need for an idealizable and/or adversarial relationship, I hear the evocation of a broader set of relational scenarios. It seems to me that Jack wants a strong other and yet also wants to dominate and control that other; indeed he "castrates" and then complains about the loss he sustains as a result of the "castration"! Jack's wish for his therapist to "have balls" is paradoxical because he is also dictating that she follow his orders (in this and so many other ways), which in my view constitutes *not* having balls. From my perspective, he "conscripts" his analyst and probably every significant other into playing out these self-cancelling wishes with him. Pardon my quip, but to be conscripted is human, to recognize and interpret it, divine. The ability to step out of such an enactment and examine its meaning as an erstwhile insider is the curative edge of what the analyst has to offer. I would have been interested to see how a transference–countertransference interpretation along these lines would have fared, whether Jack could have been helped to see how self-defeating are his efforts to dictate others' behavior.

At the same time, I agree with the authors that Jack's plea has a healthy, genuine aspect. He is asking that the analyst be an assertive, frank, benignly authoritative "other" with whom to relate. Such an experience could generate a missing positive paternal transference/ countertransference experience that would offer him the possibility of a creative masculine identification. Here is where I would be comfortable tweaking the real relationship in the service of fostering a particular transference–countertransference scenario. And in fact, the therapist sees that when she challenges him more from an adversarial position (playing out the positive paternal transference, in my terms), Jack becomes more "invigorated and engaged." My own explanation is that he needs the experience of engaging with another separate, respect-worthy self, who can "recognize" him without caving in to his wiles (Benjamin, 1995). Most important, Jack urgently needs limits to be set on his outrageous behavior (see Goldman, 2003) as the basis for developing the capacity to distinguish other from self and to begin to be able to mentalize the other's internal subjective experience. Much of his goading was unconsciously or preconsciously in the service of that very goal.

Munschauer now decides that Jack needs to experience more of her subjectivity as a separate, strong other (representing the antithesis of his childhood mother), and thus she begins to "thump" him. To my mind, however, the "thumps" we hear about are weak ones, still largely emanating from a gentle, sympathetic viewpoint. Her interventions have more of a "nudgy," stereotypic Jewish-mother quality of "I'm doing this for your own good." (Is this related to the authors' "caretaking" dimension?) This is to be distinguished from the type of "other-centered" viewpoint that would confront him with his more self-destructive and reprehensible attributes. But more to the point, I am not convinced that Munschauer's style of "thumping" achieves what she believes it achieves, as Jack still seems to feel unchanged in his toxic relationship with himself and with others. He remains full of despair.

This leads to Jack's second major challenge to the analyst and her treatment frame. He issues an ultimatum—either she gives him a "progress report" with all the answers (and presumably solutions) to his problems, or he will quit. The analyst sees her decision to meet his demands as providing the direct experience of her subjectivity (the reparative real parenting relationship) that he needs. Yet this provision, which is also a submission to his blackmail, again does not appear to do the trick of gratifying a true need and thereby strengthening his internal structure. The analyst's supposedly candid response leaves Jack still unsatisfied. On the defensive, the analyst protests that she is being as genuinely confrontive and confrontively genuine as she *can* be, and that it is his fault that he cannot recognize and be satisfied with this.

Who can blame her for objecting? The analyst has no choice but to undercut inadvertently the very thing Jack supposedly wants from her, in that she is "freely being her honest self" by doing what he has forced her to do. (And her honesty is only partial, more a worried prediction of the imminent failure of his defenses than a full-blown formulation.) Another way of saying this is that, in this moment, the analyst's own desire for her patient's approval paradoxically undermines her ability to be a good, self-motivated, agentic object within their relationship, that for which he is supposedly begging. Again, let me be clear that I see this type of enactment within the analytic relationship as thoroughly expectable. It no doubt reflects a more pervasive patterning in Jack's intrapersonal and interpersonal life spheres, and its emergence in the patient–therapist relationship could set the stage for a deeper exploration, and over time, its resolution.

I return to the interchange following the ultimatum. Reporting on her protest of the patient's continued devaluation, the analyst tells us parenthetically, "I left out the expletive 'you schmuck.'" Were I the analyst, I would wonder at the hurt and anger in my defended-against outburst. I would muse about the meaning in my spontaneous diagnosis of "schmuck." (The throw-away foreskin of a bossy penis? An impotent anti-mensch?) And I would consider why I chose not to voice it. Like the authors, I feel that it is important to withhold certain subjective reactions from the patient unless and until they are developmentally prepared to hear and make use of them (Slochower, 1996). But the reaction of deeming my patient a schmuck even sotto voce would make me wonder whether I was countertransferentially being cowed into pulling my analytic punches instead of being explicit about his deplorably self-serving nihilism, among other things. The implication for my analytic stance within our real relationship would be profound, as would the implications for the kind of transference/countertransference matrix we were generating. If he still "didn't feel anything" after I had revealed my most honest perceptions of him, perhaps I was not being a strong enough presence. Letting Jack know that he can be "a pain" would be a start, but only the tip of the iceberg of such an intervention. If I could not be comfortable being more honest about my selective hatred of some aspects of him, how could he trust my selective real regard for other aspects? I believe that it is the mutual recognition of the essential (good and bad) humanness of each other that ultimately establishes the conditions for a state of psychic growth and eventual well-being (Ghent, 1990; Benjamin, 1995). The analyst needs to provide this in the real relationship and interpret its inklings in the transferential cross-currents.

When the third big challenge comes and Jack invites the analyst on a "field trip" to his home, Munschauer agrees, noting afterward that it was informative for her and that it led to a "softening" in Jack's attitude toward her, engendering a "far warmer atmosphere" in the therapy; but as I hear it, Jack is largely the same quasi-antisocial, if suffering Jack—still full of doubt, detachment, and devaluation. We come to a revealing exchange:

"There is nothing you can do for me. I don't think you have ever done anything for me. No matter what I do, no matter what I contribute, it will not have any impact on what I receive, and that is how I see everything. You can't control other people. All I can do is lower my expectations."

The analyst answers, "Yes, it is your template; no matter what you do, you're not going to get squat back." She offers mirroring, but he is unable to absorb this and use it as a basis for a reflective mentalizing position such as "ah, it's just my template, it's not necessarily valid." Instead he replies, "With people, all you can try for is the absence of the negative. I don't care to ask for anything anymore. I don't expect anything, I don't want to be disappointed. Nothing is going to change."

As a commentary on the analyst's mirroring interpretation (see Gill, 1982), Jack is saying "yep, that's what I've been saying all along, and I'm glad you understand that but it isn't enough. I need you to bring your own maturity to bear on all that I've said, setting limits on my unrealistic wish by giving me some of your *real* subjective response to my wish to control others."

Instead of empathizing with and emphasizing Jack's frustration at not being able to "control other people," I can imagine the analyst saying, "ah, I think you're onto something there—perhaps the route to happiness lies elsewhere." If the analyst were to try being a strongly different "other" in the real therapeutic relationship, it might shake up Jack's infantile, self-absorbed posture and give him possibilities for gratification heretofore "undreamt of in his philosophy." This is akin to what a good enough ("idealizable") father could have done for him.

But as it is, the analyst's comment leaves the patient further disappointed, such that he can only react to the analyst's intervention with resignation at having to settle for "the absence of the negative," as he conceives it. This state of affairs is no longer tolerable shortly thereafter and the patient stops treatment unilaterally. I see Jack's quitting as a negative reaction to aspects of the treatment, not as a defensive response to his own increased "softness." Like the toddler during rapprochement, Jack is attempting a protest, but its meaning stays obscure. Again, like the toddler still holding out hope, he reestablishes contact several months later. But this time the connection is to be solely on his own turf—he wants to entertain his therapist as an opportunity to get needed supplies without acknowledging dependency. He will get the mirroring, the admiration, and the attention—not to mention the bending of rules—on his own terms.

When next Jack is willing to reinstate formal treatment, the analyst keeps him waiting due to her schedule demands. This turn of events is surely a frustration to him and possibly her first refusal to his terms in some time. I would be interested in how Jack processed this delay of gratification, but the analyst apparently sees it as so potentially damaging that when he counters her unavailability by again inviting her to a sumptuous lunch, she accepts. I do not see strong evidence that this new boundary crossing was essential to establishing the patient's trust. In fact, I wonder whether its unconscious intent was to lure the analyst into a deeper personal involvement in and valuation of Jack's own excessive lifestyle and narcissistic values. It is as if giving her the "royal treatment" will cause the analyst to see the error of her ways, and she will come to recognize his actual specialness and splendor.

When they do resume, Jack's focus is again concrete, for now he is insistent that his problems are biological (and readily medicated) rather than psychological. There nonetheless appears to be a breakthrough on the analytic level. When the analyst gives him the diagnosis of "Closet Sweetie Pie," Jack is hugely gratified—he has been "found." He can now tolerate the idea of more tender, weaker parts of himself and work with them symbolically. I have difficulty following this development. For one thing, I had seen no signs of the tenderness toward others that the term "sweetie pie" implies, so I find it curious that the analyst comes up with this diagnosis. In any event, the analyst and patient at this point are now said to enjoy a new parity, each with strengths and weaknesses, each learning from the other. Jack continues to show signs of greater integration and improved relatedness with others. There are additional requests for boundary bending and breaking—Munschauer ends up agreeing to treat him and his girlfriend via phone simultaneously if separately, then switches to seeing the now-wife instead of Jack, then agrees to have a session with Jack during his wife's regular time, and finally has a casual dinner with the couple and her husband at their home. Again, my objection hinges not on the concept that breaking the professional/social boundary is necessarily bad or wrong; it is that playing out the patient's wish to be loved as a personal friend in an unguarded, extratherapeutic way may not necessarily lead to optimal permanent psychic change. By being so exceptionally gratifying, the analyst's choice leaves open the question as to how much his imperiousness and omnipotence have really been modified. How long will Jack's new "humanness" last if others do not give him just what he wants?

SUMMARIZING THE POINTS OF DIFFERENCE

THE USE OF THE ANALYST'S SUBJECTIVITY
As a relationally trained analyst, I would weigh my subjective response to the patient as a partial indicator of his psychic state more heavily than Fosshage and Munschauer do. An intense, repetitive negative response to a man like Jack would tell me that he and I were embroiled in a sado-masochistic transference/countertransference matrix of great proportions. I would recognize, as did Munschauer, that my initial empathic/sympathetic stance vis-à-vis the patient had the downside of representing an enactment of the passive/maternal position that intensified his disdain and left him feeling bereft. But I would be especially concerned that this situation were reinforcing the sado-masochistic element in the patient's psyche and yielding an iatrogenic recreation of patterns of dominance and submission within the analyst/patient relationship. I would share with the patient more of my frank estimation of his infantile, destructive psychic life, and of my view of how we together were reenacting it. With respect to his own damaging behavior, I would not refrain from letting Jack see the anger he generated in me—though in modulated form—since I believe that experiences lived through in the here and now with the analyst have an especially strong therapeutic impact. Caring criticism can be offered in a benign but direct manner such that the patient can be helped to distinguish it from that offered by his or her shame-inducing, domineering internal bad object.

THE REAL RELATIONSHIP, PROVISION, AND "EXTRAORDINARY MEASURES"
Sometimes and with respect to selected issues, we should indeed give the patient a corrective emotional (or "needed" as opposed to "repeated") experience within the real relationship. Certainly

Munschauer's flexibility as to the frequency and length of session and Jack's various comings and goings from therapy were advantageous in supporting his trust that the therapeutic relationship was more in the service of his psychic needs than of the economic needs of the therapist. As I have indicated above, I believe it is still an open question—in Jack's case and in general—as to when it is more impactful to engage in the direct provision of support, approval, and affection, and when it is best to interpret (tactfully and caringly) the meaning of such wishes for provision while refraining from their direct gratification. I take it as a given that these two therapeutic approaches are not inherently mutually exclusive and that each is likely to have its place and time over the course of the analytic journey. I would say further that, often, the analyst's deep and empathic *recognition* of the patient's desires for boundary-transgressing gratification (and a recognition of the reasons behind them) can be just as or even more significant to the patient than a directly gratifying response.

Jack's case brings up the special variant of the matter, in which the patient specifically seeks the analyst's willingness to violate his or her discipline's boundaries as a means of proving to the patient that he or she is cared about. What if I agree with and am most comfortable with maintaining the prohibitions—does this mean I do not care about my patient? And should my patient's belief in herself or himself depend on my caring and on my demonstrating it in this fashion? Surely these are precarious, arbitrary, and somewhat artificial foundations on which to build a firmer sense of self. (See Crastnopol, 1999, for further consideration of the complications inherent in the analyst's professional self being a "third" vis-à-vis the analyst–patient dyad.)

Fosshage and Munschauer forcefully maintain that their clinical exemplar demonstrates the validity of employing "extraordinary measures," what some would call therapeutic parameters, to treat the intractable patient. In their view, it was only through engaging in extratherapeutic contacts and other relaxations of analytic boundaries that it was possible to break through this patient's defensive structure and ensure the analyst's survival as a good-enough object. I hope I have made it clear that I believe it is hard to draw the line between a truly needed "provision" vis-à-vis the analyst's use of an extraordinary measure (boundary bending) and a mutually gratifying submission to the patient's imperious, infantile need. In Jack's case, I think there are hints that the analyst erred on the side of too much giving in but, at the same time, some degree would have been necessary to keep Jack engaged.

Ultimately, the most important thing for a boundary-testing patient like Jack is not the upshot of the analyst's decision to give in or to hold fast; it is for the patient to experience the resilient analyst's attempt to balance respectfully his or her own needs and the patient's. It is important for the patient to experience the clinician's responsible efforts to weigh the varying factors, make a choice, and live with its consequences, as he or she holds in mind the overriding goal of furthering the patient's psychic growth while not negating his or her own human needs in the process (see Slavin and Kriegman, 1998). The patient is thus "provided" with the experience of interacting closely with a well-intentioned but not entirely altruistic "other" who acknowledges and struggles with the inevitable conflicts and compromises inherent in human relationships. This helps the patient come to terms with his or her own existential plight, shared by Everyman/Everywoman, in which some of his or her fondest needs and wishes will be met and others not by the nonetheless "good-enough" other.

CONCLUSION

This is a patient who most certainly benefited from a treatment experience that was finely tuned, competent, and humane. We can only quarterback the results in hindsight, basing our speculations on the residual areas of psychic immaturity and fixation. We learn that in the latter part and at the end of treatment contacts, Jack is still mistrustful of allowing another therapist to handle his girlfriend's (and later, wife's) treatment, is still narcissistically wanting this woman to have surgical alterations to enhance her physical attractiveness and bring her closer to his ideal, and is still concretely needing and wanting the analyst to engage in an admiring personal relationship with him outside of the treatment setting. These things bespeak the continued presence of imperious, infantile, grandiose wishes, the fixation on external concrete "fixes" for internal psychic conflict and arrests, and a debilitated sense of self. I would wonder: if the analyst had believed more fully in the implications of the patient's need for a positive, limit-setting, paternally-toned analytic relationship; if she had more fully realized this in a more assertive posture toward him within the therapeutic relationship, whether Jack could have made even more progress toward internal security and maturity. Perhaps the patient would have tested her less, and perhaps his contempt for his fellows would have receded sooner. Providing us with more unconscious material from the patient's fantasy and dream lives would have been useful in helping us gauge more fully his psychic reaction to each of the analyst's gratifying interventions. It would have helped us sort out whether the analyst's acceding to the patient's desires was enduringly curative, as the authors' maintain, or was simply the line of least resistance with such an oppositional man.

That said, let me return to my initial comment vis-à-vis the trade-offs of adopting one clinical tack versus another. There is no question but that approaching the patient in a more assertive, challenging fashion as in the stance I have just sketched would have resulted in the co-creation of an analytic relationship that would have had its own set of complications and drawbacks—different, but perhaps no less problematic than the one that was played out. I would envision Jack becoming even more defensive and competitive and having a harder time connecting with a clinician whose "analytic self" had perhaps sharper contours. Analytic technique, like life, always entails a parlay between gains and the losses that are often inextricably linked to them.

Finally, I would like to comment on an overarching issue that dogs the psychoanalytic literature. I believe that as a field, we are hampered by the infelicitous expectation that a theoretical–clinical contribution must "prove" or "disprove" a given position or school of thought. Modeling ourselves on other time-honored traditions of the arts and sciences, we feel we must use our clinical experience to further or bolster the particular set of hypotheses or beliefs we espouse. If we cannot come up with clinical material that supports one way against another, we run the risk of being unable to get an audience (it might be hard to attract enough attention to the material, find an appropriate venue for publishing, and so forth). I believe that this situation shoe-horns us into having to write articles in a tendentious fashion, which in turn ramps up the intensity of others' responses to the piece, and so on. Even an article as thoughtful and open as the present one seems to be influenced by the demand to present evidence to support a particular theoretical viewpoint as against others. If instead we could begin presenting clinical material and ideas in a studiously questioning spirit, feeling free to say "here is what I *thought* was going on, here is where I am in the dark," or "here were the virtues of what I did, here are the limitations," I believe the spirit of inquiry would be enhanced even further.

REFERENCES

Benjamin, J. (1995), *Like Subjects, Love Objects*. New Haven, CT: Yale University Press.

Crastnopol, M. (1999), The analyst's professional self as a "third" influence on the dyad: When the analyst writes about the treatment. *Psychoanal. Dial.*, 9:445–470.

Fonagy, P. & Target, M. (1996), Playing with reality: I. Theory of mind and the normal development of psychic reality. *Internat. J. Psychoanal.*, 77:217–233.

Ghent, E. (1990), Masochism, submission, surrender. *Contemp. Psychoanal.*, 26:108–136.

Gill, M. (1982), *Analysis of Transference, Vol. 1*. New York: International Universities Press.

Goldman, D. (2003), The outrageous prince: Winnicott's uncure of Masud Khan. *Brit. J. Psychother.*, 19:483–501.

Harris, A. (1991), Gender as contradiction. *Psychoanal. Dial.*, 1:197–224.

Mitchell, S. (2000), *Relationality: From Attachment to Intersubjectivity*. Hillsdale, NJ: The Analytic Press.

Slavin, M. O. & Kriegman, D. (1998), Why the analyst needs to change: Toward a theory of conflict, negotiation, and mutual influence in the therapeutic process. *Psychoanal. Dial.*, 8:247–284.

Slochower, J. (1996), *Holding and Psychoanalysis: A Relational Perspective*. Hillsdale, NJ: The Analytic Press.

Six

FACILITATIVE INTERACTION, RULES, ENACTMENTS, AND "A SPIRIT OF INQUIRY"
REPLY TO THE DISCUSSIONS

JAMES L. FOSSHAGE
CAROL A. MUNSCHAUER

We wish to thank the discussants for their careful and respectful consideration of our theoretical proposals and case material. Different perspectives enrich the dialogue through raising issues and questions and presenting alternative angles. Because a written format requires limited case material as well as limited opportunity for discussion and reply, we will be able to address only highlights of each discussion. We address first the issue of "enactments."

Because this analysis included some unusual enactments, examples of "throwing the book away" (Hoffman, 1998), we were not surprised about the mixed reviews. Unfortunately, unusual enactments (that is, poignant unconscious and conscious interactions) that are outside our "rule book" tend to serve as lightning rods. Discussions easily gravitate toward the enactments, often decontextualizing them as well as neglecting or minimizing the more traditional exploratory/ interpretive work. This occurred in Crastnopol's discussion as well as that of Trop and Burke. How much we contributed in our write-up to their misperception that we emphasize less the "spirit of inquiry" (Lichtenberg, Lachmann, and Fosshage, 2002) or how much their reaction is a counter-reaction to unusual "out of bounds" enactments is difficult to decipher. While we felt that these enactments within the contexts of this treatment were important and, in these instances, growth promoting, we presented them to remind us "how intrinsically creative the psychoanalytic encounter is and contribute to the range of possibilities not previously thought possible to facilitate the analytic process." Poignant interactions cannot be prescriptive. We can never know for sure that certain actions we take are going to be productive. We make judgment calls, hope for the best, continue to function and, at times, save the day through the use of a consistent spirit of inquiry.

In a discussion of "breaking the rules," we need to remember that analysts' agreement on rules varies from those that have a unanimous consensus (for example, the prohibition of sexual engagement between patient and analyst) to those that generate a wide range of opinion (for example, the occurrence and use of physical touch for communication [*Psychoanalytic Inquiry*, 2000]). Moreover, an analyst's clarity regarding a specific rule does not necessarily mean that a patient is cognizant of it or, for that matter, agrees with it. Too often analysts assume that the patient's perspective is the same as the analyst's (an "analystcentric" perspective) and, thereby, assess the patient to be consciously or unconsciously "breaking the rules." Keeping in mind the difference between the respective perspectives of analyst and patient substantially influences assessment of an interaction. For example, when Munschauer turned down Jack's first invitation to a party, Jack became aware of a generally agreed upon interdiction about socializing with patients—to Jack, an unexpected and, in his judgment, "arbitrary" rule that became a point of focus for the analysis.

When Jack requested that his analyst begin therapy with his girlfriend/fiancée, he was not aware of a rule prohibiting this. Moreover, within contemporary psychoanalysis the rule not to treat a spouse has become more relaxed with an understanding that it depends on the couple and the analyst. From a dynamic systems perspective, for example, one can cogently argue that analytically treating both members of a particular dyadic system not only can enhance but, in instances of deeply entrenched systemic patterns, may even be required for successful treatment. Recognizing that some rules are not so "hard and fast" and that, in this instance, the patient, analyst, and consultant did not perceive Jack's request to be breaking a rule not only impacts but even reverses analytic assessment of Jack's request and the analyst's consent. For example, in contrast to Crastnopol's assessment of a "boundary-transgressing gratification" and a capitulation to "his imperiousness and omnipotence," the patient's request was viewed as an expression of the patient's trust, sense of safety, and confidence in the analyst. The analyst's consent implicitly acknowledged, in light of Jack's history and subjectivity, and contributed to these hard-won new relational experiences (new implicit procedural learning).

PAULA B. FUQUA

In a substantially resonant reading of our paper, Fuqua questions whether or not our three listening perspectives are so clear cut. Coming from a self-psychological perspective, Fuqua advocates that empathy is the "supraordinate" listening perspective. In fact, we agree with Fuqua that the listening/experiencing perspectives are not always so clearly distinguishable and often are intricately intertwined. The empathic perspective itself—the attempt to understand from within the frame of reference and experience of the patient—is also not a sure thing, for judgments are required about what part of the patient's experience is most important at a given time. Moreover, our analytic models clearly influence our understanding of that which we hear from an empathic perspective as well. Despite these complexities, we still maintain that making these distinctions in listening/experiencing stances provides clarity in understanding analysts' varied reactions in a clinical moment.

In agreement with Fuqua, we take the position that "an overriding use of the empathic listening/experiencing perspective, whether in the foreground or background, helps us assess how and when to use information from these respective perspectives therapeutically and helps to guide us in the interaction" (Fosshage, 2003, p. 424). While analysts of all persuasions variably listen and experience from an empathic perspective, some often use other-centered information as a primary focus without distinguishing it from the empathic perspective. For example, Fuqua herself momentarily does so when she asks whether Jack's wealth, power, and attractiveness could have been a factor in "their aggressive-submissive enactment." Generally out of keeping with the tone of her discussion, Fuqua assumes at this moment, with the other-centered perspective in the forefront, that an "aggressive-submissive enactment" took place. We are sure that

Fuqua would agree that empathic inquiry would be necessary to ferret out, as best we can in light of operating conscious and unconscious processes, whether the patient experienced aggression and the analyst submission to validate her hypothesis.

Fuqua makes an important and helpful distinction between "rule-bound" and "boundary violation." Boundary violations, of course, require definition. To make this distinction, however, could militate against precipitate judgments that boundary violations have occurred when it is only rules that have been broken. In turn, to understand and assess the meanings of going outside the rules requires us to explore the experience of each participant in the analytic dyad. In addition to an empathic understanding of the patient, Fuqua importantly asserts that a "maturity, morality, and inner commitment to the growth of our patients" are required. We add that the consistent maintenance of an asymmetrical analytic relationship and a "spirit of inquiry" are centrally important factors that contribute to "throwing the book away" successfully.[1]

JEFFREY L. TROP AND MELANIE L. BURKE

Trop and Burke use systems theory (Thelen and Smith, 1994) to frame the psychoanalytic process. While not using the more formal terminology we, as indicated in our paper, consider our work to be well anchored within an interactive systems model as well. The use of systems theory, in our view, is not the central point of differentiation between Trop and Burke and ourselves. So what is the point of differentiation? While they are respectful, we feel that Trop and Burke have skewed our material and theoretical position, perhaps in reaction to the enactments, as previously described, or for purposes of differentiation. Essentially they conceptualize the "thrust" of our paper as demonstrating "an advocacy of repetitive and extreme enactments as providing the essential and necessary conditions for growth and

---

[1] We refer to selfobject relating, which Fuqua mistakenly calls "empathic relating," when mirroring and idealizing needs are in the forefront. While we use the term *selfobject* in "selfobject relating" very specifically to refer to a form of relating, we also use the term *selfobject* to refer generally to a vitalizing experience that each form of relating can generate.

development in this case." They, in turn, propose a consistent declarative analytic exploration to illuminate the repetitive patterns, explicitly creating insight and implicitly creating new relational experience. From our perspective, they have minimized our emphasis on the "spirit of inquiry" and have accentuated our "advocacy of repetitive and extreme enactments." One cannot advocate for or prescribe repetitive and extreme enactments; rather they occur with various degrees of conscious choice, including at times total lack of choice on the part of the analyst. The major difference between Trop and Burke and ourselves, in our view, is that we are convinced that facilitative analytic interaction requires analytic participation and responses that, while based on an analytic understanding of the patient, cannot be subsumed under the rubric of analytic exploration/ interpretation. Even the processes of exploration and interpretation require an analyst's emotional engagement in a far more complex way than previously recognized to negotiate successfully the analytic encounter. As Kohut (1977) suggested, we cannot function as "a well-programmed computer" (p. 252). In addition, not to be willing or available to respond more flexibly and within a broader range does, in our view, seriously limit facilitative analytic interaction (Bacal, 1985, 1998; Fosshage, 1990, 1997). Whether in the foreground or background, however, we view a "spirit of inquiry" (Lichtenberg, Lachmann, and Fosshage, 2002), as central to analysis.

We define enactment as referring to "an affectively poignant (powerful) and meaningful interaction that either can be facilitating of new growth-promoting relational experience or replicating of traumatic past experience" (Fosshage, 1995b). A patient can experience an exploratory/interpretive response, depending on its meaning and context, to be contributing either to a powerfully novel or to a repetitive interaction. Rather than advocating "extreme enactments" as Trop and Burke suggest, we (among others) are proposing that all analyses require spontaneous and creative interactions, what Lichtenberg, Lachmann, and Fosshage (1996) have called "disciplined spontaneous engagements," interactions that require us at times, to "throw the book away."

We found Trop and Burke's understandings of Jack to be generally in keeping with our own. In contrast to us, Trop and Burke propose a consistent, if not rigid, adherence to exploration and interpretation, comparable to ego psychology's singular emphasis on interpretation and insight. Emanating from this perspective, they are positioned to view any deviation from exploration/interpretation as a problematic repetition. Their position, to us, feels like a throwback to the time when the intricate complexity of the analytic interaction was yet to be recognized—rather puzzling considering their purported systems perspective. Our increased understanding of implicit and explicit domains of learning and memory clarifies that change requires not only a declaratively generated insight, but new procedural or "implicit relational learning" (Stern et al., 1998). While we understand Trop and Burke's concerns, we are convinced that analytic interaction not only entails, but requires, a much wider range of responses on the part of the analyst to facilitate an analysis, perhaps even more so for the more difficult patient (Bacal, 1985, 1998; Fosshage, 1990, 1997). Therefore, in contrast to Trop and Burke, we understood some of the enactments as quite facilitative of new implicit relational learning that typically included new insight as well.

Very early in treatment Jack announced his strongly held belief that all people would disappoint him and that his only choice was to lower his expectations. Faced with Jack's deep conviction, Munschauer responded, "Yes, it is your template; no matter what you do, you're going to get squat back." Her comment was not simply a reflection of Jack's experience. Patient and analyst were beginning to develop a mutual understanding and language that elucidated the patient's construction. It did so without challenging the veridicality of his construction, a challenge that, at this point in treatment, would have provoked aversiveness. Yet, Trop and Burke suggest that "he does not recognize his contribution to this. We would have taken the opportunity to inquire with Jack what were his own contributions to his disappointments." To our ears, their approach not only feels distant from the patient's experience and challenging of the patient but also is asking for something from the patient that he, at this juncture, does not know. We feel that their approach at this moment would have closed down both the reflective space and the patient. To help the patient perceive his constructive contribution is typically a gradual process, one in which, in our view, both patient and analyst were engaged. The questions Trop and Burke would have raised, of course, are good ones, and ones that we would explore gradually, over time, when they are closer to the patient's experience and dawning awareness.

We have a sense that, in their emphasis on exploration and interpretation, Trop and Burke neglect the idiosyncratic meanings and impact that such a singular emphasis might have on a particular analytic system—surprising in view of their emphasis on systems theory. In fact, the analyst initially tried the exploratory/interpretative approach, in part in reaction to having difficulty withstanding the patient's extreme nihilism, devaluation, and aversiveness (perhaps Trop and Burke were feeling similarly). Jack experienced the analyst's exploratory/interpretative comments as critical and as an attempt to dislodge him from his nihilistic and aversive position: that, in turn, became more fodder for his nihilism and aversiveness. When the analyst more consistently shifted into an empathic understanding position, tracking more closely the patient's experience, the patient felt better understood and subsequently was able, gradually, to emerge from his aversiveness and to express desire for more of her input.

We will conclude by considering one additional example of Trop and Burke's consistent reliance on exploration. When Jack invited Munschauer for the first time to dinner, they purportedly would have tried to explore "his motivation for the invitation." In our view, Trop and Burke take this moment out of context. The patient, in fact, had been out of treatment for several months, still under the sway of his conviction that he could not get anything out of treatment, much less his life. We viewed Jack as reaching out in a way that he could muster at that moment to contact Munschauer. To attempt to explore on the phone, of course, was a possible choice. Munschauer, however, felt that under these tenuous conditions, Jack would have experienced her exploration as her distancing herself from him and her aversiveness to him—a repetitive enactment. These moments require quick judgments that necessitate taking into account the context as best we can. In our view, we need flexibility in these situations, not a rigid adherence to the "book."

MARGARET CRASTNOPOL

In her comprehensive discussion from a relational perspective, Crastnopol presents a series of alternative formulations and interventions. We very much agree with Crastnopol that the particular subjectivities of patient and analyst create different relational fields and analytic experiences. A discussant, thus, creates a different relational field.

Crastnopol, as all analysts, certainly uses the empathic position to ferret out how Jack experiences his world. Yet, in her reading of the case material she emphasizes what it feels like to be an other in a relationship with Jack (the other-centered perspective) and hones in on the domination/submission, sadistic/masochistic enactments in the analytic relationship. We agree that other-centered data can inform analysts about problematic and self-defeating relational patterns. In fact, one of us has been urging self psychologists to make analytic use of this data (Fosshage, 1995a, 1997) and, in turn, has suggested that the American relational authors need to integrate more definitively the use of the empathic listening/experiencing perspective (Fosshage, 2003). In listening/experiencing and subsequent interventions, self psychologists more consistently lead with the empathic mode; American relationists, as compared to self psychologists, more often lead with the other-centered mode. Discussions like these provide a valuable opportunity to etch out the advantages and disadvantages of intervening on the basis of these different listening/experiencing perspectives. We are convinced of the importance of utilizing both perspectives as well as the analyst's self perspective to facilitate analytic interaction. A principal and at times difficult task is judging the timely use of each one of these perspectives.

From the other-centered perspective Crastnopol sees that Jack "wants a strong other and yet also wants to dominate and control that other; indeed he 'castrates' and then complains about the loss he sustains as a result of the 'castration'!" She says she would have been "interested to see how a transference–countertransference interpretation along these lines would have fared, whether Jack could have been helped to see how self-defeating are his efforts to dictate others' behavior." While we certainly agree with Crastnopol that this relational pattern is centrally important, the issue is how and when to address it. To address it early in treatment, we feel, would have potentiated the patient experiencing the interpretation as critical, evoking further despair and aversiveness. Remember that, at this point, the patient does not have a reflective awareness about his contribution to his "reality," nor has reflective space yet been achieved. In our view, Munschauer's reference to his template was not an "empathic mirroring," as Crastnopol saw it, but was an initial attempt to create reflective space for the consideration of his constructive contribution. It was an incipient effort to illuminate a primary pattern of organization that had emerged out of past experience. When analyst and patient had cocreated sufficient reflective space, interpretations based on the other-centered perspective were useful in illuminating this self-destructive relational pattern.

Another issue has to do with what we experienced as the bleakness in tone and content of Crastnopol's intervention. We believe that contextualizing the origins of relational patterns (emanating from an empathic perspective) increases reflection and makes the information sufficiently palatable for a patient to be able to integrate the new information. Jack needs to know why he wants to dominate and control. Not to include an explanation about the relational origins of his wish to dominate ironically and unfortunately begins to sound like he has "bad" traits—a one-person psychology, or an intrapsychic explanation of psychopathology. We, thus, would include through exploration and interpretation that his wish to dominate is most likely anchored in his relational experience of domination and submission with his father. He learned that only two positions existed—to be the dominator or the subjugated. Jack wants a strong other, yet, the strong other evokes the domination–submission relational pattern. While his domination is self-defeating on the one hand, it protects him from anticipated subjugation. Without this explanation of the relational origins of his wish to dominate, a patient can easily experience the analyst's interpretive remarks as critical, subsequently evoking the patient's aversiveness and possibly a transference–countertransference impasse. Crastnopol, in this instance, did not contextualize it.

Crastnopol is relieved that "sustaining an empathic posture is not as central to my view of the optimal therapeutic environment as it is to hers." While an empathic stance helps to inform us about what a patient may need therapeutically, in our view, and this is where we agree with Crastnopol, it has its limits when a patient wants to experience the analyst more fully as a person (intersubjective relatedness). On the other hand, not to include the empathically acquired data about the origins of the relational patterns as one makes use of other-centered data, in our view, also limits the usefulness of the interpretation to the patient. The moment-to-moment balance of the data acquired from each of these perspectives as well as the analyst's self perspective, in our view, is a central challenge in focusing and formulating interpretative interventions. When an analyst is provoked into the other-centered perspective (and certainly a patient's problematic relational patterns can do this), it is difficult for any analyst to get back into an empathic perspective. Yet, to do so enables us to be more facilitative as we anchor our interpretive understandings within both other-centered and empathic perspectives.

As Jack was shifting out of his nihilism and aversiveness, he began to "need" (from an empathic perspective) and "demand" (from an other-centered perspective) a progress report. Munschauer intuitively realized that she needed to interact with him even more fully as a "real" person and to give him feedback. Her feedback included his difficulty in "feeling" her involvement, again an incipient effort to illuminate a "template" and his use of it protectively. "At times, I showed my reaction by making grimaces of frustration and confirming that 'Yes, you can be a pain' (other-centered information directly revealed)." Crastnopol, however, wanted to up the ante and to have the analyst "confront him with his more self-destructive and reprehensible attributes." Apart from the different sensibilities of analyst and discussant, the question again pertains to timing and tone. It is possible, as Crastnopol suggests, that the analyst could have addressed even more; yet, in so doing, the danger was to become the humiliating, critical father.

We were puzzled about Crastnopol's assertion that Munchauer's "thumping" at this point in treatment did not bring about change and the patient "remains full of despair." In contrast, we reported that a new relational experience was in the making in which he felt like a "someone." "It contrasted with his father's crashing down on him and humiliating him, making him feel like a nobody, and his mother's collapsing in the face of his subjectivity which engendered contempt." These new experiences, of course, were not consolidated and the old themes were quite subject to activation. For example, showing his tenderness later in treatment triggered anxiety, nihilism, aversiveness, and a momentary departure from treatment.

We agree with Crastnopol that breaking professional boundaries is not necessarily "bad" or "wrong." The meanings of the action are the decisive factor. We have a very different understanding of the meanings. In Jack's invitation to the analyst to his home, Crastnopol perceives Jack as attempting "to lure the analyst into a deeper personal involvement in and valuation of Jack's own excessive lifestyle and narcissistic values . . . so [that] she'll come to recognize his actual specialness and splendor." She views the analyst's acceptance of the dinner invitation as "playing out the patient's wish to be loved as a personal friend in an unguarded extratherapeutic way."

We find Crastnopol's characterization to be quite suspicious of Jack's intentions, seemingly anchored in Freud's theory that (primary or secondary) narcissistic strivings for specialness have to be renounced. Her view as to the meanings of his request would certainly position the analyst not to accept the invitation, for it would be a countertransferential collusion with his narcissistic demands and a reinforcement of his grandiosity.

In marked contrast, we viewed Jack's invitation as a move out of his nihilistic reclusiveness and as an attempt to reach out to the analyst to reveal more of himself to her and to show the analyst the inanimate objects with which he had a vital connection. It was, in fact, during her first visit that Jack was "truly affectionate as he talked, with the tenderness of a loving parent, about his cars and tractors, all of which he had given pet names. In his element, surrounded by his 'things,' a softer side of Jack emerged that I had never witnessed before." Our understanding emerges out of Kohut's reconceptualization of narcissism, in which self strivings are legitimized as an essential aspect of self development. Self strivings include a need to feel "special," not in a comparative grandiose way, but in terms of feeling unique, valued, and important.

It was on the basis of seeing Jack's softer side that Munschauer came up with the powerful diagnosis, "You are a Closet Sweetie Pie." Perhaps because of her emphasis on aggression and self-destructiveness, and her implicit acceptance of Freud's theory of narcissism, Crastnopol does not see the "signs of the tenderness toward others that the term 'sweetie pie' implies" (p.13) and, therefore, is dubious about Munschauer's diagnosis. While Jack had spoken tenderly toward his inanimate objects (rather than "others"), implicitly he was revealing his softer side to Munschauer. Not to have seen these signs of tenderness, in our view, would have blunted the sensitive and fragile emergence of what Tolpin (2002) has described as "the tendrils of the self."

We disagree with Crastnopol when she suggests that she weighs her "subjective response to the patient as a partial indicator of his psychic state more heavily than Fosshage and Munschauer." All analysts use their subjective responses to their patients, for what else is there (Fosshage, 1995a)? In addition to different models and subjectivities, a distinguishing feature of subjective experience, in our view, is related to the respective use of other-centered, empathic, and self perspectives. For example, to experience Jack from the position as the other in a relationship (other-centered perspective), his invitation/request for the analyst to visit his home could easily be experienced as threatening and demanding. From an empathic perspective, the analyst is positioned better to hear the wish or need to share more of himself with the analyst, to be seen by her.

Generally, Crastnopol emphasizes Jack's aggressive, self-destructive, and more "reprehensible" qualities. She would attempt to confront and interpret those qualities relatively early in treatment. These early confrontations, in our view, would have increased his self-criticism, nihilism, and despair. In contrast, we emphasize or, perhaps more accurately, we attempt to ride the wave of Jack's emergent strivings, no matter how hidden, to grow—to become more vitally alive. We agree with Crastnopol that the "darker" aspects of Jack and the problematic relational patterns must be analytically addressed. The timing differs. In addition, to address those aspects of Jack, we emphasize the importance of contextualizing their origins so that the patient can potentially make better use of the interpretations rather than experience them as aversive or as requiring subjugation.

We were not stating, as Crestnopol suggests, that it was possible to break through this man's nihilism and aversiveness "only through engaging in extratherapeutic contacts." While we feel that the "home visits" were most facilitating in this analysis, the word "only" portrays us as asserting more certitude than we have and overemphasizes these occurrences at the expense of the considerable exploratory/interpretive work that took place. Moreover, Crastnopol's framing of these enactments as "provisions," contrasting them with exploration, obfuscates the fact that any intervention, including exploration and interpretation, can be experienced as a provision or not. Again, it depends on the meaning.

CONCLUSION

Successfully engaging an extremely nihilistic and aversive man in psychoanalytic treatment is a complex and difficult task, and this certainly was the case with Jack. Munschauer managed to cocreate with Jack a powerful transformative experience—in Jack's words, "It doesn't get no better than this." As we tried to make clear, there were many aspects of this treatment. Especially highlighted were Jack's shifting relational needs, which required various responses, based on various listening/experiencing perspectives, from the analyst.

Were the "extratherapeutic" contacts necessary? While, of course, we cannot answer with certainty, we are convinced from understanding and assessing as best we could from within the subjective experiences of patient, analyst, and consultant that these contacts, in this treatment, proved to be facilitative. We also do not underestimate the importance of having a consultant to "steady the ship" in these types of situations. In addition to offering heuristic conceptual schemas, we are attempting to open up the possibilities of interaction heretofore "undreamt of in our philosophy" in order to increase our chances of hearing patients and responding in a way that facilitates an analytically healing experience.

REFERENCES

Bacal, H. (1985), Optimal responsiveness and the therapeutic process. In: *Progress in Self Psychology, Vol. 1,* ed. A. Goldberg. Hillsdale, NJ: The Analytic Press, pp. 202–227.

———— ed. (1998), *How Therapists Heal Their Patients: Optimal Responsiveness.* Northvale, NJ: Aronson.

Fosshage, J. (1990), Clinical protocol. *Psychoanal. Inq.,* 10:461–477; Response, 601–622.

———— (1995a), Countertransference as the analyst's experience of the analysand: Influence of listening perspectives. *Psychoanal. Psychol.,* 12:375–391.

———— (1995b), Interaction in psychoanalysis: A broadening horizon. *Psychoanal. Dial.,* 5:459–478.

———— (1997), Listening/experiencing perspectives and the quest for a facilitative responsiveness. *Conversations in Self Psychology: Progress in Self Psychology, Vol. 13.* Hillsdale, NJ: The Analytic Press, pp. 33–55.

———— (2003), Contextualizing self psychology and relational psychoanalysis: Bidirectional influence and proposed syntheses. *Contemp. Psychoanal.,* 39:411–448.

Hoffman, I. Z. (1998), *Ritual and Spontaneity in the Psychoanalytic Process: A Dialectical-Constructivist View.* Hillsdale, NJ: The Analytic Press.

Kohut, H. (1977), *The Restoration of the Self.* New York: International Universities Press.

Lichtenberg, J., Lachmann, F. & Fosshage, J. (1996), *The Clinical Exchange: Techniques Derived from Self and Motivational Systems.* Hillsdale, NJ: The Analytic Press.

———— ———— & ———— (2002), *A Spirit of Inquiry: Communication in Psychoanalysis.* Hillsdale, NJ: The Analytic Press.

Psychoanalytic Inquiry (2000), 20:1–186.

Stern, D. N., Sander, L., Nahum, J., Harrison, A., Lyons-Ruth, K., Morgan, A.,
    Bruschweiler-Stern, N. & Tronick, E. (1998), Non-interpretive mechanisms in
    psychoanalytic therapy: The "something more" than interpretation. *Internat. J.
    Psychoanal.*, 79:903–921.
Thelen, E. & Smith, L. (1994), *A Dynamic Systems Approach to the Development of
    Cognition and Action.* Cambridge, MA: MIT Press.
Tolpin, M. (2002), Doing psychoanalysis of normal development: Forward edge
    transferences. In: *Postmodern Self Psychology: Progress in Self Psychology,* Vol. 18,
    ed. A. Goldberg. Hillsdale, NJ: The Analytic Press, pp. 167–190.

Part Two

WORKING IN TRAUMA

Seven

WHO DISSOCIATES? INCEST SURVIVOR OR THERAPIST?

STUART D. PERLMAN

This article describes some events in the psychotherapy of a survivor of profound childhood sexual abuse. These events involved dissociative states of the patient interestingly interacting with corresponding dissociations in myself.

In my clinical work with patients who suffer from dissociative disorders (e.g., Perlman, 1993, 1995, 1999), I have come to appreciate the power of intense affects, dissociation, and triggering of traumatic material in both the patient and myself. Each of us in the therapeutic dyad reacts to the other, mutually influencing and shaping the other (Lichtenberg, 1983; Davies and Frawley, 1992, 1994; Lachmann and Beebe, 1992, 1993; Beebe and Lachmann, 1994).[1]

THE POWER OF TRAUMA IN EVOKING COUNTERTRANSFERENCE

Herman (1992) asserts in her classic book, *Trauma and Recovery*, that "no one can hold atrocities in their mind for any length of time." For both patient or therapist, these horrors provoke too many intense affects. This truism ripples through clinical work with trauma survivors.

I thank George Atwood and Louis Breger for comments and encouragement on this chapter.

[1] The existence of mutual dissociation seriously undermines the traditional psychoanalytic assumption that the analyst's perspective is privileged over the patient's. More contemporary theories do not make this assumption, including intersubjectivity theory (e.g., Stolorow and Atwood, 1992; Orange, Atwood, and Stolorow, 1997), relational theory (e.g., Aron, 1996; Mitchell, 1997; Stern, 1997), and self psychology theory (e.g., Kohut, 1977, 1984).

When working with traumatized patients, one finds oneself gripped by the power of the traumas experienced by the patient that are acted out in the treatment process. Not only are the therapist's issues triggered by this intense work, but he or she may become involved in intense dramas that tap the core of the therapist's existence (Davies and Frawley, 1992, 1994).

As Mitchell (1988) puts it:

Unless the analyst effectively enters the patient's relational matrix or, rather, discovers himself within it—unless the analyst is in some sense charmed by the patient's entreaties, shaped by the patient's projections, antagonized and frustrated by the patient's defenses—the treatment is never fully engaged, and a certain depth within the analytic experience is lost [p. 293].

A Style of Treatment Tailored to a Severely Traumatized Patient

Kohut (1977) has helped me understand how the patient can be our best supervisor:

I advance the tenet that the analysand's capacity to assess his own psychological state is in certain situations potentially vastly more accurate than the analyst's. It must be added, however, that this assertion does not invalidate the equally cogent one that the analyst must carefully scrutinize whether the patient might not, under the influence of specific fears, wish to avoid undertaking psychological tasks that, if indeed performed, would lead to long-term beneficial results. Still, as my experience as an analyst has increased over the years, I have learned to trust a patient's wish [pp. 19–20].

For the patient described in this paper, the style used in her treatment fits with her specific request for absolute and detailed honesty. She knew what I was feeling many times even before I did. If she sensed that I was in any way withholding details or dissembling, even as part of social greetings (Ferenczi, 1932, called this professional hypocrisy), then she would lose trust and become physically ill. For example, she wrote me a message in a card one day.

> I think you lied to me today—the same kind of lie like when I asked you about abortion [I had told her I thought it was okay; but I am really ambivalent about abortions]. It makes me hurt and throw up. And I will not get better cuz then it don't meen nothing. I can't do it like that ever. Lies don't go for Buds or dr. God or the Pearlman [loving and playfully teasing names she would call me]. Only for rapists.

This form of treatment has been explicated in Perlman (1999, 2000) and is an extension of, and within the tradition of, Ferenczi's work in the 1920s and 1930s (e.g., Ferenczi, 1933). The approach with this patient included self-disclosure, even at times approximating a "mutual analysis" (Ferenczi, 1933, 1988) and, in addition, extensive discussions of the process simultaneously with my own analyst. Ferenczi emphasized how the process and needs of the analyst crucially shape treatment. According to Ferenczi, the patient therefore needs to be free to interpret the therapist's behavior and dynamics as the therapist feels free to comment on the patient's to make the treatment as helpful for the patient as possible. Ferenczi (1988) explains his reasons for using mutual analysis with a specific patient in an entry in his clinical diary in 1932:

> Was not the entire plan of "mutuality" conceived solely for the purpose of bringing to light something the patient had suspected in me and felt I had disavowed? Was it not an unconsciously sought antidote against the hypnotic lies of her childhood? Full insight into deepest recesses of my mind, in defiance of all conventions, including those of kindness and consideration? [p. 38].

This is clearly illustrated in this paper and is part of the work the patient experienced as validating her own "reality."

I also assisted the patient with various life tasks at a number of points during her therapy. These are not invariable features of my clinical practice (Perlman, 1999), but rather emerged as a way of working effectively with this particular patient.

REGINA

Several years ago I asked the patient, Regina, for permission to publish a paper, "In the Trenches Treating a Dissociated Trauma Survivor" (Perlman, 2000). As a condition to agreeing, she asked to read it. From her response, I learned that there were moments of heightened affect during our work together that she perceived as crucial, moments that I had not seen in the same way. I had noticed only specific aspects of these moments, or they had different meanings to me. Our dialogue encouraged me to ask Regina more directly about her perspective on other important incidents in her therapy and their meaning. Regina gave voice to surprising feedback and what emerged from this process inspired me to write this paper.

FEAR AND FIRST CONTACT: FAMILY SESSIONS

Long before I worked with Regina individually, her family was referred to me because of problems with her youngest son, then four years old. I came to understand that her son had developed his symptoms as a way to deflect Regina's rage at men. I worked with her, her husband, and her two sons in family sessions. Regina needed help understanding her children. She would become enraged at and attack them, and then she would feel horrible afterwards. Family sessions provided the children with an opportunity to tell their mother about what frightened and hurt them. I helped the children work out a strategy with their mother to help her manage her anger so that she was able to be more compassionate towards them. This enabled the family dynamics to improve and, after a few months, the family therapy ended.

Regina, who was in individual therapy with another therapist at that time, seemed frightened. I was struck by how hard she worked to be a caring and good mother. In the course of the family work and from the one individual session we had, it emerged that she had been brutally abused and tortured, both physically and sexually, by her father and the men to whom her father had given her when she was a child. I had felt a natural connection to and deep affection for her, a woman I saw as so earnestly trying to be a good, moral, and contributing person.

The only contact Regina and I had for many years was an occasional winter holiday card I sent and the one time I called her, asking permission of her and each member of her family to write about their family sessions in a book I was preparing. At that time, she told me that she was in individual therapy but would periodically change therapists.

REACHING OUT

Many years later, as I was walking with a patient from my waiting room to my office, I saw a frightened woman crouched, hiding behind some plants. She "reached out" her hand. I said, "Regina?"

I told her that I would help her, but she had to wait a moment and I would be back. She nodded. I took my scheduled patient into my office and said it would take a few minutes. Then I went back to Regina, who was still crouching behind the plants. She did not know where she was, who she was, or who I was. I felt torn between taking care of her and going back to the patient in my office. After a few minutes of explaining to her who I was, that I knew her and was willing to help her, I told her that I had to see the other patient first, but if she would be willing to wait in the waiting room, I would see her.

After the scheduled session, I went back to the waiting room and saw Regina under a little coffee table. She looked like a frightened and trapped cat ready to spring. I noticed that she had a sharp metal file in her hand. I asked her, "Should I be afraid of you with the file?" She seemed to indicate that I was safe. Even though I was still somewhat fearful, I coaxed her out from under the table and into my office. (Later, when she read this paper, Regina reported that while under the table in the waiting room, she had been extremely frightened and tried to "look mean" as a way to be safe.)

In my office I then saw Regina for two and a half hours, and I tried to get her back together, oriented, and able to function. As we spoke, Regina related to me as if she were a little girl of four or five, in the presence of a man to whom her father had given her to be used sexually. If she did not have sex with me, her father would punish her terribly. She felt that her father (who was dead) was waiting outside the door. After talking to the frightened child and telling her that she was safe and that I would protect her from the bad men who were after her, a more adult person, more like the Regina who had come to family therapy with me years earlier, began to talk. She told me that the "little ones" inside of her had forced her to come to see me. She told me that they wanted me to help her and she also wanted it. I agreed to help her, and we set up an appointment for a few days later.

This was a very arduous two-and-a-half hour session for me. Yet Regina remembers this session as having taken only a few minutes. I was concerned about taking on another person who was so disorganized, for I knew the depth of connection and support a person like this might need, and that at any moment a severe crisis could erupt. At the same time, I felt honored that she had felt compelled to seek my help.

Over the months of the family therapy and in the years since, I had secretly wished I could work with Regina because I felt she was not getting appropriate care from the several therapists she had been seeing for more than 18 years. I asked myself whether it was hubris and competitive zeal getting the best of me, but I felt strongly that her therapists were unaware of the depth of her splits and the horrors she had experienced. They seemed to me to lack understanding of the degree of safety she needed in order to come forth to tell of the pictures in her head, the experiences she had been through, and the devastation these experiences had wrought. In addition, I feared her therapists were unable to contain their own reactions enough to sit with her through this very difficult process (Perlman, 1995, 1999).

The sessions that followed our reconnection were filled with Regina telling me about terrible things that had happened to her that she had never told anyone before. She developed a ritual of holding my hand as a way to feel alive and connected. She said she lived for these moments, which made her life feel worth living. For the first time she felt that she could touch a man, and she trusted me enough to take in the good part and not feel like I was going to use her sexually. Young parts of her would come out, and they would remember many traumatic and brutal abuses by her father and by the men her father gave her over to for sexual exploitation.

Regina regularly got parking tickets during our sessions, because she would become disoriented, go into a child state reliving horrible memories, and lose track of time. Sometimes she would ask me to put money she provided into the meter for her while she waited in my office. Frequently after sessions, she felt too frightened to go alone back into the waiting room or to walk out to her car. I would walk with her so that she could reconstitute in a safe haven (the waiting room or her car).

All along she had difficulty remembering and putting together the pieces of her experience into a cohesive whole. As a result, we both started to create summaries of our work together, which I would write. She would carry the summaries around and reread them. She would then discuss her ideas about what I had written in terms of our relationship and her inner dynamics. Much of this paper is an extension of the shared summaries of our experience in the course of her treatment.[2]

BLOODY PUNISHMENT

An incident that occurred four months into our work together disturbed me greatly. When I went out to put money in the parking meter for her one day, I came back to the office to find she had stabbed herself in her arm with a knife and was bleeding extensively on my carpet. This was a powerfully upsetting moment for me. In an instant, many images and thoughts passed within me. I was horrified at the sight of the blood. Now looking back, I realize it triggered a physical reexperiencing in my body of an accident I had when I was ten years old in which I was run over by a car. I could feel the physical impact. All I could see was the blood, the blood of the car accident and the blood dripping from her arm onto my carpet. It felt to me almost as if she had hit me with a physical blow. It made me frightened of her, until I later realized that what I was reacting to was not what she was doing to me but rather included a reliving of the car accident.

I recovered quickly and told her that everything was okay, and that I was not angry. I gave her tissues to put on the cuts, brought peroxide and bandages, and cleaned her up. She was frightened I would not want to see her any more. I told her it was okay, but that I was concerned for her and did not want her to do it again. I had to keep reassuring her that I was not angry. She was frightened I would never trust her and never be willing to put money in her meter. I told her I would, and did so the following session. Later Regina told me,

---

[2] Yalom and Elkin (1974) describe a similar process of each member of a therapeutic dyad writing summaries of the therapy sessions, but in Yalom's process he did not have each member read and respond to the others' summaries.

The Exacto-knife cut was a major deal that you didn't keep
bringing it up. I didn't think you would trust me. You didn't
hit me or yell. You fixed me up. You put stuff on—peroxide.
I can remember watching Stuart, like a dream. Thinking
that you were so nice to me after I got blood on your carpet.
You said you were concerned about me. Then you cleaned
it up. It was a magical thing. You should have been beating
me up and forcing me to clean up the blood. Instead of
being mean—you said you didn't have to clean it up, you
cleaned some up but left some there. That was weird. You
never seemed to care if I spilled on the carpet—I would
look at it every time and see if it was still there. I would
remember thinking how weird that you left it there a long
time. And let me still come. Then the blood was not there.
You said, "I don't care about the rug but I care about you."
I was blown away that you were so nice to me. Blown away.

It astounded her that I was so nice to her then and in many
other ways as well, such as putting money in her meter and sometimes
giving her food when she was hungry. Being treated in this way was so
unusual to her that she began to worry and consulted another therapist
she had seen in a workshop. The workshop leader told her it was
wonderful that she found someone who was being kind to her, and it
was not weird. This relieved her.

She explained in a hesitant manner that Max, a male part of her,
was against her telling me about her experiences. It was Max who had
stabbed her and was threatening that continued discussion might
trigger the same "bloody punishment." This male part of her hated me
and was punishing her by stabbing her for engaging in this process in
which she told me many things that she was never supposed to tell
anyone. I realized that I had to develop some sort of connection with
the male personality who wished to kill her. I then made several
attempts to ask him to come out and talk with me. He did finally
emerge and said that Regina and the little ones deserved punishment
for trusting me and being so stupid and weak. He said he did not
trust me.

To hold my course I needed support and soothing from my own
analyst. My analyst emphasized that Regina was opening up to me in
a deeper way, which clearly let me see how she functioned inside,

what she had experienced, and what her daily experience on a moment-to-moment basis was like. She was telling me about experiences she had never revealed to another human being and this was unquestionably a profound deepening of the process. My analyst continued by saying that a patient coming in contact with this deeper experience of himself or herself could become disorganized for periods of time. This was one stage of Regina's treatment in a very intense, powerful, and long process.

I showed the draft of the present manuscript up to this point to Regina. In the next section, I describe what ensued.

REGINA'S SURPRISING REVELATION

I found myself telling Regina that one of the crucial elements in my being able to help another person, especially one with dissociative disorders, is the basic feeling that this person does not want to destroy me. I have worked with multiple personalities who have had alters who have been too vicious and who wanted to hurt or kill me, and I could not work effectively with these patients.

In this context, Regina asked hesitantly, *"Do you really want to know what happened in the treatment?"* She then told me about an experience that she felt was critically important to her in going deeper in the process and continuing on in her therapy. Regina told me then that Max, this male personality, had come out in an earlier session months before her "bloody punishment," stood over me as I sat in my seat, and verbally attacked me. It was only at this point that the angry male alter decided he could allow treatment to continue with me.

Regina explained, *"Trust thing is mega with Max. Why Max allowed the reliving and child little ones to come out is because Max is always watching. I know Max can beat you up; so little ones can come out."* When I asked how Max could know that he could beat me up, she told me the following:

You were sitting in your chair with your legs crossed. You were looking at me. Max standing over you. You were listening and you said 'All right already. All right already.' You took a big breath of air all puffed up. Then you let out all this air, dropped your shoulders, your energy dropped, head went down, you looked at floor, and turned away on the swivel chair. I backed off. Like you were really scared and hurt and like your soul popped out." I asked how long I was in this state. She told me 15 to 20 seconds. I asked Regina about my soul popping out, and she told me that "your body crumpled and your soul had left" for that period of time. She said, "Max knew he could destroy you psychologically, so then he didn't feel afraid and could let the little ones out."

I was shocked to hear this. I realized that I had been trying not to think about this powerful male alter personality as a way to feel more comfortable and safer in my interactions with Regina. It was clear to me that much was going on of which I was not fully aware.

The following session I asked Regina what Max had said to me that scared me so much. She told me she "didn't remember exactly," but that Max was "Mean. Monotone. Threats. He told a story about coming close to killing someone. Cut your heart out and rip your guts out and cut your jugular vein. You will die. Cross the line of okay behavior and this is what will happen to you." She then went on to tell me about a series of real events in her life. It was a long description that boiled down to her having lived with a man who kept threatening to kill her and who threw her against the wall. She had endured this abuse passively for a long time but then, "I took a big sharp knife. Put it to his throat. Right on the jugular vein. Told him, 'Fucker you'd better get your ass out of here and never come back or I'll kill you for sure.'" She told me "Max's job is survival and physical living" in crisis situations.

Discussing this material with my analyst, I began to associate to my father, a violent man who would, when angry, physically assault his children. He had been a professional boxer. On some occasions I would watch him cut open, butcher, and filet the deer he shot on hunting trips. He had a delicatessen and grocery store that I worked in from age 11 to 21. I remembered how my father, when he was angry with me, would bang and point the razor-sharp carving knife at me. I remember at those moments being afraid that he would cut my stomach open, pull out my guts, and filet me like a scared deer. It was not surprising to me that this angry male alter threatening directly or indirectly to filet and cut me open, as my father seemed to be threatening, caused me to momentarily dissociate.

Over the next weeks and in discussions with my analyst, I came to integrate this experience. I thanked Regina for her help in pointing this out to me. I explained how I thought it was useful for me that she had done this. She seemed confused that I was grateful rather than angry with her. I was confused about why my previous therapy and analysis had not fully explored my fears of being killed.

The following occurred after she had read the paper for a second time. Her response astounded me. Regina said, "You've asked me what I really think and there is something I've been thinking for long time. Is it all right if I tell you?" I told her, "Absolutely!" with my best therapist voice. But inside I was afraid of whatever new revelation she might articulate. Regina continued,

> I usually feel most comfortable with people who have been sexually abused and can tell if they have been sexually abused many times even before the other person knows. And we get along amazingly well. I think you were sexually abused after you were hit by that car and you were in your body cast and unable to move.

First I was struck by how coherently, directly, and fluently she spoke. Then I immediately said to myself, "No way! She's got to be wrong."

Then I had an immediate body experience of being back in the full body cast that went from my neck to the end of my toes with a hole in it around my genitals and my behind. This occurred at the start of puberty when I had a sense of heightened vulnerability and sensitivity to humiliation. I remembered how, due to the body cast, all these people would have to wipe me after I defecated and would wash my genitals and behind. Nurses would come in abruptly and pull off the bed sheets and wash me as though I was not a person who had rights over his own body. Later, when I went home from the hospital, my mother had to do this for me for months until a smaller cast was put on my leg. Though in some sense I was not sexually abused legally or technically, I felt profoundly violated, helpless, and physically imprisoned by the medical and physical care I received.

For the next three days after Regina told me this, I experienced myself in a regressed place, overpowered by the feelings of invasion, violation, helplessness, and humiliation. Even though I had talked about this experience with previous therapists, I had never explored the specific sense of invasion and violation and its meaning to me. It also helped me to understand more fully that the ways I behave in certain situations are not as linked to my parents as I had previously assumed. This revelation changed my view of myself, helped me feel my own skin as more of a protective shield creating more of a sense of body integrity, and reduced some of my resentment towards my parents. It also highlighted for me the importance of understanding the impact of some medical procedures on the future experience of children and adults.

I thanked Regina for her help in pointing this out to me. I explained how I thought she was right in this way and how it was useful for me that she had done this. I also explained that it had taken me some time to integrate. I mentioned the last idea because she was always critical of herself for how long it takes her to integrate our understandings of her own history and psychological functioning. I also thought it was useful to have told her that because she sensed that I had been more distant from her for about a week and I knew it was because I was feeling trepidation about her next revelation about my experience. She seemed confused that I was not angry with her. I was indeed grateful to her and confused again about why my previous therapy and analysis had not explored this fully.

Three years have passed since the interactions described in this paper. Regina's trust in the therapeutic process has continued to deepen during this time, and she has progressed from her initial state of overwhelming reliving to one of increasingly integrating her traumatic history and achieving a greater sense of perspective on her life as a whole.

MUTUAL DISSOCIATION AND INTEGRATION

This treatment description, I believe, illustrates how two human beings in the treatment room can powerfully affect each other. The treatment is for the purpose of helping the patient, and I am responsible for monitoring the process. But I am also a vulnerable, embedded participant in a process that is larger than both of us.

It is my experience directly and as a supervisor that intersubjective phenomena such as mutual dissociation and triggering frequently occur in the work with survivors of extreme trauma. The specific interactions on which I have focused came to light because of the rather unusual process of feedback that occurred between Regina and myself in the course of her therapy. Ordinarily these interactions tend to be unacknowledged and unexplored, and sometimes are even collusively denied. The potential of the therapy to then facilitate healing and emotional understanding for both participants is accordingly limited and circumscribed.

I have a central belief, born of clinical experience and validated by my early experience with self and humanistic psychologies, that to do deep work with severe trauma survivors, the therapist needs to be exquisitely sensitive to the patient's intense fear and to the human relationship being developed between patient and therapist. The budding relationship with me stimulates expectations based on the patient's past relationships. These patients have often experienced people as sources of betrayal, danger, and harm. My behavior needs to communicate that I am trying to help them, treat them with respect, understand their needs, and recognize their validity as human beings with their own perspectives, and it is this that I believe enables the integration of affects and traumatic experience.

Regina and her self-states and alters profoundly intruded on and provoked my issues, and triggered deep dissociated traumatic experiences that I began to relive. Some of these experiences were so painful that I forgot or dissociated them. Having experienced this with her was very humbling. But I also believe that it was helpful for me in understanding the depth of pain Regina felt, the psychotherapeutic process, and many important new things about myself. I believe that, no matter what therapist had worked with Regina, she would have provoked some profound parallel experience.

This treatment reminds me of Mitchell's (1997) comment:

> One of the best-kept secrets of the psychoanalytic profession is the extent to which analysts often grow (in corrective emotional experiences) through a surrender to the influence of patients whose life experiences, talents, and resources may be different from their own [p. 26].

REFERENCES

Aron, L. (1996), *A Meeting of Minds: Mutuality in Psychoanalysis*. Hillsdale, NJ: The Analytic Press.

Beebe, B. & Lachmann, F. (1994), Representation and internalization in infancy: Three principles of salience. Psychoanal. Psychol., 11:127–165.

Davies, J. & Frawley, M. (1992), Dissociative processes and transference-countertransference paradigms in the psychoanalytically oriented treatment of adult survivors of childhood sexual abuse. Psychoanal. Dial., 2:5–36.

———— & ———— (1994), Treating the Adult Survivor of Childhood Sexual Abuse: A Psychoanalytic Perspective. New York: Basic Books.

Ferenczi, S. (1933), Confusion of tongues between adults and the child: The language of tenderness and passion. In: Final Contributions to the Problems and Methods of Psychoanalysis, Vol. 3, ed. M. Balint. New York: Basic Books, 1955, pp. 156–167.

———— (1988), The Clinical Diary of Sándor Ferenczi, ed. J. Dupont. Cambridge, MA: Harvard University Press.

Herman, J. (1992), Trauma and Recovery. New York: Basic Books.

Kohut, H. (1977), The Restoration of the Self. New York: International Universities Press.

———— (1984), How Does Analysis Cure? ed. A. Goldberg & P. Stepansky. Chicago: The University of Chicago Press.

Lachman, F. M. & Beebe, B. (1992), Representational and selfobject transferences: A developmental perspective. In: New Therapeutic Visions: Progress in Self Psychology, Vol. 8, ed. A. Goldberg. Hillsdale, NJ: The Analytic Press, pp. 3–15.

———— & ———— (1993), Interpretation in a developmental perspective. In: The Widening Scope of Self Psychology: Progress in Self Psychology, Vol. 9, ed. A. Goldberg. Hillsdale, NJ: The Analytic Press, pp. 45–52.

Lichtenberg, J. (1983), Psychoanalysis and Infant Research. Hillsdale, NJ: The Analytic Press.

Mitchell, S. (1988), Relational Concepts of Psychoanalysis: An Integration. Cambridge, MA: Harvard University Press.

———— (1997), Influence and Autonomy in Psychoanalysis. Hillsdale, NJ: The Analytic Press.

Orange, D., Atwood, G. & Stolorow, R. (1997), Working Intersubjectively: Contextualism in Psychoanalytic Practice. Hillsdale, NJ: The Analytic Press.

Perlman, S. (1993), Unlocking incest memories: Preoedipal transference, countertransference, and the body. J. Amer. Acad. Psychoanal., 21:363–386.

———— (1995), One analyst's journey into darkness: Countertransference resistance to recognizing sexual abuse, ritual abuse, and multiple personality disorders. J. Amer. Acad. Psychoanal., 23:137–151.

———— (1999), The Therapist's Emotional Survival: Dealing with the Pain of Exploring Trauma. Lanham, MD: Rowan & Littlefield.

———— (2000), In the trenches treating a dissociated trauma survivor: A detailed process analysis. Presented at the Annual Conference on the Psychology of the Self, October, Chicago.

Stern, D. (1997), Unformulated Experience: From Dissociation to Imagination in Psychoanalysis. Hillsdale, NJ: The Analytic Press.

Stolorow, R. & Atwood, G. (1992), Contexts of Being: The Intersubjective Foundations of Psychological Life. Hillsdale, NJ: The Analytic Press.

Yalom, I. & Elkin, G. (1974), Every Day Gets a Little Closer: A Twice Told Therapy. New York: Basic Books.

Eight

TRAUMA AND RECOVERY
A STORY OF PERSONAL TRANSFORMATION AND HEALING AMIDST THE TERROR OF SEPTEMBER 11

TODD F. WALKER
STAN T. DUDLEY

The terrorist attacks of September 11, 2001, changed life, as we knew it, forever. The American sense of security and invulnerability was destroyed along with the World Trade Center Towers and the west wing of the Pentagon. The killing of more than 3000 people, most of whom were never found, has left hundreds of children without parents and spouses without partners. Television brought the atrocious images of trauma into our homes such that much of the world shared the experience of horror, disbelief, and fear. Terrorism had finally dealt America a severe blow, scarring the American psyche and leaving many people feeling that things would never be the same.

On September 11, we witnessed the destruction of the naïve American belief of security and invulnerability and the disintegration of the illusion that the horrors of war and terrorism were something that happened beyond our borders. The tidal waves of the horror and nationalism in our country reached people around the world, creating a strong sense of international unity in many people. This is the context of terror created by the September 11 attacks on America and the resulting destruction of the sense of certainty, security, predictability, and ongoingness-of-being.

The authors are grateful to Lindsey Slaughter for her insightful critique and editorial comments.

During the discussion of the impact of September 11 at the International Conference on the Psychology of the Self in 2002, Anna Ornstein and Ernst Wolf told us how the terrorist attacks brought back memories of a life they had lived during the Holocaust. While it is no surprise to us that the pandemonium of September 11 triggered traumatic memories and pain, the possible therapeutic effect of the terrorist attacks is less imaginable without a microscopic analysis of the healing process of a trauma survivor.

We use Stolorow's (1999) conceptualization of the nature of trauma as a model to understand the potential mutative impact of September 11. Additionally, we use Ornstein's (1985, 1994, 2003) model of how traumatized individuals can recover through the transformative nature of sharing, reconstructing, and integrating recovered memories. These two models illustrate the process of post-traumatic self-integration in a previously traumatized patient whose healing was catalyzed by witnessing the unthinkable events of September 11.

Stolorow (1999) shared his experience of trauma following the death of his wife, Daphne. He believes that the profound sense of estrangement and emotional isolation that he felt separates many traumatized individuals from others. Trauma can destroy one's pre-traumatic organization of reality—no one would ever crash airplanes into the World Trade Center Towers and destroy the buildings and their inhabitants. The absolutisms or rules of non-terrorist existence not only play a central role in stabilizing everyday life, these beliefs also provide a context of safety, harmony, and continuity.

When trauma shatters these everyday absolutisms, one's sense of certainty and safety is destroyed. A concomitant threat occurs to one's sense of continuity with the exposure to "the unbearable embeddedness of being" (Stolorow and Atwood, 1992, p. 22), where reality is random and unpredictable, if not chaotic. Further, trauma may leave the victim feeling isolated due to the real and perceived difficulty that others will have in trying to empathize with the victim's unique experience of the trauma. A traumatized individual may have difficulty imagining that anyone else can truly feel what it is like to walk in his shoes. Stolorow (1999) believes that the trauma victim cannot trust that anyone else's horizons of experience are commensurable with his; and therefore others are not in possession of the requisite empathy for understanding his unique experience of trauma. Stolorow's belief is reminiscent of John Locke's epistemology in his 1689 *Essay Concerning Human Understanding:* "No man's knowledge here can go beyond his experience" (cited in Miner and Rawson, 1994, p. 116).

Many traumatized people are convinced in their belief that nontraumatized, or "normal," people live in a world with different rules of existence. Therefore the traumatized person may feel exiled to an alien existence with no hope of an understanding connection, or twinship, with another. Thus, there is the initial traumatic event and the secondary traumatogenic process of disconnection from one's previous world of self-selfobject bonds. While Stolorow was in a familiar context with his "old and good friends and close colleagues," like some trauma victims, he felt alone in an alien world without the possibility of any visitors who might resonate with his experience. He described his search for twinship with the analyst he sought out in his own recovery from trauma: "I remembered how important it had been for me to believe that the analyst I saw after Daphne's death was also a person who had known devastating loss and how I implored her not to say anything that could disabuse me of my own belief" (p. 465).

The terrorism of September 11 was a shock that provided a new context of being for many people. However, the catastrophic happenings and horrendous loss catalyzed a fervent sense of patriotism that promoted an increase in American cohesion, vitality, and direction. This national reintegration, despite the expected episodes of acts of prejudice and narcissistic rage against individuals, led numerous people to put aside their differences and unify to struggle to regain the ideals of security, freedom, and a promising future. Profound trauma that impacts a community, like the terrorist attacks of September 11 or other national disasters may unite victims and empathizers alike into a selfobject milieu that offers support as well as the potential for healing and growth to all members. These communities are built upon a common experience—an intersubjectivity of traumatic experience.

By contrast, individual trauma is usually perpetrated behind closed doors and endured in solitude. As Ornstein (2003) states, "The secrecy surrounding the childhood abuse created a profound sense of emotional isolation in these patients (adults abused as children) while survivors of collectively endured trauma were able to share their experiences throughout the ordeal" (p. 96). It is often very difficult for the person who experienced private trauma to imagine that anyone else can understand their unique lived experiences. There is usually no communal or shared experience and the possibility of the therapeutic effects of empathically responsive others may not be immediately present. Many traumatized individuals have lost their senses of safety, freedom, and a positive future as they feel alone and in an ongoing state of chaos, vulnerability, agony, and despair. Shame, often experienced by the victim, can further stymie the telling of one's incomprehensible story, as one feels that, even if listeners can understand, they will confirm the victim's shameful self-image.

Feeling irrevocably shackled to their unique traumatic experience, these individuals frequently feel estranged from their pre-traumatized selfhood, and others may be seen as living in a world governed by different rules of existence. The rules or absolutisms of trauma may create a sense of separation from others who have not lived through the individual's feeling of incomparable pain. Often there is a strong sense of alienation, such that the traumatized cannot fathom that anyone else could empathically understand their inner world. As noted by Ornstein (1994):

> Survivors of trauma have every reason to expect that their story will evoke fear, confusion, horror, and disbelief and that therapists will protect themselves from these affects by resorting to generalizations, quick explanations, or praise for the survivor's heroism or special qualities [p. 139].

Therefore, the traumatized self is often shattered, emotionally overwhelmed, and feels alienated from others, who might provide the desperately-needed selfobject experiences of twinship, cohesion, and revitalization. Sharing lived experiences of trauma with a community of others creates a strong and therapeutic intersubjectivity of traumatic experience. Victims of trauma that is endured alone may need to first put their story into words. They may then overcome their belief that they cannot be understood by others and have their longed-for selfobject connection with someone. Ornstein (2003) states "The integration of traumatic memories into the flow of one's life narrative depends on the healing of the split between experiences as they are lived and as they are remembered" (p. 138). She believes this process is a function of the therapeutic dialogue, in which patient and therapist attempt to articulate and reconstruct images and memories in order to integrate the past with the present.

Fortuitously, the trauma of September 11 decontextualized life in America such that the worlds of the traumatized and other human beings could be temporarily merged. The dramatic and unending media blitz made the horror of September 11 experience-near for many who witnessed it. The horizons of experience of the traumatized and nontraumatized could be merged, thus creating a context in which some traumatized individuals might feel less alienated and more connected with others in the world. Ornstein (1994), a Holocaust survivor, cites the old Hasidic saying, "Memory is the key to redemption" to emphasize how empathic listeners facilitate victim acceptance, remembering, feeling, and then self-integration of previously split-off traumatic experiences. Healing from trauma requires the emotional presence of another who listens from an empathic perspective and accepts the horrific images and pain as real, thereby allowing the victim to reconnect with trauma in a way that is nontraumatic and integrative.

Stolorow's (1999) description of the phenomenology of trauma and Ornstein's theory (1985, 1994, 2003) of healing and recovery help us to better understand the unforeseen transformations in self-integration and emotional vitality in a severely traumatized patient. This woman seemed to have a twinship kind of selfobject connection, via television, with the trauma victims of September 11. Her renewed opportunity for healing followed her capacity for empathic connection with the September 11 victims. This connection facilitated the reawakening of her capacity to feel, the recovery of traumatic memories, renewed self-integration, and the beginning of her experience of feeling bonded with, rather than alienated from, other human beings.

THE CASE OF HEATHER

Heather is a 43-year-old woman who sustained unthinkable trauma throughout her childhood and adolescence. She had been physically and sexually abused beginning at age four and ending when she was 16 years old and pregnant after being raped. At that time, she eloped with the man who is now her husband. The degree of traumatic experience in Heather's family was evidenced in her repeatedly diving off the swing on the playground during elementary school "to hit my head so hard [that] it would kill me." This also put her in contact with a gentle and loving school nurse "who would take care of me like my mother should have." Her youngest brother had jumped out in front of and been hit by cars many times before his tenth birthday and her other younger brother was hospitalized as a young teenager after plunging his right arm into a cement mixer being used in a nearby road construction. Incredibly, no one understood the meaning of these poignant cries for help, and Heather and her brothers were not rescued from their horrendous familial trauma. One of Heather's early recollections was being only two years old and asking an unfamiliar couple to take her and her bag of belongings home with them to start a family where she fantasized being loved. Heather was first referred to me (TW) 10 years ago, at age 33, by her gynecologist after she cut her genitals "to get rid of all those horrible memories of being raped." She presented with symptoms of self-cutting, suicidality (e.g., holding a handgun in her mouth for five hours and taking a near-fatal overdose of Ativan), alexithymia, avoidance of social contact, and an inability to be emotionally or sexually intimate with her husband. Her impenetrable wall of shame and self-loathing was evidenced by her angry and hostile outbursts at her husband when he said that he loved her. She reported,

> I feel like I'm walking around empty and dead. I can't feel anything. I don't want to feel anything—it would probably kill me. And I really don't want to be close to anyone because I just feel like I'm from a different planet. No one is like me. Why should I think that anyone can understand me? If I wasn't me I wouldn't want to know me either. I'm glad that nobody has lived through what I have, but it's pretty lonely. I can't even imagine that [my husband] can understand me. What a great wife I am—I don't sleep with him and I walk away from him when he wants to talk to me. I just can't handle it! I wish God would just realize that I've been through enough and take me to Heaven. But I know what would happen, I'll go to Hell and life wouldn't be any different.

Over the next three years, I listened to Heather's shame, self-hatred, despair, and fragmentation anxiety as she told her life story— being severely neglected by her mother, physically abused as a young child by her father, and leaving her "house of pain" pregnant with a child of rape. Her mother had actually forced Heather to go out with the rapist when she was first allowed to date. The baby was stillborn, and she was told that she could never have other children. Her mother visited her in the hospital and told Heather that the baby had probably died because Heather had smoked a cigarette during the third trimester. Despite Heather's caring for her two younger brothers during most of her childhood, her mother told her that the baby was lucky not to have been born to an incapable young mother. Heather felt extremely ashamed about her sexual abuse and not being able to give her husband, her rescuer, the child that he longed for. She therefore withdrew from him emotionally as well as sexually. These were a few of the horrid fragments from her childhood that had kept her fragmentation-prone and too vulnerable to be emotionally alive before entering treatment. She and I understood that her self-hatred and longing to escape the childhood trauma that tortured her in her adult life resulted in her attempts to cut her genitals out of her body in order to "let me start my life all over again or kill me."

She was seen two or three times per week in individual psychotherapy for three years and weekly in group treatment for the last 18 months of her first treatment. After three years of treatment, Heather had ceased to cut herself and was more able to talk, laugh, and cry about moments in her current life with her husband, although not with members of her therapy group. She was much closer and happier with her husband, including being sexually intimate for the first time in more than ten years. I remember being very encouraged by the emotional fluency that she had developed with her husband and by her feeling more comfortable in sharing day-to-day life experiences with him. This newfound marital harmony led Heather and her husband to adopt a three-year-old boy and a four-year-old girl, both children of chemically addicted and abusive parents. For the first time since childhood, she was able to enthusiastically use her artistic talent in painting murals for a local interior designer. Despite Heather's significant growth and her experience of "coming back to life" during her psychotherapy, I believed that she remained rather vulnerable. Due to her understandable reluctance to face the full spectrum of the traumatic pain that she had survived, it did not seem that many of the traumatic memory fragments had been sufficiently analyzed or integrated. Her basic mistrust of others and her resulting social anxiety continued to plague her interactions outside of her nuclear family. However, I respected her decision to cease therapy after her significant growth and newfound intimacy with her husband and I knew that her deep and trusting connection with me would allow her to return to treatment if she felt that it was again needed.

In April of 2001, seven years after her termination, Heather called for an appointment due to her grief regarding the recent death of her alcoholic brother, the one who had jumped in front of cars as a child. Her insurance company had referred her to an EAP counselor who, according to Heather,

> could only listen to me for a few minutes before telling me that my main problem was just my negative attitude. He seemed like he didn't believe me about what I was telling him about my life. He started to squirm in his chair and I knew he wasn't gonna be able to handle what I was going to tell him. He went on to this speech about how he had had a lot of bad things happen to him and he was still positive bout his life. He even talked about how bad the Holocaust Jews had it! He made me feel so bad about myself. He was asking me to be more positive and get over the things in my life that I couldn't; and he just made me feel even worse. I came back to see you 'cause I knew you would understand me if anybody could.

I remembered how difficult Heather's story had been for me to hear and I could relate to this counselor's reported inability to venture into her horrific and threatening history. I also realized how crucial it was for me to be psychologically available to Heather to journey back into traumatic experiences that would not be easy for either of us to endure.

Heather went on to describe her curative fantasy:

> I wish you could press my cry-button and make me feel the sadness I should feel for my brother. Over the last few years I've been able to have fun with [my husband] and my kids. But I have to admit, I do retreat to bed when the bad memories start to come back. But now, I feel like my heart is frozen and I can't cry. I couldn't even cry at my brother's funeral after spending two weeks next to him dying. Todd,

it was so horrible—he would puke bowls full of blood and just cry and cry waiting to die. He was my little brother, the one whose diapers I used to change and fix meals for after my father died, and my mother was spending the night at her boyfriend's house. I'm so worried that I'll go back to the way I was before I met you. I don't want to be frozen— I want to be able to feel sad and then happy again.

In the five sessions before September 11, Heather and I explored her self-experiences triggered by her brother's tragic and gory death. His death activated memories of her severe neglect, her sexual abuse, and her only *raison d'être* as a child—to protect and care for her brothers. While she had vivid visual memories of these events, she again felt emotionally broken, as she could not feel or cry in reaction to these traumatic images. I attempted to empathically interpret that I could understand how her factual, emotionally flat experience of these memories may be protective. While she was intellectually cognizant of my interpretations, there was a noticeable lack of deep emotional resonance. Our therapeutic dialogue before September 11 had not opened the door to a deeper exploration of her traumatic memories and pain, which seemed necessary for the process of reintegration and recovery.

SEPTEMBER 12 SESSION

Heather began the session by describing her personal experience of the events of September 11, which she had witnessed on television while alone in her home:

I was in the kitchen listening to the radio yesterday. I heard that the plane had crashed into the World Trade Center. I ran over to the TV to turn on the news. It was weird— I hadn't felt that curious about anything for a long time. I just felt that something really bad had happened and I wanted to see what it was. When I turned on the TV, the second plane was just flying into the second tower and I couldn't believe what I was seeing. Todd, I remember standing there like I was watching history happen. I'm almost embarrassed to admit it but I felt like I was alive again—like something big was happening in the world. Anyway, they showed pictures of people running around in a total panic. I remember this one guy who looked like the Devil was trying to catch him from behind, like he was running as fast as he could to stay alive. I hope you don't take this the wrong way, like I'm melodramatic, but I could really feel the terror in that man's eyes. It made me remember how I felt running away from my father when he was drunk and after me. . . . [long pause for retrospection].

It sounds kinda sick or selfish, but I had this strong reaction to the terror in his face. I could, or at least I felt I could, feel what he was going through. My heart and mind were racing like I was back in those old crazy days as a kid. It was like this guy's struggle to stay alive put me in a time machine and took me back to the horrors of my childhood when I would run around in circles trying to get my little brothers and me away from whatever dad was going to do to torture us. Beat us. Throw a plate at us. I remember when I was nine years old and my parents had to run away [to keep] my dad from being arrested. We stayed on a farm in the middle of Nebraska for a whole summer. I remember my cousins when there was a tornado coming. They seemed so scared and so nervous about being killed. I remember thinking how it would be okay if I was killed and that every day of my life felt like a tornado in my house. Except, we never had a warning about when it was coming. It just blew in with my dad and turned everything upside down. I remember wishing [that] my ten-year-old cousin could understand and that my parents would let me live with them in Nebraska—I wouldn't mind the tornadoes at all. They were nothing like the storms in our house. And we never had any siren warnings so we could hide. I had to always stay on guard to protect my brothers. But, I knew my wish [to live with her cousins] would never come true. No one could understood what my life was like and I wasn't gonna try and tell them either. That guy's face and all the craziness and uncertainty I felt watching him brought all the pain back. After all of these years, my heart was beating, no pounding, again. It was just like I felt so long ago as a kid. It's even weird to tell you how much I could feel for that guy.

I responded, "I can understand how this man's face reminded you of many horrible moments in your life. While you and I have been trying to press your cry-button because you wanted to cry for your brother and learn to feel again, the events of September 11 were something you could relate to. I sense a hope that maybe you can move from feeling dead to feeling alive again and sharing a real life with others."

I was amazed at how her witnessing the events of September 11 had reawakened her capacity to feel and allowed her to cry. Her experience of other people's trauma had brought to the surface many of the traumatic memories in their full imagery and emotionality, which had previously not been accessible to us. It seemed that our previous therapeutic dialogue about these matters had not yet provided the experience-nearness and intensity needed to evoke her true lived experiences. Despite her long-standing trust in and engagement with me, witnessing the traumatic events of September 11 provided Heather with the necessary experiential context of trauma and intensity of affect needed to evoke her empathic resonance to the face of the man she saw on television struggling to survive. Her empathic connection with this man was therapeutic in reawakening her capacity to feel, thereby rescuing her from her experience of emotional deadness and aloneness.

She went on to describe her feelings of being connected with her fellow Americans on September 11:

> I couldn't pull myself away from the TV. You know I never watch it. I'm not interested in the news, those ridiculous "As-The-World-Turns" shows, and I don't watch sports with [my husband and son]. But, let me tell you, I couldn't tear myself away from the television that day. I watched the people jump out of the World Trade Center buildings. It reminded me of how my brother tried to kill himself by running out in front of cars on the highway in front of our house. Anything was better than the hell inside our house. I wanted to be there and help. I felt so bad for all of those people who were trying to get out of there. For the first time in I don't know how long, I felt like I was part of something. Can you believe I'm saying this? I wanted to be right there with those people. I wanted to scream through the television and let them know that I was there with them!

I was sitting there, feeling like I was there, like I wanted to be there and I all of a sudden realized that I was about to wet my pants and I ran to the bathroom.

When I was walking back through the kitchen, I saw the Tower collapse. It was like I couldn't breathe, like the wind had been knocked out of me. I just sat down on the floor and found myself sobbing. I couldn't believe what I was seeing! They showed it again and again and I just sat there crying. [Looks at me and smiles.] Yes, Todd, I found something to cry about! The Frank Sinatra songs and the movies didn't work, but watching television that day . . . I couldn't help but cry. It was like my heart finally opened up. The horror that all of those people were going through was enough. That man running for his life, those people jumping to their death, and that building collapsing with my mind imagining all of the children left without fathers and mothers . . . I couldn't help myself. I wanted to cry for them—they deserve to have everyone cry for them. [Begins to cry hard.] I'm sure you know what I'm crying about. [Looks up at me.]

I offered, "Your baby?" She continued to cry and talk about how much she has missed her baby, with whom she never got the chance to share any life.

I've been thinking about him lately. I never got to hold him. The doctor just gave him to the nurse and she and [my husband] went out into the hall. I caught a glimpse of him on the way out of the [delivery room]. He looked like me. God, I have missed him every day of my life. I can understand how those mothers who lost children must feel—it's the worst pain in the world!" . . .

And, they [the September 11 victims] let me cry for my brother. It's too bad it took such a horrible thing for me to really cry like I needed to.

At the end of this session, Heather asked if I was still running the group therapy in which she had participated seven years earlier. I stated that I was cofacilitating a group, but that no one that she knew was still a member of the group. Although seven years earlier, her anxiety and despair about relating with others had been extreme, she asked me whether she could join my current group stating,

> I'm ready to see if I can really be a normal person or not. I feel like I'm ready to put myself to the test; can I talk to people and can they understand me or not? I better sign up tonight before my courage disappears. Yesterday gave me the strength to hope that maybe I'm not the only one who has had a horrible life. I'd like to see if I can relate to people better now than I did in the last group

Impressed by the powerful sense of connection with the victims of September 11 and her hope of being able to relate with others in the world, I offered the following interpretation to Heather: "Yesterday was quite a day. It is wonderful to hear how the terrors of yesterday brought your heart back from the dead and gave you the courage to hope that you could stop feeling like a Martian and again be able to relate and feel close to people here on Earth."

With a radiant smile she replied, "Yeah, I do feel alive again! Welcome back, Heather!"

SUMMARY

We agree with Stolorow (1999) that traumatic life experiences can alienate individuals from others with whom the victims feel that they can no longer relate. Heather, severely traumatized as a child and emotionally estranged and isolated as an adult, struggled to find tears and feelings for her brother who had recently died an agonizing death. Her brother's death seemed to re-expose Heather to many traumatic memories from her past that we had not analyzed in her first treatment, including the profound pain and loss related to her stillborn baby. His death triggered many traumatic images and a flood of painful affect that threatened to shatter Heather and destroy the tenuous stability in life that she had achieved over the last decade. The protective wall of disavowal, the psychological defense that had allowed her to survive an extremely traumatic childhood, had returned in the face of overwhelming vulnerability and pain.

As stated by Ornstein (1994), "Disvowal appears to create a state of mind in which emotional detachment, that is, the numbing of affects, makes adaptation to and survival of traumatic experiences possible." Her brother's death had knocked the life and her sense of being-with-others out of her. She had lost a sense of closeness with her husband and children and her interest in the pursuit of her artistic ambitions. She no longer experienced the contentment, hope, and joy that she had worked so hard in her first psychotherapy to attain, and the next seven years to maintain. In the five sessions of therapeutic dialogue before September 11, Heather was unable to affectively connect with her grief. However, in our previous work together she had developed a mirroring and idealizing transference and a strong therapeutic alliance. We believe that, after her brother's death, her continued selfobject connection with Walker allowed her to return to therapy even after feeling misunderstood and shamed by a previous therapist.

Witnessing the unspeakable events of September 11 brought her back to life. As a survivor of severe and chronic trauma, the vivid media display of the screams and faces of terror evoked vivid memories and intense pain served to facilitate her empathic resonance for victims and their traumatic context of being. We believe that Heather's immediate, experience-near empathic connection with September 11 victims provided her with a community of trauma and a reality of terrorizing absolutisms that made her feel right at home. No longer was she an alien; she was facing the reality of trauma as a seasoned veteran alongside other victims with whom she was experiencing a variety of twinship. We believe that witnessing the events of September 11 on television provided Heather with the experiential context for the development of these mutative twinship selfobject bonds that rescued her from her estrangement and psychic deadness. Not only was she rescued from her current emotional deadness and exile, but her newfound twinship experiences and supportive selfobject connections allowed Heather to return to her own museum of childhood trauma. As noted by Ornstein (2003) "Once psychic pain (anger, sorrow, and grief) replaces numbness and detachment, the integration of traumatic memories is in progress" (p. 140).

While she had been able to tell me about her traumatic past, she was not able to go home with me, which she felt able to do with her new trauma soul mates. As Heather had repeatedly stated before September 11, "Talking about what happened doesn't really tell the whole story of my life." This was especially true for Heather given that much of her trauma had never been put into words and was therefore insulated from therapeutic dialogue. Being exposed to others whom she felt shared a common bond of trauma allowed Heather to access the previously split-off and intolerable images and disavowed pain of her traumatic childhood. Heather now felt connected to a community of other victims, which facilitated her emotional connection with the trauma associated with the deaths of her brother and stillborn baby and the unresolved remnants of the previous horrors in her life. She no longer felt emotionally dead or like an alien with others.

Heather's strong alliance with me and our years of therapeutic dialogue facilitated an intellectually rich but emotionally limited reworking of her traumatic past during the five sessions before September 11. The overwhelming events of September 11 helped her to recover disavowed traumatic affect and imagery. She was able to restart her thwarted need to feel connected with and understood by fellow human beings. As Ornstein (1985, 1994) describes, the capacity to verbalize traumatic images is the by-product of the process of self-integration and recovery. With her current capacity to articulate her traumatic images and affect, she has come closer to realizing her lifelong dream of being a member of the human race, with experiences of enjoyment, contentment, and intimacy in her life pursuits and bonds with others.

REFERENCES

Miner, M. & Rawson, H., eds. (1994), *The New International Dictionary of Quotations*. New York: Signet.

Ornstein, A. (1985), Survival and recovery. *Psychoanal. Inq.*, 5:99–130.

———— (1994), Trauma, memory, and psychic continuity. In: *A Decade of Progress: Progress in Self Psychology, Vol. 10*, ed. A. Goldberg. Hillsdale, NJ: The Analytic Press, pp. 131–146.

———— (2003), Survival and recovery: Psychoanalytic reflection. In: *Explorations in Self Psychology: Progress in Self Psychology, Vol. 19*, ed. M. Gehrie. Hillsdale, NJ: The Analytic Press, pp. 85–105.

Stolorow, R. (1999), The phenomenology of trauma and the absolutisms of everyday life: A personal journey. *Psychoanal. Psychol.*, 16:464–468.

———— & Atwood, G. (1992), *Contexts of Being: The Intersubjective Foundations of Psychological Life*. Hillsdale, NJ: The Analytic Press, pp. 131–146.

Part Three

MULTICULTURALISM

Nine

WORKING WITH
INTERCULTURAL COUPLES
AN INTERSUBJECTIVE–CONSTRUCTIVIST
PERSPECTIVE

LUIS A. RUBALCAVA
KENNETH M. WALDMAN

*I*n this time of increasing cultural diversity, therapists often find themselves working with couples who come from different ethnic and cultural backgrounds. A number of articles have been published (Baptiste, 1984; Carter and McGoldrick, 1989; Ho, 1990; Ibrahim and Schroeder, 1990; Falicov, 1995; Biever, Bobele, and North, 1998; Crohn, 1998; Perel, 2000; Hsu, 2001; Tseng and Streltzer, 2001) on working therapeutically with these couples, but paradoxically, little has been said about the role of culture and the experience of culture in influencing the individual and couple psychodynamics in these marriages. The literature correctly emphasizes the importance of sensitivity to cultural differences but is lacking in an explication of how the experience of growing up within a culture structures the unconscious ways in which individuals will experience and respond to each other. This article integrates contemporary psychoanalytic perspectives with interpretive anthropology to offer a coherent approach to working with intercultural couples. Expanding on the work by Ringstrom (1994), Trop (1994), and Shaddock (2000), the authors use intersubjectivity theory and self psychology to illuminate the unconscious organizing principles, specifically those organizing principles grounded in culture, that shape the individual subjective experiences of the marital partners and the therapist. Awareness of the unconscious cultural organizing principles facilitates the therapist's ability to help the individuals to understand their differences and co-construct their own distinct marital subculture.

FREQUENCY OF INTERCULTURAL MARRIAGES

We are adopting the term "intercultural marriages" generically to refer to marriages between partners from different racial, ethnic, national or religious backgrounds (Ho, 1990). Recent census data on interethnic and interracial marriages attest to a demographic shift of seismic proportions. The 1960 census indicated 149,000 interracial marriages within a total population of 179 million. This small figure is not surprising, since entering into an interracial marriage was considered a criminal activity in more than a dozen states at that time (Wu, 2002). Laws prohibiting interracial marriages were declared unconstitutional by the United States Supreme Court in 1967. Since then, the number of interracial and interethnic marriages has rapidly increased (Ho, 1990).

The 1990 census showed more than 1.46 million interracial marriages out of a total population of 281 million (Wu, 2002). According to Wu, mixed marriages constituted about 3 percent of all marriages nationwide in 1980, and an estimated 5 percent in 1990. In California, which leads the mainland United States, about one out of six marriages are between partners of different races or ethnic backgrounds. Among Asian Americans under the age of thirty-five who are married, half have found spouses who are not Asian. Experts forecast that more than 20 percent of all marriages will be mixed by 2050. The 2000 census counted about 6.8 million people of mixed race background, making up 2.4 percent of the population (pp. 263–264). The increase in mixed marriages is changing the American cultural landscape and the expectations that many individuals bring to their marriages.

THE ROLE OF CULTURE AND LANGUAGE IN THE CONSTRUCTION OF SUBJECTIVITY

Anthropologists have long recognized that how we experience ourselves, our internal subjective world, our relationships, and our emotions, as well as how we organize experience and construct personal meaning, is grounded in culture. "Culture is thus the orientations of a people's way of feeling, thinking and being in the world—their unself-conscious medium of experience and interpretation, and action" (Jenkins, 1999, p. 99). D'Andrade (1984) argues that cultural meaning systems have three functions, which he calls the "representational, the directive, and the evocative." By representational, he means the role of the meaning system in mapping reality. Directive refers to the normative aspects of the meaning system—their role in shaping human action. The evocative functions refer to the capacity of the meaning system to stimulate affective responses (pp. 88–119).

In other words, our experience of culture plays a central role in how we perceive reality, how we behave in our social and interpersonal worlds, and how we express and experience our emotions. Thus culture, with its socially established structures of meaning, provides the symbolic knowledge we use to interpret experience. Our ideas, our world view, our values, our actions, and our very emotions are culturally rooted. Culture is experienced as a realized signifying system embedded in everyday life through social relations, activities, and institutions. Life as humanity lives it would be impossible without individuals internalizing the signifying systems of their particular culture, and all humans interpret the world in accordance with these signifying systems.

Culture, therefore, represents a complex system that structures our subjective experience (LeVine, 1984). Culture constitutes "a relatively stable system of shared meanings, a repository of meaningful symbols, which provide structure to experience" (Kashima, 2000, p. 21). Culture represents for us a supraordinate organizing principle; it is a mode of organizing daily life and a world view (Frankenberg, 1993). Culture provides primary schemas or templates which we use to structure our thinking, feeling, and behavior, often outside of our awareness. "We see the world through our own cultural filters and we often persist in our established views in spite of clear evidence to the contrary" (Carter and McGoldrick, 1989, p. 69).

We subscribe to Triandis's notion of *subjective culture* that:

> It is not as if each of us has been dropped into some monolithic culture, which then asserts its inexorable effects upon us. Rather, we are raised in a plurality of cultural

subgroups, each exerting a multiplicity of influences upon us. For example, each of us belongs to a racial group, a socioeconomic group, a sex group, a religious preference, and a political constituency. The subjective culture of each of us is strongly influenced by the degree of contact we have with people and institutions that focus on (or see the world in terms of) their own subcultural perspectives [cited in Howard, 1991, p. 192].

Central to our approach to culture is the notion that human psychological processes and subjectivities are contextually specific, culturally mediated, historically developed, and embedded in social and interpersonal activity (Miller, 1999). In our view, the psychological self is culturally and linguistically constructed, and personal subjectivities are created and grounded in language and culture (Markus and Kitayama, 1991). It is impossible to separate the cultural from the personal. Moore (1999), a psychoanalyst and constructivist, asserts that "although we are guided in our constructions by the larger society and culture, to a significant degree we actively create everything we know. It is obvious that there are an infinite variety of collective and individual ways and styles of creating our subjective experience of reality" (p. 161). Thus the creation of meaning is simultaneously cultural, personal, and idiosyncratic. Neither domain of experience is autonomous from the other.

Constructivists insist that an individual's subjectivity is created out of the linguistic and cultural narratives in which he or she is embedded (Neimeyer, 1995). Language is the primary organizer of our experience. According to Gadamer (1976), humans are quintessentially linguistic beings, enclosed in a linguistic world which we have constructed. Language, however, is inherently a social activity and can never be the exclusive property of the individual. The way we think and organize experience is structured within the symbolic and linguistic dialogues of our culture.

Perez Foster (1998) describes language as "a cultural template for organizing the world" (p. 15). She posits that those individuals who possess two or more languages have in fact two or more linguistic organizational schemas by which to organize experience and create meaning. Thus bilinguals possess two symbolic systems for organizing internal and external experiences resulting in two distinct self-states.

Furthermore, according to her, each language is unique in evoking the specific relational and social contextual experiences at the time of the original acquisition and usage. For this reason, in cases where English is the second language of one or both partners in a couple, it is essential for the therapist to be sensitive to the issue of language both in the marriage and in the therapy. Indeed, recent social psychological research has demonstrated that bicultural individuals who have been socialized into two distinct cultures have acquired two cultural meaning systems or networks of cultural constructs, "even if these systems contain conflicting theories" (Hong, Morris, and Benet-Martínez, 2000, p. 710). The significance and importance of dealing with the bilingual self in psychotherapy cannot be underestimated.

OUR THEORETICAL PERSPECTIVE: CONTEMPORARY PSYCHOANALYTIC THEORIES

In addition to interpretive anthropology and multiculturalism, our thinking has been influenced by the relational and hermeneutic perspectives in contemporary psychoanalytic theories, specifically self psychology and intersubjectivity theory. We agree with many of the tenets of intersubjectivity theory as formulated by Stolorow, Brandshaft, and Atwood (1987), Stolorow and Atwood (1992), and Orange (1995). Intersubjectivity theory articulates an overview of the psychological processes that are operative in significant relationships—parent–child, primary partners, and therapist–client. In infancy, every individual's awareness of his or her personal subjective experience of life is developed in relationships with the primary caregivers. Each individual's emerging self, and fundamental ways of organizing the experience of self, other, and world, develop in this interaction. Developmentally, these early organizing principles—the ways that an infant organizes his or her experiences—become invariant principles for organizing subjective experience. Humans define their personal reality, most often unconsciously, through the operation of their personal psychological organization, which is developed in a cultural milieu (Waldman, 1995).

Human experience is always personal and subjective. Orange (1992) surmises that subjectivity "includes both the process, the activity of organizing experience, and the product, the organization of experience understood as relatively enduring configurations that shape and limit a person's future experience and activity" (p. 190). A person's subjectivity is, therefore, defined by his or her attempt to organize experience and construct meaning. The product of these activities, which are necessarily personal and idiosyncratic, are referred to as "central organizing principles." Organizing principles are thus defined as unconscious schemata that are "psychological structures [of meaning] into which a person assimilates his current experience" (Stolorow and Atwood, 1992, p. 63). However, each individual, as noted above, creates personal and subjective meaning within the parameters of his or her particular culture and life experience.

Kohut's (1959, 1977) self psychology has given us a theory for understanding the dynamics of primary intimate relationships. His concept of the selfobject and the significance of selfobject experiences throughout the life span describes the significance of intimate human relationships and the needs that individuals bring to their primary relationships. The need of individuals to feel understood, mirrored, supported, and included by others is universal in humans, though individual cultures will define the social relationships in which these needs are to be met in a variety of ways.

Kohut's delineation of the significance of "selfobjects" in human life provides a description of how human beings use selfobject relationships "to maintain, restore or consolidate their organization of self experience" (Kohut, 1984; Stolorow, Atwood, and Brandschaft, 1994). The concepts of a self-selfobject relationship and a selfobject transference are ways of conceptualizing relationships in human life in which the self-concept, self-organization, self-experience, and sense of self are evolved and shaped. The infant's earliest caretaker(s) clearly fall into this category, as do marital relationships and therapeutic relationships in which strong transference bonds are developed. According to Bacal (1995), the selfobject experience is "the glue that holds the self together." Kohut (1971) defined selfobjects as "objects which are either used in the service of the self . . . or which are themselves experienced as parts of the self" (p. xiv).

The concept of a self–selfobject relationship describes a fundamental condition of human life, which is that our personal, subjective, psychological realities are cocreated in our most significant relationships. A critical element in the concept of the self-selfobject relationship and its myriad of implications is the impact on human beings *of being—or not being—understood empathically and affirmed by significant others.* This is critical during significant developmental periods and is important throughout the life span. Psychotherapy is effective when it is able to provide the client(s) with a new selfobject experience, one that will promote a reconsolidation of self experience. Marriages are successful when each of the partners is able to provide the other with sufficient selfobject experiences to affirm and support a healthy sense of self.

It is through selfobject experiences that an individual internalizes the meanings and values of the culture, as parents, extended family, teachers, and important others will be the providers of both cultural and selfobject experiences. They are inseparable. Our culturally and psychoanalytically informed work with intercultural couples, therefore, entails illuminating the unconscious organizing principles of the couple, which have their origin in their early developmental and familial histories and respective cultures. We have found that the experience of becoming aware of the unconscious organizing principles that shape the intersubjective field of the marital relationship has the effect of changing the shape of the field and increasing the possibilities for creating selfobject experiences for both partners.

According to Stolorow, Brandchaft, and Atwood (1987), "selfobject functions pertain fundamentally to the integration of affect into the organization of self-experience, and . . . the need for selfobject ties pertain most centrally to the need for attuned responsiveness to affect states in all stages of the life cycle" (p. 66). The propensity for empathic ruptures and selfobject failures is intensified in intercultural marriages. Partners in a good-enough marriage are able to provide each other with such vital and necessary selfobject functions as affect attunement, validation of each other's subjective experience, tension regulation, and soothing. Ringstrom (1994) states that:

> A picture of an optimal marriage might entail two adults who, without too many disruptions, reciprocally share in admiring one another's style of expressiveness and expansiveness; take comfort in each other's soothing; have a sufficient mix of common qualities, interests, and beliefs; encourage one another's verbalization of feeling and experiences; reckon with and tolerate inevitable disappointments; and *utilize their strong feelings as signals*

that indicate something to explore within themselves, instead of becoming fixated in blaming their spouses for their disappointment [p. 163; emphasis added].

The mutual provision of such selfobject functions becomes more problematic and difficult in intercultural marriages because culture plays a significant role in the very construction of emotion. For example, in terms of emotional expression, Saarnie (1993) notes that, in all cultures, children learn the rules and guidelines for where and how to express what emotion with which people. According to Saarnie, acquiring emotional competence partly entails the following: the ability to discern others' emotions based on situational and expressive cues that have some degree of cultural consensus as to their emotional meaning; the ability to use the vocabulary of emotions and expressive terms commonly available in one's culture; awareness of cultural display rules; and capacity for empathic involvement in others' emotional experience.

In order to sustain an optimal marriage, intercultural couples must learn to enhance their emotional competence by becoming aware of their respective cultural organizing principles centered around emotion and emotional expressiveness.

For purely heuristic purposes we have identified two primary types of organizing principles, familial and cultural. Cultural organizing principles "are fundamental constructs which shape the perceptions, beliefs, and behaviors of members of a group" (Hardy and Laszloffy, 1995, p. 229). For example, a powerful cultural organizing principle among some American ethnic populations (such as German, Greek, Irish, Jewish, Polish, Norwegian, and British) is that of individualism. This contrasts with collectivist organizing principles found among other American ethnic minority groups (such as Asian, African, Latino, and American Indian). Individualism is characterized by the subordination of a group's goals to an individual's own goals. In contrast, "collectivism may be characterized by the individual's subordination of their personal goals to the goals of the designated collective" (Ho, 1990).

In fact Plath (1983) has argued that the very definition of human development in Eastern cultures is different from that in Western cultures, beginning with the definition of a person as a social being and defining development as growth in the human capacity for empathy and connection. By contrast, Western cultures begin with the individual as a psychological being and define development as growth in the human capacity for differentiation (McGoldrick, 1989, p. 69).

We may safely posit that persons coming from individualistic cultures who are married to individuals from collectivist cultures will find it especially difficult to make sense of each other and cocreate a harmonious family culture.

Cultural organizing principles are also applied to gender, class, race, and religion, and are used by individuals in their interpretation of daily experience and subjective construction of reality. Sapriel and Palumbo (2001) offer the following examples in terms of the role of culture in the organization of experience:

> It is axiomatic that Western cultures favor individuation, separateness, and goal directed behaviour (coincidentally, identified as "masculine" goals). In contrast, many Asian or Arab cultures prize communal goals: connectedness, relatedness, and non-verbal attunement (often identified as "feminine" qualities) [p. 86].

In their original, unedited manuscript, Sapriel and Palumbo highlight other significant cultural organizing principles as identified in McGoldrick, Giordano, and Pearce's (1996) book, *Ethnicity and Family Therapy*. They discuss the stereotypic nature of these organizing principles, such as the English fear of dependency and emotionality, the Italians' emphasis on family loyalty, the Chinese focus on harmony, the Jews' emphasis on their children being successful, and the Arabs' anxiety regarding their daughters' virginity.

THE CULTURE OF THE THERAPIST: OBSTACLES TO EMPATHIC UNDERSTANDING

How do we go about illuminating the cultural and familial psychological organizing principles that are actively operating in the intersubjective field formed by the intercultural couple? The process of illuminating personal and subjective meaning involves the therapist making empathic interpretations. Since we cannot directly know another's subjective world, Stolorow suggests that the therapist embark on an "analog search," in which the therapist searches his or her own subjective experiences for potential analogs of what the client is presenting. Sapriel (1998) describes Stolorow's analog search in more concrete terms. She notes that:

> We reflect on relational history to arrive at the closest approximation of the other's experience. We search our memories, affects, philosophies, etcetera, and reflect such understanding back to the patient. . . . The therapist attempts to convey a close enough approximation of the other's experience, honed through dialogue [p. 6].

In other words, empathically derived knowledge is a product of subjective and personal reflection derived from the therapist's own experience and cultural surround.

Transference is conceptualized by Stolorow (1994) as having two basic dimensions:

> In one dimension are the patient's yearnings and hopes for selfobject experiences that were missing or insufficient during the formative years. In the other dimension, which is the source of conflict and resistance, are his expectations and fears of a transference repetition of the original experience of selfobject failure [p. 52].

These same hopes and fears will be present in marital and intimate relationships. Stolorow contends that, when the client experiences the therapist as unattuned or unempathic, "foreshadowing a traumatic repetition of early developmental failure, the conflictual and resistive dimension of the transference is frequently brought into the foreground, while the patient's selfobject longings are driven into hiding" (p. 52). Likewise, this same dynamic will be present in intimate relationships, and is often a basis for marital conflict. Differences in language and culture add to misunderstanding in marriage and in psychotherapy, increasing the probability of selfobject failures. Often, speaking in the client's native tongue facilitates the emergence and consolidation of the selfobject dimension of the transference. Therapists unfamiliar with a client's culture and language are more susceptible to the activation of the resistant or repetitive dimensions of the transference.

Since the therapist's subjectivity is also culturally constructed, the more dissimilar our client's cultural background is from our own, the more difficult it is to understand his or her experience. According to Strozier (2001), Kohut concluded that: "There can be little doubt about the fact that the reliability of empathy declines, the more dissimilar the observed is from the observer" (p. 145). Gorkin (1996) also forewarns that in "treating a patient from a very different background, the therapist is prone to countertransference errors that reflect his cultural assumptions and values. He is likely to err at times in understanding or construing the meaning of some of the patient's statements and behavior" (p. 170). According to Perez Foster (1998), cultural countertransference includes both cognitive and affective factors and consists of culturally based life values, academically based theoretical beliefs and clinical practices, emotionally charged biases about ethnic and racial groups, and biases about the therapist's own ethnic self-identity. Perez Foster (1996) similarly cautions that "the more disparate the respective cultural worlds of the members of the therapeutic dyad, the more the work must be undertaken as a joint quest for understanding and meaning making, with the therapist needing to be cautious against rushing to apply his or her personal assumptions and metapsychology about minds at large" (pp. 9–10).

In the process of interpreting the central organizing principles of intercultural couples via sustained empathic inquiry, the therapist must reflect on his or her own subjectivity. As Stern (1994) observed, therapists cannot step outside of their own organizing principles "because they are the only means of understanding we have" (p. 446). Such subjective reflection invariably results in coming to terms with the cultural and linguistic construction of our own subjectivity. Working with intercultural couples requires therapists to expand their own cultural horizons.

THERAPY WITH INTERCULTURAL COUPLES:
PROCESSES AND PROBLEMS

Intercultural couples have two very distinct and divergent ways of organizing experience based on their respective cultural backgrounds and familial developmental history. Sometimes these distinct modes of organizing experience collide, creating disjunctions and failures in validating selfobject experiences. Each partner's way of organizing his or her subjective experience is based on unconscious and taken-for-granted cultural organizing principles. An example of how these different, culturally determined structures of meaning can lead to disjunctions and misunderstanding in the marital relationship can be seen in the subjective experiences of an Italian-English couple. The English man views the emotional expressiveness of his Italian wife as hysterical, whereas the wife will organize her husband's more restrained emotional expression as cold, wooden, and distant (McGoldrick, 1989). Each partner will make sense of the other's affect, behavior, and expression in terms of their own unconscious cultural organizing principles. Therapy with these couples requires that the therapist understand each individual's experience empathically. The therapist must be able to articulate that experience so that each partner is able to more fully understand the experience of the other as well as those factors which will influence his or her own individual construction of meaning and interpretation. The illumination and description of those organizing principles—the cultural and idiosyncratic ways of interpreting and creating meaning of the other's behavior—invariably result in the reconstruction of the marital subculture.

Intimate partners will cocreate an "intersubjective field," a unique blend of meaning, communication, emotion, and feeling in the relationship. The field may be harmonious and fulfilling to both partners, or it may be filled with conflict, misunderstanding, and unfulfilled longings. It may be flexible and open to change, or it may be rigid and stuck in repetitive behaviors. Most often the couples we see in therapy will have had the mutual experience of love and fulfillment with each other at some time in the past, or even in the present, and yet they are presently caught in a seemingly irresolvable conflict and repeatedly find themselves angry and resentful. When the relationship is not satisfying the desires of one or both of the partners, resentment is bound to grow over time. When a couple presents for therapy, one or both of the partners has declared the need for change in the relationship. Quite often one (or both) will argue that the other must change. When the therapist is able to enter the couple's field and understand the selfobject needs and failures in the relationship, the possibility for change in the couple's "intersubjective field" is created. It is our view that when an intercultural couple comes into therapy, the cultural organizing principles of each of the partners and the therapist become significant, even critical, components of the therapy. Illuminating the cultural, as well as the individual organizing principles offers each of the partners the opportunity for a greater understanding of themselves and each other. Though often subtle and unconscious, the cultural roots, meanings, and expressions can be discussed by the therapist, and each of the partners can become more conscious of his or her own part in creating the couple's intersubjective field.

It often helps to educate both partners about the impact that culture has on their relationship. When a therapist is able to hear and understand how the cultural organizing principles are influencing the experience, behavior, and meanings of each partner—and is able to articulate this in a manner that is understandable to both partners— the interaction will have beneficial effects on several levels of the couple's interaction. De-pathologizing behaviors can reduce shame in one partner while increasing understanding in the other. It is vital in this process not to apply cultural stereotypes to an understanding of either partner. Even when one partner is behaving in ways that are "typical" of his or her culture, the problem for the therapist is to understand how this individual has internalized some aspect of the culture and how that internalization is influencing his or her behavior and experience of the other.

CLINICAL EXAMPLES

ED AND CARLOTTA

Ed came into my office for personal therapy, feeling that his life had been stuck for some time. Ed grew up in Beverly Hills. His father was a Jewish lawyer, his mother a Catholic businesswoman. He was in his mid-forties, had a low-level management job with little future, and had been seeing Carlotta for four years, on again-off again living together.

Carlotta had been born to a large Mexican-American family, had developed considerable secretarial and bookkeeping skills, supported herself, wanted badly to get married, and was enraged at Ed's distancing and unwillingness to participate in any way with her interests. She had been in therapy for some time, but change was not happening.

As Ed's story unfolded in individual therapy, it became apparent that he had felt himself to be an outsider. His father had been a successful lawyer; his parents had divorced; he spent a few years in college, had a business of his own for awhile, and spent his time surfing or sitting in front of the television, drinking beer. He had not done well in school, either academically or socially. He typified the alienated American male—low self esteem, angry at people's "phoniness," and afraid of intimacy. At the same time, he was honest, well-meaning, and willing to learn something new.

After a year of individual therapy, Ed was feeling much better about himself. By understanding his experience, I had been able to provide sufficient selfobject experiences for him, and he was able to develop a level of trust that he had never had with his father or mother. He came to understand that his problems in school were not due to a lack of intelligence and there were things about himself that he could really feel good about. It was time for him to take a closer look at Carlotta to see if he wanted to stay in the relationship. She came to a few sessions and we examined how they communicated with each other. Ed discovered that he really did "talk down to her," belittling her intelligence and her emotionality. Carlotta was understandably angry about this. We also discovered that, over the years, they had stood by one another at times when each of them experienced difficulties in their lives.

The cultural organizing principles were operating in subtle and paradoxical ways. When I pointed out how their different cultural values were sometimes interpreted as character flaws, while at the same time were attractive, both of them became more open to understanding the other and were less angry about their differences. Carlotta's warmth and loyalty to family gave Ed a feeling of security he hadn't known in his childhood. Ed's independence supported her desire to individuate. Carlotta's desire to feel like an insider supported her cultural interests, which initially Ed had rejected because he had defined himself as an outsider in childhood. When he was willing to join her in some of her interests, he discovered that he could both enjoy the experience and learn something. They decided to make another try at living together.

I saw Ed for a little over two years. Carlotta came for an occasional joint session, while Ed and I worked on many aspects of their relationship. In this case, some of the cultural differences were an integral part of their attraction. Ed's early alienation from the cultural mainstream as a result of his parents' divorce and his difficulties in school supported his unconscious desire to bond with someone who was different from the "phony Beverly Hills chicks" that he had grown up with. Carlotta's attachment to family supported Ed's trust in her and offered him security. They were both willing to try something new. Things were going well between them when Ed got an offer to go into business in another state. They decided to get married and start a new life in a new place.

JOHN AND LAKSHMI

John and Lakshmi had been married for 25 years, were successful professionals, and had raised two children when they arrived in my office. Lakshmi had a long list of grievances, beginning with how she had been rejected and suffered humiliation at the hands of his family for many years. She was fed up and did not know whether she still loved John or wanted out of the marriage. John was convinced that he still loved Lakshmi, could now acknowledge that his family had hurt her, though he had not seen it at the time, and did not understand why she was still so angry. Neither partner was aware of how their cultural and family organizing principles were unconsciously impacting their marriage in the present.

John had grown up the eldest of five siblings, the son of a Protestant minister in a small town in the American Midwest. Lakshmi was the daughter of an East Indian international businessman. Her mother had been killed in an automobile accident when Lakshmi was eight years old. She had married John, whom she met in New York, against her father's wishes when she was twenty. John's mother had presumed that Lakshmi would convert to Christianity—which she did not do—and the marriage got off to a difficult start. Although each of them entered the marriage with a conscious desire to have something different from what they were familiar with, they were unaware of how much their unconscious organizing principles were influencing their expectations and understanding of each other. As a result, they were unable to consistently provide each other with selfobject experiences.

I introduced the idea that their communication difficulties were exacerbated by their cultural differences, and pointed out how their expectations of marriage and each other were rooted in their cultures of origin. Developing an understanding of how cultural differences and misunderstandings led to a pattern of relating that limited their ability to be with each other in ways that were nourishing and mutually satisfying played a critical role in helping these individuals to resolve their difficulties and transform their marriage. Each of the partners was willing to immerse himself or herself in the therapeutic process in order to save their marriage. John was motivated by the love he still felt for Lakshmi and the recognition that he had been blind to many of her needs. Lakshmi was motivated by her very real fear of falling out of love and having to survive on her own. In the beginning of treatment I saw them both individually and jointly, endeavoring to help them build a way of communicating and responding to each other that was more supportive and honest.

In her individual sessions, Lakshmi revealed that, after her mother had died, she spent several months with another Indian family in the United States while her father was in the hospital, and then was sent to live with an aunt in India, where she was separated from her brothers. The aunt resented having to care for her, and treated her accordingly. She also revealed that she had other aunts who loved her and treated her with great warmth. When I asked why she did not live with one of those aunts, she replied that it was what her father wanted. Although she knew that she did not like this arrangement, she was powerless to do anything about it and simply accepted this as the way things were. She was told not to complain and simply to get on with her life, which she resolved to do. It had not even occurred to her that she had a very difficult childhood.

The combination of cultural norms and life experiences helped to create a matrix of organizing principles in Lakshmi that made it difficult for her to be honest whenever she felt that honesty was at odds with what the other person wanted. It became apparent that there were deep conflicts between her Indian self, which accepted that women had very little power, and her American self, which had successfully raised two children and developed a professional career. There were many times in sessions when I was able to point out that her expectations and behaviors were based on Indian cultural norms, which were only barely understood by John and not at all by his family. I was also able to show her that her anxieties about telling John how she honestly felt about things were rooted in her experiences of loss, rejection, and the messages she got from a resentful caretaker aunt.

John had grown up in a cultural environment that emphasized duty and responsibility to family and community over and above personal needs or desires; adherence to a Christian ideal; and suppression of personal feelings that differed from these values. Prior to meeting Lakshmi, he was consumed with a struggle to find personal meaning in being devoted to helping others. When he fell in love with Lakshmi, he made a conscious decision to change his life without realizing that his cultural and personal organizing principles were still very much in operation. He devoted himself to providing for his wife while attempting to retain his ideals of community service by becoming a teacher in a boarding school. Lakshmi felt completely out of place in the restricted white middle class environment of the school. When their first child was born, it became apparent that they could not comfortably survive on a teacher's salary. John went to night school to earn a business degree and eventually became financially successful, but he remained cut off from many of his emotions.

Once freed from the school environment and their financial hardship, Lakshmi developed many relationships in the local Indian community. John dutifully went along with Lakshmi to many social events where he was the only Anglo. Initially, he was excited to find himself in a social environment very different from the one he grew up in, but he often felt himself to be an outsider and was unable to fully understand or articulate his feelings to Lakshmi. His cultural organizing principles did not value the expression of feelings and emotions. Her cultural organizing principles did not allow her to say anything that might hurt John's feelings. Both of them began to feel as if they were prisoners in their marriage, and resentment grew on both sides.

It was readily apparent to me that neither John nor Lakshmi wanted to end their marriage, and it was equally apparent that neither one of them knew how to honestly communicate their feelings and concerns to each other. In a paradoxical way, one of the fortunate aspects of their marriage was that their individual organizing principles required the maintenance of politeness, and neither one of them expressed their anger in overtly destructive ways. Although both of them were filled with disappointment, they had not beaten each other up verbally or with passive aggressive behaviors and, as a result, they were not stuck in a pattern of continual fighting or demeaning of one another.

Initially, the joint sessions consisted in helping each of them articulate their feelings and understand how the other might feel as they did. Both of them were surprised at how much their unconscious cultural and personal organizing principles led them to misunderstand each other's motives and feelings. Although John had realized that his family had been hostile to Lakshmi in many ways, he did not understand how difficult it was for her to simply ignore them as he had learned to do. Lakshmi was able to convey how much she had expected to be welcomed into the family as the wife of the eldest brother and how disappointed she had been when this did not happen.

I functioned as both guide and interpreter, pointing out how their individual expectations and understanding of each other's expressions were rooted in their childhood experiences and cultural differences. Although I was not personally very familiar with Indian culture, my willingness to try to understand Lakshmi, and to articulate my understanding without judgment, helped her to be more open in expressing her thoughts and feelings, and helped John to increase his understanding of her. At the same time, helping John to understand how he had suppressed his own feelings and emotions simultaneously helped Lakshmi to understand that his reticence was not a personal response to her, but was rooted in the cultural milieu in which he grew up.

At one point I inquired how it might be that Lakshmi was able to be strong and assertive in some contexts, but withdrawn and passively accepting in others. We discovered that she felt very differently, depending on what language she was thinking in at that moment. Although Lakshmi was thoroughly fluent in English, she had spoken one of the Indian dialects during significant periods of her childhood. It was in this session that we both became aware of how much her experience of herself depended on whether she was in the identity of her English-speaking American self or her Indian-speaking self. This helped her to clarify much of the confusion that she had long felt about herself.

Lakshmi had a dream about one year into the treatment in which the search for meaning illustrates a subtle and yet profound way that culture is interwoven with identity and one's sense of self. In the dream, Lakshmi discovered that she had not been legally married to John even though they had been together and had children. She was very upset, but she was to marry another man. The marriage had been arranged as traditional marriages are in the Indian culture. She was visibly upset by the dream. When she had brought a previous dream in, she had alluded to taking dreams at face value, so if God was speaking to her in a dream, it meant that God was indeed speaking to her. She could not understand the present dream, "because I've really been discovering that I love John, and he's been making changes since the treatment that have really been good for me and the marriage." I asked her what her wedding ceremony had been like twenty-five years ago. She was marrying outside of culture and tradition, against her father's wishes, and John was leaving the church and also marrying some distance from the expectations of his family, particularly his mother. She briefly described a wedding that was neither Christian nor Hindu, but some hodgepodge that had elements of both. We both discovered that she had never felt married in the way that she, as a young girl, had always imagined it would be. She realized that she had never felt fully married to an equal partner the way she was beginning to now. Then she realized that the meaning of the dream was that she and John should get married again—now—and in a way that truly represented who they were as individuals.

She asked if they could have a joint session for her to raise this issue with John. She was still afraid that John would somehow ally with his family and reject her. When she presented the idea to John, in a session, John's immediate and spontaneous response was, "What a good idea!" which had the effect of further confirming for Lakshmi that he was changing and really listening to her.

This case illustrates that a therapist who is sensitive to how cultural organizing principles contribute to misunderstandings between marital partners will be able to facilitate the development of greater understanding and acceptance of differences in the marriage. When couples are able to better understand and communicate with each other, the potential for providing selfobject experiences is greatly enhanced, and marital satisfaction is increased. John and Lakshmi were fortunate in that the foundation of their marriage was still intact, and their affection for each other had not been destroyed by the difficulties that they encountered.

CONCLUSION

This article underscores the importance of understanding the influence of culture on the psychodynamics of intercultural couples if one is to help these couples to develop increased understanding and acceptance of their individual differences and facilitate the co-construction of their own unique marital culture. What is unique in our approach is our understanding of the role of culture in the construction of subjectivity, the illumination and interpretation of such unconscious organizing activity, and how such processes impact intercultural marriages.

Conjoint therapy with intercultural couples challenges the therapist to develop a stance that allows him or her to develop an empathic understanding of each partner's cultural organizing principles along with the personal and familial organizing principles that underpin the intersubjective field created in the relationship. In order to do this, the therapist must be aware of how his or her own cultural values will color his or her understanding of the clients. Raising the issue of culture and demonstrating how one may increase one's understanding of the other through empathic inquiry enables the individual partners to develop more acceptance, tolerance, and respect for each other. This further enables each of the partners to provide selfobject experiences for each other.

Intercultural couples come to therapy with the range of problems that any couple might face, with the added challenge of unconscious, culturally grounded, psychological organizing principles that make communication and mutual understanding especially difficult. We have applied the construct of the cultural organizing principle to our understanding of the psychodynamics operative in the intersubjective field of intercultural couples, and we have found that illuminating these organizing principles helps a couple to more consciously co-construct their own unique marital subculture.

REFERENCES

Bacal, H. A. (1995), The essence of Kohut's work and the progress of self psychology. *Psychoanal. Dial.*, 5:353–366.
Baptiste, D. (1984), Marital and family with racially/culturally intermarried stepfamilies: Issues and guidelines. *Family Relations: Journal of Applied Family & Child Studies*, 33:373–380.
Biever, J., Bobele, M. & North, M. W. (1998), Therapy with intercultural couples: A postmodern approach. *Counseling Psychology Quart.*, 11:181–188.
Carter, B., & McGoldrick, M., eds. (1989), *The Changing Family Life Cycle*. Boston: Allyn & Bacon.

Crohn, J. (1998), Intercultural couples. In: *Re-visioning Family Therapy; Race, Culture, and Gender in Clinical Practice*, ed. M. McGoldrick. New York: Guilford Press.

D'Andrade, R. (1984), Cultural meaning systems. In: *Culture Theory: Essays on Mind, Self, and Emotion*, ed. R. A. Shweder, & R. A. LeVine. Cambridge: Cambridge University Press, pp. 88–119.

Falicov. C. J. (1995), Cross-cultural marriages. In: *Clinical Handbook of Couple Therapy*, ed. N. S. Jacobson & A. S. Gurman. New York: Guilford Press, pp. 231–246.

Frankenberg, R. (1993), *White Women, Race Matters: The Social Construction of Whiteness*. Minneapolis: University of Minnesota Press

Gadamer, H. D. (1975), *Truth and Method*, ed. & trans. G. Barden & J. Cumming. New York: Seabury Press. Orig. pub. German, 1960.

Gorkin, M. (1996), Countertransference in cross-cultural psychotherapy. In: *Reaching Across Boundaries of Culture and Class*, ed. R. Perez Foster, M. Moscowitz & A. J. Javier. Northvale, NJ: Aronson, pp. 159–178.

Hardy, K. V. & Laszloffy, T. A. (1995), The cultural genogram: Key to training culturally competent family therapists. *J. Marital & Fam. Ther.*, 21:227–237.

Ho, M. K. (1990), *Intermarried Couples in Therapy*. Springfield: Charles Thomas.

Hong, Y., Morris, M. W. & Benet-Martínez, V. (2000), Multicultural minds: A dynamic constructivist approach to culture and cognition. *Amer. Psychol*, 55:709–720.

Howard, G. S. (1991), A narrative approach to thinking, cross-cultural psychology and psychotherapy. *Amer. Psychol.*, 46:187–197.

Hsu, J. (2001), Marital therapy for intercultural couples. In: *Culture and Psychotherapy: A Guide to Clinical Practice*, ed. W. S. Tseng & J. Stresetzer. Washington, DC: American Psychiatric Press, pp. 225–242.

Ibrahim, F. & Schroeder, D. G. (1990), Cross-cultural couples counseling: A developmental, psychoeducational intervention. *J. Comparative Fam. Stud.*, 21: 193–205.

Jenkins, J. H. (1999), The psychocultural study of emotion and mental disorder. In: *Handbook of Psychological Anthropology*, ed. P. K. Bock. Westport, CT: Greenberg Press, pp. 97–120.

Kashima, Y. (2000), Conception of culture and person for psychology. *J. Cross-Cultural Psychol.*, 31:15–32.

Kohut, H. (1959), Introspection, empathy, and psychoanalysis. In: *The Search for the Self, Vol. 1*, ed. P. Ornstein. Madison, CT: International Universities Press, pp. 205–232.

——— (1977), *The Restoration of the Self*. New York: International Universities Press.

——— (1984), *How Does Analysis Cure?* ed. A. Goldberg & P. Stepansky. Chicago: University of Chicago Press.

LeVine, R. (1984), Properties of culture: An ethnographic view. In: *Culture Theory: Essays on Mind, Self, and Emotion*, ed. R. A. Shweder & R. A. LeVine. Cambridge, England: Cambridge University Press, pp. 67–87.

Markus, H. & Kitayama, S. (1991), Culture and the self: Implications for cognition, emotion, and motivation. *Psychological Rev.*, 98:224–253.

McGoldrick, M. (1989), Ethnicity and the family life cycle. In: *The Changing Family Life Cycle*, ed. E. Carter & M. McGoldrick. Boston: Allyn & Bacon, pp. 69–89.

———— Giordano, J. & Pearce, J. K. (1996), *Ethnicity and Family Therapy*. New York: Guilford Press.

Miller, J. G. (1999), Cultural psychology: Bridging disciplinary boundaries in understanding the cultural grounding of the self. In: *Handbook of Psychological Anthropology*, ed. P. K. Bock. Westport, CT: Greenberg Press, pp. 139–170.

Moore, R. (1999), *The Creation of Reality in Psychoanalysis: A View of the Contributions of Donald Spence, Roy Schafer, Robert Stolorow, Irwin Z. Hoffman, and Beyond*. Hillsdale, NJ: The Analytic Press.

Neimeyer, R. A. (1995), Constructivist psychotherapies: Features, foundations, and future directions. In: *Constructivism in Psychotherapy*, ed. R. A. Neimeyer & M. Mahoney. Washington DC: American Psychological Association, pp. 11–38.

Orange, D. (1992), Subjectivism, relativism, and realism in psychoanalysis. In: *New Therapeutic Visions: Progress in Self Psychology, Vol. 8*, ed. A. Goldberg. Hillsdale, NJ: The Analytic Press, pp. 189–197.

———— (1995), *Emotional Understanding*. New York: Guilford Press.

Perel, E. (2000), A tourist view of marriage: Cross-cultural couples—challenges, choices, and implications for therapy. In: *Couples on the Fault Line: New Directions for Therapists*, ed. P. Papp. New York: Guilford Press, pp. 178–204.

Perez Foster, R. (1996), What is a multicultural perspective for psychoanalysis? In: *Reaching Across Boundaries of Culture and Class*, ed. R. Perez Foster, M. Moskowitz & R. A. Javier. Northvale, NJ: Aronson, pp. 3–20.

———— (1998), *The Power of Language in the Clinical Process*. Northvale, NJ: Aronson.

Ringstrom, P. A. (1994), An intersubjective approach to conjoint therapy. In: *A Decade of Progress: Progress in Self Psychology, Vol. 10*, ed. A. Goldberg. Hillsdale, NJ: The Analytic Press, pp. 159–182.

Saarnie, C. (1993), Socialization of emotion. In: *Handbook of Emotions*, ed. M. Lewis & J. M. Haviland. New York: Guilford Press, pp. 435–446.

Sapriel, L. (1998), Can Gestalt therapy, self psychology and intersubjectivity be integrated? *Brit. Gestalt J.*, 7:33–44.

———— & Palumbo, D. (2001), Psyche and culture: An exercise in peer supervision. *Brit. Gestalt J.*, 10:86–96.

Shaddock, D. (2000), *Contexts and Connections: An Intersubjective Systems Approach to Couples Therapy*. New York: Basic Books.

Stern, D. B. (1994), Empathy is interpretation (And who ever said it wasn't?): Commentary on papers by Hayes, Kiersky and Beebe, and Feiner and Kiersky. *Psychoanal. Dial.*, 4: 441–471.

Stolorow, R. (1994), The nature and therapeutic actions of psychoanalytic interpretation. In: *The Intersubjective Perspective*, ed. R. Stolorow, G. Atwood & B. Brandchaft. Northvale, NJ: Aronson, pp. 43–55.

———— & Atwood, G. E. (1992), *Contexts of Being: The Intersubjective Foundations of Psychological Life*. Hillsdale, NJ: The Analytic Press.

———— ———— & Brandchaft, B., eds. (1994), *The Intersubjective Perspective*. Northvale, NJ: Aronson.

———— Brandchaft, B. & Atwood, G. E. (1987), *Psychoanalytic Treatment: An Intersubjective Approach*. Hillsdale, NJ: The Analytic Press.

Strozier, C. B. (2001), *Heinz Kohut: The Making of a Psychoanalyst*. New York: Farrar, Straus & Giroux.

Tseng, W. S. & Streltzer, J. (2001), *Culture and Psychotherapy: A Guide to Clinical Practice*. Washington, DC: American Psychiatric Press.

Trop, J. (1994), Conjoint therapy: An intersubjective approach. In: *A Decade of Progress: Progress in S elf Psychology, Vol. 10*, ed. A. Goldberg. Hillsdale, NJ: The Analytic Press, pp. 147–158.

Waldman, K. (1995), The intersubjective perspective. *Transpersonal Review, 2*: 12–15.

Wu, F. H. (2002), *Yellow: Race in America Beyond Black and White*. New York: Basic Books.

Ten

AN ATTACHMENT SYSTEMS PERSPECTIVE TREATMENT OF A BICULTURAL COUPLE

SALLY A. HOWARD

*F*rom its inception, self psychology has asserted the belief that development is possible throughout life. The nexus of development, according to Kohut, is certain relational experiences. Kohut's focus on development within the analytic relationship provided a rich and ample context for further theoretical cultivation, evidenced by the eight broad paradigms now considered a part of contemporary self psychology. In addition to traditional self psychology (Kohut, 1977), these paradigms include intersubjectivity and contextualism (Stolorow, Atwood, and Orange, 2002), self and motivational systems (Lichtenberg, Lachmann, and Fosshage, 1992), specificity theory (Bacal, 1985), attachment/infant research (Beebe and Lachmann, 2002), developmental systems self psychology (Shane, Shane, and Gales, 1997), nonlinear dynamic systems theory or complexity theory (Trop, Burke-Trop, and Trop, 1999; Coburn, 2002), and relational self psychology (Fosshage, 2003). In this paper, I discuss the treatment of a bicultural couple—Tyler, a Caucasian woman, and Ben, a Japanese man, from an attachment systems perspective. This theoretical base incorporates nonlinear dynamic systems theory, attachment/infant research, and some additional currents outside self psychology which I believe enrich our dialogue.

Tyler first captured my attention as she sat on the edge of a parenting group I was teaching for those brave parents anticipating entry into the land of adolescent children. She stood out in this manicured crowd as a self-revealing, somewhat anxious, unruly and flamboyant flower child. She was concerned about the effects of commercialism, TV, Barbie, and nonorganic products on her children. I liked her and admired her courage to be herself, although I found her difficult to follow at times and a challenge to contain within the group. As the parenting class progressed through its eight-week course, her differences from the group became more pronounced, and she became even more of an outsider, with some members ignoring or withdrawing from her. She appeared highly anxious, and her comments became overly expansive, less connected to group discussion, and more idiosyncratic. As I approached my car after the last parent meeting, Tyler approached me and asked me if I would see her and her husband for marital counseling. She appeared acutely distressed and frightened, stating, "We are having so much trouble. I'm not sure what's going to happen." I agreed to meet with them for an initial consultation.

My first meeting with Tyler and Ben introduced me to a very divergent and interesting couple. He appeared as highly contained as she was expansive, as carefully stated as she was fluid and spontaneous. When I asked them to tell me what concerns brought them to treatment, Tyler waited briefly for Ben to speak and then began speaking herself. She complained that Ben worked too much and that the house they had purchased was too big, too materialistic, too expensive, and the cause of Ben's excessive work schedule. She described Ben as irritable and withdrawn. She said she felt very alone and that Ben barely spoke to her and rarely expressed any feelings. As a full-time mother, she felt isolated with the children. Tyler said that, when Ben did talk, he was critical of her for not keeping a cleaner house or for not getting a job. She stopped every so often, looking at Ben to confirm or deny her statements. He did neither, but looked painfully embarrassed. Tyler then began to speculate about what Ben might be feeling and why he behaved the way he did. Maybe he had lost interest in her; maybe he was angry with her. Maybe he wished he had never left Japan or that Tyler would be more like Ben's mother. She was worried he wanted a divorce. The more Tyler talked, the quieter and more withdrawn Ben appeared. He folded his arms across his chest, drew his shoulders forward, crossed his legs, and stared painfully ahead. She in turn, became more emotional, more animated, tilting her body towards him to gain access to his field of vision, gesturing in a larger more rapid way. I thought, at that moment of the "chase and dodge" interactions filmed by Beebe and Lachmann (in Shore, 1994), as Tyler looked to me like the anxious mother, desperate to gain access to her child and Ben looked just as desperate to escape. I wondered about Ben and Tyler's history of attachment and about the cultural meanings and patterning of their emotional exchange. They appeared acutely distressed and uncomfortable to me, and I felt it was important to intervene.

At this point, I asked Tyler if she could pause for a moment, stating that I could see how desperate she felt to make contact with Ben and how shut out I thought she felt. I then addressed Ben, saying "I wonder what this has been like for you and how you feel about what Tyler is saying?" He responded that Tyler's descriptions were not the way things were, that he had to work to support the family. "She's not reasonable," he said. " I don't know what she wants. We have bills that have to be paid." Tyler began to object. I stated to Tyler, "I know that there is a lot you want and need to say and it's very important to hear all of it, but I know also that you want very much to have Ben tell you more about what he feels and thinks, and I think he is trying to do that right now." Ben looked relieved, Tyler dubious. I continued, "I'd like to understand both of you more and help you feel better together. You both seem to feel quite bad and I would like to help. May I share with you my initial thoughts about what's happening between the two of you?" They assented. "Tyler, I think that you feel very left out, shut out of Ben's life and it makes you feel very frightened and upset. I know it is very important to you to feel that you can connect to Ben and that he is connecting to you." Tyler nodded with tears. "Ben, I am aware that you did express yourself today, and I don't know how easy that was for you. When you say Tyler doesn't make sense to you, I believe that is true, that it really is difficult for you to understand what she is about. I have a sense that there is more that you think and feel that you might like to share if we can make it feel safe for you to do so."

Ben said quietly, "I think that is right."

In my presentation of this case, I want to show how attachment and systems theory have informed the way I work and how I understand some of the changes that occurred in the course of treatment. A primary principle from an attachment perspective is the importance of establishing a sense of safety or a secure base for each partner of the couple in therapy. This idea, originally developed by Bowlby (1988), conveys that a sense of safety provided through reliable, contingent responsiveness is not only prerequisite to, but the primary engine of, optimal development and therapeutic change. Attachment theory and the idea of secure attachment have been further articulated by many theorists. Fonagy et al. (2002), for example, describes attachment as the context that allows for development of interpersonal understanding. Attachment determines the depth to which the social environment may be processed and understood. In his opinion, secure attachments and productive therapeutic intervention are characterized by mentalization, or the ability of the therapist to recognize the mind of the patient and vice versa. In this opening session, my verbal intervention was an initial attempt to recognize the subjective experience or mind of each person, letting each person know that this is a place where being heard and understood is possible and protected. Boszormenyi-Nagy and Ulrich (1981), describe this stance as "multidirected partiality" (p. 52). The goal of such action is to articulate attention, interest, and respect for each person's experience. The therapist's ability to do so is the cornerstone of building trust between patient and therapist. Heavily influenced by Martin Buber, Nagy spoke of this experience as one of dialogue or I-Thou, the foundation of which is deep recognition of and respect for the other. Initiated by the therapist's recognition of each person's experience, a developmental process begins that one hopes will result in collaborative dialogue for the couple: getting to know another mind and taking it into account in constructing and regulating interaction.

A second aspect to my intervention in the first session is in the enactive realm. I responded to regulate Ben and Tyler's affect as well as my own. As I observed what I experienced to be a painful, probably repetitive pattern of Tyler's escalating attempts to reach an increasingly withdrawn and escaping Ben, I felt an urge to respond. Byng-Hall (1995) emphasizes the importance of the therapist's willingness to intervene or *act* in crisis as foundational to a sense of security. The willingness to respond to a crisis or to the patient's perception of danger is essential from an attachment perspective. With couples this may mean fairly active and direct attempts to reduce distress and intervene to alter patterns of mutually alienating interactions. This creates a safe environment that is prerequisite for new, more adaptive regulation of interpersonal experiences.

Beebe and Lachmann (2002) emphasize that therapist and patient simultaneously, although asymmetrically, create an affectively well-regulated system. Thus the therapist's own regulatory needs, strengths, and weaknesses play a part in the system that develops. The regulatory system that emerges contains verbal and conscious components as well as procedural and dynamic unconscious components. For example, the desire I had to alter the escalating negative affect between Ben and Tyler reflected my own complex procedural history, culture, and socialization, as well as my training. I am an American female, a mother, I was a child who acted as mediator in a blended family of origin, I am married to a man who immigrated as an adult to the United States, and I am an analyst trained in infant and attachment research. All of these past and current experiences (record of finitude, as Gadamer, 1976, would put it) inform my affective responses. The hope, of course, when one acts in the analytic relationship, is that the action will be based in self-reflective capacities or "mentalized affectivity" (Fonagy et al., 2002)—an ability to understand the subjective meanings of one's own affect states and therefore to direct one's actions towards therapeutic ends. Yet as Lyons-Ruth (1998) has written, much of the relational procedures and processes that affect change occur out of awareness. The verbal intervention I have described was accompanied by particular tones of voice, vocal rhythms, facial expressions, and body movements—all ways I have of being with, emergent in this context, most of which I cannot tell you now, and could not have fully articulated then. The result, however, was in the moment to provide some measure of relief, affect stabilization, and scaffolding for further developments.

One last note about my own experience as I began treatment with Ben and Tyler: I was aware of the excitement and mild anxiety that I have come to associate with doing analytic work, particularly analytic work with couples and families. I relate this excitement and anxiety to the nonlinear nature of therapeutic experience. The triadic system of the therapist and couple is necessarily more complex than that found in individual work, and I am often surprised by what happens. Although I identify certain global processes or patterns that I find useful in understanding treatment, growth, and development, unpredictability is always present on the local level of a particular treatment triad. (Thelan and Smith, 1994). An understanding of nonlinear systems theory has increased my tolerance for the unpredictability of therapeutic work and supported an increased sense of openness to novelty, divergence, and context dependence.

Within the first two months of treatment, I knew the following historical information about Ben and Tyler: They had met in a major east coast city where Tyler was working and Ben was attending graduate school. Ben was raised outside Tokyo, the only child of a middle-class Japanese family. Tyler was the third of four girls in a well-to-do Caucasian family from upstate New York. Both had experienced significant parental loss in childhood, Ben through his father's death when he was 11 and Tyler through her father's career, which took him away from the family frequently, and through the father's eventual departure from the family after an affair. Ben's mother had been depressed, and Ben recalled that he often heard her crying in her bedroom. Tyler described her mother as frequently stressed, during which times she would "yell." Her mother was very busy with so many children, and Tyler thought that the most unruly child got the attention. Everyone argued a lot, and they were loud.

Tyler and Ben were married after two years of courtship. Tyler described Ben as different from previous men she had dated in that he was stable, faithful, and committed. She admired his intellect, as he did hers. She also commented that she enjoyed their sexual relationship. Ben stated in his more minimalist emotional style that he wanted to marry Tyler and that he thought she would be a good mother and wife. He agreed with Tyler that their intimate relationship had been enjoyable. It was not until later in treatment that Ben expanded his emotional expression to include words like sadness, love, or excitement.

Shortly after they married, Ben and Tyler had moved to Japan where they lived for four years. During their second year there, they had the first of two children. Tyler stated that this time had been very difficult for her. She felt isolated and very much like an outsider. She stated she often felt judged for not "being Japanese enough." She complained that Ben had not been understanding or supportive of her experience. Things worsened for her with the birth of their baby, and she felt "locked in a box" in the small apartment in which they lived. When she became pregnant with their second child, they moved to the United States. Although Tyler wanted to move to the east coast to be close to her family, they chose the west coast due to a career opportunity for Ben. When I asked them how they had made the decision about where to live in the United States, neither person could offer a very detailed or coherent narrative about it. They did state that where they lived and where they spent their vacations continued to be a painful source of conflict.

On the west coast, Ben and Tyler purchased a home in an exclusive area. Tyler saw the house as too burdensome: she felt alienated both from her neighbors and from her past. I suspected that Ben, too, must have feelings about living away from his family and country of origin, but they were not accessible at this time in treatment.

I wondered about Ben's (from my point of view) restricted emotional expression. I formulated that this style reflected a pattern of interaction emergent from a number of contexts, including the domain of interaction we think of as attachment and the domain of culture and language. Here I was faced with a dilemma: how much of Ben's demeanor was an expression of cultural codes and norms with which I had limited experience, and how much did it reflect his personal attachment history? This is a dilemma we all face when we meet a person from a different culture. I thought it was possible that Ben's emotional expression might be patterned by traditional Japanese cultural norms such as an emphasis on harmony, masking negative facial expressions, and displaying less facial affect overall. In this cultural context, a universe of feelings may exist between individuals, feelings that are acknowledged, though not spoken or expressed in the explicit way so typical of American culture. How well did traditional Japanese norms describe Ben? It remained to be seen. On the other side of the dilemma, understanding Ben only through a cultural lens would miss him as an individual and leave out consideration of such important developmental contexts as attachment experiences. Along these lines, I wondered about Ben's attachment history and the impact of the loss of his father. Did the loss of his father impede him from risking a deep attachment to his wife? Did Ben's relational and affect repertoire reflect an avoidant attachment and consequent lack of connection to certain feelings and self states? Lastly, I was aware of the interesting parallel in my position to that of Tyler: we were both western females who valued verbal and emotional expression, and we were both trying to understand what Ben was about.

I found it easier to formulate a picture of Tyler. Perhaps this was because I already had experiences of her, but certainly also because of her cultural familiarity to me. I hypothesized that she was an anxiously attached person with concerns about betrayal by important men. She appeared to me to be prone to affect dysregulation and to becoming increasingly upset in the face of Ben's self-containment. She appeared very anxious that she would be abandoned and read most of Ben's behavior as indicative of impending rejection. I added a note of caution to myself, that the ease with which I felt I could understand Tyler did not make my formulations necessarily more accurate or helpful. I felt very aware of my own cultural and contextual embeddedness.

Finally, looking at Ben and Tyler as a couples system, I postulated that they were engaged in a pattern of insecure attachment, with Tyler displaying an anxious attachment pattern interacting with Ben's avoidant or minimally expressive affective style. Both appeared limited in their ability to self-reflect or to reflect on the mind of the other. Without this capacity to recognize the other person's initiatives or communications, little dyadic regulation or collaborative dialogue was possible. The implicit procedures each brought to the table for negotiating affectively charged exchanges were mutually dysregulating. I held open the possibility that they were further challenged by cultural differences and the attendant differences in procedural learning and meaning systems pertaining to affect display.

During the first several months of treatment, Ben and Tyler often displayed the chase and dodge pattern observed in the first session. Even though I would sometimes begin the session by asking Ben about his experience, shortly thereafter, Tyler would begin talking, followed by Ben's increased withdrawal and Tyler's increased anxiety, an interaction sequence which culminated in both people feeling affectively dysregulated. I continued intervening to disrupt this cycle by offering my observations of the pattern and by articulating each person's experience. With Ben, my work often involved trying to make a connection between what I thought to be his self states and his awareness of them. For Tyler, it often involved affect mirroring to reassure and calm her rather than to intensify her affective experience. For example, Tyler was quite distressed by Ben's working in the evening. She was lonely at the end of a day spent in the company of her children and wanted to be with Ben. He often worked until eleven o'clock, after Tyler had gone to bed. I said that I thought Tyler must feel very lonely and agitated when the day ended with a lack of connection to Ben and that I knew the sense of urgency this caused in her. I then stated to Ben that I thought he must feel puzzled and perhaps unappreciated because he was working so hard to take care of the family, yet Tyler did not experience his care for her in this way. Tyler appeared calmer and Ben more alert. This was one of the moments in which I felt we were making progress.

There were other moments in which I did not feel we were making progress. There were sessions in which I felt as stuck as I think they did, unable to facilitate much sense of connectedness. At times, I found myself guessing what I thought Ben might be thinking or feeling, in a fashion that was reminiscent of Tyler, with little sense of what Ben felt or thought about what I said. When Ben did respond to my formulations and ventured some thoughts of his own, Tyler felt threatened and upset that he would not do the same with her. At times I felt agitated by Tyler's escalating affect and I struggled to find ways of listening to her, as I thought Ben did. I wondered also if she feared she might lose my attention, as I thought she must have felt with her mother. I found it difficult to help Tyler feel safe. This kind of emergent, at times turbulent, self-finding process felt like traveling with a map that lacked the detail necessary to navigate the turns. It reminded me of Lyons-Ruth's (1998) description of "complex empathy":

> Empathy is not a simple apprehension of one person's state by another but a complex outcome of a number of [skilled] communicative procedures for querying and decoding another's subjective reality. Another's mind is a terrain that can never be fully known. The difficulty of knowing another's mind guarantees that communication will be fraught with error and require many procedures of disambiguating messages, detecting and correcting misunderstandings, and repairing serious communicative failures [p. 584].

Yet with continued effort and commitment on all of our parts, things began to change. The repeated experience of affect mirroring and affect regulation led to each person anticipating a positive and emotionally safe experience with me that allowed us to explore the

immediate interactive patterns and the way each experienced the other
in them. For example, I eventually was able to ask Ben and Tyler if
they were aware that, often when Tyler began to talk, Ben became
quiet. They were able to see that, too. I then asked Tyler if she was
aware of becoming louder and more upset as Ben grew quiet. She was.
She was also able to describe how his quietness made her think he
wanted nothing to do with her. I asked Ben if he was aware that this is
how Tyler experienced him. He said no. In turn, I asked Ben if he was
aware of how he felt when Tyler became more upset. He stated that it
made him uncomfortable and that it was hard to understand her. As
he said this, he brought his shoulders toward his ears. I asked him if
her voice felt too loud to him, and he said yes. Tyler did not take this
information well at first. She became defensive, feeling criticized by
Ben. I responded by pursuing repair, both between Ben and Tyler and
between Tyler and me. I emphasized that I thought it was quite a
difficult task I was asking of them. I emphasized that I saw each person's
mode of affect expression as different but of equal value; that neither
was wrong or bad. I said that, in order to improve things, it was
important for each person to understand the meaning and experience
of that style for the other. Lyons-Ruth might describe this process as
the active bridging of dialogue to new levels of awareness. I also offered
that I was concerned that she felt criticized and hoped to improve
things so that she would feel criticized much less often.

With this reassurance, Ben and Tyler expanded their exploration
of how they experienced each other in moment-to-moment
interactions. They discussed facial expressions or the lack thereof;
the tone of voice that caused each to feel criticized; and how to tell
the other they were not finished with expressing a thought or feeling.
Later, they began trying to identify what kinds of experiences made
each feel safe and understood. For example, Tyler expressed a desire
for more eye contact when she spoke; Ben asked her not to stare at
him when it was his turn. I was aware of the cultural dimensions in
some of the differences they discussed and felt at times that I was
assisting in a translation of some kind. I thought about the cultural
linguist, Michael Tomasello (1999), and his theory of language
development. From this perspective our work could be thought of as
creating a new culture by entering into joint attentional states, taking
each person's perspective and describing it linguistically. Over time,
each person became more articulate about his or her individual

experience and also began to understand more about the intentions and communications of the other.

Ben and Tyler also developed new procedures for negotiating affectively charged interactions. They made fewer critical and guilt-inducing remarks in stressful situations. As Ben became more able to talk about his own experience, Tyler made fewer "guesses" about his inner state, and he felt less cornered by her. Each appeared better able to understand the mind of the other and to take it into account in constructing and regulating interactions.

As the couple's sense of safety with me and each other increased, they began sharing more deeply, including narratives of childhood experiences. This began rather abruptly following a discussion of greeting routines. Tyler was expressing her distress at Ben's lack of acknowledgment of her in the morning and when he returned at the end of the day. She expected a hello, a kiss, a "how are you?" This seemed not only reasonable but universally understood to her. Ben claimed he acknowledged her and was puzzled and annoyed at her complaint. At this juncture, I asked each of them to tell me about greeting routines in their respective families of origin. Keep in mind that I had tried several times prior to this point to initiate a more in-depth discussion of family history, but to no avail. Ben began by stating that he usually got himself out of bed in the morning, particularly after his father had died. His mother often did not arise until he had left for school and that he often heard her crying in her room. Greetings upon arriving home were brief, with a hello or nod of the head. He had some memory of things being different before his father died, although he seldom saw his father in the morning and not until late in the evening after he came home from work. He stated that he assumed his father loved him and his mother by the way that he took care of them and worked so hard. He knew his mother loved him even though she never spoke those words. Ben thought he was a very responsible and independent child. He remembered feeling very sad when his father died, but he did not recall ever talking about that with anyone until now. As he was speaking, Ben began to look sad, as did Tyler. I shared my observation that they both looked sad. I asked Ben if he had felt alone when his father died, and he stated that he had. I expressed my sadness that Ben had experienced this painful loss and that I was glad he could share his feelings with Tyler and me. I added that I thought he had had to be alone with too many feelings and experiences in his life. Tyler also expressed her sadness that Ben was sad and that he had been by himself so much as a child. She added that she was always up early and would be happy to do something, such as make him breakfast

I was aware again of feeling the complexity of our work in understanding individuals in a multicontext way. Ben was clearly experiencing pain associated with the death of his father. Had he also experienced his father as distant before he died? He also seemed to be describing a norm of paternal love demonstrated through hard work and material provision that he understood as an expression of his father's love. When he told us that he had never spoken of his sadness to anyone, was he describing a culturally influenced way of processing emotion that was more internal and less public than is emphasized in American culture, but nonetheless consensually understood and acknowledged as real? I entertained the idea that the consensual recognition of emotional experience that is not explicitly expressed might nonetheless facilitate connection to internal feeling states. Given all of these factors, I still thought Ben was indicating a family history in which there were less than optimal self-with-other regulating experiences, and that this experience with me and with Tyler represented a powerful new experience of affect regulation within the context of a relationship. It was also a moment for Ben of knowing himself in the context of being known by another.

The session when Ben talked about his father's death was a watershed event for Tyler and Ben's relationship. Tyler began to develop greater empathy for Ben and to take less personally many of the things that she had previously experienced as rejecting. It also appeared to usher in an increased vulnerability and willingness to share on Tyler's part. When we returned to the issue of greetings during another session, Tyler recalled that, although there had usually been some kind of greeting in her family after separations, it was difficult to get much attention because of the number of children in the house. She added that it was worse when her father was away, as he often was. I asked her to tell me more about her father. She described her father as irritable and preoccupied. He was rarely affectionate, and she felt it was very difficult to please him. She described having written numerous letters to him when he went on business trips, letters that she initially asked her mother to send. He never responded to or mentioned the letters. She kept writing them but eventually, instead of sending them, stored them in a box in her room, hoping that someday she could give them to him and he would read every one. Three years after her parent's divorce, her father ceased contact with her and her siblings. I said how sad it made me feel to hear her story and to hear about the painful longings she had had to be close to her father. I then asked her if she felt some of those same longings with Ben. She agreed tearfully that she did. I asked Ben if he was aware of Tyler's sadness and of how much she longed to feel close to him. Ben responded that he was aware of her wanting to be close to him and that he wanted to be close to her too. For the first time in treatment, Ben took Tyler's hand.

Ben and Tyler continued to expand their capacity for open and collaborative dialogue. For example, each began to create a narrative about his or her own family and was able to relate it to current experiences between them. Tyler realized not only how difficult it was to get her parents' attention as a child, but also that it left her feeling uncertain that anybody would really want to attend to her. She understood that this made it hard for her to believe that Ben loved her. With this awareness, she began to accept and feel his love and to view his ways of expressing love as real. In turn, Ben felt more successful with her and with his own increased affective capacities and understanding of Tyler; he expressed his love in ways she could more easily recognize. Ben began to formulate an awareness that, as a child he had always kept very busy and had relied on himself and his hard work to feel good. He realized that keeping so busy then and now had been a way to self-regulate in the absence of needed comfort from, and connection to, his parents. He began to express his needs to Tyler, including wanting increased time with her and wanting her to listen to some of the stressful things that happened at work. She responded readily to him. Each person was getting to know the mind of the other and was able to take it into account in constructing and regulating interactions. I noticed that certain nonverbal and procedural components of the relationship had changed, too. A rhythm developed between them conversationally, with a greater ease in taking turns and expressing points of view. Tyler's tempo of speech slowed down, Ben's became faster and more fluent. They began to smile. Their bodies appeared more relaxed together, they touched more, they made more eye contact.

After 18 months of hard work and sustained commitment, Tyler and Ben had established a significantly increased sense of intimacy and safety together. Not only had they grown as individuals, but the relationship itself was becoming one that was developmentally enhancing. From an attachment systems perspective, these changes reflected the establishment of an attuned and well-regulated system, or in Bowlby's terms, the establishment of a secure base. The therapeutic stance of multidirected partiality is a key component in creating a sense of safety and optimizing development. Of particular importance is the recognition and articulation of, as well as respect for, each person's intersubjective experience. For Ben and Tyler, this included exploration of cultural differences in both the declarative and procedural realms. What followed in the remaining months of treatment were some truly dramatic and surprising changes, including expanded individual capacities and enhanced relationships with their children. The nature of these changes reflect emergent and nonlinear properties of living systems, systems which sometimes develop in leaps and bounds that are unpredictable and noncontinuous with past development.

REFERENCES

Bacal, H. (1985), Optimal responsiveness and the therapeutic process. In: *Progress in Self Psychology, Vol. 1*, ed. A. Goldberg. Hillsdale, NJ: The Analytic Press, pp. 202–227.

Beebe, B. & Lachmann, F. M. (2002), *Infant Research and Adult Treatment*. Hillsdale, NJ: The Analytic Press.

Boszormenyi–Nagy, I. & Ulrich, D. N. (1981), Contextual family therapy. In: *Handbook of Family Therapy*, ed. A. S. Gurman & D. P. Kniskern. New York: Brunner/Mazel.

Bowlby, J. (1988), *A Secure Base: Clinical Applications of Attachment Theory*. London: Routledge.

Byng-Hall, J. (1995), *Rewriting Family Scripts: Improvisation and Systems Change*. New York: Guilford Press.

Coburn, W. (2002), A world of systems: The role of systemic patterns of experience in the therapeutic process. *Psychoanal. Inq.*, 22:655–677.

Fonagy, P., Gergely, G., Jurist, E. L. & Target, M. (2002), *Affect Regulation, Mentalization, and the Development of the Self*. New York: Other Press.

Fosshage, J. L. (2003), Contextualizing self psychology and relational psychoanalysis. *Contemp. Psychoanal.*, 39:411–448.

Gadamer, H. G. (1976), *Philosophical Hermeneutics*. Los Angeles: University of California Press.

Kohut, H. (1977), *The Restoration of the Self*. Madison, CT: International Universities Press.

Lichtenberg, J., Lachmann, F. & Fosshage, J. (1992), *Self and Motivational Systems: Toward a Theory of Psychoanalytic Technique*. Hillsdale, NJ: The Analytic Press.

Lyons-Ruth, K. (1998), Implicit relational knowing: Its role in development and psychoanalytic treatment. *Infant Mental Health J.*, 19:282–291.

Shane, M., Shane, E. & Gales, M. (1997), *Intimate Attachments: Toward a New Self Psychology*. New York: Guilford Press.

Shore, A. (1994), *Affect Regulation and the Orgin of the Self: The Neurobiology of Emotional Development*. Mahwah, NJ: Lawrence Erlbaum Associates.

Stolorow, R. D., Atwood, G. E. & Orange, D. (2002), *Worlds of Experience: Interweaving Philosophy and Clinical Dimensions in Psychoanalysis*. New York: Basic Books.

Thelan, E. & Smith, L. B. (1994), *A Dynamic Systems Approach to the Development of Cognition and Action*. Cambridge, MA: MIT Press.

Tomasello, M. (1999), *The Cultural Origins of Human Cognition*. Cambridge, MA: Harvard University Press.

Trop, G., Burke, M. & Trop, J. (1999), Contextualism and dynamic systems in psychoanalysis: Rethinking intersubjectivity theory. *Constructivism Human Sci.*, 4:202–223.

Part Four

COUNTERTRANSFERENCE

Eleven

THE ANALYST'S SHAM(E)
COLLAPSING INTO A ONE-PERSON SYSTEM

JENNIFER LEIGHTON

The susceptibility of being affectively impacted and regulated by the patient is situated at the very base of the analyst–patient relationship.

—William J. Coburn

Not one of us escapes the experience of failure and the shame that often accompanies it. Sometimes it happens like this: We are struggling with an impasse that is not being resolved. Every time we seem to undo one knot, two others appear in its place. We find ourselves suddenly—or not so suddenly—angry and frustrated with our patient at the same time we sense we are failing him. We consult with our colleagues, once again centering ourselves, creating a new strategy, only to fall into a similar conundrum two sessions down the road. Eventually, the patient leaves treatment, perhaps in a rage or perhaps even through mutual agreement. We are left without enough awareness of our contribution to the impasse, yet feeling we were part of something that went very wrong. Or maybe it happens, without any warning that is obvious to us, a patient walks out mid-treatment and never comes back. For years to come we may find ourselves at odd moments pondering what happened—stymied because, of course, we cannot conclude anything definitive without the participation of the patient. And my guess is that most of us have

For all their helpful comments, I wish to thank Donna Gould, Marg Hainer, Barbara Kane, Jean Owen, Lynn Preston, Kathy Roe, Ellen Shumsky, Lucy Slurzberg, and Dori Sorter.

been saddened as we realize that today we could probably better help someone we were unable to help twenty years ago.

This sense that we have failed our patient is beyond the familiar impasse that we confront on a somewhat regular basis and from which we are able to right ourselves in a reasonably timely manner. We as analysts occasionally become stuck in dissociated self-experiences that we are unable to process at the time of treatment and that interfere with our capacity to function as therapists. It does not happen very often. But when it does, even though we are able to move on, grateful for our successes and for the fascination of our work, something of the experience of failure lingers. Something rankles when we cannot say a proper good-bye to a patient.

Postmodern epistemology rejects notions of Cartesian objectivism and the autonomy of the isolated mind and embraces that which is pluralistic, subjective, and perspectival (Stolorow, Atwood, and Orange, 2001). Accordingly, we view neither the patient nor the analyst as solely responsible for the derailment of the treatment.

In this chapter I argue, however, that in spite of our commitment to a two-person theory, we as analysts can still feel and act on notions that the patient has caused the stalemate, is making unreasonable demands of the analyst, is refusing to take us in, and so forth. Or, alternatively, we can blame ourselves, feel inadequate, unskilled, or insufficiently analyzed. At first glance, it may seem contradictory that, on the one hand, our view is that enactments "flow from both sides of the couch" (Jacobs, 1991, p. 31) and, on the other hand, we can be stuck in the conviction that either the analyst or the patient is the cause of the impasse. How can we blame the patient (or ourselves, for that matter) for treatment failure when we believe all clinical events are co-constructed? Yet this is what happens all too frequently in our profession. Many of us are treating patients from previously derailed treatments with analysts who were committed to intersubjectivity in theory, yet those patients were left holding the blame for enactments that were coconstructed.

I am positing that this apparent contradiction can be explained, at least in part, by understanding that the analyst's cognitive and affective states have become dissociated from each other. I agree with Bacal and Thompson's (1998) assertions that, when the analyst disavows her selfobject needs, she can lose empathy and thereby contribute to treatment derailment and experience shame, which can also sometimes be disavowed. In addition I believe that the analyst's affective states can become derailed in a way that can no longer be linked to complex, relativistic, perspectival cognitions concerning the analytic dyad. At this point the analyst is vulnerable to collapsing into a one-person psychology. Sometimes we experience the dissonance—thinking in intersubjective terms while simultaneously feeling stuck in shame/blame affective states—and sometimes the experience is effectively dissociated; that is, we collapse into a one-person system without knowing it.

To clarify what I mean by a two-person theory, I am referring to the assumptions that, in a dyad, both realities are valid, though they may be different, and both mutually influence each other. My view of two-person theory does not exclude our frequent focus on the investigation of the patient's reality, history, and culture, even though the analyst's subjectivity is present in formulating and shaping the patient's narrative. Collapsing into a one-person psychology is about losing the affective/cognitive integration of the assumptions of this two-person theory. Another way of saying "collapsing into a one-person psychology" is: "slipping out of the co-constructed stance into positivism" (Marg Hainer, 1999, personal communication).

I believe that at the root of this collapse is an experience of shame (sometimes disavowed) that we have lost both our empathy and our ability to remain affectively engaged with our patient. The sham is that, when we fail to acknowledge and process our shame, we become vulnerable to returning to a one-person system in which we may diagnose intractable pathology and stop making it safe for the patient to think about the analyst's limitations. (Lansky, 1992, believes we "evacuate" our feelings of inadequacy—our shame—by blaming or shaming the other [p. 47].) We may accomplish this by overtly pathologizing and shaming a patient, dispensing interpretations about his devaluation or envy of the analyst. Or we may hold the patient responsible in more subtle ways, such as interpreting along the lines of his transference and repetition compulsion only, leaving the possibility of our own contributions out of the dialogue. Subtler still, we can sometimes collude with a patient's rationale for leaving treatment as a way of backing off—disconnecting—from a treatment stalemate. I am aware that for many, sham can feel like a harsh term.

Let me clarify here that I do not believe that the sham is about the intent of the analyst, since I believe the analyst is in some way fragmented, having lost cognitive and affective cohesion. (I agree with Lachmann [1985, personal communication] that it is important not to confuse intent and effect, and that that applies to the analyst as well as the patient.) Rather, the sham is that patients get stuck with the blame for the treatment impasse, or at the very least get stuck in shame/blame affects from which they cannot extricate themselves.

Next I would like to suggest that we have not been able to find our way out of this murky terrain by employing private solutions (personal analysis and supervision) only, though these are indeed essential in negotiating the agonies and uncertainties of our profession. Shame's power to upend the reflective and creative aspects of the analyst begs for broader solutions—solutions that address the historical entrenchment of our professional narcissism. I believe we need more actual, complex, self-revealing case material in our analytic journals, which are in fact the meta-communicators of our professional values and standards. If we agree that the analytic community is always in the room (Zeddies, 2001), and if in our professional journals our complex processes and failures remain hidden, then that which is hidden is also in the room in its hidden form. That which is hidden remains shameful. (Not only does shame lead to hiding, but what is hidden often provokes shame.) That which gets stuck in shame does not find creative and enlightened resolution.

The fact is, the most accepted style of case presentation does not reveal the mess and the agony of the analyst. It is called the "brief vignette." The brief vignette has the very important function of elucidating clinical theory. The problem is that it is often labeled "case material." In fact it is not case material, but rather a distilled concretization of abstract theory. As important as this function is, it should not be confused with showing what happens in the room between analyst and patient. In mistaking the brief vignette for case material we are, I believe, adversely affected, from the time we begin to train as analytic candidates. We know our own process is so much messier, deeper, longer, and sometimes even intractable with a given patient. We cannot identify with the author of the vignette because we do not experience our own process as being as "clean" (affectively simple) as that which is in the written presentation. So we feel ashamed of the messiness of our affective states, and we hide. Ultimately we can become accustomed to hiding—at least to some degree—from our supervisors, teachers, colleagues, and then, because we have no place to take our agony, we hide from ourselves.

And if our own mess is well enough hidden, we will begin looking clean while our patients will look a mess, and our evacuation of shame onto our patients will be that much more likely. At this point the blame of the patient may also be hidden, because it, too, is unacceptable in the cognitive states in which our two-person theories lie.

I would therefore like to make a strong appeal to our professional journals to find ways for us to make it safer for analysts to write more openly, revealing our own affective states and organizing principles and thereby demonstrating the difficulties and complexities of the treatment process. Morrison (1994) asserts that we help our patients emerge from their suffusion in shame by restoring the "sense of our shared humanity" (p. 33). He is speaking about the needs of the patient, but of course the same is true for the analyst. We all have times when we lose our ability to function as therapists. When we bring this fact out of hiding, we support the notion that we can recover, heal, and become better at what we do. Opening our journal writing in this way can provide positive selfobject experiences for the analyst that reduce and help process shame states. (The other reason to reveal our cases more openly is that, without specificity, there is no way to think together about complex cotransferences [Orange, 1995]. These complexities include both the cognitive and affective realms of the analyst.)

Later I will present a case of chronic treatment impasses in which a difficult patient's persistent criticism and disconnection triggered in me a painful loss of selfobject connection. After a positive start, this severely traumatized patient gradually began to deflect everything he was offered in a way that evoked in me an old horror that every attempt at authentic connection would go sliding off the surface of the other, leaving me feeling invaded by someone who only wore the face of contact. I was left in a dysphoric state and could not fully process this traumatic (for me) repetition until sometime after termination. I believe that my experience can be both illuminating and comforting to other analysts. I also believe, after all I have said about the necessity of extended case presentations, I need to put my money where my mouth is.

BACKGROUND

Early on, Kohut (1977) recognized the ubiquity of narcissistic vulnerability, which also included that of the analyst. Later, according to Bacal and Thompson (1998) Wolf recognized more specifically the bidirectionality of the selfobject needs of patient and analyst. I am locating my theoretical discussion within three articles that progressively elaborate these ideas: Bacal and Thompson, 1998; Coburn, 1998; and Preston and Shumsky, 2000). Each of these authors has helped me to formulate what I consider to be the most salient ideas in this paper: (1) The analyst contributes to the derailment of treatment and is vulnerable to collapsing into a one-person system; (2) Self psychology and trauma theory help us think more precisely about why this happens; and (3) Solutions involve more open, process-orientated case presentation in the literature. (I recognize that there is a staggering amount of literature on all these subjects, some of which I will cite in passing and some of which I have so fully assimilated into my own thinking that I have forgotten where those ideas came from. My apologies to those I leave out.)

Developing Wolf's thinking about the bidirectionality of selfobject needs, Bacal and Thompson (1998) provide us with an excellent paradigm (explicated above) describing the analyst's vulnerability to disturbed cognitive and affective self states in reaction to the patient's withdrawal of selfobject needs. These authors assert, that in dealing with unacknowledged and/or unprocessed shame, the analyst may step up interpretive activity, particularly transference interpretations, because in our analytic culture these actions are seen as valuable—as evidence that we are doing useful work. This is what I call the sham—the analyst's use of otherwise legitimate interpretive functions to avoid dealing head on with her shame. Furthermore, they emphasize that in order to get back "on track" with the patient, it is not helpful at this point to focus on decentering or empathic immersion in the patient's process. Instead they assert that only by having selfobject needs legitimized can the analyst once again empathize with the patient.

I would like to unpack some of Bacal and Thompson's ideas to help us think further about why analysts get stuck in their process and collapse into one-person theory. I think these authors are referring to the dissociation of cognitive and affective self states due to shame and disavowal of affects. Shumsky (2003, personal communication) has said that shame is "the antithesis of selfobject experience" and needs to be dissociated for self-cohesion to be restored and maintained—especially, I would add, in the absence of an empathic self or other. I think what Bacal and Thompson are referring to when they say the analyst is knocked off track is that, when she feels her selfobject needs are not legitimate, she disowns a part of her affective experience. Her empathic resonance with the patient is no longer in her affective foreground, even as the need for an empathic stance remains central to her cognitive agenda. The affect and cognition concerning empathy are thus dissociated (unlinked) from each other. What happens when the analyst at this point tries to decenter or to make transference interpretations is that those cognitive actions are driven by something entirely different than the empathic attunement that was operating before the disruption in the analyst occurred. These cognitive actions now have the function of self-righting in the face of affect dis-integration—"derailment by shame" (Morrison and Stolorow, 1997). This is not fertile ground for the analyst's empathy for the patient. The capacity for empathy, which includes a full respect for the patient's separate subjectivity, is threatened when the analyst is destabilized or dis-integrated.

What Bacal and Thompson say is legitimizing the analyst's selfobject needs is equivalent to attending to our self state—first owning our shame and then providing self empathy for our own needs for connection, to feel useful, to have our specific invariant organizing principles matched, and so forth. To accomplish this healing of our self states the authors also suggest going further than analysis and supervision. They think a safe professional group is helpful. I agree but, as I have said, unless the wider analytic community, represented chiefly in our psychoanalytic journals, takes on the project of making it safer for analysts to reveal more specifically their own limits and failures, they will continue to reinforce the kind of dis-integration I am talking about, one that collapses us into a one-person psychology.

Coburn (1998) also takes up the difficulties inherent in the analyst's narcissistic vulnerabilities. He notes that it would have been easy to attribute the deadness in the field between himself and his patient, Nathan, all to Nathan's projective identification—putting the feelings into Coburn—or alternatively to miss Nathan's feelings altogether by assuming the deadness was due solely to Coburn's narcissistic vulnerability. He is saying, in different language, that he had to struggle not to collapse into a one-person psychology.

Coburn asserts, and I agree, that discarding the notion of projective identification does not ensure that the analyst will not hold the patient responsible for cognitive/affective states that he seeks to disavow, but Coburn offers a useful construct to help us remain within a two-person psychology. He suggests we view countertransference as the affective intersection in the analyst of both the patient's unconscious communication and the analyst's narcissistic vulnerability. He elaborates the idea of unconscious communication partly along the lines of Beebe and Lachmann (1994), who say that unconscious affective communication is a "sensori-motor dialogue" in which cognitive/affective states can be mutually experienced and regulated. Coburn's assumption here is that, in order for the analyst to participate affectively in the treatment, he must be open to affective impact and regulation by the patient (i.e., the patient's unconscious communication). This is the sine qua non of the analyst–patient relationship. In the affective intersection, the analyst is experiencing (affectively receptive to) both the patient's communication and his own narcissistic vulnerability (possibility of frustrated selfobject needs). These are separate events that coexist simultaneously. Viewing these two events as both separate and simultaneous is such a gem of a cognitive tool because it forces the question: what is each of us contributing to the difficulty in the relationship? This concept also argues against the assumptions underlying what Lachmann (2000) says (and I agree) are outdated ideas about induced countertransference: that there are "universal expectable reactions" that form the "insider information" (pp. 192–193) about the patient's transference.

In addition, this construct makes it clear that we need to explicate both the analyst and patient contributions to impasses in the relationship. We are usually shown only the unconscious communication of the patient and then perhaps told that the analyst also had difficulties that he then overcame in personal analysis or supervision. We need also to be shown the specific vulnerabilities and invariant organizing principles of the analyst. Coburn (1998) begins to do this when he speaks not only of the specific unconscious communication underlying Nathan's diatribes against all those who attempt to "cure" him, but also of how Coburn felt "hurt, belittled, and cheated out of [his] role as viable practitioner" (p. 25). In general I think that being told about something feeds our cognitive states, while being shown feeds both cognitive and affective states. Getting the cognitive half is only helpful and integrative if we are able to do our own affective linking. Furthermore, when an author is able to explicate his process more specifically, it enriches us and stimulates our affective identifications, leading to twinning experience and shame reduction, and thus it invites a higher level of affective and cognitive integration and expansion.

Preston and Shumsky (2000) develop further the ideas and implications of psychoanalytic bidirectionality as they assert: "Both partners struggle to provide what the other needs for partnership and both struggle to accept what the other has to offer" (p. 72). They go on to legitimize the analyst's use of his treatment with his patient to gain access to aspects of himself that have been heretofore unformulated or out of awareness. In fact, Preston and Shumsky argue, it is precisely this opportunity to grow that can help the analyst remain engaged in and therefore move along a treatment that has become stuck. The analyst's self-awareness helps him provide a new experience that contributes to new relational possibilities in the dyad. "The analyst steps out of rigidified interactional patterns and broadens his own self-regulatory range, simultaneously impacting on the patient" (p. 79). In other words, both analyst and patient are invited to change in the treatment relationship and, in order for the patient to change, the analyst must expand his relational capabilities.

In keeping with these ideas, we see in Preston and Shumsky's work that in every vignette the analyst's organizing principles are shown to us. We are shown how the analyst expands his regulatory capacity as well as what happens when he does not. It was enriching to be shown specifically what the analysts had to tangle with in themselves.

The "well-kept secret" as Mitchell (1997) would have it, is out. We are in this profession to grow. (What is the shame in this?) We are mere humans enhanced with fabulous skills and limited by our own invariant organizing principles. I would just like to add that sometimes we do not grow in time, to move along a stuck treatment. This was so in my case, and I experienced it as a painful failure. However, in writing this paper, I was able to learn that sometimes growing happens later. We cannot always control our readiness.

CASE MATERIAL

I began seeing Jack ten years ago. We ended the treatment three years later. I had pursued consultation tirelessly as soon as I saw the treatment was at an impasse. But I was not able to process adequately my contribution to the stalemate, until a year after treatment ended, when a dream I had took me back to Jack. It was then that I felt a need to write about my experience and had some ability to work on what it was about Jack—or Jack and me—that led to what Bacal and Thompson (1998) would call "disturbed self-states" in me.

In my dream it became clear to me that various aspects of myself were represented in the form of various selves, and there was an "I" that was interacting with each. It was a rich dream, the first half full of interesting and joyful intellectual and artistic exchanges. But the most compelling part of the dream was coming upon a self that I started to hug (because that is what I thought I should do), but then felt frightened and backed away. She seemed disconnected and bizarre. Her body was misshapen—lumpy in places where people do not have lumps. Her face was strange and empty looking. She was not someone I could imagine ever wanting to hug. As the dream insinuated itself into my consciousness on the following day, it gradually became clear to me that I could no longer just let this strange creature sit off by herself, rejected and neglected (and projected!) as was my impulse in the dream. Her disconnection and dysphoria were manifestations of a self that was starving for engagement, a self that was not contacted and embraced, but had instead been used and expelled by a mother who could neither embrace nor engage. I have known for a long time that, in my early developmental strivings to find connection any way I could get it, I thrust aside this misshapen self and fled from my early mother with a contempt borne of my need for connection so that I could thrive and develop. Although along the way I have discovered and integrated pieces of this self, this was perhaps the first time I was able to recognize her in full-person (if also misshapen) form.

When I first began to see Jack I had two distinct reactions to him that perhaps, had I been able to think further about their significance, might have signaled my internal struggle with the acceptance of my heretofore misshapen (unembraced) self. I had an initial physical revulsion to him. One eye turned slightly inward and his hair fell over his face in greasy clumps. His face looked to me like a pasty-complexioned mask, hiding whatever might be lurking beneath. He seemed both self-conscious and aggressive as he stumbled onto my couch, announcing his exhaustion from his trip to my office—a subway ride from downtown. (A colleague, reading an earlier version of this paper, reminded me that this unilateral way of describing a patient is very typical in our field. It is an example of how easy it is to slip back into one-person theory. The description of Jack only appears to be uninfluenced by my own organizing principles. What I notice in Jack and what I select to convey to the reader is not only about him, but also reflects my own subjectivity. I am already feeling contempt toward him, probably fearing things in him that are misshapen in a particular way that sets me off. I did not know then that an important underlying question in treatment would be: who is misshapen?)

At the same time I had immense admiration for Jack. I thought he was scrappy—possessing a fierce will to get better. He was 43 years old when he first consulted me but had been in therapy since he was 17. Early in treatment, as Jack invited me into the bleak interior of his childhood, I empathized with his relentless terror and "catastrophic loneliness" (Grand, 2000). His parents had little contact with the outside world and were paranoid about both neighbors and extended family. As an only child, he wandered around neglected and isolated, locked away from a potentially rescuing outside world. At the same time his parents could be extremely intrusive. When they did pay attention to him it never seemed to be about him. Instead they projected their own internal terrors onto Jack. For instance, they would accuse him of wanting to kill them when he was merely frowning in puzzlement or concentration. He felt unrecognized his entire childhood. Likewise, he never felt he could get beneath the surface of either parent. He did not know who they were. I was struck by the fact that he had somehow managed to survive such a bleak and suffocating childhood.

Early on, Jack showed me pictures of himself as a little boy with his parents. I noticed the lack of interaction, of bonding—evidenced in lack of eye contact and body fit—particularly between Jack and his mother. I told him I was moved, and he said he felt I understood how bleak his early existence was. What I did not tell him was how chilled I felt, chilled because the picture so resembled those of me with my mother and, not surprisingly, those of my mother with her mother. In each sequence, the child looked thin, lost, empty, and needy. How could one hold such a child, I thought.

And whereas I had a few fleeting worries that Jack might be like my mother (and his mother) in some essential way—like Teflon deflecting all but surface contact—the first six months of treatment seemed to go well. His mode of interaction felt choppy to me, as he often leapt from one topic to another without any apparent association. For a moment I would feel jolted and unable to think clearly about what he was saying. However, as I regained my equilibrium, I was then able to help us make meaning out of his style of relating. He dreamt about frozen babies needing to be rescued. He would not associate to the dream and wanted to talk about something else entirely. I felt jerked around. I had already begun to ache for the frozen babies and then felt compelled to try to follow him to the place he went next. When I regained my senses, I told him I thought he had brought me an important and precious dream, yet was obscuring its significance by jumping to other topics. He was grateful for my observation and said: "I know I do that. I keep things in pieces. I'm afraid if I come to life I'll die." He talked about needing to keep all his pieces separate because of his fear of overwhelming anxiety (unto death), were he to bring them together. I identified with and felt empathy for the little boy who had had to regulate his emotional life all by himself. This was the kind of meaning making that kept us going during the first phase of treatment.

What I did not know at the time was how pervasive and seemingly unshakable was Jack's organizing principle that he would die if the pieces were brought together. Most patients—particularly those who have experienced severe trauma—have aspects of themselves that are afraid of knowing, and yet somehow analyst and patient manage to negotiate how to trust and how to put the pieces together (make meaning) over a period of time (Brothers, 1995). This is some of the difficult work that we do. My own accumulated experience is that indeed time passes and negotiation takes place, and that helps me through multiple levels of interpersonal disconnection—the necessary disruptions that come with the psychoanalytic territory. However, it is now clear to me that the tenacity of Jack's organizing principle was in direct conflict with one of my organizing principles: I need to move towards knowing. For me the closing off of knowing—the despair about never being allowed to know, to bring the pieces together so that I can eventually connect to an other—feels like my death. By the treatment's end, my difficulty was that I could not survive the despair of feeling that we would never again be able to forge a connection. Regarding Jack's part in the treatment failure, my experience throughout the years is that often patients will lend their help in time to rescue a stalemated treatment. And it felt to me that Jack could or would not.

In the transference, he feared that I would be like his mother, who would take over conversations. His mother would listen to Jack for a few seconds and then say "oh, that reminds me," but it would always be a bogus association to what Jack was saying, and Jack would lose himself as his mother went off on her own track. So, among other things, his fear of taking in from me was that I would go off on my own track, leaving him with his untold story, or more importantly, alone with unmanageable affect. His way of "keeping things in pieces" made increasing sense to me. It was too frightening to know how the pieces fit (to link and shape them into something more whole) and too potentially retraumatizing to be left alone with his known story.

After about six months, the treatment began to shift. It was gradual, but eventually we were no longer able to make meaning together. He would race with apparent incoherence from one topic to another, leaving me so stymied I was no longer able to think in fluid and creative ways. And he would no longer acknowledge that this was what he was doing. I listened to Jack describing his mother's taking him off the track of his own thinking and I can now see that, due to my own organizing principles, I was having the same experience with him: his mother destroyed his capacity to think, and he was destroying mine. I want to make it clear here that I am describing the effect on me of what he was doing, not the intent. In fact, I experienced what he was doing as destructive because my mother destroyed my capacity to think in much the same way. (This is a good example of Coburn's affective intersection—the separate and coexistent unconscious communication of the patient and the analyst's narcissistic vulnerability.) "Oh, that reminds me" were the very same words my mother would use as she went off to "entertain" us with a story that would leave me bored and disconnected and unable to stay fluid and on track with my own thoughts. As Jack took on more and more aspects of his mother, the fit with my mother and the fact that I could only tolerate that kind of disconnection for just so long augured trouble for our relationship.

In a session late in treatment he walked in with a dream. He was being chased by a pack of dogs. I was not part of what was chasing him, he said, but he needed me to run with him. His mother never followed. He told me he had been rejecting me in the previous day's session. His topics were a smokescreen. I had not been following him. Although I understood the context of his need for me to run with him in the dream, I had no idea what he was referring to in the previous day's session, so I questioned him. He became furious, telling me I was pulling him off course, confusing him. Eventually he stopped yelling at me and told me that he thought he had been doing a wonderful job telling me something, and now he experienced me as angry—demanding that he be clearer. He said I was too stuck on the content of what he was saying. At the time I remember thinking that Jack was onto something important—struggling with a mother who would always pull him off course. Yet I also remember feeling frustrated. He continually leapt from topic to topic, and it seemed no crime at the time that I was trying to understand what he was saying when I could not follow his leaps.

As I view from this distance, it seems clear to me that while I was struggling so hard to understand the content of what he was saying, I was actually losing my empathy. Now, of course, I wish I could have said something like: "In my trying so hard to understand the meaning of your words, it must feel to you like I am putting my agenda before yours. And you feel pulled off course by this, just like with your mother." In fact it is possible that I might have said words like that, but if I did I was not emotionally behind them. (In other words, I would have been using a cognitive technique that was not linked to the corresponding affect—empathic identification.) I was unable to understand that his raging at me probably came from his experience of my destroying his thinking; if I had understood that this particular rage might have been good news, it might have moved the treatment along. It might have helped him to shape what was heretofore unformulated. I was unable to shape for myself at that time that I was stuck in a parallel trauma of feeling continually pulled off course by a mother. And my organizing principle was that, unless I got her to stop pulling me off course, I would not be able to think. I would therefore lose my connection not only to her, but also to that part of myself that thinks, which for me felt (and feels) catastrophic. That is where I was stuck with Jack and, I presume, he with me. I was too disrupted, too much in the grip of my own trauma with my mother to get back to the fact that he was reliving his trauma with his mother. Unbeknownst to me at that time, it seems we were in a life-and-death power struggle, each fighting for the capacity to shape our own thinking so that we could maintain connection both to the other and to ourselves. And, in our failure to move beyond impasse, we were left—both of us— misshapen.

The issues of our disjunction that I describe might have been enough to derail treatment, but I also suspect something else was at stake, which may have had something to do with the tenacity of Jack's inability or refusal to put the pieces together. Occasionally, he would express a kind of disembodied anxiety that, if he brought the pieces together in a way that would help us to know what had happened to him, I would tell someone else and that someone would come and kill him—or me. Over the three years I saw Jack, he may have spoken about his father six times, and I could never get more out of him than an occasional fragment he would drop in my lap in a dissociated way, never to be revisited. One time he told me that his father had killed his cat in his presence. Much later, he left a message on my answering machine describing a dark place where ritual abuse occurred, where he was made to cut someone, and where his father sexually abused little girls and boys. This bit of information, too, he was unwilling or unable to revisit in any subsequent session. Were his father's rage and sadism the "pack of dogs" in the dream? I never knew what was true about his father, and I wanted to know. (In my organizing principle, I had a need to get past the dissociation of my parents and know their traumatic origins—malignant trauma that they only indirectly visited on me. I wanted to know and heal my parents.) I have a capacity in my practice for listening to and processing evil. But Jack could not tell me about this, and we were not far enough along in the treatment to shape this aspect of his father. Perhaps our inability to negotiate our impasse influenced his distrust. Perhaps his mother always took him off course intentionally to keep him from speaking about his perceptions of his father. My guess is, since he experienced me as his mother in a way that we were never able to move from, we never got to find out how much I was capable of hearing about his father. On the other hand, he may not have been ready at the time to take on something that may have been more malignant than the mother's destructiveness.

I do not believe I can know for sure without Jack's participation how his relationship with his father influenced the treatment difficulties between us. What follows is speculative and thus must remain part of what was heretofore unformulated. But there were signs of Jack's sadism. He would insist that I read something that was important to him, but then I could not get him to talk about what I had just spent my time reading. He began to criticize me in what felt like a relentless fashion. His grating, disembodied observations of my appearance and behavior—the scarf I wore, the juice I drank—sent cold shudders down my spine. "I see you wear the same shoes every day," he insinuated, in a tone difficult to describe, yet it was the tone itself more than what he said that got under my skin. My conscious experience at the time was that of being invaded by someone who was faking a connection, but who actually had no ability to be concerned about who I was. When I asked for his experience of what I felt to be his insinuations and criticisms, he found no meaning. Any inquiry on my part sent me skidding off a slippery surface. And I could not keep to the task of analysis. It is clear to me now that my selfobject needs for connection and meaning-making were not being met and I had lost perspective. I lost my empathy and withdrew emotionally. Perhaps another contribution to the impasse was that I was not able to negotiate more effectively my own outrage and sadism—not able in this case to, in Preston and Shumsky's terms, expand my self-regulatory range.

For me, I think the last straw came when we reconvened after my summer vacation in our third year together. I had left him in the care of a colleague and, when I returned, he announced that he wanted to see her because she was so much more knowledgeable about obsessional thinking (a symptom he and I had worked on) than I was. He was upset by her refusal to treat him on an ongoing basis and wanted me to intervene on his behalf. She seemed so competent, he said. He saw no meaning in his sudden wish to leave me, ignoring any attempt at making meaning of his wish to switch to my colleague. Suddenly he dropped his request to see my colleague, refusing further conversation, which made me feel that his request had been a straw man all along. Yet I had no way to think with him about what he was doing. I felt imprisoned by what I experienced as his incessant demands for my response which, once given, he would then deflect.

Was this his wish to turn the tables on me after I had just returned from leaving him? Did his insinuations and criticisms stem from the therapeutic stalemate? Or were they manifestations of an unreachable and sadistic father entering the treatment zone in a way that Jack could or would not formulate? I asked him if his wish to move to a new therapist had to do with the fact that I had just left him for vacation. I also asked if this wish had to do with his hopelessness about our treatment. His response, each time, was to change the subject to something I was unable to follow. And I knew my insistence on such interpretations, without his agreement, in the middle of therapeutic embattlement, would have been acting out of a one-person system and would have served only to shame him and leave him holding the blame. We would have had to be farther down the road (out of the impasse) to reflect creatively on these questions.

Eventually it became clear to both of us that we had to terminate. He became more and more critical, and I became more and more frustrated by not being able to make meaning together out of his criticisms and by his "keeping things in pieces." Behind all my attempts to understand his communications to me, my empathy was ebbing fast, even though I did not want that to be the case. Although I was feeling stonewalled and imprisoned in my relationship with Jack, I was simultaneously aware that our enactment was cocreated. (My cognitive and affective states remained dissociated in spite of the fact that I was aware of their dissonance. I was unable to process what was needed for me to link them back up again.) I did what I could to convey that where we were stuck had to do with both of us. I said it felt to me like I was a rock and he was the ocean, and the rock was finally becoming dislodged. Another rock would not have moved, I said. I doubt this helped much, and I am sure he felt blamed. How could he not?

The reader may want to know more precisely how this treatment ended. I think if I try to answer this question I would be in danger of sounding like I know "who did what to whom" (Bromberg, 2001). I strongly believe, along with Stolorow, Atwood, and Orange (2001), that not only are psychoanalytic events co-constructed, but also the analyst cannot know by herself what happened. I embarked on the project of writing this paper to show as honestly as possible where I got stuck with this patient and to assert how important it is to reveal our humanity as analysts. At the same time, I realize that, by discussing where I got stuck and surmising where Jack got stuck with me, I continually flirt with the danger of sounding objectivist. No matter how postmodern we are, we seem not to be able to sever all our posivitist tendrils. My version of what happened at the end is that Jack was the first to bring up the idea in a serious way of terminating the therapy. Although I insisted that we spend some sessions discussing and processing the treatment, I did not resist his suggestion and, as I have said, I did everything I could not to fault him for the impasse. The higher therapist part of me did not want him to be stuck with my incapacities any longer than he already had been (and another part of me did not want to be stuck with the experience of failure any longer), and I did not know how long it would take me to extricate myself from my muddle. I could see from his past therapies that he could move himself along quite well. That was the scrappy, resilient part of him that I admired. But having said all this, I have no idea what his version of termination would be. Perhaps he would say that I brought it up and blamed him for our impasse.

The sorrow I feel over our termination is immense. Jack believed that I understood him as no one else had. Also, he knew I had years of experience with trauma, which gave him great hopes for our treatment. It is painful for me to think of his hopes so dashed as a result of an up-ended treatment. But it is now sorrow I am left with—no longer the shame that I felt in the last stages and in the time after termination. Often in the midst of writing this paper, I would turn away, thinking these were things I could never say out loud. As I was writing, I sometimes felt a general anxiety and depression and a feeling of, why am I doing this? I would rather be gardening, or drawing, or playing Scrabble. But here is what I have discovered: as I made my shame experiences specific and imagined writing them "out loud," they were transformed. They became a part of me that has faults, incompetencies, "ailing internal objects [needing to be healed] . . . over and over again" (Davies, 1999, p. 187). I no longer feel suffused with shame or its manifestations—anxiety and depression. I have had a lived experience of something we all know, that a large part of shame's power is in its secretiveness. Shame revealed is only a mistake, a weakness (however sad the consequences might be), not a condemnation and dislodging of an entire self. I know it is in the recognition of shame and of the shared sorrow of our particular "affective incompetencies"

(Russell, 1998) within the analytic community that we can heal ourselves and do better next time.

REFERENCES

Bacal, H. & Thompson, P. (1998), Optimal responsiveness and the therapist's reaction to the patient's unresponsiveness. In: *Optimal Responsiveness: How Therapists Heal Their Patients*, ed. H. Bacal. Northvale, NJ: Aronson.

Beebe, B. & Lachmann, F. (1994), Representation and internalization in infancy: Three principles of salience. *Psychoanal. Psychol.*, 11:127–165.

Bromberg, P. (2001), Treating patients with symptoms—and symptoms with patience: Reflections on shame, dissociation, and eating disorders. *Psychoanal. Dial.*, 11: 891–912.

Brothers, D. (1995), *Falling Backwards: An Exploration of Trust and Self Experience*. New York: Norton.

Coburn, W. (1998), Patient unconscious communication and analyst narcissistic vulnerability in the countertransference experience, In: *The World of Self Psychology: Progress in Self Psychology, Vol. 14*, ed. A. Goldberg. Hillsdale, NJ: The Analytic Press, pp. 17–31.

Davies, J. M. (1999), Getting cold feet, defining safe-enough borders: Dissociation, multiplicity, and integration in the analyst's experience. *Psychoanal. Quart.*, 68: 184–208.

Grand, S. (2000), *The Reproduction of Evil: A Clinical and Cultural Perspective*. Hillsdale, NJ: The Analytic Press.

Jacobs, T. J. (1991), *The Use of the Self*. Madison, CT: International Universities Press.

Kohut, H. (1977), *The Restoration of the Self*. Madison, CT: International Universities Press.

Lachmann, F. (2000), *Transforming Aggression: Psychotherapy with the Difficult-to-Treat Patient*. Northvale, NJ: Aronson, pp. 192–193.

Lansky, M. R. (1992), *Fathers Who Fail: Shame and Psychopathology in the Family System*. Hillsdale, NJ: The Analytic Press.

Mitchell, S. A. (1997), *Influence and Autonomy in Psychoanalysis*. Hillsdale, NJ: The Analytic Press.

Morrison, A. P. (1994), The breadth and boundaries of a self-psychological immersion in shame: A one-and-a-half person perspective. *Psychoanal. Dial.*, 4:19–35.

———— & Stolorow, R. (1997), Shame, narcissism, and intersubjectivity. In: *The Widening Scope of Shame*, ed. M. R. Lansky & A. P. Morrison. Hillsdale, NJ: The Analytic Press, pp. 63–87.

Orange, D. (1995), *Emotional Understanding*. New York: Guilford Press.

Preston, L. & Shumsky, E. (2000), The development of the dyad: A bidirectional revisioning of some self-psychological concepts. In: *How Responsive Should We Be? Progress in Self Psychology. Vol. 16*, ed. A. Goldberg. Hillsdale, NJ: The Analytic Press.

Russell, P. (1998), The role of the paradox. In: *Trauma, Repetition, and Affect Regulation: The Work of Paul Russell*, ed. J. Teicholz & D. Kriegman. New York: Other Press.

Stolorow, R., Atwood, G. & Orange, D. (2001), World horizons: A post-Cartesian alternative to the Freudian unconscious. *Contemp. Psychoanal.*, 37:43–61.

Zeddies, T. (2001), On the wall or in the ointment? The psychoanalytic community as a third presence in the consulting room. *Contemp. Psychoanal.*, 37:133–147.

Twelve

WHO TORE THE WEB?
THOUGHTS ON PSYCHOANALYTIC AUTHORITY
AND RESPONSE-ABILITY

LYNN PRESTON
ELLEN SHUMSKY

*P*ostmodern challenges to taken-for-granted ideas of objectivity, neutrality, truth, simple cause and effect, and reliable sequential stages of development have left psychoanalysts scrambling for solid ground. Practitioners are confused and bewildered by the myriad ways in which the complexity of the psychoanalytic situation can be understood and managed. In the vulnerability and frustration of embattled treatments and unyielding impasses, we are especially in need of guidelines to comfort us, certainties to direct us, and firm principles to reassure us. In a world devoid of "immaculate perception" (Stolorow, Atwood, and Orange, 1999, p. 386), concepts such as authority, responsibility, and correct technique have lost their traditional underpinnings.

As the idea of the analyst's objectivity is relinquished, we feel the need for new concepts and a different kind of language—a language of systems and processes rather than verities and entities—in order to talk about issues such as analytic authority and responsibility. This paper is the most recent in a series in which we have been pursuing the expansion of self-psychological concepts and language in keeping with this post-Cartesian thrust (Preston and Shumsky, 2000, 2002). These papers also reflect a desire to be part of the cross-fertilization process that is taking place between self psychology/intersubjective systems theory and other relational theories.

We became intrigued with the challenge of thinking further about issues of responsibility and authority in response to recent clinical presentations by Maroda (1999) and Davies (2002). (These will be discussed later.) As we pursued this interest, we became aware that these topics have not attracted much recent attention from the self psychology community. Donna Orange (2002, personal communication) commented to us that this may be the case because self psychology and intersubjective systems theory are phenomenologically based and therefore not concerned with authority and responsibility as "things in themselves," but rather in the *experience* of authority and of responsible participation. In this paper we offer some reflections on the experience of analysts and patients struggling to negotiate issues of responsibility and authority in a new paradigm of psychoanalysis.

RESPONSIBILITY

Buber (1985) writes, "The idea of responsibility is to be brought back from the province of specialized ethics, of an 'ought' that swings free in the air, into that of lived life. Genuine responsibility exists only where there is real responding" (p. 16).

This quote addresses shifting understandings of the nature of responsibility. Responsibility has traditionally been defined as accountability—as being able to answer for one's conduct, or to fulfill one's obligations. In the realm of moral responsibility it is generally acknowledged that "we are not responsible for what we were forced to do or were unable to avoid no matter how hard we tried" (Audi, 1995, p. 280). Accepting responsibility from this perspective is related to whether it is within the individual's control to act in such a way as to avoid a problematic outcome. We experience the legalistic tone of this dictionary terminology as typifying a more Cartesian way of thinking somewhat like Buber's reference to "specialized ethics, [of] an 'ought' that swings free in the air." It seems to us that these "specialized ethics" are predicated on positivist assumptions of simple cause and effect, objective reality, separate self, and bifurcation of right and wrong. Buber appears to be pointing in the direction of the idea of contextualism, in which he turns away from a prescribed "ought," and looks to the complexities of "lived life" which press for "real responding." Of real responding, Buber (1985) speaks of

> entering upon this situation . . . which has at this moment
> stepped up to us, whose appearance we did not and could
> not know, for its like has not yet been. . . . A newly-created

concrete reality has been laid in our arms; we answer for it. A dog has looked at you, you answer its glance, a child has clutched your hand, you answer its touch, a host of men moves about you, you answer for their need [p. 18].

In other words, real responding is a spontaneous answering to the message of the moment.

As psychoanalysis relinquishes its positivist foundational cornerstones—the solidity of objective truth, the autonomy of isolated mind, and the predictability of causal sequences—the concept of responsibility takes on a different shape and tone, perhaps more in keeping with Buber's understanding. We can no longer simply pinpoint who is doing what to whom. We are instead tossed into the complexities, ambiguities, and paradoxes of "lived life," in which we experience ourselves as shaping and being shaped by each moment. In this milieu of microadaptations and mutual influence, considerations of responsibility seek to understand the complex, often contradictory impact that people have on each other as they touch and engage, like ripples on a pond in the rain. Taking responsibility no longer points to individuals' having created a situation, or being able to avoid or fix it, but suggests instead a commitment to attend to the complex threads of circumstance, personality, and the psychological vicissitudes that have shaped the interaction. Stern (1997) writes about:

> looking for a degree of responsibility . . . suspended between undiluted personal agency and absolute destiny. . . . We do not move or purposively "stride" in and out of self-states, nor are we simply transported. It is the interactive combination of . . . ourselves and the influence on us of each person we encounter that calls out a particular interpersonal field [p. 156].

A systems view of the idea of responsibility shifts discourse from a focus on "whose fault is it?" to "how did we get here?" or "what is the meaning of this?" It assumes a web of connection in which the question "who tore the web?" (i.e., which one of us is responsible for this rupture?) is impossible to answer. It is like asking the question, "What is the sound of one hand clapping?" The web metaphor includes as a given that all of us in some way contribute to the creation and to the destruction of the web. The question of responsibility then becomes, how did each of us participate in the tearing and how can we mend it? In assuming that life processes emerge out of and create systems and subsystems of human interaction, responsibility is embedded in initiating, facilitating, and pursuing a commitment to mutually regulated personal responsiveness.

The issue of psychoanalytic responsibility is rendered yet more complex by the asymmetrical nature of the analytic engagement. It is very different to be a responsible analyst than to be a responsible patient. Stephen Mitchell (2000) eloquently describes the different role responsibilities of analyst and patient:

> One of the most important distinctions between the role of the analysand and the role of the analyst pertains to the claims on each to be responsible. . . . It is the analysand's job in some very important ways to be irresponsible. That is, we ask analysands to surrender to their experience, to show up and discover what they find themselves feeling and thinking. We ask analysands to renounce all other conscious intents. . . . The analyst is trying to be responsibly analytic, trying to do the "right thing" [p. 131].

Self psychology, with its developmental underpinnings, is particularly sensitive to issues of asymmetry in the analytic relationship. Self psychologists, embracing a conceptual framework that assumes the centrality of selfobject transferences, have traditionally approached the issue of responsible analytic participation by attempting to decenter from their own needs for validation and shared responsibility. They tend to deal with problematic interactions through a model of rupture and repair. In this approach, which wears the clear stamp of a self psychological sensibility, the analyst takes responsibility for initiating and facilitating a repair by deeply understanding the meanings of the difficulty for the patient.

SHAME AND BLAME

It was more than ten years ago that Morrison (1989) brought into the psychoanalytic dialogue, the central importance of shame as a primary motivating affect experience. He pointed out that "shame is, by its very nature, confounding" (p. 180). The immediacy of the bodily grip of shame fills one with paralyzing dread, unmitigated badness, withering inadequacy, and a conviction of unlovability. This annihilation of self-esteem, self-cohesion, and connection stands in sharp contrast to the vitalization, consolidation, and sense of secure belonging associated with selfobject experience. Shame is the antithesis of selfobject experience. Bacal and Thompson (1996) point out that the analyst's shame is as potentially lethal to an analytic selfobject connection as the patient's shame.

An analytic investigation of responsibility is exquisitely balanced on the cusp of agency and shame. Therapists often try to tease apart interpersonal conflicts and impasses by investigating the question "who is doing what to whom?" When this approach is framed as an attempt to decipher some objective reality, it is but a breath away from the slippery slope of fault with its overtones of demoralizing shame and blame. The attempt at a broadened perspective of expanded awareness and sense of agency that could be gained by the illumination of individual contributions to a problematic interaction may just as easily disrupt as enhance forward movement. Consideration of one's contribution may lead to a greater sense of self awareness, agency, and intimacy, but in a fragile, narcissistically vulnerable system where there is sensitivity to feeling judged and criticized, it can as easily lead to feelings of defensiveness, blame, shame, or being left holding the bag of badness and inadequacy. For those who can accept their participation in the creation of a disruption, an exploration of a problematic interaction may feel like a way to engage and connect. But if it is experienced as the attribution of "fault," with its implication of culpability and badness, it may instead lead to feelings of condemned isolation because a sense of fault implies that, if one were good, developed, or smart enough, the ruptures, glitches, disappointments, and disconnections would not have happened. (This point will be illuminated further in the case presentation that follows.) It is for this reason that self psychologists have tended to approach the tearing of the web through a lens of rupture and repair.

One way of attempting to minimize the pitfalls of shame and move a stuck interaction in the direction of nonjudgmental meaning-making is to pursue "we" questions such as, "How did we get here?" "What does this mean to us?" "What are its impact, precursors, antecedents, implications?" These questions are less about "reality" and more about personal and dyadic subjectivity. This effort to link responsibility with personal meanings has the potential to embed the discussion in "no-fault" assurance which can consolidate selfobject experience and minimize shame-prone self-protective defensiveness. The therapist's ability to negotiate her own shame is crucial here. Atwood, Stolorow, and Trop (1989) speak of impasses in the psychoanalytic process as a "royal road": "Whether these intersubjective situations facilitate or obstruct the progress of therapy depends in large part on the extent of the therapists capacity to become reflectively aware of the organizing principles of his own world" (p. 555). In other words, the therapist and patient have cocreated the stalemate, and an exploration of the difficulty must include the therapist's serious self-reflection. Such an introspective capacity rests on a sturdy sense of self-acceptance.

There are some patients for whom the experience of a non-blaming therapist lends permission to be blaming in a way that offers a developmental opportunity. Freedom to blame assumes one's entitlement to belonging, care, and respect: "I have a secure membership in this family, deserve love and appreciation, and can protest when it is not forthcoming." It suggests that the relational other is big enough and strong enough to tolerate challenges to self-esteem without collapsing or retaliating. For patients who grew up taking responsibility for their parents and for the mutual regulation of the family, and for patients who are trauma survivors, finally being able to blame the analyst/parent/perpetrator is a developmental achievement. To foster such a corrective experience, the analyst needs to be able to be blamed without falling into states of shame that press for blaming back. An analyst who can manage to shoulder blame facilitates the creation of a more flexible, resilient, and resourceful analytic dyad. Bacal and Thompson (1996) point out that analysts need a professional milieu of nonjudgmental, open discourse to be able to perform this counterintuitive task.

The arena of greatest debate between self psychologists and other relationalists is perhaps in understanding and managing aversive reactions in embattled treatments. Self psychologists, assuming the reactive nature of aggression, view aggression as a defense against shame. Other relationalists, who think of aggression as spontaneous and central to human motivation, think of shame as a derivative of aggression. This difference informs the analyst's approach to responsible analytic participation. In contrasting Mitchell with Kohut, Lachmann (2001) says,

> Mitchell emphasizes engaging the patient interpersonally to mobilize relational patterns in the transference and thereby to help the patient move beyond them. . . . Kohut places greater emphasis on the analyst's affective resonance with, communication of, empathic understanding of the patient's experience [p. 199].

Relationalists such as Bromberg (1989) consider adherence to an empathic stance to be a straitjacket, whereas Teichholz (1999), a self psychologist, criticizes interpersonalists for losing sight of the patient's needs for empathic attunement. Both traditions can lose touch with what is commonly taken for granted outside the realm of psychoanalysis—namely that "I" and "we" statements are an essential component of taking responsibility in a conflict. Speaking in the first person can allow us, as analysts, to stick up for ourselves and the analysis without sticking it *to* the patient.

Davies (2002), in a gripping case presentation, described a session in which she was feeling sick, vulnerable, and barely able to manage her challenging patient's angry demand for a schedule change. The patient accused Davies of being an "icy bitch" who never went out of her way for her. Davies both resented the patient and went into a state of self-recrimination about her own feelings of punitive withholdingness. Davies and her patient stared at each other in icy silence until the patient finally said, "You hate me don't you?" Davies pulled herself together and managed to reply, "Sometimes we hate each other. We'll have to see where we get to from here." In the next session, surprisingly, the patient brought hot tea, and as Jody drank in the "hot milky goodness" she struggled with whether and how to reintroduce the disruption of the previous session. She asked, "Can we be the same people who hated each other yesterday?" The patient said, "That was awful wasn't it." Davies then went further by telling her patient that the worst part for her had been her own feelings of self-hatred. The patient was amazed and intrigued and wanted to know more about Davies's experience of self-hate. The atmosphere changed to one of confiding trust, and the patient admitted that her states of self-hatred were only ameliorated in moments of vehemently hating her therapist.

Davies embeds this case in an object relations framework (a comparison of this framework with our own is beyond the scope of this paper). But, from a self-psychological perspective, what is striking to us is that Davies was able to decenter from a polarized position with her patient by introducing the idea of an "us"—"we sometimes hate each other." In other words, she took responsibility by including herself in the stalemate. It empowered the patient "to respond" with a caring offer of tea. The therapist took another step of responsibility by reintroducing the couple that had hated each other the day before. She went further still by sharing her vulnerability and telling her patient that the worst part for her was hating herself. This offering moved the dyad into a twinship in which the patient, feeling the weight of a "shame and blame" deadlock lift, could take the risk of describing her own experiences of self-hate. The patient/analyst system opened into a state of intimacy and aliveness.

AUTHORITY

Issues of authority and power are closely linked with responsibility. Responsibility is an acceptance of the obligation to respond. Authority, which includes elements of expertise, leadership, and the power to influence others, is a vehicle for the impactfulness of a response. Authority used to reside in a belief that the patient was ill and the properly analyzed analyst was healthy. The trained and theoretically informed psychoanalyst was an expert on human psychological dynamics. Mitchell (1993) has pointed out that, in these postmodern times, "the realm of psychoanalytic debate entails a fundamental redefinition of the very nature of psychoanalytic thought and of psychoanalysis as a discipline" (p. 42). He says that this philosophical upheaval has caused a crisis of confidence in the underpinnings of analytic authority. Relational theorists (Aron, 1996; Benjamin, 1997; Hoffman, 1998) have been struggling with new understandings of analytic authority and responsibility. They pose the question, if authority does not reside in claims on truth, where does it reside?

Karen Maroda (1999), another relational psychoanalyst struggling with the issue of authority, wants to believe there is still something positive about positivism. She says she is uncomfortable with "the philosophy that we cannot be sure of anything, that our opinions and judgments are so subjective that everything we say and think should be questioned and scrutinized" (p. 161). Although we share Maroda's concerns about the lack of spontaneity that accompanies scrutinizing everything one thinks and does, we would submit that, just as one cannot be a "little bit pregnant," one cannot be a little bit subjective. Kohut (1977) insisted that psychoanalysis is delimited by the scope of empathy and vicarious introspection (p. 303). In other words, all we as analysts have is our subjectivity. Anything else is outside the realm of psychoanalysis. Maroda wants to give the analyst her due in terms of expertise, authority and power. Referring to her treatment with a challenging and dismissive patient she says, "I told her that if I was going to continue to treat her she had to be willing to acknowledge that all the money she was paying me was for a professional service that I did, indeed, know how to provide" (p. 166). Maroda's confidence in her ability to work with this patient seems to be based on her belief in her superior grasp of reality: "Without my own convictions regarding 'reality' and my willingness to take many stands regarding my authority in the relationship, this treatment would most certainly have failed" (p. 167). Maroda believes her authority is based on her ability to keep her feet firmly planted on the solid foundation of her relational objectivity. While we acknowledge that Maroda's authoritative stance may have been helpful, even crucial, for this treatment at this particular juncture, we think there are other interpretations as to why her positivism turned out to be so positive. For example, it is equally plausible that, in "laying down the law" to her patient, the service she was providing was that of facilitating a needed idealizing selfobject experience.

The question Mitchell voices is, if we do not have a greater grasp of objective reality, on what do we base our authority? The following are some tentative directions we have been investigating

RELATIONAL PROCESS SKILLS

As we see it, a reformulation of the basis of analytic authority within a relativist paradigm is a shift in focus from content to process. We cannot rely on the ultimate truth of what we know, but we depend on our commitment to the process of opening ourselves to multiple layers of both subjectively and intersubjectively acquired understandings. Not only can we not be sure of the correctness of our interpretations of the patient and the analytic relationship, we also cannot know whether those interpretations will be useful or not. We rely on the process of intimate dialogue, self -reflection, making ourselves more comfortable with not knowing, and negotiating the tension between spontaneous participation and thoughtful, considered responsiveness. We no longer believe ourselves to be antiseptic scientists with a bead on reality, healthier than our patients. We are more like skilled artisans crafting our trade in an impactful type of conversation. Mitchell (2000), in exploring concerns about analytic process, is pointing to what may be thought of as an analytical skill when he cites Loewald. Loewald refers to the analyst's expertise as "the capacity to navigate among and bridge different developmental and organizational levels . . . primary and secondary process, self and other, past and present, reality and fantasy" (p. 51). This kind of versatility can be thought of as a particular analytic conversational skill. In our previous paper (Preston and Shumsky, 2002), we spoke about analytic expertise as centrally involving the capacity to navigate the tension between the poles of empathy and authenticity. These empathic, relational, and interpretive capabilities certainly do not save us from narcissistic vulnerabilities, blind spots, or self-limiting emotional convictions. But they become well-worn, trustworthy tools that both analyst and patient can rely on in times of desert barrenness, torrential floods, dangerous mountain passes, and erupting earthquakes.

THE THERAPEUTIC POWER OF IDEALIZATION

Hoffman (1998) believes, and we are inclined to agree, that the analyst's authority is part and parcel of the ritual asymmetry of the analytic relationship. "The analyst's personal involvement in the analytic situation has, potentially, a particular kind of concentrated power because it is embedded in a ritual in which the analyst is set up to be a special kind of authority" (p. 84). This ritual asymmetry promotes an element of idealization. Hoffman refers to the "magical power of the analyst's relative anonymity" that invites the patient's longings for a wise, knowing, loving parent (p. 234).

This "magical power" and the longings it invites may also be understood as an idealizing selfobject transference experience. In this transference the patient invests the analyst with comforting or reverential authority. It is in keeping with the nature of a selfobject transference attribution that the analyst accepts and wears the mantle of awesome power in a kind of transitional space. She is a representative of authority that derives from a role that the analytic situation has constructed. The therapist might say, "It was not right that you were blamed for that as a child," which is an important validation of the child's suffering, but the analyst cannot really believe that she knows what was right or wrong. In working with idealization, the therapist accepts the patient's authorization of her in order to ultimately give the authority back to the patient's inner experience.

Mitchell (1993) challenges the idea that the patient's inner experience is any more authoritative than the analyst's knowledge of him or her. He asserts that human experience is fundamentally ambiguous (p. 52). We would submit that the authority of the patient's inner experience rests not on some ultimate correctness—the uncovering of a singular, pristine, unambiguous self—but rather on the power of the unambiguous *experience* of a ring of truth, a sense of emotional conviction that is at the core of agency. Kohut's (1984) famous statement that his rightness was superficial and his patient's rightness was profound (p. 94) speaks to the wisdom of staying close to the patient's felt experience of the moment. It is not that the analyst or the patient has a truth which by its absoluteness can set the patient free but that, through the enlivening power of the sense of freedom in the analytic micro-moment, we recognize the authority of the patient's subjective truth.

CLINICAL EXAMPLE

Carol, a gifted, creative, and accomplished musician, was being seen by me (E. S.) for both individual and group therapy. She was the newest member of the group, quiet at first as she tentatively felt her way into the new experience. Walking home from the group session one night with another member, Louise, Carol mentioned that before the next meeting she was going into the hospital for a surgical procedure. The following week, in group, Carol thanked the members for their concerned messages. Louise then explained that, after hearing about Carol's surgery, she had taken it upon herself to call all the group members and leave a message informing each of them of Carol's health crisis. She told each one that she thought it would be nice if they called Carol to wish her well. Myrna, another group member, took great issue with Louise's message. In fact, she was furious and said she felt manipulated by Louise. A very uncharacteristically raw, angry exchange erupted between the two women and I, with some anxiety, moved in to try to manage it.

At the next group meeting Carol said that she had felt hurt in the previous session and had said so. She went on angrily, "I don't understand why nobody responded to me." The group members and I reacted to Carol's challenge by explaining that we had been so swept up by the explosion of anger that, although with hindsight many of us could recall hearing Carol express hurt, her voice had been so small relative to the intensity of the storm of fury that it had not fully registered.

Carol was devastated. She felt that not only had she been painfully ignored by the group when she was taking the risk, for the very first time, of expressing a vulnerable feeling; but additionally, she was being blamed by everyone for having created, with her small voice, her traumatic experience of painful inconsequence and invisibility. This event was processed and reprocessed in Carol's individual therapy, and, when it felt safe enough to do so, with the group. Most group members understood why Carol was upset that her expression of vulnerability had been ignored, but they wanted her to understand how, by approaching them with the statement, "I don't understand," she was inviting the very explanations that then felt blaming and invalidating.

Throughout this process, I heard the group members struggling with a complex array of feelings that included their defensiveness along with identification and empathic understanding; their annoyance and frustration about Carol's tenacious refusal to let go of the experience along with apologies, expressions of regret, and a new awareness of and sensitivity to her. From my perspective, there was a rich evolving tapestry of connections, affects, and behaviors. Carol, however, continued to hear only defensiveness, blame, and invalidation. In her individual sessions she expressed herself in a logical style which had the effect on me of limiting our discourse to legalistic arguments about the "facts" of what had happened. I could not seem to find a way to move the discussion into an arena in which I could wholeheartedly empathize with her feelings of hurt and betrayal. I tried to share with her my perceptions of the group process, including my own participation, but this as well was experienced by Carol as blame for having created her own pain. I was struggling to understand, through Carol's condemning eyes, her traumatic experience with the group and with my leadership. Were we so heartless and unconcerned? I wanted Carol to see the complexity of what "really" happened and for her to own her part in this multidimensional drama.

As Carol and I continued to explore and attempt to deconstruct the situation, she became increasingly silent and hopeless. She reported recurrent, terrifying nightmares of her home being invaded and her property and person being mutilated and destroyed. She began to consider leaving the group, and I began to fear that this might be necessary because she seemed traumatized at being required to handle the multiperson perspective necessitated by group interaction.

During yet another exploration with Carol of the traumatic group experience that was now beginning to focus more closely on my participation in it, I explained to her that I had missed her small, hurt cry in the group because I had been feeling anxious about managing the unusual (for this group) explosive anger. The result was dramatic. Her whole demeanor changed. Her urgent tone disappeared as she expressed immense relief at knowing that I had culpability. The problem was no longer her muted affect but my anxiety. The blame was no longer with Carol but with me. At this point, her dream imagery began to include the presence of police who were called to rescue her but who ended up rendered impotent by the audacious nefariousness of the perpetrators. Carol associated the impotent police with me, because I was, from her vantage point, helpless in getting the group members, including myself, to shift the blame for her violation from Carol to ourselves. I had been feeling deeply troubled by Carol's spiraling anguish and fragmentation, and I was immensely relieved finally to understand and accept the attributions of passivity and impotence symbolized by the dream. I was then able to acknowledge how greatly I had failed her. I began to grasp how my offered perception of complexity in the group process was slipping through the filters of her organizing grid, which included only victim and victimizer. In her world there was only a blaming one and a blamed one.

Carol, from birth, had been cared for by a nurse whose attitude—which she imparted to Carol's anxious, inexperienced mother—was that children should be taught that they could not control their caregivers. Carol's cries were never answered, and the family story, told by Carol's mother with a sense of considerable pride and accomplishment, was that by the age of six weeks Carol had stopped crying and never cried again. For 50 years Carol had been disavowing her pain. From her perspective, she had finally been feeling safe enough in group, because of her tie to me and because of Louise's protective concern, to resume a cry—"I'm hurt." For the group, who knew nothing of Carol's childhood, this was a peep that hardly registered. For me, anxious about anger management, it was also hardly discernable. For Carol, silent for 50 years, it was a life-affirming birth cry that carried the hope of resuming an early aborted aliveness. When it went unheard and she felt blamed for not making it heard, it was a devastating confirmation of her complete invisibility and disempowerment.

As I was able to decenter from my experience of the "complex reality" of the group event and take in the bare bones experience from Carol's perspective, I could feel along with her the traumatic repetition of the annihilation of her agency and understand her hopelessness about ever finding a responsive, validating other. As I relaxed into receiving her experience, she told and retold and retold again the story of the group trauma which now included my failure to make it safe for her. With each retelling I acknowledged my part in the creation of her nightmare experience. I did this both privately with Carol and also in the group. I spoke of how it was my "job" to learn how to read and respond to Carol's self-expression. In this phase of our relationship, I sometimes thought of Carol as a traumatized child replaying over and over again the horrific story of abuse so that she could work it through and integrate it.

I was also, however, working it through and integrating it. In the repeated retellings, the traumatic story and my participation in its creation were slowly and inexorably embedding themselves in my psyche. During this time, though sessions were less tense, Carol's nightmares continued unabated. One night after a group session, I recalled that, out of the corner of my consciousness, I had been aware of her fidgeting in her seat. The image stayed with me and troubled me deeply, so much so that I followed an impulse to phone her at home to say that I was concerned. She said she had, in fact, been feeling very angry about something going on in the group and was pleased that I had noticed and felt upset enough to call her. That night, her nightmares ended. Carol had experienced a concrete demonstration that her cry—in this case in the form of agitation—could be received and responded to by me. It disconfirmed her expectation of invisibility. Very slowly in the ensuing months tendrils of nuance and complexity started showing up in her narratives.

DISCUSSION

I first replied literally to Carol's challenge—"I don't understand why nobody responded to my experession of hurt." I said "I didn't hear you because the anger was so loud and your voice was so small." Carol organized this as "I, with my small voice, am to blame for being unattended to." I had in effect, presented myself as a victim of circumstance with no culpability. Carol was in a bind: she had to accept blame and the ensuing shame in order to have a shared reality with me, but it was a reality in which she was the cause of her own difficulties and was unentitled to redress or legitimization. In Carol's inner world, she existed as a vessel holding all the blame for her mother's deprivation and shame. In such a world there was only blamer and blamed. Multidimensionality did not exist. A measure of her integrity, and perhaps of the effectiveness of her therapy experience, was that in this interaction she refused to play the role of vessel with me, even though she risked giving up connection. She was unwilling to be placated into carrying the blame and persisted in a refusal to let me off the hook. She pushed me to examine and speak from my inner experience ("I was anxious") to take personal responsibility for her trauma.

Initially I thought that Carol was blaming other people and refusing responsibility for the way she had participated in creating her own suffering. Arguing about facts was, for me, an all-too-familiar early idiom, and I slipped into it with Carol as easily as an immigrant who, upon encountering a compatriot, starts speaking their common tongue. As the process unfolded I began to understand the impasse as a dense, complicated, roiling stew whose ingredients included Carol's hope for a caring place in the group; her traumatic group experience; her wish for a strong parent/analyst to care for and defend her; the group's defensiveness; their empathic strivings; their competitiveness about the special attention Carol sought from me; my empathic failure; my concern about being seen by the group as favoring Carol; my discomfort with confusion; and my shame-proneness about failing Carol. It was a far cry from the clear soup of simple old-paradigm ownership of fault. I wanted Carol to join me in my project of deconstructing the cocreated trauma and I was frustrated by her self-preserving intransigence. To make a bridge to her world, I had to join her in her organization of experience. I had to be the parent/analyst who could say, "I am to blame," and to translate my acceptance of responsibility into statements and actions that reached Carol. "It is my job to learn how to make meaning of your self-expression." "I called because I sensed and was concerned about your agitation." In so doing, I discovered a shameless acceptance of responsibility that laid the groundwork for a new approach to relational repair.

How did I finally get to the place of being able to do this? I am not sure. With hindsight I can suggest the following plausible process: I think that, over time, Carol's tenacious, urgent, repeated refusals to accept my explanations, which were essentially defensive and unemotional, coupled with my genuine if often self-serving and misguided desire to understand and address her pain broke through my analytic reserve, pushing me into more direct, explicit, personal self-disclosure—"I was anxious!" At the time that I said this, I was not consciously aware that it was different from saying, "I didn't hear you because the anger was so loud." It was only in experiencing her dramatic new response and reconstructing the conversation that led up to it that I realized I had at last brought something new, vital, and "response-able" to the impasse.

This case illustrates how, for patients like Carol, the potentially growth-producing exploration of the patient's contribution to the question of "who tore the web?" must be postponed until the dyad is able to avoid the pitfalls of demoralizing shame and blame. Navigating through the tumultuous waters of retraumatization, I was ultimately anchored by a framework of rupture and repair, fueled by *my* understanding of the shame-laden meaning for Carol of my empathic lapse and by my willingness to convey this understanding—not through interpretation, but through meaningful action.

CONCLUSION

In this paper we have considered the impact of postmodern contextualism on concepts of responsibility and analytic authority. It is part of a series in which we are exploring the unique contributions of self psychology to the broader relational community of which it is a member. We have emphasized the empathically responsive nature of a self-psychological model of responsibility and we have sought to demonstrate the need to protect explorations of process that include the patient's participation in conflict or impasse from slipping into the clutches of culpability that collapses into shame. We have also explored the idea of analytic authority from a self-psychological vantage point in which the power of an idealizing selfobject transference is used to hand authority back to the patient's inner experience. The analyst's expertise shifts from content to process, residing in skills inherent in responding to the uniqueness of the moment and the specificity of the dyad.

REFERENCES

Aron, L. (1996), A Meeting of Minds: Mutuality in Psychoanalysis. Hillsdale, NJ: The Analytic Press.

Atwood, G., Stolorow, R. & Trop, J. (1989), Impasses in psychoanalytic therapy: A royal road. Contemp. Psychoanal., 25:554–574.

Audi, R., ed. (1995), The Cambridge Dictionary of Philosophy. Cambridge, England: Cambridge University Press.

Bacal, H. & Thomson, P. (1996), The psychoanalyst's selfobject needs and the effect of their frustration on the treatment: A new view of countertransference. Basic Ideas Reconsidered: Progress in Self Psychology, Vol. 12, ed. A. Goldberg. Hillsdale, NJ: The Analytic Press, pp. 17–35.

Benjamin, J. (1997), Psychoanalysis as vocation. Psychoanal. Dial., 7:781–802.

Bromberg, P. (1989), Interpersonal psychoanalysis and self psychology: A clinical comparison. In: Self Psychology: Comparisons and Contrasts, ed. D. Detrick & S. Detrick. Hillsdale, NJ: The Analytic Press, pp. 275–291.

Buber, M. (1985), Between Man and Man. New York: Macmillan.

Davies, J. M. (2002), Whose bad objects are these anyway? Repetition and our elusive love affair with evil. Presented at the International Association for Relational Psychoanalysis and Psychotherapy Conference, January 19, New York.

Hoffman, I. (1998), Ritual and Spontaneity in the Psychoanalytic Process: A Dialectical-Constructivist View. Hillsdale, NJ: The Analytic Press.

Kohut, H. (1977), The Restoration of the Self. New York: International Universities Press.

——— (1984), How Does Analysis Cure? ed. A. Goldberg & P. Stepansky. Chicago: University of Chicago Press.

Lachmann, F. (2001), Transforming Aggression: Psychotherapy with the Difficult-to-Treat Patient. Northvale, NJ: Aronson.

Maroda, K. J. (1999), *Seduction, Surrender, and Transformation: Emotional Engagement in the Analytic Process*. Hillsdale, NJ: The Analytic Press.

Mitchell, S. (1993), *Hope and Dread in Psychoanalysis*. New York: Basic Books.

———— (2000) *Relationality: From Attachment to Intersubjectivity*, Hillsdale, NJ: The Analytic Press.

Morrison, A. (1989), *Shame: The Underside of Narcissism*. Hillsdale, NJ: The Analytic Press.

Preston, L. & Shumsky, E. (2000), The development of the dyad: A bidirectional revisioning of some self-psychological concepts. In: *How Responsive Should We Be? Progress in Self Psychology*, Vol. 16, ed. A. Goldberg. Hillsdale, NJ: The Analytic Press, pp. 67–84.

———— (2002), From an empathic stance to an empathic dance: Empathy as a bidirectional negotiation. In: *Postmodern Self Psychology: Progress in Self Psychology*, Vol. 18, ed. A Goldberg. Hillsdale, NJ: The Analytic Press, pp. 47–61.

Stern, D. (1997), *Unformulated Experience: From Dissociation to Imagination in Psychoanalysis*. Hillsdale, NJ: The Analytic Press.

Stolorow, R., Atwood, G. & Orange, D. (1999), Kohut and contextualism: Toward a post-Cartesian analytic theory. *Psychoanal. Psychol.*, 16:380–388.

Teicholz, J. (1999), *Kohut, Loewald, and the Postmoderns: A Comparative Study of Self and Relationship*. Hillsdale, NJ: The Analytic Press.

Part Five

GENDER AND SEXUALITY

Thirteen

THE CASE OF DAVIDA

MICHAEL D. CLIFFORD

*I*n this chapter, I present the treatment of a woman I call "Davida." I have chosen the name "Davida"—the feminized version of "David"—because my patient also has a barely feminized version of a masculine name. I point this out because I think in this case it is an indication of her parents' own preoccupation with gender and their inability to consider with empathy her experience in carrying a name even more unusual than Davida.

We have worked together for 14 years. We began twice a week, quickly accelerating to three and then four times a week. In addition, we soon moved to an hour-long session, because 45-minute sessions "didn't feel right" to Davida.

I am her 11th therapist. She was with some therapists for a short time, others for years. Frequently, these treatments were stalemated. It was rare that she left these therapists; rather, she was told by a number of them that they could no longer be of help to her. Evidently, they felt stuck and frustrated with her; she felt abandoned and "fired" by them.

Although I will give more history in a moment, I'll state now that she was the eldest child of parents who were both prominent psychotherapists in their community. Her first experience with therapy was when she was at the age of six, when she was referred to treatment because she dropped kittens from the roof of her apartment building to see whether they would survive the fall. Also, she threw rocks at other children. Finally she injured one when she hit him in the head. This first treatment ended quickly when the therapist suggested there might be family issues involved. Insulted, her parents withdrew her from that treatment, an act that she has mourned in the course of our work together.

In this kind of treatment, clearly, there are many issues involved. In this paper, I try to give an adequate background picture of the main movements of the treatment and focus on issues of gender and sexuality, especially as manifested in the treatment relationship.

When we began treatment, Davida was in her mid-30s, a temporary employee unable to hold even short assignments because she felt too unstable. Now she is holding a prominent position in finance. I think this is due to our work together, which has included medication, and also to her own tremendous innate abilities that have been freed up during the course of treatment. She is a person of great, nuanced emotional depth, with a fine mind. What she has lacked is a stable selfobject environment, and that is what we have struggled with throughout the treatment: my ability to provide her with stability, so that she can create and sustain this stability on her own.

THE EARLY TREATMENT

Davida first came to me when I was covering for a friend who was on vacation. Upon her return, my friend told Davida that she was adopting a baby. Davida found this idea intolerable. Davida called to ask if we could work together. After consulting with my friend, Davida and I started the treatment.

We had both felt we clicked when I was covering for my friend. During the first few months of the treatment there was what I now see as a honeymoon period. She felt affirmed, enthused, and delighted by our sessions.

This honeymoon was over, for me at least, when she came to a session with a sense of anticipatory glee, with an undercurrent that I must not break this spell. She stated that she wanted to change her name. "To what?" I inquired. She replied, "I want to change my last name to Clifford, to your last name." This took me aback, since it was said without the analytic self-consciousness I would have expected, although there was what struck me as a pretense of coyness. Exploration of her desire to change her name did not reveal much at this point; I thought it might be evidence of an idealizing selfobject transference.

From this point, her attachment to me continued to grow quickly. She asked to be my last patient in the evening, and, following uneventful exploration, I agreed. Soon, I discovered she made this request because she had difficulty ending the session. Indeed, often she would not leave my office when the session was over. This is when we extended the session to an hour from 45 minutes, prorating the fee accordingly. Often Davida would still stop at my office door without leaving, saying she could not leave until she felt "right," or until she could "be sure things were all right between us."

I attempted a variety of interpretations to end the session. For example, I said I knew from our work together that separations were difficult for her. Did it help to think that this separation between us was only temporary, that we would see each other the next night? She responded by saying that to see each other the next night was not soon enough—could she call me if she needed to before the next appointment? And she would say, "Isn't the separation difficult for you, too?" Here was what seemed to be her desire to know my subjectivity, but with the proviso that we must have the same experience.

After many months of this, at those times that interpretations were not successful, I fell back on action. Eventually, I would close my office door on her standing in the waiting room, saying I needed to get ready to leave the office. Then when I was ready to leave a few minutes later, I would find her standing outside my door, waiting for me. At these times she said she could not move, and I would escort her out of the building and put her into a cab, telling the driver her address.

In the background of this difficulty were the troubling states she would get into at home. She reported she could lie for hours on her apartment floor "frozen," unable to move. At these times, she often called me, and we had a telephone session. Loss of hopefulness and loss of a feeling of connection with me often contributed to her falling into these states. Essentially, the reconnection with me and our focusing on her desire to get herself going again would enable her to get up off the floor and continue with her day. The selfobject functions the treatment was providing for her are clear.

Also in the background was my own sense that, although indeed disorganized, she was refusing to engage in the treatment to the extent that she was capable. She was relying on me exclusively to organize her and refused any of my efforts to help her organize herself. Yet to explore this idea, too, was not possible, for she took this as my distancing myself from her, which provoked further disintegration. I began to find this treatment situation untenable.

These issues came to a head when, from her work, she called me seven times in one day, reporting that she felt disrupted and saying she wanted me to call her. I thought about it, and then I did call her. I said I very much wanted to continue to work together, but that I could not work this way, that she needed to try to help herself with her feelings also, and to begin to try to contain them so that we could work together on them during sessions. She agreed that she would try to work in this way. I suggested that perhaps to her being taken care of meant being cared for, a feeling she might have experienced very little in her life. This was an interpretation she could accept.

At this point, Davida had a strong reaction to the patients that preceded her in my office. If the patient was a woman, it was intolerable to her. Intensely jealous and fearful that I liked the other patient more than her, she could not bear the smell of another woman's perfume in my office. These feelings grew until she threatened to physically attack a woman patient who had a session before her. Despite my best efforts, she would not try to contain herself or even to be curious as to why she would not. My response, then, was that I would need to call the police to protect her and the other patient, if she would not or could not restrain herself. She did not believe this. She thought that I should interpret this more than I had. I stuck to my guns, and she relented that she would not attack this patient. Setting limits was organizing to her behavior, although it did not affect her fragile sense of her own worth. Her self-worth was measured in how attractive she was to me, which she constantly questioned.

As a result of her extensive experience in therapy, Davida was what I call an expert patient. It seemed to me she drew on the conventions of treatment to thwart the work of treatment. Appropriately, she would state, "Treatment is only about my talking about my feelings." But she would only *express* her feelings; she refused to reflect upon them. In an aversive way, she held her thoughts and feelings to be absolutely true; there was no modulation to their intensity. If she felt the woman patient before her was a harridan, then she *was* a harridan. Period. Alongside the absolute truth of her feelings was an absolute sense of timelessness about them. If they were absolutely true, they were true forever. Yet this also meant that she could not think that her profound depressions, for example, would ever end. She could only experience and express her feelings; she could not reflect upon them or conceptualize their meanings.

Her hold on her feelings was modified somewhat by my interpretations. She responded when I said that perhaps she needed to hold onto her feelings so fiercely because she felt they were devalued when she was growing up. Somewhat reluctantly, she agreed when I said her feelings were not sacrosanct, but rather were a system of perceptions that could be as accurate or inaccurate as any other set of perceptions. From a self-psychological perspective, I think she used her severe affects as a reliable, if devastating, system that provided her with a selfobject experience. She *knew* how to be hopeless and severely depressed; it was organizing to her. Tellingly, she was often confused as she began to feel better because it was too different from her usual experience.

Davida and I began to get trapped in a very problematic pattern, in which she demanded that I tell her I loved her more than my wife. This would escalate to the point that she would sit within a couple of feet of me, and shout, "You must love me. You must love me more than your wife." I did not know how to react to this at first. I fell back on avoidance—trying to buy time through standard analytic reflection. This did not work for long, because she saw it for what it was. Clearly caught up in an enactment, I countered by rearranging my office between sessions and put a coffee table between us. *She* countered by pounding the table, shouting, "You must love me more than your wife. God damn it, I am lovable."

I tried different tactics to take refuge from these assaults. I said that treatment was not about *my* talking about *my* feelings, but rather *our* talking about *her* feelings. I said this since she demanded not just to know my feelings, but also demanded I say what she wanted to hear. She began to become self-conscious about these demands and worried I might not like her any more. I said that my feelings about her had not changed since the beginning of treatment. She countered that that could mean that I had never cared for her. But she remembered that I had told her very early in the treatment that I thought we could have been social friends if we had not met within the framework of treatment. She often used this to reassure herself of her worth.

She tried different tactics. She would say, "If you don't love me more than your wife, at least you have to love me as *much* as your wife," or, "Could you adopt me? Could I at least be part of your family?"

Again, there was no metaphorical dimension to these questions. She was incredulous that I might not love her. In those moments I would wonder to myself what I was missing, so strong was her self-righteousness. She implied—no, she stated—"Beyond being a bad analyst, you are a bad person unless you love me, as I deserve to be loved." And yet I stuck to my reality: I did not love her as much as my wife.

It was very difficult to find a way to explore her feelings, for Davida felt that if I wondered *why* it was so important for me to love her, then I must not love her. Finally, I was able to make some room for exploration by stating that my asking these questions did not have to mean that I did not love her, or that she did not love me, but rather that I was trying to understand her more deeply. At last themes could be isolated: she wanted to be a member of my family so that she could have a family; she wanted to be the most special person to someone because she had never felt that way before. Often, these statements were heartbreaking as Davida revealed her deep unmet needs.

Alongside these direct episodes between us, we were also doing ordinary analytic work. We worked on helping her learn how to self-regulate, especially how to soothe herself. I monitored her eating, as she often did not feed herself regularly. We explored until we hit upon her taking warm baths to help soothe herself. From a motivational systems perspective, her psychological regulation of physiological requirements was awry. We also worked on her reconceptualizing time so that an appointment in 24 or 48 hours did not seem so distant, and I reminded her of her own fantasy that there was a cord that connected us no matter how far apart we were.

Further, I was working on my own self-regulation. One way I was doing this was trying to encourage her to lie down on the couch. I believed her lying down would enable us to work on stabilizing her without her looking at me (and thus working toward her ability to stabilize herself when we were apart). Further, I needed relief from being looked at by her, so that an errant eyebrow twitch on my part would not become an issue in the treatment. At first she said, "I'm not lying down unless you lie down right here beside me." But eventually she became interested enough in what she thought of as "a real analysis" to try it and now she usually uses the couch.

At this point in the treatment, there was an unadulterated idealized selfobject transference. There were also strong elements of a mirroring selfobject transference, seemingly of a merger type, as I *had* to feel as she did because any sense of separate subjectivities would threaten her stability. But besides experiencing this transference, she also used it as a defense against working on issues of intimacy with others. She would tell me that, since I was the handsomest man on earth, how could she be interested in anyone else, that no one could compare with me. In more recent years, her idealizing transference has been modified—she has had a wish I had broader shoulders but, as she says, you can't ask for everything.

HISTORY

As I have stated, Davida was the oldest child of psychotherapists who were prominent in their community. For her father, treatment extended into his own family life. If she wanted to talk to him, for example, he would announce that she wanted a session.

Apparently, her father hated talking to his own clients when they called him at home, even though he gave them his home number. Davida said he would speak to them in a "normal way," and then afterward would degrade them to his family, ridiculing their problems. This hypocrisy disturbed Davida greatly, and she wondered if I did the same when she called me at home. I told her I did not and, over time, this calmed her worry.

Although her parents promoted the view that they had an ideal family to the outside community, her family was remarkably dysfunctional. For example, she has no memory of her family ever having a meal together. Each person, even the children, would cook for himself or herself. Her father disciplined his children by beating one with a belt, forcing the other children to watch before it was their turn.

Her parents' relationship was deeply troubled. They had a gender-stereotyped relationship typical of the postwar era. Her father worked outside the house and, before her mother became a therapist, she worked inside it. His job was to be the head of the house and hers was to serve him. This gender rigidity extended to their views of their children's gender roles.

Her father was abusively critical of her mother, undercutting her authority with their children, belittling her opinions and intelligence, and ridiculing her weight problems. Even as a young child, Davida suspected that her father was involved with other women, a suspicion that was borne out when her parents divorced when she was a young adult. Clearly, her father's unfaithfulness contributed to her hypervigilance of my authenticity in our relationship, which was evident by her difficulty believing that I cared for her. Her father's denigration of women did not stop at her mother. Davida remembers being in her bedroom, quietly playing with her sister when her father appeared at the doorway and muttered something Davida understood to mean "little whores." This was crushing to her, since it came completely out of the blue.

She remembers as a young girl consciously thinking that it was better to be a boy if being female meant being so powerless and abused. She remembers becoming a tomboy as a way to avoid being female. Feeding this avoidance was the flip side of her father's denigration of her—what she calls "dates" with her father. As a girl, beginning when she was about 12 and continuing until she left home for college, her father would insist she dress up and would take her to supper clubs, clearly pretending that she was his date. Her only bond with her father was as his "date." His positive regard of her, then, was based on this fantasy; she was desired only as something she was not.

Her relationship with her mother did not offer her much refuge. She has an early memory of trailing her mother throughout the house, repetitively asking her if she loved her. The image was of her mother's back, as she walked from room to room, away from Davida. Later, she felt her mother was competitive with her due to her father's attention. Davida remembers her mother usurping her place in the few relationships with other girls and women that Davida was able to make. Davida's friends soon became better friends of her mother.

Another important memory was from about 9 years of age. Davida decided to run naked into the living room when her parents had their best friends over. She had an unquestioned expectation that she would be adored. Instead, she was greeted by her father's harsh yelling: "Get out of here!" This is an example of her desperate attempts to break through to be "the apple of *someone's* eye."

Not surprisingly, Davida has had difficulty with interpersonal relationships. In her twenties, she had a series of relationships with men. These were intense, marked by her severe jealousy, and ended when the men left. Apparently they had had enough. In order to try to secure men for these relationships, she was indiscriminately promiscuous. She has also had what she calls two lesbian "flings." "It wasn't working out with men, so I thought I'd try women," she said. These relationships ended as her relationships with men had ended. She feared that I would be repulsed by these relationships because it would mean that I would see that she did not desire me, a man, and I would not desire her if she did not desire me. We had to have the same feeling in equal quantity.

Davida also reported that there were intense verbal fights in all these relationships. Into the night, she would badger the other person to agree that her point of view was right whatever it might have been, until finally, in exhaustion he or she would turn away from her. At this point she would physically attack her partner. Her fear of being separate could lead to her being aggressive, even violent.

From her early experience, Davida developed a hatred and fear of being a woman. She had a terrible dilemma: she knew she was going to become a woman, yet to be a woman meant being denigrated, as her mother's experience had shown. Then what kind of woman could she become? A siren? Yet her experiences of dates with her father could not be of use to her because she was never desired and seen as herself at the same time. She had an empty oedipal victory. Inevitably, her experiences were brought into our work together. She required me to be genuine with her, but demanded confirmation in a way that I could not provide in the treatment relationship. And if we *just* had a treatment relationship, then she was a patient like any other. In her experience, this meant being reduced to a secretly despised object.

MID-TREATMENT

A few years into the treatment, I told her I would need to be away for a week because my wife and I were going to have a child. My announcement precipitated a breakdown—she fell apart, screaming and crying. This was particularly traumatic for her because her previous therapist had adopted a baby, and Davida had ended the treatment with her. She said, "I'm a baby too, you know." I said I did know that. Slowly she came together. Finally, at the end of the session, she asked if she could hug me. I said yes, and she did. This is to date our own only physical contact. There was an intense vice-grip to this hug, a desperate, life-or-death quality. She asked that I call her when my wife went into labor so that she would know when our work would be disrupted, and I said I would. I did call her that day; she asked if I would think of her. I did say I would, although in truth I did not.

Unfortunately, my son's birth was difficult and life-threatening to both my wife and son. When I returned to my practice a week later, Davida asked, "First, is everybody okay?" "Yes," I replied. Then she said, "I wish they had died!" I said, "I'm sorry, but I can't hear that."

Introducing my own subjectivity into the treatment at this point seems to have had a mollifying effect on Davida. She did not pursue her desire that my wife and child had died, but our son's birth did precipitate another round of demands on her part that lasted for many months. This time it was: "Why can't we have a baby? Aren't I an attractive enough woman for you? If I were attractive enough for you then you would have a baby with me. Can't you just tell me if you hadn't met your wife, you would have married me? You said that we could have been social friends—couldn't we have been lovers, too?" Here was another dimension of her gender development: she thought of herself as female, but questioned her attractiveness as a woman. But she was also using her sexuality to prove her gender. The formulation was, If you are sexually attracted to me, then I am a woman, an attractive woman.

Again, I tried a variety of interpretations and interventions. I tried to distinguish between the ideas of being attracted to her and having that be so tied to having a baby together. I pointed out that I could not be sexually involved with her, because it would be unethical to do so since I was her psychoanalyst. Again, I could not marry her because as well as being her analyst, I was already married.

This intense psychological tug-of-war continued for some time. But finally I could not beat her at her own game. She was desperate to secure permanently her tie to me. She stated: "Even if we cannot be married on earth, we will be married forever in heaven."

And finally for me, enough was enough. I had had it with this psychic fencing. I became furious with her, and threw my pad to the floor. Enraged, I said, "God damn it! That is enough. I am sick of this pattern. We are not doing any work!" Astonished by and ashamed of myself, I said, "Neither one of us can speak until I have regained my temper." After a few moments, I said, "This is getting us nowhere. We have to figure out another way to work. For starters, it's important for you to know that I don't take kindly to being told what to do or being told what to say."

Interestingly enough, *this* combination of intervention and action got her attention. I think that I could have an impact on her because Davida was becoming secure in our relationship, because I had generally kept to the technique of exploration and interpretation, and because we had a shared history of my efforts to understand her. For the first time, once we began the pattern of her needing concrete statements from me, we did not always have to continue it. I could interpret to her that for some reason she felt insecure about our relationship, that she was caught up in a state, and that I needed her help to get her out of it.

Alongside these difficulties, there were signs of progress in the treatment. After considerable deliberation, Davida decided to adopt a cat. As a child, she had come to hate cats because she associated them with her being seen as evil when she dropped them from the roof. She was uncertain she could care for another being, but decided to give it a try. I was very touched when she named her cat "Michael," after me. Also, I was astonished when she referred a friend to me— first that she had this friend (I did not know that she had been developing relationships outside the treatment) and second that she was able to share me with another woman.

Davida had not given up all thoughts of our being together, however. She began to refocus on her idea that we would be married in heaven. This idea began to gather in frequency and intensity, especially since there was little progress in her intimate relationships with men here on earth. She had begun to notice that men were noticing her, but since none came close to my level of perfection, it was no use, she concluded, to pursue any kind of relationship with them.

This was about 10 years into the treatment, and she had not had sex since the treatment began. Nor did she have any masturbatory life. Masturbation necessarily involved fantasy, and her experience of fantasy was that it was a trap: if she had a desire, even in fantasy, it would not be fulfilled. In addition, in her conceptualization, fantasies could not come true, so they were prohibitive in that way also.

After being stalemated in this way for many months, I concluded that her idea of heaven was thwarting her life here on earth. This was especially so in light of her wish to marry and perhaps have a child. I decided to confront her with the idea that by focusing on our being together in heaven, she was neglecting living life on earth. Again, she strongly reacted: "You are saying we can never be married!" I pointed out that my emphasis was different—I focused on the fact that we *did* have a relationship and that we *were* together, although not in all ways.

So she began "dating"—with a vengeance. An only somewhat diluted version of the intense desire she directed at me was also directed at other men, apparently frightening many of them. During this time we came to understand that she had kept herself out of other intimate relationships because she would be too possessive and jealous, and she knew this could scuttle the relationship. But her feelings about our relationship began to change. She began to feel that our relationship was stable and that I had continued to accept her despite her deep fear that, if I knew too much about her, I would be repulsed.

Davida fell back into the pattern of her early twenties, in which she was promiscuous in order to try to secure a man for a relationship. But we had more freedom to explore her feelings, to try to understand what propelled her to go out looking for men. Usually, this was a collapse in her self-esteem brought on by professional and personal slights, and sometimes by a feeling that I was too distant. We were able to work through these crises, so that she could independently decide whether she wanted to go out. She learned to use the treatment to evaluate her states. She could ask herself: Do I feel desperate without knowing it? Should I stay in and protect myself? Am I safe enough to go out? (She could be reckless with her personal safety, both in terms of the men she picked up and in not practicing safe sex.) Sometimes this desperation reached the point that she had to pick up a man in order to see his erect penis, as a way to reassure herself that she was attractive. We have been able to work through this, as well, so that her self-esteem does not need to rest so exclusively on a sexual response. Nor does it need to rely on the response of an outside other, but can also be reasonably generated from within.

There has been a progression to her relationships with men. A wealthy businessman offered to keep her, but his availability only on his terms made this untenable for her. Besides, she did not want to be kept; she wanted a relationship.

This year, she had a brief relationship with a man, who, surprisingly, *she* felt was too intense. Although she loved that he was head-over-heels in love with her after just a couple of dates, she felt that this was not quite believable given the short time they had known each other. I wondered if the intensity of feeling that he felt for her might be off-putting in the same way that men had felt that her intensity of feeling had been off-putting to them. She was able to wonder about this too, and agreed.

CONCLUSION

Alongside beseeching me to tell her I love her, Davida has often pleaded with me to tell her I am sexually attracted to her. Although I have always concurred when she says she is an attractive woman, I have never answered her directly. At the beginning of the treatment, when she began making her demands, I did not find her attractive at all. Once she stated, "I am paying you to love me." I replied, "My love is not for sale." Over the years, however, as she has been able to soften these demands and become more vulnerable, she has indeed become more attractive to me. She has begun to take much better care of herself. She dresses more attractively and displays her good taste in jewelry. She no longer even asks me to tell her I love her; now she wonders why, at a particular moment, she is not able to feel the caring she knows I feel for her.

Recently, the treatment has been characterized by a variety of new experiences for her as well. The recent revival of interest in World War II made her wonder about her father's experience. Acting on my encouragement, she asked him what it was, and was empathic to him when he told her of being on Iwo Jima, desperate to survive in a landscape drenched in blood. Her social circle has widened considerably. Now she has friends who like her more than she likes them, which I think is real progress. She is able to date with more ease, although she complains that "men are such dicks" (another sign of her gender consolidation, as she is grouping herself with other women, against men). She has developed a sense of humor and can even laugh at the intensity of her feelings. She is more frequently able to feel joyful and to take pride in her accomplishments. Some happy memories have emerged from her childhood, such as being at summer camp, in a tree with a boy who also felt like an outsider, sharing bubble gum by passing it mouth to mouth. Finally, just this week she brought in a picture of herself at about nine years of age, the only one she has from her childhood in which she is smiling. I wish I could show it: She had just cut her hair herself, cutting off the bangs her mother wanted her to have. Now it was the way *she* wanted it. She has a wide self-satisfied grin.

Fourteen

GENDER AND TRAUMA
A DISCUSSION OF MICHAEL D. CLIFFORD'S CLINICAL CASE

VIRGINIA GOLDNER

*F*eminism and the postmodern turn have vaporized the commonsense meanings of gender and sexuality, both in psychoanalytic theory and, for many, as lived experience. Yet the so-called anatomical difference—a social distinction that fixates on the genitals, determining our sex assignment as man or woman— remains the first fact that matters about personhood. This foundational act of categorization exaggerates and mythologizes the relatively small anatomical differences between men and women, creating *The* Difference: a singular polarity of counteridentities that slip from body to mind, such that Man/Woman is made equivalent to the nominal gender categories Male/Female, which become conflated with the ideologically charged psychosymbolic categories of Masculinity and Femininity.

Note that even here, within our psychoanalytic community, gender has been installed in a taken-for-granted way. Much of our thinking has been *organized* in terms of nominal gender oppositions— male analyst/female patient—a format that conflates sex assignment (man/woman) with gender categorization (male/female) and makes the a priori assumption that likeness and difference can be mapped onto gender in some self-evident way, as in "same" or "opposite" sex pairs. But gender does not "speak for itself," to borrow Kim Leary's (1997) memorable phrase about race. Rather, she continues, it "is worn and lived similarly *and* differently by each one of us, flourishing in the tension between universal and unique experience" (p. 185).

There are a multiplex of intrapsychic, intersubjective and cultural processes that are engaged in the act of simply inhabiting a taken-for-granted gender category. Nominal gender—the category through which we are named and name ourselves male or female—is not an inert label, the "given" from which we *then* begin psychoanalytic inquiry. Rather, the intersubjective act of naming and being named a gender is a fraught dialectic. Messages and counter-messages about gender and sexuality are continuously being exchanged in conscious and unconscious registers between parents and children, romantic partners, and between each individual and the cultural archetypes that beckon. "In the dialectic of seeing and being seen," Adrienne Harris (1999) writes, "the body is the receiving and transmitting instrument . . . struggling in the rough and tumble play of visual contact" (p. 7).

From this social, intersubjective perspective, the question shifts from what gender "is" to how it is "used." From gender *per se* to (a) the *psychic and intersubjective work it is being deployed to do; and (b) how rigidly and concretely it is being used in an individual mind, family context, or treatment situation.* Put in Ogden's (1986) terms (a framework shared by Stern, 1985; Benjamin, 1988; and Fonagy, 1998), the important question is whether the subject experiences herself as personally investing gender and sexuality with meaning, or whether gender and sexuality are "meanings happening to her."

Which brings me to Michael Clifford's "heartbreaking" (his word—and so apt) case of Davida, whose concreteness about gender and sexuality reflected her pervasive inability to conceive of herself, or anyone else, as a center of subjectivity—a personal meaning-maker with intentionality and interiority. Davida's impairments in thinking extended to the psychoanalytic situation, since her limited capacity for mentalization and reflective function meant that she could only intermittently work symbolically and metaphorically in the transitional space of analytic treatment.

These handicaps of mindedness and of relatedness point to fissures in her self and sense of personhood that are evidence of traumatically induced deficits and of dynamically inspired identifications with an abusive parent and his perverse misuse of psychological speech. The extremity of the story that Clifford tells about the terrifying and hellish circumstances of daily life in Davida's household take us far beyond the psychic injuries we ascribe to gender stereotyping. Rather—and here is the reason for my extended theoretical introduction—gender conventions appear to me to have been merely normative conveniences through which Davida's father could structure his various methods of sadistic emotional abuse, all of which seem to have been aimed at destroying the personhood of family members, patients, and anyone else over whom he had power.

Whether or not Father took gender literally, he *used* it to hurt. Mental torture was his specialty—gender a means to that end.[1] But whatever his dynamics, gender served his tortured sensibility far too well. Davida's family story is a chilling exemplification of the pathogenic processes that are activated when gender is used to evacuate and project the intolerable onto other persons who are rendered without subjectivity. For all that feminism has accomplished, Benjamin's (1988) original insight still stands: the gender binary is not literally about masculinity and femininity, or even about activity and passivity, it is about the use of gender to divide persons into subjects and objects, producing the complementarity Male Subject/ Female Object. In this arrangement, masculinity is constituted as an illusory state of omnipotence that is sustainable only because dependency and vulnerability are projected onto femininity. Reduced to its pure form, woman's position as Other to the male Subject comes down to this: femininity "is" whatever masculinity repudiates.

In Davida's household, the heterosexual gender paradigm had devolved into its most primitive form: the Hegelian erotics of Master and Slave. In the psychic economy of that family, Father was Everything and everyone else was Nothing. Davida could have no mental contents of her own, no subjectivity independent of her father's mind, with its chronic needs for psychic evacuation. Father names her and everything about her—without me you are Nothing and with me you are Nothing. That is why, when the sisters are playing on their own, he calls them "little whores." It is intolerable for them to exist

---

[1] We do not, of course, know this man from the inside. He was not Clifford's patient, nor does the case presentation take up the question of how and why Father had become such a sadistic person—a line of inquiry that would not be unusual over years of work with such a severely abused person. We can only speculate about how the father's "being in Iwo Jima, desperate to survive on a landscape drenched in blood," was being reenacted daily in the family.

just for themselves, outside his orbit. If they can "go on being" without him, *he* is Nothing.

All this is repeated in the transference. While the analyst continually works to create a relationship of mutual recognition between subjects, Davida continually defaults to her Father's all-or-nothing, subject/object paradigm. In Benjamin's terms, this means one person asserting and demanding recognition, the other being forced to submit and to grant it. In this sense, Davida's insistence that the analyst can only think and feel as she does is a reflection of more than her primitive fear of difference. It is fear bred of an inability to conjure mental freedom itself. In her world of complementarities, if the analyst has a mind of his own, *she* will be negated.

This is why, whenever Clifford asserts his unique subjectivity—whether by departing, even momentarily, from his mirroring function or simply because he goes on living and working outside her sphere of influence, Davida becomes a petty tyrant, a pale imitation of her tyrannical father, but such are the limits of femininity. What is being repeated is actually quite literal—she is not only attempting to control the analyst's *mind,* but to control his actions as well. Thus she oscillates between demands that the analyst be enslaved in masochistic mirroring of her subjectivity and offering herself up as a sexual object for him since, in her primitive calculus, sex is also not volitional, but an addictive state that would keep the analyst enslaved. In all these gambits, we could think of Davida as trying to force Clifford into knowing first hand what total defeat and submission to another's will feels like.

It would, of course, have been catastrophic for Davida to succeed in corrupting the analyst or in obliterating his personal truth, an insight Clifford distills in one matchless statement: "My love is not for sale." As Benjamin (1988) demonstrated, once the partner forfeits subjectivity, he or she loses the ability to grant the other the recognition that true subjecthood requires.

But the damage had been done long before analyst and patient began their existential tug-of-war. Davida's fate was sealed when her father succeeded in destroying her mother. This shadowy, victimized woman, chronically debilitated by tending to and protecting herself from her sadistic husband, was in no condition to recognize or even tolerate her daughter's intelligent voice and palpable need. Davida got nothing but shame for wanting recognition in the family—

remember the desperate naked run into the livingroom—nor could Mother provide what Clifford calls "refuge," not even the "mother–daughter" bond that is sometimes the only consolation prize for the insults of patriarchy. Davida belonged nowhere—not as daddy's little girl, not as mommy's little helper.

Her experience of invisibility and objectification (really *thingification*) begins with maternal nonrecognition. Remember that the scene of the young daughter trailing her mother from room to room demanding to know whether she was lovable was played to her mother's *back*. Father's methodical rituals designed to underline that she really was a nonperson came later. In the dating ruse, one of the most novel and chilling versions of his strategies of gender objectification, it seems Davida is not even real enough to her father for him to actually desire her sexually—that would mean sharing some kind of intimacy in which he would be revealed as needing and enjoying her.

No. Father's aim is to constitute her an empty shell, a cardboard facsimile of a woman who is a sexual trophy in name only. His pleasures are only sadistic—the profound insult to his wife, the destruction of the mother–daughter bond, and the enthrallment with deception and betrayal above all. Father's relations with patients were structured around one simple cruel deceit: You think I care about you but I despise you. But in this oedipal masquerade, mendacity doubles back on itself. There was not only the simple deception: You think this beautiful woman is my lover, but she is my daughter. There is the further sham: She is my daughter-in-name-only, play acting at being my lover-in-name-only. In truth, she is a mannequin and a puppet that I brought to deceive you.

Which takes us to the horrifying story of the kittens that launches Clifford's case discussion and constitutes, in my mind, the central trope of the treatment. The cats were *her* of course, and the pseudoscience of throwing them off the roof to "see if they would survive the fall" was not only a reflection of how her self-estrangement alienated her from the murderous rage she must have felt about being negated. It was also, I believe, a reflection of her mental struggle with an authentic ontological question: can one be alive if one is not meaningful to another person? Since Davida was invisible, maybe she was a nonperson, an object. Alive perhaps, but not real. This is Kohut's territory—a child must not only be human, but *feel* human—not a "non-human monstrosity" (Kohut, 1977, p. 287).

Fonagy (1998) reports that maltreatment can produce deficits in mentalization that can cause a person to treat others like physical objects. It is poignant to imagine Davida on that roof, trying to think her way through the process and experience of objectification. Cognitively she knows the kittens are alive, but psychologically they exist only as objects to her, which is of course her experience of her parents' experience of her. If the animals died, would the actuality of their death make them (read her) come to life in the minds of her caregivers? Can sadism kill you? How far do I have to go to get someone's attention?

Since questions like these could not be consciously thought, they were repeatedly acted out in the analysis, as Davida found more and more ways to push the frame to its limits in order to see who and what would survive. None of this could be represented linguistically because words and speech, especially speech that mattered, could put a person at extreme risk for humiliation and worse. Father's psychotherapy practice was an object lesson in betrayal—when he was not lying to patients, he was exposing and degrading them. Moreover, he showed his contempt for clinical work by collapsing the metaphor of the treatment frame onto personal conversation, corrupting the integrity of both. When "needing to talk" is derisively relabeled as "wanting a session," heartfelt speech of either sort is rendered absurd and suspect.

No wonder Davida was an "expert patient, drawing on the conventions of treatment to thwart the work of treatment." She was taught by a master. But I also see her incessant challenges to the frame, including her inability/unwillingness to abandon concrete thinking in favor of reflectivity, as motivated, paradoxically, by her fervent desire to make the analysis honest and true. Her provocations were meant to drive the analyst out into the open. By making him angry enough to be "really real," she was probing for his uniquely personal subjectivity in order to make sure he was not another malingering imposter, hiding inside the conventions of analytic ritual and role. Only the specificity of the "spontaneous gesture" of the analyst's anger could reassure her that his empathy was also genuine, reflecting a personal choice to know her up close, rather than a technique-driven, guilt-ridden, or evasive maneuver.

As Clifford moves through the Stations of the Cross—from empathy to interpretation, limit setting, revelation, and finally to outburst, we see him working his way toward full participation. Early in the process, his personal anger at being browbeaten is still expressed coyly, as a procedural chiding: "treatment is not about *my* talking about my feelings, but *our* talking about *yours*" But finally when, as he writes, "enough was enough", we have this extraordinary sequence: "God damn it! I am sick of this!" followed by the mutually containing, bidirectional intervention, "neither of us can speak until I have regained my temper," and finished off with a small, but strong dose of (his) personal reality, "You should know that I don't take kindly to being told what to do or what to say!"

In these singular, pivotal moments, it is not the analyst's disclosures or bursts of aggression per se that are transformational. It is the *transparency of his working process* and what it reveals about him—his genuine struggle between the necessity for analytic discipline and need for authenticity. The richness of Clifford's internal process, and his willingness to reveal it in *statu nascendi*—as it is happening—gives Davida the critical data she needs. "This guy is real, his work is very hard (on him), he obviously cares about me and believes in this work."

Paradoxically, as the analyst takes incremental risks becoming more real, the patient returns his generosity by moving increasingly into the symbolic: from threatening to steal his last name in a unilateral and concrete move to become his adopted daughter, she ultimately gives his first name (the one reserved for personal relations) to the newly adopted cat, the transitional analytic object that could only now, in the context of their hard-won mutuality, come into being.

In the poetry that, retrospectively, shapes this story, we can see how the action of this case operates in the dialectic between empathy and authenticity, metaphor and actuality, the concrete and the symbolic, the reparative and the repeated.

But finally it is the marvel of Michael Clifford's staying power that warrants our deepest consideration. In lending himself to this project with such steadfast personal vitality, Clifford gave Davida the chance to destroy him and see him survive over and over again, thus resolving the lifelong paradox of the kittens, making life down here with the rest of us start to seem like a chance worth taking.

REFERENCES

Benjamin, J. (1988), *The Bonds of Love: Psychoanalysis, Feminism, and the Problem of Domination*. New York: Pantheon.

Fonagy, P. (1998), Male perpetrators of violence against women: An attachment theory perspective. *J. Applied Psychoanal. Studies*, 1:7–27.

Harris, A. (1999), Gender as a soft assembly: Feminism meets chaos theory. Presented at New York University, March.

Kohut, H. (1977), *The Restoration of the Self*. New York: International Universities Press.

Leary, K. (1997), Race, self-disclosure, and "forbidden talk": Race and ethnicity in contemporary clinical practice. *Psychoanal. Quart.*, 66:163–190.

Ogden, T. (1986), *The Matrix of Mind*. Northvale, NJ: Aronson.

Stern, D. (1985), *The Interpersonal World of the Human Infant*. New York: Basic Books.

Fifteen

REPLY TO DISCUSSION

MICHAEL D. CLIFFORD

I want to begin my reply to this discussion by thanking Virginia Goldner for her thoughtful response to my paper, in particular for her appreciation of my clinical work with Davida. This was a difficult treatment to conduct, and it was difficult to decide to present this case. So, I was very pleased to find in the discussion that Virginia responded with understanding and compassion for both Davida and me.

Goldner and I certainly agree that it was crucial for the treatment for Davida to push the limits of the frame, while needing me to push back. Goldner tended to think of this in terms of Davida's search for authenticity and my becoming more "real" in the treatment. There is a linkage here, however, that I would like to question. I hope that my discussant would agree with me that maintaining an analytic role (with its commensurate frame) would not necessarily be correlated with being inauthentic, or that breaking an analytic role (or frame) is inherently authentic. I think what makes the difference in this case was the context of the relationship between Davida and myself, which included a great deal of run-of-the-mill analytic work that was done by us as well as the crises I described.

Goldner has raised other questions to which I want to respond. I will make comments about three areas—two of which may seem odd—of the discussion. These are: general comments on gender and sexuality; a defense of the father; and a defense of objectification.

GENERAL COMMENTS ON GENDER AND SEXUALITY

Goldner begins her discussion by stating that "feminism and the postmodern turn have vaporized the commonsense meanings of gender and sexuality, both in psychoanalytic theory and, for many, as lived

231

experience." It may be that feminism and postmodernism have influenced *our* area of psychoanalytic theory, but I doubt that this is true of *all* areas of psychoanalytic theory. Further, as psychoanalysts per se, I think we live in rarified strata and, for better or for worse, do not represent the thinking of anyone but ourselves. Certainly, as an American psychoanalyst, I know my beliefs do not reflect many parts of American culture. We are all painfully aware of the power gender and sexual stereotyping have over parts of our country. The murder of gay men because they are gay is but one example of this. Even within the last couple of years, the Southern Baptist Convention—as the largest Protestant demonination, it represents some 40 million Americans—voted a theological position that a man is the head of the household and the woman and their children are subservient to him.

I raise this issue because, to oversimplify, I think we need to be careful that we do not believe too strongly that psychoanalysis is a better route to "the truth" than any other discipline. Further, I believe we need to be careful as analysts that we do not believe we have greater access to "the truth" than anyone else does. This self-confirming tendency coincides with how we view gender and sexuality. I think there *is* something unique about our own experiences of gender and sexuality that make our beliefs—and thus our theories—about them deeply held. Perhaps this is a reflection of our personal experiences as men and women, both in terms of gender and sexuality, and how most of us experience these areas as central to our selves.

That being said, I do believe that psychoanalysis and self psychology in particular can contribute a great deal to understanding gender and sexuality. I think this is particularly true for self psychology *because* our area of psychoanalysis focuses on self experience, and self experience is so central to both sexuality and gender, just as sexuality and gender are so central to self experience. I think we can make this contribution by continuing to do what we as self psychologists do best: through conducting treatments that focus on understanding the patient's *individual* experience. I believe this empathic focus can, to some degree, mitigate the tendency in all psychoanalytic theories toward reification.

A DEFENSE OF THE FATHER

Although it is clear that, *in my patient's experience*, her father is a first-class son of a bitch, nonetheless, I think we need to be careful not to correlate her experience with "the truth" and thus demonize him.

Indeed, the challenge with this man is to try to see his humanity. If we do this, we can see there is no reason to believe he did not come by his psychology as honestly as anyone else does. However, it has been difficult in this treatment to garner much information about the father. For much of the treatment, my patient experienced exploration of any issue other than *her* feelings as dreaded evidence of my disinterest in her. Part of my own thinking about the father is that his grandiosity was not appropriately reflected by his parents (perhaps for some reason connected with their experience as immigrants). Probably also his experience in the Second World War as a very young man was thoroughly traumatizing to him (and this before post-traumatic stress syndrome was recognized, and thus socially sanctioned, so he was more alone with his experience). We need to remember that he was only 17 or 18 years old when he lived through Iwo Jima. We may also dislike him because he was a therapist; this may be an additional insult to us, as we want our colleagues to be idealizable.

But I think it is not helpful in constructing a theoretical understanding of this case (and it certainly has not been helpful clinically) to see the father as anything else but a tortured human being who does what most tortured human beings do: in turn, they torture others. Indeed, to begin to empathize with her father has been a turning point for Davida. Not only does she not have to expend so much of her time and energy hating him (and thus is increasingly freed from the struggle of seeking recognition from him), but her own humanity is expanded by considering him as a person.

Along these same lines, it seems to me that Goldner correlates the master–slave relationship to male–female relationships too strongly. (At least she does not state that there can be exceptions to this correlation.) But we have all conducted treatments that involve male–female relationships that do *not* involve a master–slave correlation, and indeed have conducted treatments involving same-sex partners in which there *was* a master–slave correlation. Here, too, I do not see the mother only as a victim. There is something about seeing her only as a victim that feels as though it is another way to take away her subjectivity.

A DEFENSE OF OBJECTIFICATION

We live in a time and a culture that prizes individuality, and we practice a profession from a perspective that amplifies subjectivity, either of the patient or the patient–analyst dyad. Conversely, we tend to see objectification as antithetical to subjectivity, and thus only a negative thing.

Goldner emphasizes one kind of objectification in her discussion, an existential objectification that robs the person of humanity. She writes that my patient could "only intermittently work symbolically and metaphorically in the transitional space of analytic treatment." I agree, and what particularly interested me as her analyst was her *intermittent* ability. To me, this meant she sometimes had this ability, and what we needed to understand was what enabled her to work analytically and what led her to refuse to do so. My experience of this patient was that her objectification by her father—and her mother— was not so extreme that she lost her humanity (although her objectification was indeed extreme).

I would like to conclude my reply by suggesting that we need to remind ourselves that objectification does not have to be antithetical to subjectivity. Indeed, I would suggest that it is a common part of human experience to objectify other people without untoward consequences. To a degree, we objectify even when we so automatically categorize each other as men and women. We need to organize the world, and this is one way we do it. Thus, it is not surprising that most people see male/female as equivalent to masculinity/femininity and then with man/woman. I would argue that these are not *inherently* problematic equations. Further, it is a common experience for us to want to be seen by others as an attractive man or woman. I think this is a kind of normal self-objectification.

Finally, it is the experience of many people to objectify others by thinking more or less consciously, "I'd really like to fuck that woman (or man)." I would suggest that this is harmless in itself, and becomes problematic when it becomes an exclusive reaction. What we often see, however, is that patients will report these thoughts with intense shame. In these situations, if all else is equal, we need to help patients normalize this experience.

Sixteen

SEXUALIZATION IN A CLINICAL CASE

NANCY VANDERHEIDE

"*T*think I'm in love with you." The words hung in the air, and I knew it was a crucial moment in the course of the treatment. What to do? Interpret them? Ignore them? Refer? I hope to demonstrate with this case presentation that my appreciation of the hope-filled nature of the sexualized transference allowed my client, Josh, access to and flexibility with a greater range of affect states, and thereby an increased sense of self-cohesion. I believe that the sexualization occurring in this case expresses hope that injuries to the self can be healed, hope for engagement in self-vitalizing relationships, and hope that a relationship can in some way be a vehicle of self-transformation.

Sexualized phenomena manifest in many forms and represent various dynamics in the clinical setting. Recognition of the multiple roles sexualization can play, even in the course of a single analysis, provides invaluable perspectives within which to organize dynamic material. Kohut (1977) proposed that:

> The increased sexual activities and especially the so-called sexualization of the transference encountered in the early phases of some analyses of narcissistic personality disorders are usually manifestations of the intensification of the patients' need to fill in a structural defect. The manifestations should not be understood as an eruption of drives *but as expressions of the patients' hope that the selfobject will now supply them with the needed psychological structure* [pp. 217–218; emphasis added].

It follows that an openness to the possibilities inherent in such a profound expression of desire for human contact enables the analyst to work with the individual in a manner in which compassion, commitment to understanding the needs communicated, and the opportunity for a mutative, intensely affect-rich therapeutic relationship form the basis of the analysis.

Self psychologists and intersubjective systems theorists continue to broaden the roles ascribed to erotic phenomena by the classical traditions and object relations theories, which primarily emphasize oedipal dynamics and sexualization of maternal functioning (Blum, 1973; Person, 1985; Wrye and Welles, 1994). In an exceptionally clear paper, Trop (1988) differentiates between eroticized and erotic transferences, calling specific attention to the sexualization of selfobject needs for mirroring as well as to the developmental need to consolidate a sexual sense of self, respectively. The use of sexualization for a variety of self-regulating and self-vitalizing functions is essential. Sexualization can function as a primary source in the provision or maintenance of self-cohesion. Orange, Atwood, and Stolorow (1997) articulate the "antidotal function" of erotic phenomena when they prevent a calamitous disintegration of the self in the face of intolerable organizing principles. Josh declared his love and desire for me as we entered the second year of his analysis. As the process unfolded, I experienced Josh's contributions to the relationship as an expression of hope for emotional healing in a fragmentation-prone self and a chance for a new life characterized by enriched interpersonal relating. I approached his sexual feelings and fantasies in the same way I would deal with any intense emotions: by exploring with Josh their many and complex meanings. In doing so, I attended to the unique set of dynamics contributed by Josh, by myself, and by our relationship to the analysis, as urged in Bacal's (1998) specificity theory.

Though certainly fraught with management difficulties, awkward moments, boundary dilemmas, and downright discomfort, the relationship that emerged served multiple functions. Josh described himself as feeling alive only when he is deeply in love with and erotically attracted to a woman he experiences as emotionally attached to him. His sexualized feelings for me served as a vehicle for his attempts at relatedness. His sexualized idealization expressed deep needs for connection with an omnipotent other. Additionally, this idealization allowed him not only to make the one kind of connection that feels familiar and self-enhancing to him, but also brought his profound inability to form any other kind of emotional attachment directly into the therapeutic process.

An attractive man in his mid-forties, Josh introduced himself to me following a presentation I made to a lay audience, gave me his card, and asked if he could call me to make an appointment for psychotherapy. Within half an hour he called me from his cell phone asking to make an appointment as soon as possible. My sense of Josh's desperation and urgent need was reinforced at our first meeting, but it was not until we increased the session frequency to three and finally five times a week that the force of that need was focused directly upon me.

Josh's initial presentation was a catalogue of painful, failed relationships, excruciatingly low self-worth, tremendous anxiety, and overwhelming confusion about his place in his own life. A marginally successful small business owner with aspirations toward writing and playing music, Josh seemed torn between efforts to make intense contact with me and avoidance of contact by way of tangential, cryptic responses, remarks, and stories. He stated that he had been extremely impressed by my presentation, particularly my demeanor, which he experienced as confident, poised and calm—reflecting, I believe, his compelling search for an idealizable selfobject.

Josh described in a convoluted manner the difficulties he was having in his relationship with the mother of his six-year-old son. They had never married and he had moved out of the house they shared because their confrontations had grown increasingly destructive. They continued to have very close contact, however, as they shared caretaking responsibilities for the child. Josh was still in love with her and extremely accommodating to her wishes and needs, tentatively hopeful that his efforts would induce her to be nice to him and allow him more access to her. His requests for mutuality were met with scorn, derision, and withdrawal. Their contact was to be on her terms or not at all. When Josh came to see me, he was experiencing tremendous conflict between his enormous need for increased contact with her and his excruciating sense of loss and rage as he sacrificed aspects of his self to maintain his tie to her.

The other major aspect of Josh's initial presentation was his almost unbearable anxiety and crippling incapacity to self-soothe. A recovering alcoholic with more than ten years of sobriety, he relied on cigarettes, fantasy, and masturbation to manage his affect and anxiety. He felt something soothing in my voice and presence as I gave the lecture, and his ability to find a kind of calmness through his relationship with me continues to this time. Historically for Josh, to feel close to someone is to feel in love with and sexually desirous of her, desired by her or yearning for her desire. When experiencing these sensations, Josh feels vitalized, cohesive, and valued; as he says, at times like this he knows God loves him.

Josh has a twin sister and a brother three years his senior. Apparently his mother did not know she was pregnant with twins and was dismayed to give birth to the second baby, Josh. The family lived a somewhat isolated life in a harsh, rural environment. Both parents were physically abusive alcoholics. Josh was quieter and more sensitive than his rugged older brother and felt he was a disappointment to his father, who enjoyed the hunting, daredevil-type amusements, and sporting activities favored by his brother. Josh could rarely keep up with them. He was frequently injured, sometimes seriously, during these adventures and felt humiliated and scorned for his ineptitude. He has no memories of having felt liked or admired by his father; rather, he experienced a pervasive sense of deficiency, especially in comparison with his brother, who was also physically abusive to Josh.

Josh's mother seems to have had an extremely fragile sense of self-esteem; she frequently felt insulted and abused by those around her, and flew into scornful, contemptuous, violent rages at such times. Josh felt he was able to elicit intermittent positive attention from his mother only by providing her with self-enhancing supplies. His impression is that she was frequently overwhelmed by the demands of her family, poorly equipped to meet them, and that he was the primary cause of her difficulties. The experience of being a nuisance to his mother contrasts with memories of overstimulating, seductive qualities that she brought into their relationship. A vague, early memory of some kind of sexual stimulation by his mother around the age of three coalesced into a "peak experience" of bliss and self-worth, of being loved and accepted that Josh is understandably loath to relinquish. He recalls more clearly from older ages many incidents of his mother's drunken, flirtatious behavior with him, including making him dance closely with her. These are not pleasant memories as he felt exploited and coerced into serving self-enhancing functions for her.

Over the course of the first year of treatment, session frequency increased from once to three times and finally to five times a week. The increased contact greatly magnified the ever-present sexual undertones and associations of our interactions. Two months after increasing session frequency, Josh said that he realized he had a "crush" on me that felt somewhat juvenile to him, reminding him of the way a schoolchild might pine after a favorite teacher. Over the next two months the crush abated, to be followed by discrete periods of longing and daydreaming about me that finally coalesced into a continuous sense of being in love with me and desiring me sexually. I wondered how Josh would manage the intense affects involved in our relationship. I was also aware of the thin line between providing space for the frequently graphic content of his fantasies to unfold and contributing to an unbearably stimulating or depriving situation in the analysis. His capacity to tolerate his confusion regarding his deep and often painful preoccupation with me was encouraging, and I was heartened by the curiosity Josh evinced about the meaning of his fantasies and of my multi-layered importance to him.

From the outset, power themes materialized frequently in the work, as Josh continually strove to establish which of us had it and which lacked it. Early in the second year Josh was overwhelmed by discrepancies in our positions relative to one another. During this period of time he portrayed himself as a little boy infatuated with an omnipotent and unobtainable goddess. The following process notes reflect this experience. After several minutes of studious attempts to avoid meeting my eyes and halfhearted bids to engage me in conversation, I offer:

A: It seems kind of hard for us to get connected in here today. Are you aware of having some discomfort in making eye contact with me?

J: I can't look at you, I'm afraid of what I'll see in your eyes. You couldn't want to connect with me.

A: Do you think that what you will see in my eyes will shame you?

J: I'm already ashamed. I feel so pathetic; I couldn't bear to see your contempt or pity.

A: You seem very certain that those are the only options right now . . . what's going on?

J: [Bitterly] Goddesses don't generally have much interest in little boys.

A: Oh, I'm a goddess and you're a little boy? You feel ashamed; can you say more?

J: I'm in love with you, and have nothing to offer you that's worthy of you, I'm just a pathetic little boy and you can have any man you want. You already have me, for whatever that's worth. So I come in here and grovel about wanting you and your love so much. It just feels awful.

A: It feels awful to be seen by me as wanting so deeply.

J: And I can't ever hope to have what I want because I don't have what a goddess would want!

A: What does a goddess want?

J: She wants a man who is as strong as she is; no, stronger, who can carry her away and give her what she needs, everything she desires, things she doesn't know she desires.

A: Well, yes, I can see how that feels like an impossibly tall order . . . and it feels very black and white. Like in order to be loved you have to be big and strong and in control, as though there's nothing lovable about smallness, and needing something for yourself.

J: When you're small you can't do anything, I can't give you anything that would win your love.

A: Have you always felt that being loved depended on giving the other person something?

J: I don't know what you mean, isn't that how it works?

A: I get that you haven't had much experience in feeling loved for who you are, outside of what you do, or provide.

J: Once my ex realized that I wasn't going to get rich or win an Oscar she totally turned on me, I was worthless to her. I think she only wanted me for the sex, which got weird pretty quickly, and then she only wanted me because she wanted a baby. Once she saw that I couldn't provide the glamorous life she wanted she started to hate me. My other girlfriends loved me because of how I made them feel, special and good about themselves. Like my mother. As long as her esteem level was high, she was okay, but if you were in the way when she didn't feel good, watch out, that's when she would beat you up or be just wickedly nasty.

A: So of course you would do what you could to keep her as happy as possible. Which sounds like it wasn't easy, you must have really had to keep track of her moods.

J: [Animated] Oh yeah, I was scanning all the time, everything and everyone. I still do.

A: I imagine that's how you knew what would make your girlfriends feel special, you must have gotten very good at reading people for what they need or want. You also learned to be hypervigilant for any sign of potential trouble. Are you aware of scanning in here, with me?

J: Are you kidding? I am constantly taking your temperature. From the time I hear you opening the door to when I leave, and the rest of the day, I'm checking to make sure you're okay.

A: Okay with you?

J: Just okay in any way, mostly with me, but when you look like there's something going on at home or like you didn't get much sleep, I want to know what you need and I for sure don't want to add to your burdens. Like that idiot that is here before me sometimes, who messes up the waiting room. I get so full of fury when I see that, and I wish he was still here so I could tell him not to make more work for you. But I just say, "Josh, just clean it up and let it go."

A: It looks like it makes you angry even talking about it.

J: I just want to say to him, "How dare you come in here and give her more work to do? She doesn't need to be cleaning up after you when she has so much to do.

A: So much to do?

J: Yeah, I guess taking care of me. I'm so afraid you're going to get fed up and "graduate" me. So I don't want anything or anybody making anything harder for you.

A: So in addition to feeling as though you have nothing to offer me, you also feel like you could easily be a burden and make it even harder for me to be here for you. And then you feel like you have to clean things up for me, make things easier for me.

J: I *want* to do things for you, give you things, bring that smile to your face—it brightens up my life to see you smile at me. It makes me feel like I can do anything.

A: When you feel like someone you need or love is pleased, or likes you, you feel stronger.

J: No, when *you* are pleased or I can feel the warmth of you liking
     me, I feel more like a man, not a pathetic little boy, like I could be
     somebody.

A: It is so hard for you to feel anything but contempt for a little boy
     who wants and loves and wants to grow and heal. And you think
     that is how I feel too. I wonder what comes to mind when you
     think of Joey [his six-year-old-son] and how it is to be with him
     when he is hurting, or needing you?

J: [Breaking into a sob, cries for awhile. Silent for a minute.] I just
     had a picture of me coming over and sitting by your chair, with my
     head in your lap and you putting your hand on my head and just
     comforting me.

A: What does that feel like?

J: Good. Like maybe there is something good about me. God, I am
     so lonely [starts crying again]. I hurt so much.

A: I know. I think you've been alone, and lonely, for a very long
     time. And it really hurts when you let go of your scanning and
     wind up feeling all the loss and sadness and loneliness you've lived
     with since you were very little.

J: No way I could do that with my mother or any of the women in
     my life. It was definitely "I'll give you something to cry about."

A: Exactly.
     [We were silent for a few moments before the session's end drew
     near.]

J: [Wonderingly] Right now I can almost feel loved by you.

A: I think you are experiencing what it is like to feel lovable.

Early in our work together, I discovered that an effective way to
work with Josh is to frequently "wear the attributions" (Lichtenberg,
Lachmann, and Fosshage, 1992) in order to facilitate an understanding
of the way Josh organizes his life experiences. Invalidation of his
experience contributes to his compliance with the dictates of others.
His emotions are then driven further out of awareness and rendered
even less available for his constructive use. Therefore, I tend to allow
the qualities, fantasies, characteristics, and motivations he attributes
to me to go neither challenged nor validated. There is, thus, more
room to generate and explore the associations he has to them.

The impact of this stance on the analysis has been profound in
many ways. I will now relate three interactions that illustrate this

impact. The first incident revealed in an affect-laden way for both of us an important element in Josh's experience of relationships. During a break before a session with Josh, I did some errands outside the office, and he saw me as I was walking back to my building. His first comment as we got settled into the session was, "Wow, I nearly crashed my car getting here. I was driving along and saw this gorgeous blonde with a great figure walking down the street and then I said, 'Oh my God, that's Nancy!'" He was laughing as he said it, but was clearly shaken in some way. His conclusion was that I had separated from my husband and "had my lures out" to land a new guy. I acknowledged the impact this event had on him and wondered what other feelings it evoked. He replied that for some weeks now, he had noticed that I dressed up more on Wednesdays and he'd been thinking that maybe I was going to some kind of singles event on Wednesday nights, and that he imagined I was getting a lot of male attention and men asking me out. I observed that he felt that with the way I was dressing I would be successful in attracting attention. He laughingly said that I was certainly being successful in getting his attention and that he almost had a wrecked car to prove it.

I said, "I know you're laughing about this, but I can't help wondering if you are having some more feelings about it." He said yes, that it felt very frustrating because here he was, seeing someone who really turned him on, but there was nothing he could do about it. Additionally, he felt humiliated because I was getting so many ego strokes and so much admiration from him. He was angry, he said, that I was getting my need for attention met through his attraction to me. He then fell silent and grew somewhat agitated.

I said, "I wonder if in some way what happened has compromised your sense of safety in here today." He asked what I meant, and I noted that he seemed to be referring to something dangerous in talking about almost crashing his car and that somehow my motives in dressing the way I had were implicated in that danger. That is, my appearance provoked sexual attention, and was undermining his sense of safety in our relationship in ways that seemed important for us to explore. He agreed that he wasn't feeling safe but didn't know how or why. I mused that he was feeling somewhat used, in a way that he had also mentioned in the past, that his admiration of me provided me with ego strokes and ways of feeling good about myself without concern about the pain this caused him. He added that it was even worse because it involved sexual feelings and he always was punished when he talked about feeling sexually attracted to women, even when it was clear that they were doing something to arouse him. It appeared to him that they got the affirmation they needed, and he was left feeling like a fool.

I said, "Then, in a way we are doing something with each other that you've had a lot of experience with. Through my dressing a particular way, I am being the seductive exploitative woman using you to fill my ego needs, and you are the seduced, exploited victim left frustrated and rejected."

He said, "My God, you could be describing my relationship with my ex-girlfriend, my ex-wife, my mother."

Josh's experience of being exploited in relationships with enticing, frustrating others thus became a live part of our engagement with each other. Interestingly, I did wind up feeling as though I were in some way being seductive: he certainly was interested, and quite frankly, I was flattered; my sense of self *was* enhanced. I felt the power inherent in that position and knew in a visceral way just what he was up against and how powerless he was to resist his attraction. In effect he was held hostage by his compelling need and desire for me.

A second illustration comes from my observation that attributions evoked in different but similar circumstances changed with the state and context of the analytic relationship. For example, at a time near the initial disclosures of Josh's erotic feelings about me, he interpreted the new artwork hanging in my office in the following way: I had separated from my husband, largely on Josh's account, and moved into an apartment not suited for the newly relocated pictures. This new situation rendered me available and willing for courtship, and he was ready to proceed with it.

By contrast, at a later point in the analysis, when he was absolutely convinced that my romantic interest in him was finally stronger than my ethical and legal obligations, his reaction to a similar situation evoked terror of being suffocated by my neediness and demands for him to accommodate to the various sexual and emotional needs he perceived I required. Again, allowing his attribution to go unchallenged permitted us to arrive at a juncture wherein I could say to him: "You are worried that my availability to you gives you no other choice than to forever sacrifice your own needs, wants, and self to meeting my needs."

The third vignette took place a year and a half into the analysis. Josh had to deal with an extremely important business situation that held potentially devastating consequences for him. For some time he had been discussing the painful experience of having fallen in love with me. A few weeks before the business event he began to describe the evidence mounting in his mind that I had fallen in love with him as well. Each time we met he was more convinced that I was leaving my husband and considering abandoning my career as a psychotherapist. Regardless of my approach with him, Josh construed my every move as validation of the deep, enduring love I held for him, my commitment to his victory, and my desire to be with him as much as he wanted to be with me. The upcoming event took on the feel of a grand battle and on the evening prior to it, he called and left me a voice message reiterating his deep love for me, and excitedly telling me he now understood the relationship we had: He was Lancelot, galloping off into a battle where the righteous would prevail, and I was his Guinevere, holding my secret love for him to my heart, and prevented from betraying King Arthur (i.e., my husband and sense of ethics) by a pureness of spirit that was being sorely tried by my heart's burning love for him. He had something to live for regardless of the outcome. I was concerned about the manic tone of his communication and wondered about the degree to which his connection with reality was seriously impaired, but decided that challenging him at that time would not be useful. Additionally, it seemed possible that Josh was utilizing a "fantasy selfobject" (Bacal, 1981), in other words, a selfobject created by his own particular needs rather than by a function I was providing, to maintain a sense of self-cohesion during this extremely frightening time.

Josh survived the challenge, though it did not resolve in his favor. Significantly, he was no longer Lancelot when we next met; nor was I Guenevere. In retrospect, he evinced a certain amount of confusion regarding his conviction of the last few weeks. He was devastated by the event's outcome, which held for him implications that seemingly validated his sense of himself as defective, worthless, and dangerous. These feelings were now more available for processing.

Throughout the analysis I have concentrated on developing and maintaining an awareness of my contributions to Josh's experience in the relationship. My reactions and emotions do play across my features, and Josh readily observes and makes meanings of them. He often shares his observations about my behavior, and I am frequently able to see the proverbial kernel of truth in what he sees as well as the way his interpretations emerge in the context of his current needs and fears. It is readily apparent that my process has been significant in the development of our relationship. I hope to demonstrate this in the following, and final, section.

Sometime into the second year of the analysis, my own mother was suddenly hospitalized for acute respiratory failure triggered, apparently, by a routine bronchoscopy. This event and what followed were of great significance to my process in this analysis. In my urgency to cancel my patients for the day, I did not provide much information about the circumstances, merely that I had a family emergency to which I had to attend. Josh's return call both acknowledged the session cancellation and voiced more than a little concern and anxiety, especially with regard to my own health and well-being. He requested that I call him back as this occurred on a Friday and he would be anxious all weekend. My mother's condition was shocking and deeply unsettling to me. It did, in fact, portend the steep decline that would culminate in her death within six months from what was finally diagnosed as lung cancer.

My return call to Josh had the unexpected effect of providing the leverage for pivoting our relationship into a new dimension. As I found out some time later, my disclosures of the circumstances of my absence, which included what I had felt to be sufficient but minimal details regarding my mother's situation, were experienced by Josh as my opening up to him in a very personal and intimate way. In retrospect I realize that I was receiving comfort from his heartfelt concern for my family and me; his responses were, as usual, deeply attuned to my state of mind. For his part, he was elated and immediately developed an unshakable experience of me as quietly but desperately needing him, giving him the opportunity to provide me with sustaining selfobject supplies. He became very solicitous in the sessions, imploring me to be sure to take care of myself during these trying times.

Interpretations to the effect that he was putting my needs ahead of his, thereby shifting the focus of attention to me, or that he was naturally worried about my state of mind partly because my therapeutic availability to him was contingent on my emotional well-being were met with a cross between acquiescence and a lovingly patronizing attitude that he knew, and he knew I knew he knew, just how delicate I was. He began treating me with utmost tenderness and accepted my interventions with gratitude that I could continue to focus on him in spite of my own pain.

As I processed the enormous changes that were, in fact, occurring in my life, I finally realized that Josh's solicitations were involved in evoking archaic needs of mine to be cherished, adored, and taken care of. My mother's obviously impending death was reemphasizing a sense of longing and loss of the opportunity to feel special and important enough to her, and Josh's continual, ever-more-finely attuned attention and obvious adoration provided an environment for the emergence of selfobject needs and longings of my own. These needs met with his in the intersubjective field with startling impact. I believe that I began colluding with his ever-present desire to move away from both his own threatening selfobject needs and long-buried grief and towards the warmer climes of ostensibly discussing the analytic implications of his expressions of love and desire for the most beautiful, intelligent, gifted, and otherwise wonderful woman in the world—namely, me. This phase lasted a number of weeks before I realized how much I looked forward to the sessions, and the nature of the collusion dawned on me. I was chagrined to realize that, despite all I knew about Josh's time-honored tendency to play to the vulnerabilities of his audience, I had succumbed to this combination of high idealization and well-directed flattery. But I also knew that we were engaged in a powerful drama that was the chorus of Josh's entire life's score.

I proceeded to outline for Josh some of what I thought was going on in terms of our joint efforts to ward off working in painful areas by seeking pleasurable experiences in the guise of exploring his erotic and idealizing fantasies. The only portion of this brilliant interpretation that registered was confirmation to Josh that I was indeed looking to him for solace, comfort, and enlivening and that, in fact, I had fallen deeply in love with him and was now considering leaving my husband and career for him. His initial jubilation at this turn of events slowly began to trigger anxiety and ultimately terror as the ramifications of actually considering the consolidation of our lives in a romantic relationship became very real for him. Now he was experiencing me as the woman for whom he would have to sacrifice himself, in order to provide the physical, sexual, and emotional support necessary for the maintenance of my precarious self-worth, upon which his survival depended. We moved firmly into the repetitive dimension of the transference, characteristic of all of his relationships with the valued women in his life.

My every behavior was seen by Josh as exemplifying my neediness and/or denoting unconscious denial of my feelings. Observation of certain physiological phenomena such as my blushing, averting my eyes, or some other form of body language were interpreted by Josh as absolute proof that I was desiring him in an erotic way and disowning that desire. His experience of what he felt to be my (possibly unconscious) sexual desire for him placed him in an untenable bind. On the one hand, he wanted in some way to force his way through my denial and fear of sacrificing my stable but mundane existence for a more fulfilled life as "his woman." On the other hand, but often simultaneously, he felt a desperate need to escape his palpable sense of revulsion and contempt for my neediness and terror of my suffocating feminine wiles. These opposing needs frequently appeared as extremely rapid oscillations between his fear of losing my interest in and care for him, and what he described as "deep contempt for [my] solicitousness," which he experienced as a seduction aimed at trapping him into sacrificing his self to meet my needs. At times these oscillations were slow enough to be quite clear to both of us and easily seen as triggered by changes in the levels of closeness experienced in the relationship. He was surprised at the degree of his repulsion at the mere thought of actual physical intimacy with me and associated to previous relationships in which sexual consummation was attended by a loss of his sense of self, which he experienced as co-opted by the woman he was now "servicing."

Fortunately, he had acquired sufficient affect tolerance and curiosity about his processes (as well as a certain amount of trust in me) that we were able to suffer through this incredibly painful time without any breaks in the sessions or the analysis, although such interruptions appeared perilously close many times. He was quite brutal in his castigations of me for abandoning my duty to him and my ethics by falling in love with him. He made continual reparations out of fear of having damaged me with his rage and sense of betrayal (such as calling me with apologies and endearing sentiments after particularly harsh sessions), and felt confused by being drawn in so many discrepant directions. That this was the course of all of his significant relationships provided a context in which to examine the status of our own relationship. Focusing primarily on the bind in which he was caught, we were able to explore the emotional outcome of seemingly getting what he thought he wanted, and upon which he had always pinned any hope he had of relief from his inner torment. This portion of the work exposed his abject horror of the intimacy that Josh had claimed from the start was his only salvation.

My observations that he quickly found a way to distance himself whenever he felt we were particularly close or that I had made an unsolicited move in his direction were supported by countless examples that became increasingly identifiable to him. For example, my coming to a session without my wedding ring was immediate and absolute proof to him that I had separated from my husband. And, in contrast to his many pleas that I take a chance and do just that, he was terrified that I would "show up on his doorstep" and became enraged with me for abandoning my duties as both wife and therapist. His own curiosity about his reversal provided a counterbalance to his felt experience of me as wishing to hold him in my power to meet my own needs, enabling us to explore his feelings without either discounting or validating his perceptions. He came to the conclusion himself that my appearing ringless could actually have many other possible meanings. His reaction to that realization was tinged with both relief and sadness. Of significant importance was his ability to hold those discrepant feeling states simultaneously, allowing us to exist for periods of time in conscious awareness of the enormous conflicts existing in his relationship to personal intimacy.

Feelings of loss, grief, sadness, futility, and despair began emerging more discretely, along with his recognition that he has spent nearly his entire life looking for someone to protect or distract him from those feelings or, at other times, to "plug into himself" in order to provide a sense of vitality and self-cohesion. His thorough familiarity with the fact that he has used other substances and behaviors for the same purposes mobilized his interest in continuing to explore, rather than to act on or run away from, his feelings and urges.

DISCUSSION

For a significant portion of Josh's analysis, his sexualization of our relationship and of me served as his sole vehicle for attempts at relatedness. We engaged in unique forms of relating which served different functions at different times. At times the sexualization seemed to provide an antidotal function (Orange, Atwood, and Stolorow, 1997), that is, to protect Josh from self-fragmentation upon the activation of catastrophic organizing principles involving his sense of self-worth, or from exploration of other areas of intense fear and grief. However, much of the time it expressed Josh's hope that deep involvement in our relationship would function as a process of self-transformation similar to the function that mutual self-and-other regulation in the mother–infant dyad serves in moving the infant from states of distress to states of well-being (Beebe and Lachmann, 1994). Finally, it was always a primary means of communicating affect states and intersubjective experiences that permitted the understanding and illumination of Josh's patterns of involvement with others, facilitating positive self-state changes.

As is true in the case of any relational pattern, the so-called erotic transference conveys information available for analytic use. Much as a patient whose only available means of relating is through anger or hatred would be ill-served by being forced, cajoled, or interpreted out of that way of being with the analyst, Josh needed my willingness and ability to engage with him in intensely erotic feelings and understand them as a means of self-expression. Transitional space (Winnicott, 1951) emerged within which we could explore the many levels of feelings involved, the relational needs being conveyed, significant organizing principles, and prevailing motivational systems. Both the repetitive and developmental, forward-edge dimensions of the relationship emerged in this space, available for analytic processing and transformation. Gradually, Josh is awakening to the nature and legitimacy of some of his deepest needs for safe self-expression, positive mirroring, and a calm, reliable environment in which he can begin to experience a transformed sense of self.

Bacal, H. A. (1981), Notes on some therapeutic challenges in the analysis of severely regressed patients. *Psychol. Inq.*, 1:29–56.
———— (1998), Optimal responsiveness and the specificity of selfobject experience. In: *Optimal Responsiveness: How Therapists Heal Their Patients*, ed. H. Bacal. Northvale, NJ: Aronson.

Beebe, B. & Lachmann, F. M. (1994), Representation and internalization in infancy: Three principles of salience. *Psychoanal. Psychol.*, 11:127–166.

Blum, H. (1973), The concept of erotized transference. *J. Amer. Psychoanal. Assn.*, 29:61–76.

Kohut, H. (1977), *The Restoration of the Self.* New York: International Universities Press.

Lichtenberg, J., Lachmann, F. & Fosshage, J. (1992), *Self and Motivational Systems: Toward a Theory of Psychoanalytic Technique.* Hillsdale, NJ: The Analytic Press.

Orange, D., Atwood, G. & Stolorow, R. (1997), *Working Intersubjectively: Contextualism in Psychoanalytic Practice.* Hillsdale, NJ: The Analytic Press.

Person, E. S. (1985), The erotic transference in women and in men: Differences and consequences. *J. Amer. Acad. Psychoanal.*, 13:159–180.

Trop, J. (1988), Erotic and erotized transference—a self psychology perspective. *Psychoanal. Psychol.*, 5:269–284.

Winnicott, D. W. (1951), Transitional objects and transitional phenomena. In: *Collected Papers: Through Paediatrics to Psycho-Analysis.* London: Tavistock, 1958, pp. 229–242.

Wrye, H. K. & Welles, J. (1994), *The Narration of Desire: Erotic Transferences and Countertransferences.* Hillsdale, NJ: The Analytic Press.

Seventeen

MIRRORING AND MENTALIZING
A DISCUSSION OF NANCY VANDERHEIDE'S CLINICAL CASE

HANS-PETER HARTMANN

*I*n connection with this case report I would like to quote Christel Schöttler (1993, personal communication), who observed with regard to such difficulties as are described here: no development without involvement.

Josh quickly develops the form of relationship to his analyst that he experienced as vitalizing with his mother: He feels erotically attracted to his analyst, idealizes her, and does everything to bring her to a state in which she would reciprocate his desire. The repetitive aspect of the transference thus comes into the picture, together with Josh's lack of conviction that he can experience himself in any other way. This repetitive transference mode represents a form of bondage which is also reflected in Josh's addiction problems. Addictive behavior originates with the incapacity to be able to soothe the self.

In Josh's case, the early affect mirroring (Gergely and Watson, 1996) appears to be severely disturbed by a narcissistically abusive mother as well as physically abusive parents. In contrast to Kohut's mirror transference, affect mirroring is described quite differently first by Gergely and Watson (1996) and later by Fonagy et al. (2002) as a process in which the parents in reaction to the infant's emotion expression "mark their affect mirroring displays to make them perceptually differentiated from their realistic emotion expressions" (p. 177). Thus the infant notices this markedness. According to Dornes (2000): "They [the parents] confront him/her with an 'as-if' joy. . . . They 'play' with his/her smile in their response [pretend play]. The markedness that results from this exaggeration allows the infant to realize that the parents are representing something and not only expressing something of their own" (p. 196). As a result of this markedness, according to Gergely and Watson, a referential decoupling occurs; that is, through this exaggeration, the infant can perceive the mirrored affect as not belonging to the other.

Finally, referential anchoring occurs, whereby the infant recognizes his/her own affect in the other. In this model of affect mirroring, affect regulation at an elementary level is also possible. In a further step, according to Gergely and Watson, the infant's emotional state becomes representable through the affective reactions (facial expression) of his or her caregivers. According to Dornes (2000), the facial expression of the parents thus becomes a representation of the infant's own emotional state. "In the further course of development, whenever the primary affect arises, to which the parents react with mirroring, the (secondary) representation of the affect is also activated . . . [this representation] now carries out signal functions, informs the subject of ongoing processes and contributes to their regulation" (p. 202). The secondary representation thus takes over all affect regulation functions of primary affect mirroring. Via this externalization of his/her own affect state, the infant learns to regulate his/her affective impulses. This may correspond to the feeling of infant omnipotence—being able to cause and control events (Fonagy and Target, 2002).

When mothers have difficulties with their own affect regulation, as we may assume was the case with Josh's mother, who showed symptoms of a borderline personality disorder and was addicted to alcohol, they are overwhelmed by the negative affect of their children, and congruent affect mirroring occurs without markedness. When confronted with the distress of their infants, such mothers tend to express the same affect in a realistic way, and not marked. The child therefore does not develop secondary representations of his or her primary emotional state, which results in deficits in self-perception and affect control. No regulative limiting of the child's negative affect can occur through the parents, and this results in traumatization instead of containment. In terms of self psychology, the regulative function of an archaic selfobject is missing.

Additionally, in the case of Josh's mother, incongruent mirroring was also marked, evidently when she was drunk. She mirrored her own sexual and tender, needy side to him, and thus did not match his affect as an infant: that is, her mirroring was incongruent, although emphasized and thus marked. The purpose of this oblique mirroring was her own vitalization through her son. Thus she framed Josh's experiences as a toddler, but did not mirror the boy's masculinity in a phase-appropriate way. She was searching for a partner over whom she would have control and who would mirror her femininity through his sexual reactions. Such children are later fully adapted to referencing the expressive behavior of the caregiver as though it were their own. They deliberately seek out dependent relationships in later life in order to, as Fonagy and Target (2002) express it, restore the situation of adaptive subjugation and, in this way are able to experience a feeling of their own existence.

Josh seems to have no organized working model of attachment; through compulsive sexualization, he attempts to exert control over his essential selfobject, the loss of which he constantly fears. He wavers between control of the beloved, sexualized analyst and being controlled by her.

The rejecting father renders a loving and idealizing relationship with him impossible and makes the process of mentalization, which could help him distance himself from his seductive and exploitative mother, more difficult. He has no alternative to her. To be able to establish a triadic relationship, the child must be in the position to imagine how his relationship to his mother is perceived from the perspective of a third person outside the relationship. That is, the child must be able to imagine how a third person might feel when he or she experiences an exclusive interchange between two others.

This situation resembles Piaget's (1983) Three Mountains experiment, in which he asks the children what perspective of the "three mountains" the doll will "see" from the other end of the table. The development of a feeling for the mental presence of the other in the mother–child dyad is, however, a prerequisite for such mentalization processes. Thinking about the mental state of the primary caregiver is only possible when the caregiver is not hostile and abusive toward the child. Therefore it was not, or not sufficiently, possible for Josh to acquire a complete theory of the inner life of either his mother or his father, both of whom physically and mentally (especially narcissistically) abused him. Without the acquisition of such an adequately resilient and reliable theory, it is not possible to see one's own affects and fantasies in relative terms and to put oneself in the place of the third person.

Considering Josh's life story, it is hardly surprising that his sexualized feelings touch the analyst, flatter her, and increase her self-esteem or that she falls under his spell. I have asked myself whether a small clue to this development is found in the text in the form of a slip of the pen. VanDerHeide writes: "I felt the power inherent in that position and knew in a visceral way just what he was up against and how powerless he was to resist his attraction" (instead of *her*—presumably what was meant was his attractiveness to her!). I wonder whether she is communicating some aspect of the erotic countertransference. For me, the psychopathology of everyday life, as demonstrated by such a slip, is the most convincing sign of enmeshed relationships.

The difficulties the analyst encounters with such a sexualizing transference also become clear at another point. Although VanDerHeide emphasizes how much she attempts to carry out one of Lichtenberg's principles (Lichtenberg, Lachmann, and Fosshage, 1992), namely to wear the attributions, she does not apply this principle in a moment of intense meeting. Josh says: "Right now I almost feel loved by you," and VanDerHeide responds: "I think you are experiencing what it is like to feel lovable."

This well-intentioned remark, which was intended to help Josh with the clarification of his feelings, instead detached him from these feelings. I assume that at this moment VanDerHeide found herself in considerable emotional proximity to Josh and—for whatever reason—distanced herself from this closeness. Possibly a "moment of meeting" (Stern et al., 1998) was missed since a "now moment" seems to me to have occurred.

At another point, VanDerHeide aptly interprets the sexualized aspect of her relationship: "Through my dressing a particular way, I am being the seductive exploitative woman, using you to fill my ego needs, and you are the seduced, exploited victim left frustrated and rejected."

My impression is that Josh uses the feeling of efficacy that he can experience through sexualizing relationships to increase his cohesion because the fundamental attachment relationship, his inner working model of attachment, is not organized. Thus his erotic transference is a consequence of a threatened sense of self or, as Wolf (1994) expressed it: "Sexualization occurs in selfs that defend against fragmentation . . . by reorganizing regressed and excited sexual fantasies into a replica of the original self-sustaining selfobject configuration." Josh feels abandoned, but he is also annoyed that he does not withhold his participation. Josh behaves like a codependent which, as the child of his addictive mother, he also was, and as such he develops a bondage in his relationship to the analyst through which he attempts to maintain the relationship and to gain control over her. Otherwise he would have to bear his own painful emptiness inside. Thus his own neediness and the realization of his selfobject needs, particularly with regard to his affect regulation (attachment), remain neglected, as was the case earlier with his mother.

Finally, I would like to comment briefly on the specific problems of the combination of a female analyst and a male patient. In the case of Josh, it is obvious that he rapidly falls into the relationship pattern with the analyst that he had toward his mother. Sexualization would not have occurred with a male therapist and, presumably, as a result of his experience of violence and rejection on the part of his father, he would not have sought out a male analyst. Josh remains in a "confusion of tongues" (Ferenczi, 1933) towards his therapist in that he speaks the language of passion and seeks tenderness. Thus, in his manifest behavior and expression of his needs, he remains caught in the common stereotype of masculinity found in western culture: sexuality and eroticism toward women are basically given prominence at the expense of sensuality. Sexuality or sexualization is possibly the (predominant) male form of symbolization of infant requirements. From the point of view of developmental psychology, the characteristics of showing signs of weakness as well as concern and care for others are more likely to be ascribed to girls than to boys and, in fact, by their mothers (Bischof-Köhler, 2002). In an analysis of American films, Gabbard and Gabbard (1989) determined that there is a stereotype of what happens when a male patient consults a female analyst: in American cinema, a female analyst only successfully treats a male patient when she falls in love with him and vice versa, and according to this stereotype, male patients then heal their female analysts—they actively do something instead of being passive recipients. Men evidently have extreme difficulty showing their passive requirements and reconciling them with the traditional active male sex role. In Josh's case, this basic problem is certainly compounded by the physically and narcissistically abusive mother and the rejecting father. In our western culture it is much more forbidden for men to be in dependent relationships with women than to talk about sexual feelings with them. But in Josh's case the development of sexual feelings in the transference is not or not only a consequence of his need to find a way out of powerlessness and shame but also a source of suffering.

REFERENCES

Bischof-Köhler, D. (2002), *Von Natur aus Anders. Die Psychologie der Geschlechtsunterschiede [Different by Nature: The Psychology of Gender Differences]*. Stuttgart: Kohlhammer.

Dornes, M. (2000), *Die Emotionale Welt des Kindes [The Emotional World of the Child]*. Frankfurt: Fischer.

Ferenczi, S. (1933), Confusion of tongues between adults and the child. In: *Final Contributions to the Problems and Methods of Psycho-Analysis*, ed. M. Balint. London: Karnac, 1980, pp. 156–167.

Fonagy, P., Gergely, G., Jurist, E. L. & Target, M. (2002), *Affect Regulation, Mentalization, and the Development of the Self*. New York: Other Press.

———— & Target, M. (2002), Neubewertung der entwicklung der affektregulation vor dem hintergrund von Winnicotts konzepts des "falschen selbst" [Evaluation of the development of affect regulation from the perspective of Winnicott's idea of the "false self"]. *Psyche-Z. Psychoanal.*, 56:839–862.

Gabbard, G. O. & Gabbard, K. (1989), The female psychoanalyst in the movies. *J. Amer. Psychoanal. Assn.* 37:1031–1049.

Gergely, G. & Watson, J. S. (1996), The social biofeedback theory of parental affect-mirroring: The development of emotional self-awareness and self-control in infancy. *Internat. J. Psycho-Anal.*, 77:1181–1212.

Lichtenberg, J. D., Lachmann, F. M. & Fosshage, J. (1992), *Self and Motivational Systems*. Hillsdale, NJ: The Analytic Press.

Piaget, J. (1983), Piaget's theory. In: *Handbook of Child Psychology, Vol. 1*, ed. W. Kessen. New York: Wiley, pp. 103–128.

Stern, D. N., Sander, L. W., Nahum, J. P., Harrison, A. M., Lyons-Ruth, K., Morgan, A. C., Bruschweiler-Stern, N. & Tronick, E. Z. (1998), Non-interpretive mechanisms in psychoanalytic therapy: The "something more" than interpretation. *Internat. J. Psychoanal.*, 79:903–921.

Wolf, E. S. (1994), Narcissistic lust and other vicissitudes of sexuality. *Psychoanal. Inq.*, 14:519–534.

Eighteen

ENMESHMENT, ENACTMENTS, AND ENGAGEMENT
REPLY TO DISCUSSION

NANCY VANDERHEIDE

*T*hough there is considerable difference between Hartmann's ideas about my work with Josh and my own, I heartily agree with his citation of his analyst, Christel Schöttler, to which he refers in his discussion: "No development without involvement." It is not clear from this phrase whether she is referring to the analyst, analysand, or both, but I would venture to say that it is descriptive of the entire relationship. My involvement with Josh's processes resulted from my deep interest in the co-creation of a therapeutic relationship, one in which the processes of self-transformation would find fertile soil. Josh's growth was not solely mediated through interpretation; rather it occurred naturally during the course of analytically following the twists and turns of our relationship.

It is that theme of involvement to which Hartmann refers. His references to that involvement are far from positive: he terms it "enmeshment." Ironically, his illustration, pointing to the validity of using that term, is not accurate. There was no "slip of the pen," as Hartmann presumed; I actually did intend to say that Josh was powerless to resist *his* state of attraction to me. Rather than my being irresistible, I felt it was his own needs and desire that compelled him. The potent nature of his need was fueled by intense selfobject longings for both mirroring and idealization, as well as his pull for enactment in the repetitive dimension of the transference. Nevertheless, the concept of enmeshment is certainly relevant to my involvement with Josh, as is the notion of enactment.

Enmeshment and enactment are words that can connote less than healthy interpersonal situations. Hence, family systems theory refers to enmeshed families in describing the permeable boundaries of subsystems within the family that mark over-involvement of the members with one another. In psychoanalysis the word would probably imply a strong emphasis on separation and individuation as the goals of maturation.

Enactments, too, have a checkered past (Newman, 1988). The success a patient has in inducing a complementary countertransference response in the analyst can serve merely to confirm a persistent organizing principle. Certainly, many impasses in therapy occur as a result of the unconscious reenactment of old and addictive patterns of interpersonal relating. These patterns may eventuate in a sense of validation of the patient's belief that, for example, closeness always leads to exploitation, or his belief in the conditional nature of the analyst's relationship to him—that is, that he will only obtain needed selfobject experiences upon compliance with the analyst's narcissistic needs. The end result is the patient's need for self-defense.

Whereas Hartmann focuses on the potential for re-injury contained in my deep engagement with Josh, I found essential to the analysis the emergence of transitional space that grew from Josh's and my immersion in the process. The factors that determine the outcome of such engagements are the analyst's capacity for self-reflection and recognition that something of immense relevance to the patient's self-organization is taking place and must be explored.

Additionally, in this case, it was essential that I recognize my need for ongoing consultation with others. I was particularly influenced by Gabbard and Lester's (1995) recommendation that, when one is on the slippery slope of intense emotional involvement, it is important to disclose to trusted others the very feelings one is most reluctant to share. Such discussions—with colleagues, consultants, and analysts—permitted me to enter deeply into a relationship with Josh as I was linked to the world outside the relationship. In fact, a recurring image during these times was of descending into an unfamiliar cave, secured as though by ropes to my support team on the surface, with whom I shared my ongoing struggle to make sense in this affect-laden world.

In addition to different opinions about the clinical value of enactment, or engagement, as I prefer to think of it, Hartmann's discussion also illustrates a competing view of sexualization in the analytic relationship. He appears to reductionistically take the traditional perspective on sexualization, which is that it indicates resistance. In working with Josh, I preferred Kohut's (1977) explication of transference as a domain of developmental longings rather than simply as resistance. Stolorow, Brandchaft, and Atwood (1987) enhanced this concept by distinguishing between two organizing dimensions of the transference, the selfobject or developmentally striving dimension and the resistive, repetitive (or representational, as per Lachmann and Beebe [1992]) dimension. Also informative in my work with Josh was (and continues to be) Tolpin's (1997) conceptualization of the "forward edge" of the transference. She is referring here to vulnerable tendrils of growth that can precariously reach out of a safe and nurturing relationship. This is in contrast with the trailing edge, which pertains to expectations of reinjury and non-nurturance.

It is in the context of Tolpin's forward edge of the transference that I made the intervention I did in the dialogue I presented at the beginning of my paper. Hartmann objected to what he construed to be my fearful avoidance of a "now-moment" by neglecting to wear the attribution ascribed by Josh when he recognized, "Right now I almost feel loved by you." My sense of this moment was that Josh, consciously unfamiliar with, and unconsciously fearful of, the experience of being loved, was in a very vulnerable state, apropos of both himself and me. His communication to me was of the forward-edge variety, and he needed the respect and care of a safe response. My feeling is that any response resembling an admission of love on my part would have been overstimulating, frightening, and derailing of the process. The optimal response (Bacal, 1990) here comprised neither a confirmation nor a denial of his attribution of being loved by me; by virtue of the way in which I wore that attribution, Josh was permitted to have the experience of (almost) feeling loved by me. Bacal defines optimal responsiveness as "the therapist's acts of communicating to his patient in ways that that particular patient experiences as usable for the cohesion, strengthening, and growth of his self" (p. 361). Following this engagement, Josh demonstrated access to a wider range of affectivity.

Contemporary psychoanalytic theory maintains that the patient's sexualization of the therapeutic relationship can embody both developmental and repetitive dimensions.

One aspect of the repetitive dimension for Josh lay in his fear that anything resembling my need and love for him would culminate in his suffocation at the hands of a devouring, narcissistic woman. Also, at times his bids for my attentions served to elicit what Orange, Atwood, and Stolorow (1997) term an "antidotal function" or a palliative response that would protect him from self-fragmentation upon the activation of catastrophic organizing principles involving his sense of defectiveness or from exploration of other areas of intense fear and grief.

Sexualization manifests as the developmental dimension of the transference when it represents a longing for a mirroring response to sexual aspects of the self (Trop, 1988). Josh's inability to consolidate his sexual self through age-appropriate mirroring by his parents left him vulnerable to great doubt about his capacity to attract positive responses to his physical self. The nurturing quality of the analysis remobilized his developmentally appropriate longing to be admired and desired.

The analyst must be aware of the coexistence, indeed, the simultaneous existence of the repetitive and developmental dimensions of the transference in order to avoid over-focusing on either dimension. Emphasizing one dimension to the exclusion of the other eliminates the context within which each dimension arises. Unrelenting interpretation of the resistive aspects of sexualization may be experienced as shaming and injurious. Too much focus on the selfobject dimension clouds the picture and risks immersion in the palliative effect of a non-growth-producing collusion that neglects underlying selfobject needs. Illumination of foundational organizing patterns is thus possible only if the two dimensions of the transference are understood both to inform one another and to contribute to the patient's patterns of relatedness.

My experience with Josh was that his sexualization of the analytic relationship embodied both repetitive and selfobject dimensions, creating a tragic bind that has occurred in all of his significant male–female relationships; when his attempts to win the affections of another fail, he experiences himself as a pathetic little boy. However, if his attempts to attract are successful, he feels immediately vulnerable to the inevitable exploitation or abuse at the hands of an insatiable, narcissistically vulnerable, needy other. Much of our work has entailed explorations of these invariantly organized expectations, engendering greater awareness of himself and higher levels of safety in the relationship with me.

However, for a significant portion of this analysis, Josh's sexualization of me and our relationship served as his sole vehicle for attempts at relatedness. It expressed his hope that deep involvement in our relationship would function as a process of self-transformation similar to the function that mutual self-and-other regulation in the mother–infant dyad serves in moving the infant from states of distress to states of well-being.

In agreement with Davies (1994) and Benjamin (1994), I believe that the erotic transference can make possible a relational space within which conflict and longing might be expressed. Wearing the attributions, wherever feasible, facilitated the creation of space within which re-enactments could slowly unfold, be explored, and finally be understood. This potential, or transitional space, provides ideal components for the move from reflexive enactment to reflective analytic work.

Additionally, time spent in that relational space permitted the experiences upon which the unexpected developments surrounding the death of my mother could be built. The enactment that occurred created a scenario in which reflection of my own emotional reactions allowed the emergence of opportunities to disprove one of Josh's most salient organizing principles: that a needy woman will exploit and ultimately destroy him.

Continued work with Josh has enabled him to recognize vital patterns present in his relatedness with others, something he has come to call "echoes" of the original interactions with his parents. Well into our fifth year of his analysis, manifestations of Josh's tendency to sexualize me occur only occasionally and have acquired for him the status of affect signals.

REFERENCES

Bacal, H. (1990), The elements of a corrective selfobject experience. *Psychoanal. Inq.*, 10:347–372.

Benjamin, J. (1994), What angel would hear me? The erotics of transference. *Psychoanal. Inq.*, 14:535–557.

Davies, J. M. (1994), Love in the afternoon: A relational reconsideration of desire and dread in the countertransference. *Psychoanal. Dial.*, 4:153–170.

Gabbard, G. & Lester, E. (1995), *Boundaries and Boundary Violations in Psychoanalysis.* New York: Basic Books.

Kohut, H. (1977), *The Restoration of the Self*. New York: International Universities Press.

Lachmann, F. M. & Beebe, B. (1992), Representational and selfobject transferences: A developmental perspective. In: *New Therapeutic Visions: Progress in Self Psychology, Vol. 8*, ed. A. Goldberg. Hillsdale, NJ: The Analytic Press, pp. 3–15.

Newman, K. M. (1988), Countertransference: Its role in facilitating the use of the object. *The Annual of Psychoanalysis*, 16:251–285. New York: International Universities Press.

Orange, D., Atwood, G. & Stolorow, R. (1997), *Working Intersubjectively: Contextualism in Psychoanalytic Practice*. Hillsdale, NJ: The Analytic Press.

Stolorow, R., Brandchaft, B. & Atwood, G. (1987), *Psychoanalytic Treatment: An Intersubjective Approach*. Hillsdale, NJ: The Analytic Press.

Tolpin, M. (1997), Compensatory structures. *Conversations in Self Psychology: Progress in Self Psychology, Vol. 13*, ed. A. Goldberg. Hillsdale, NJ: The Analytic Press, pp. 3–19.

Trop, J. (1988), Erotic and erotized transference—A self-psychology perspective. *Psychoanal. Psychol.*, 5:269–284.

Part Six

PERSONAL REFLECTIONS

Nineteen

PERSONAL REFLECTIONS
FIFTY YEARS OF PSYCHOANALYSIS

ARTHUR MALIN

*I*n this article I review developments in psychoanalytic theory and practice over the past fifty or so years. Of course, I will present these developments from my own experience and my own perspective, demonstrating my involvement with American psychoanalysis as it evolved, beginning with ego psychology, and then moving to the theories of Melanie Klein, object relations (both British and American), self psychology, intersubjectivity, and the relational theories. My focus is on the special significance of self psychology in the theoretical evolution I experienced, and I will offer some ideas about the angry character of the debates that surrounded these developments. The role of the psychoanalytic organizations in Southern California will be highlighted as exemplifying nationwide trends in the field. I attempt to give this history chronologically and as concisely as possible, interspersing some important events in slightly greater detail.

I applied for psychoanalytic training at the Los Angeles Psychoanalytic Society and Institute (LAPSI) in the fall of 1949. Only physicians could apply, and there were many applicants. Psychoanalysis was popular, and physicians who had served in the Second World War were applying, as well as many recent graduates of medical school, such as myself. Less than one-half were accepted. I was accepted in February 1950, and less than one month later I was told that the Institute had split and asked which one was I going to be in. Welcome to the world of psychoanalysis!

This chapter was originally presented as the Kohut Memorial Lecture at the 2001 International Conference on the Psychology of the Self.

To offer a perspective on the meaning of fifty years, I recall the first day of my residency in psychiatry in July 1950 at the Veterans Administration in Los Angeles which is now a part of the UCLA Medical Center. I was assigned to the women's building, which housed about 150 patients of this 2200 bed hospital. I was shown around and eventually taken to the basement, where we entered a room in which there were fifteen very elderly women who were very senile. World War I had ended 32 years before (1918), and I supposed that the women were nurses from that war. I was told that they were nurses, but from the Spanish American War, 1898!

To understand what was going on at the Veterans' Hospital in 1950 I suggest the book, *I Never Promised You a Rose Garden*, by Hannah Green. This is a description of the experience of a patient at Chestnut Lodge in Washington, DC, and the woman psychiatrist in the book is Frieda Fromm-Reichman. The book also describes what was going on in most mental hospitals in 1950: shock treatment, wet packs, insulin coma, and the use of sodium amytal—the so-called truth serum. In other words, everyone was trying their best to do something for these very psychotic patients. These were not very humane treatments. But the hope was that they would help because, occasionally, a patient seemed to go into remission after undergoing such a treatment. For almost everyone going into the field of psychiatry in those days, psychoanalysis was the real hope. Perhaps we all oversold it since we tried to apply it to everything we did. There were case presentations about working only psychoanalytically with autistic children and people with other kinds of diagnoses that are now known to have a biological component.

When I arrived in Los Angeles in July 1950, I went to a meeting of all the psychoanalytic candidates from the now-split institutes. At this meeting there was an outraged group of perhaps 30 or 40 candidates who were very disturbed that the institute was splitting and that they had to make decisions about what to do.

Why was there a split in the institutes at that time? It was an argument between one group, which stood for strict rules on training and standards and frequency of visits for analysis, versus a less strict group that held that perhaps analysis did not have to be five times a week and that questioned some of the classical theoretical orthodoxy. The latter seemed to be influenced by the work of Franz Alexander. Nonetheless, all were ego psychologists in both groups. There were splits around the same time in other cities: New York, Boston, Philadelphia, and Washington D.C. The situation in LAPSI was often represented by Ralph Greenson of the more strict conservative group and Martin Grotjahn of the more "liberal" group. Interestingly the liberal group was more adamant about psychoanalysis being a part of the medical field, and the first name for their organization was the Southern California Institute for Psychoanalytic Medicine. Most of the non-medical psychoanalysts, particularly those who came from Europe in the late 1930s, were at the Los Angeles Institute.

I had made arrangements for a training analysis with Ralph Greenson and therefore was in the Los Angeles Institute. I started analysis in September 1950. Since the Korean War had broken out in June of that year, I realized that I would probably have to go back into the armed forces soon. I had been in the Army in World War II but mostly in schools and as a ward boy in a hospital. Greenson suggested that I start seminars immediately. This was unusual. The training analyst would decide when you could start seminars, usually after one year of analysis. Actually the acceptance to training was provisional, depending on a six-month trial in analysis. The training analyst spoke about his analysands at the Education Committee, determining when they could start seminars, take control cases, or any other advancement. Whatever you told your analyst was essentially an open book. The training analyst was in complete control of the destiny of the candidate, including deciding if he or she was no longer acceptable for further training. The candidate's professional career was in the hands of the training analyst. If you were not able to make it through an analytic institute, you were almost hopeless as far as developing a career in private-practice psychotherapy.

The reporting analyst approach did not end until the 1960s and 1970s. Even in a report from 1961 the Board of Professional Standards (BOPS) was trying to get "more information from the applicant's analyst to provide the committee with the appropriate and indispensable information" for granting membership in the American Psychoanalytic Association. There were 366 applications to American Psychoanalytic Association institutes for training in 1960–1961, 151 acceptances, and 196 rejections. The New York Psychoanalytic Institute had 49 applications and accepted 16. That is less than one in three.

I was in the Air Force from 1951 to 1953 during the Korean War. I then returned to Los Angeles and resumed my analysis. I might

mention what it was like for me to be in analysis in the beginning. I
desperately tried to understand and accept what the analyst said. I
was anxious and wondered, as I talked about myself as best I could,
what this would mean for my career in psychiatry and in psychoanalysis.
The concern of knowing that your analyst was also your evaluator
made things quite difficult. I had had nine months of analysis before
going into the service. I resumed in 1953, and seven to eight months
later, Greenson suggested that the analysis was not going well and
that I should find another analyst. He made the point that he was not
suggesting that I leave the field, but that I change analysts because
"something" was interfering in the treatment that he did not
understand.

When I first started in analysis, at 25 years of age, I thought of
this much older man, who was 39 at the time, in idealized terms. Dr.
Greenson was charismatic, and one of the best teachers, if not *the*
best teacher, in the institute. However, in the analysis, he said very
little. My memory is that, near the end of each session, he would spend
two or three minutes in some kind of summation. But I never felt
much contact with another human being in the room, only an evaluator
who was doing his job, and I felt quite anxious about the whole
experience. By the way, Dr. Greenson agreed to a relatively low fee at
the time: $15 per 50-minute session.

Being told that I was not making it in analysis was quite a
terrifying experience. However, being told that I should try again with
a different analyst was somewhat unusual. That implied that the
training analyst was perhaps not able to analyze the candidate and, if
the candidate was successful with another analyst, this would call into
question the ability of the first training analyst. It was easier to say
that the candidate was just impossible and therefore should be
cashiered out of the institute. If there were difficulties in the analysis,
they had to be kept quiet. A number of candidates told me of the
problems they had in their analyses. They felt they could not express
themselves fully for fear of upsetting the analyst and consequently
ruining their own careers. I was thankful to Dr. Greenson that he let
me have the opportunity to try with another analyst.

In my analysis with Greenson I reported a dream: There was a
ship that was at the dock, sort of wedged in. That was the substance
of the dream. My analyst told me that the ship represented my mother.
I will return to that later.

I started an analysis with Ivan McGuire, whom I had met when he was an instructor in my seminars. The analysis with McGuire was a very different experience. I cannot say that McGuire was a self psychologist, or any other kind of "theoretical" analyst, but I felt he made connections with me and listened carefully to everything I said, and I did not feel that it was for the purpose of evaluating me. He would talk to me about aspects of myself and occasionally give me opinions of his own. For instance, he felt that candidates should be reading other than classical psychoanalysis. He was concerned about true believers. He suggested that there were other contributors to psychoanalysis, including the Kleinians and the independent group in England, which included Winnicott and Fairbairn. McGuire became well known for second analyses of graduate psychoanalysts, and he was very instrumental with many of his analysands and supervisees in opening their view of psychoanalysis from a more narrow drive-structure paradigm, as Greenberg and Mitchell would put it, to a more relational-structure view. In this way McGuire helped inspire the movement in Los Angeles toward other points of view, starting with Melanie Klein and British object relations. Many analysts thought of McGuire as a "Fairbairnian," but I do not think McGuire would say that about himself. His approach did seem to indicate an awareness of the importance of relationships and the need for connections with others.

Soon after I ended with Greenson and started with McGuire, Greenson had a heart attack on a tennis court. I remember feeling I gave it to him. Enough about that.

A few years after I graduated, however, I told Greenson how grateful I was to him that he felt that I should try with another analyst, and I felt very good about my further analysis and my own progress. I told him that I knew many other training analysts would have just stated that the candidate was unsuitable and that that would be the end of their training. He appreciated my gratitude to him. We became friends and were participants in a psychoanalytic poker game that met once a month for perhaps twenty years. That was a much more satisfying experience with Greenson than the analysis.

Here is a sense of the atmosphere at that time: in the late 1950s, a group of recent graduates of the Los Angeles Institute had started a private study group and asked to present to the society membership about their explorations. They were scheduled to have two sessions to discuss the work of Melanie Klein. After the first session, there was so much criticism about the theoretical ideas that the second session was postponed and ultimately was never held. This was an example of how difficult it was even to consider any other point of view.

In 1960, four recent graduates of the institute (James Grotstein, Bernard Bale, Marvin Berenson, and I) formed a study group that met twice a month. We were very dissatisfied with our seminars and were eager to learn. Our seminars were restricted to classical Freud and very dull with few exceptions. There was a whole world of psychoanalysis out there, and we wanted to learn. We studied the British independent group, including Winnicott, Fairbairn, Guntrip, Balint, as well as Klein, Searles, Kernberg, Ferenczi, Jacobsen, and many others. This group continued for about eight years and then expanded into a larger group when a Kleinian, Albert Mason, moved to Los Angeles in 1969. Incidentally, in 1962 Winnicott visited Los Angeles and delivered two excellent papers. It was a special experience to meet him and hear him present his work. Starting in 1964, under the leadership of Bernard Brandchaft, a number of us helped to sponsor visits from Kleinians from London: Herbert Rosenfeld, Hannah Siegel, Wilfred Bion, and Albert Mason.

The point to studying Klein was that many of us were looking for ways to improve our work. We were not satisfied with what we had learned in our training and with our clinical results, and many of us were interested in working with much more disturbed people—people who are sometimes referred to as having more primitive mental states.

I have described the psychoanalytic institute of the 1950s when I was in training. I have also described some of what was going on in the 1960s, when there was a sense of exploration of new ideas or at least different ideas in psychoanalysis in Los Angeles. It is definitely my impression that this exploration was led by Los Angeles and that it was not as common in the rest of the country. We have to remember that the Kleinian approach made a significant step in understanding object relations. The object—the person—was much more significant than it had been under Freud's instinct theory, which had to do with source, aim, and object, and in which the object was rather interchangeable: "If I'm not near the person I love, I love the person I'm near." (Thanks to *Finian's Rainbow*, with some small changes in lyrics.) Also, in Klein's view, the attachment of instinct to object was emphasized, although the object was not personified as it would be later on by Fairbairn.

Many of us in the 1960s were very interested in trying to work with borderline and psychotic patients from an analytic perspective. We studied the writings of Harold Searles, Bryce Boyer, Peter Giovacchini, and many others. Some interest in Klein's work, especially that expressed by Herbert Rosenfeld and Bion, helped us in that direction. Over time, in Southern California, a number of analysts became very influenced by the Kleinians. Albert Mason and Wilfred Bion immigrated from England to Los Angeles around 1969. John Lindon and I were in supervision with Bion for one and a half years. We were not going to miss the opportunity to learn from one of the most significant figures in psychoanalysis.

Mason is still a very significant presence, more than 30 years later, in Los Angeles. After 10 years, Bion returned to England, where he died a few months later. However, Bion and Mason analyzed a number of analysts, including a second analysis for many graduates of both the LAPSI and the Southern California Psychoanalytic Institute (SCPI).

Fast forward to 1989. The lawsuit against the American Psychoanalytic Association by four psychologists was settled and training was opened to mental health professionals other than just physicians. The International Psychoanalytic Association could certify institutes in the United States. There were a number of analysts in Los Angeles with strong Kleinian interests, and they formed a new institute called the Psychoanalytic Center of California (PCC), which is an ongoing institute in Southern California today and a member of the International Psychoanalytic Association.

In addition, there was a group of psychologists in Los Angeles who had felt ostracized by the American Psychoanalytic Association, which had not accepted them for training. They had obtained training on their own. That was not too difficult, because they went into analysis and supervision with training and supervising analysts of the American Psychoanalytic Association. Eventually, in 1970, they formed the Los Angeles Institute and Society for Psychoanalytic Studies. They were primarily a group of psychologists, but they have expanded to include social workers, and marriage family therapists, and a few psychiatrists. This institute has also been approved by the International

Psychoanalytic Association. That makes for four official institutes in Southern California, official in that they are members of the American Psychoanalytic Association or the International Psychoanalytic Association.

In the 1960s, while there was a beginning interest in other points of view, particularly in Melanie Klein and her followers, there were also very disturbing political problems in the Los Angeles Psychoanalytic Institute. There was a problem of personalities, and two groups formed, each around a national figure in psychoanalysis who was a member of the Los Angeles Psychoanalytic Society and Institute. This split made it impossible to appoint new training analysts, and the institute became bogged down.

A group of members, led by Mike Leavitt and Mel Mandel, started a committee of concerned members that, over a few years' time (1968), led to a complete reorganization of the LAPSI, including how training analysts were chosen.

The certification process came about in the 1970s when there was a movement to have a more formal type of qualification for membership in the American Psychoanalytic Association. Before then a graduate of an institute submitted outlines of a case report and the American asked the supervisors and the institute about the applicant's qualifications. Certification was a matter of standards and the setting up of an elite analytic group. The local institutes could not be trusted to train analysts adequately, especially given the beginning theoretical interest in other than traditional American ego psychology. Arnold Richards (2001) editor of the Journal of the American Psychoanalytic Association (APsaA) stated:

> I think the system [of certification] was driven by the need
> to exclude graduates whose theoretical training was suspect,
> for example, interpersonalists from the William Alanson
> White division of the Baltimore/Washington institute,
> adaptationalists from Columbia, and Kleinians from Los
> Angeles [e-mail, open line, APsaA].

Certification by the American Psychoanalytic Association was required for anyone wanting training analyst status.

On the American Psychoanalytic Association members' electronic bulletin board, there have been many discussions recently about certification. A number of analysts believe that there has never been any objective way of evaluating how one works psychoanalytically and that the matter of how to write up a case report becomes a special, learned ability. In other words, many applicants have failed in their first written reports. When they received help in rewriting the report, rewriting it two or three times, they would finally be accepted. Henry Friedman has especially pointed out the fallacy in this procedure. The only thing that happened was that an applicant learned how to write a report that satisfied the committee's view of psychoanalysis.

In the late 1970s there was discussion of letting noncertified members into the American. This was finally approved after many years of debate. There was some principle of inclusion involved, but also there was an economic reason. New members were needed to increase revenues.

One of the functions of the American Psychoanalytic Association was to make site visits, which meant that every seven years about four or five members of the Board on Professional Standards would visit a local institute and study their procedures and standards. In 1972 there was a site visit to the Los Angeles Psychoanalytic Institute. This was just a few years after the reorganization and liberalization of the institute. It also seemed clear to many of us that the group came to root out the Kleinians that they had heard were influencing institute training. Recall that Wilfred Bion and Alfred Mason had arrived in Los Angeles a few years before. The institute leaders were told by the American Psychoanalytic Association to change the situation so that the Kleinians would not be influential. The attempt by the LAPSI to comply caused great difficulty, and there was a threatened law suit. Finally in 1976 a group of ten ego psychologists tried to split off and form another new institute (this is mitosis!) that would be free of Kleinian influence. The American Psychoanalytic Association sent in a special committee to help keep the institute whole, but they also restricted the activities of accepting candidates, graduating candidates, or appointing training analysts for four years. Through the leadership of a few members, headed by Mel Mandel, the institute was finally released from the oversight of the American Psychoanalytic Association in 1980.

I found myself in a difficult position during that time. I did not want the Kleinians or anyone else thrown out. I was willing to work with all of the analysts in the LAPSI. That was not a politically correct position. One had to be for the Kleinians or against them. I was chair of a major committee of the LAPSI, the Candidate Progression committee, and I was one of the analysts who worked with Mel Mandel to help the institute to right itself and remain whole. Then, as now, I believed that we should not suppress anyone but look at all points of view. I believe that the most helpful ideas in our field will eventually come to the fore, and that even newer ideas will eventually add to our knowledge. I decided to join a number of my friends in the more open and liberal SCPI in 1977, although I remained a member of the LAPSI and was even elected president of LAPSI from 1981 to 1983.

This was a very difficult time for the Los Angeles Institute. You can read all the gory details in the book *Unfree Association: Inside Psychoanalytic Institutes,* by Douglas Kirsner (2000). Chapter 4 is entitled "Fear and Loathing in Los Angeles." However, many members of the LA Institute, including me, would disagree with some of the author's facts and conclusions.

Around 1985 a lawsuit was instituted against the American Psychoanalytic Association by four psychologists. On April 17, 1989,

> the American Psychoanalytic Association and other psychoanalytic medical groups reached an agreement in a class action lawsuit. The APsaA agreed to admit psychologists to APsaA training institutes, to allow APsaA members to teach in non-American Psychoanalytic Association institutes, to allow psychologists to join the International Psychoanalytic Association, and to pay the court costs of the plaintiffs [e-mail, open line, APsaA].

This was a watershed event for American psychoanalysis.

Since 1939, the institutes of the American Psychoanalytic Association had admitted only medical doctors for training. An agreement existed with the International Psychoanalytic Association that, in the United States, only members of the American Psychoanalytic Association could join the international organization. Almost everywhere else in the analytic world, nonmedical analysts were trained. There were problems with how this was implemented at first. Every request for training by a nonmedical applicant had to be approved by the American Psychoanalytic Association. This was very burdensome for all concerned, and slowly the rules were changed so that at the present time, I believe, anyone with a doctoral degree can be approved at the level of the local institute and automatically be accepted into the American Psychoanalytic Association. It may have been liberalized even more in the last couple of years. Psychoanalysis needs more candidates.

Soon after the settlement of the lawsuit the SCPI accepted three nonmedical candidates for training: one had a Psy.D. and the other two had M.S.W degrees. They were turned down by the American Psychoanalytic Association. They all had further supervision, reapplied one year later, and were again rejected. The Institute defied the American and accepted them for full training. This led to a battle and negotiation with the American Psychoanalytic Association. The candidates were finally accepted. The successful leader of that battle was Richard Rosenstein of the International Council for Psychoanalytic Self Psychology. I believe it was the only time that a local institute defied the American Psychoanalytic Association.

This rebellion developed into a power shift in the Southern California Psychoanalytic Institute, and another imbroglio ensued. Those who had been the leaders were voted out by the majority (of one) who wanted to defy the American Psychoanalytic Association. Many of the new leaders were interested in self psychology. Although the usual difficulties and angry accusations developed, something new was added, and that had to do with an interest in self psychology. This was all the more remarkable because the SCPI was the more liberal institute. I believe that the so-called "self psychology problem" was only a disguise for the concern over the power shift. I believe there is no prejudice against self psychology at the SCPI now.

In 1991, in the midst of these difficulties, Louis Breger, a Ph.D. psychologist and a training analyst in the Southern California Institute, gathered together a number of analysts to start the Institute of Contemporary Psychoanalysis (ICP). The Founders consisted of eight training analysts from the Southern California Institute, two training analysts from the LA Institute, a regular member of the LA Institute, and Robert Stolorow. They were the founding fathers and mothers of the ICP. They included Estelle Shane, John Lindon, Morton Shane, Richard Rosenstein, and Robert Stolorow, who are all members of the International Council for Psychoanalytic Self Psychology.

The ICP in Southern California has had a remarkable career. They have drawn many mental health professionals into psychoanalytic training. They have a very welcoming attitude toward candidates, and they have prospered. They usually have from 12 to 25 or more in a class. Many analysts from the four other institutes have joined. A significant feature of the ICP is that it would never be a part of a national organization that involved setting standards from the outside. In other words, the institute wanted to control its own destiny. The ICP also insisted that they would have a very democratic organization, including significant input from the candidates. Here you might think that we had paradise regained, but as psychoanalytic history would predict, the ICP has had its fair share of problematic issues, though at this point many of them appear to have been resolved.

Around 1975, at the meeting of the American Psychoanalytic Association, Joe Lichtenberg introduced me to Anna and Paul Ornstein, Ernie Wolf, Paul and Marian Tolpin, and Evelyne Schwaber. I got into a discussion at dinner with Paul Ornstein and told him of a challenging analytic case. He graciously supervised me at dinner. I had only a very limited exposure to self psychology at that time, but Paul helped me a great deal. I went home and was better able to understand my patient. I have written up this case (Malin, 1993). At Paul Ornstein's invitation, I came to Cincinnati to participate in a one-day visit by Heinz Kohut. By then I had read and discussed self psychology with many of my colleagues, and I realized that Bernard Brandchaft and Estelle and Morton Shane in Los Angeles were also thinking differently about psychoanalysis and had been influenced in particular by self psychology. I was invited into a group that met with Kohut for a weekend in Chicago twice a year. The group included Arnold Goldberg, Michael Basch, Ernie Wolf, Marian and Paul Tolpin, Anna and Paul Ornstein, Evelyne Schwaber, Bob Stolorow, Estelle and Morton Shane, Bernard Brandchaft, and me. The discussions were wide ranging and thoughtful. I learned a great deal, as I am sure everyone did. This was also the time of the first annual conference in 1978.

SELF PSYCHOLOGY AND THE AMERICAN PSYCHOANALYTIC ASSOCIATION

THE FATE OF NEW IDEAS

> *First they will say it is all wrong*
> *Then that it is unimportant and trivial*
> *And finally that they knew it all the time.*
> —William James

In many ways the well known quotation from William James describes the fate of self psychology within American psychoanalysis. It was unusual to have an "insider" in the American Psychoanalytic Association, a former president, start describing a different approach to psychoanalysis. Because he was an insider, the reaction to Kohut was mainly confined to individuals; he was not excommunicated by the American Psychoanalytic Association as an organization. Kohut's 1959 paper, "Empathy, Introspection and Psychoanalysis: An Examination of the Relationship Between Mode of Observation and Theory," seemed reasonably acceptable to mainstream psychoanalysts, even though it contained many of the roots of self psychology. The 1966 paper, "Forms and Transformations of Narcissism" also created a change from prior attitudes. Narcissism, he said, did not evolve only into object love, but also into wisdom, humor, and empathy. Now, all of these ideas did not arouse too much controversy among American psychoanalysts. However, that 1966 paper was presented at a plenary session of the American Psychoanalytic Association and, according to the report I heard, when Kohut asked one of his colleagues after the presentation what he thought about it, the colleague replied, "I did not understand a word of it."

In 1968, Kohut discussed the idea that there was a spectrum within the character and personality disorders, the narcissistic personality disorders, which could be analyzed if dealt with from a different perspective than the usual classical drive/structure theory (Kohut, 1968). Kohut still conceptualized this approach as complementary to the drive/structure/oedipal neuroses; in other words, he never threw out the classical approach. All this time, Kohut basically continued to view himself as an ego psychologist, even teaching the course on ego psychology at the Chicago Institute. But with the publication of The Analysis of the Self (1971), many in the psychoanalytic world began to hold a different view toward Heinz Kohut.

Kohut himself thought of his ideas as advances in mainstream psychoanalysis, similar to Heinz Hartmann's ideas of the "average expectable environment" and the problems of adaptation. However, very few analysts saw his work in that way. In the 1972 paper on narcissistic rage, Kohut described the source of aggression without reference to instinct theory, though this was a time when others also were questioning instinct theory.

In *The Restoration of the Self* (1977), Kohut took a different tack. He stated that the self, in the broad sense, could be seen as the "center of the psychological universe." There was a definite break with classical analysis and the elaboration of a different approach to psychoanalytic work. Self psychology could now be thought of as applying to the wide spectrum of disorders helped by psychoanalysis. However, Kohut never quite gave up the concept of complementarity.

It was at this time that a number of papers were published that criticized Kohut's work. It has been reported to me that there was a stormy meeting of the program committee of the American Psychoanalytic Association at which a vote had to be taken to determine whether Kohut would be invited to be on a panel at the American. I believe it was at the winter meeting in 1978 that Kohut finally was invited, and he did appear before a packed house at the ballroom in the Waldorf.

At this same meeting, a paper was presented describing the narcissism of individuals who offer new points of view in psychoanalysis. It was obviously meant to be a paper critical of Kohut. There was a large audience, with a number of people speaking up. Many of them said they found Kohut's work significant, that it expanded their own psychoanalytic theory and practice. There was also a statement from the author of the paper, who was chairing the meeting, to the effect that the first analysis of "Mr. Z" (Kohut, 1979) was obviously not an adequate ego-psychological analysis. Merton Gill took the floor, remarking that we should be aware that many of our respected colleagues have found the concepts in self psychology very useful and that we ought to listen to them. In addition, Gill said he believed that the first analysis of Mr. Z was exactly what is taught in the psychoanalytic institutes. At the same meeting, Kurt Eissler made a clearly negative comment about Kohut's work, concluding with a question about the kinds of ideas that come out of Chicago. I was at that meeting, and it was my understanding that Eissler was referring to the problems engendered by Franz Alexander and the concept of the corrective emotional experience that had been introduced in Chicago thirty years earlier. Another member of the audience, speaking directly to Eissler, said that many analysts question psychoanalytic ideas that come from New York! This was a reference to the New York Institute's reputation as the most conservative institute in the country, the hotbed of orthodoxy, if you will.

There again, there was no institutional excommunication by the American Psychoanalytic Association, but there was the feeling that individuals were unhappy with Kohut and his ideas. A colleague close to Kohut told me that Kohut had remarked that people literally turned their back on him when he walked into the room, including some of the most prominent members of the psychoanalytic community and people who had been his friends. Kohut clearly was hurt by the response.

If Kohut was not formally banished from the American, what were the informal consequences of this attitude toward Kohut's work? Many people believe that the consequences were felt in the certification committee of the American Psychoanalytic Association. There were many of us who felt that the certification committee would not accept a self-psychological approach in a report of an analysis. Although this was never official policy, a former member of the certification committee reported that a self-psychological perspective would not be accepted by the committee—that the report would be received with prejudice.

Today there are a number of analysts influenced by self psychology who are prominent on the programs of the national meetings of the American. They include Paul and Anna Ornstein, Arnold Goldberg, Joe Lichtenberg, Ernie Wolf, Estelle Shane, Marian Tolpin, Robert Stolorow, and many others. There is an annual self psychology conference, now in its 24th year (at the time of this writing), which routinely has from 500 to 650 participants, many of them members of the American Psychoanalytic Association. Self psychology is a required seminar for candidates in most institutes.

A last point I would like to make about self psychology and the American Psychoanalytic is that, because of Kohut being an insider, and because many people who were influenced by self psychology and by Kohut's work were members of the American and training analysts in their own institutes, as well as members of the International, they stayed within the American Psychoanalytic Association. No one was "kicked out." Since a different approach can now be acceptable within the American Psychoanalytic Association, or at least tolerated, I believe other points of view are also acceptable by the American. For instance, I do not believe that the interpersonal perspective and the William Alanson White Institute were ever accepted by the American until the influence of self psychology was felt. I believe that attachment theory, and even a good part of the Kleinian approach now recognized by the American Psychoanalytic Association, came in the wake of the forward movement of self psychology within that organization. Of course this also includes the relational perspective, intersubjectivity, systems theory, and social constructivism. In today's more pluralistic world of psychoanalysis, I believe the influence of self psychology is seen everywhere. The concept of the selfobject and the selfobject transference, and the expansion of self psychology into intersubjective and relational points of view are significant parts of American psychoanalysis today. The analyst's empathy is now considered an absolute requirement, and the empathic stance of listening is now practically a shibboleth of psychoanalysis. The recognition of the significance of shame is also part of self-psychological ideas. In other words, we are at that point where "we knew it all the time."

Why are there so many problems in psychoanalytic organizations and in psychoanalysis itself, even in organizations that are set up to counter the problems of other psychoanalytic organizations? In a recent e-mail from the open line of the American Psychoanalytic Association, the problem of theory and the arguments about theory were described as narcissism, narcissism, narcissism. And someone else, I believe Henry Friedman, added, politics, politics, politics. I believe politics means power.

A number of the political and theoretical leaders in psychoanalysis appear to require acolytes, followers, loyalists to maintain their own sense of self—power as selfobject experience. I believe this situation can be easily observed in most of our organizations. It is so well recognized that most psychoanalytic institutes limit the number of candidates in training with a particular training analyst at one time.

Let us look at the concept of selfobject experience. This concept is fundamental for those of us who have been influenced by self psychology. We all know that we need continuous nourishment from our outside world to maintain and develop our own sense of self. One of the definitions of so-called "cure" in analysis is when we have the capacity to find appropriate selfobject experiences in our lives. We never give up the need for selfobject experiences. Of course, the theory to which we ascribe also has a selfobject function. And when we are told that our theories are wrong or bogus, or that we are not really analysts, but psychotherapists, we might feel frustrated and angry. Our sense of self has not been affirmed but denigrated. I believe that having conferences affords us the sense that we are part of a group of people who can think and work in different ways—hopefully without condemning one another. The conference itself can be thought of as a selfobject experience that bolsters one's sense of self. At the present time and for several years, initial self-psychological theory and ideas have been modified and expanded. There is disagreement and even rancor because, for some, when others go in different directions or emphasize different ideas, it is experienced as a selfobject failure, a threat to the sense of self. Most of us, I hope, can continue to grow and experience differences without being threatened. We can expand the sense of self.

Many other points of view in psychoanalysis employ the concept of selfobject experience, but they use different words. I am suggesting that, when we hear what appears to be a different point of view, we might be able to recognize that often the language could be translated into ideas that we find understandable. I am not being a Pollyanna and saying that every theory is fine. Actually, I see a fundamental difference between the drive/structure point of view and the relational point of view. Here I am following Greenberg and Mitchell (1983). I see self psychology as one of the relational points of view. In ego psychology, which adheres to the drive/structure model, a major attitude seems to be that the psychoanalyst knows the truth, which is very different from the relational point of view, which recognizes that the experience of the analysand is fundamental. However, if we look closely, it is quite clear that self psychology has influenced the entire psychoanalytic world, including ego psychology.

One way to look at theoretical differences is to try to define what we mean by psychoanalysis. There have been attempts at a definition recently on the e-mail open line of the American Psychoanalytic Association, but it has become clear that many so-called universal concepts, such as intrapsychic conflict, does not resonate with every psychoanalyst. Leon Hoffman (2001), who is a member of the New York Psychoanalytic Institute, has suggested,

> could this be an (almost universal) acceptable, brief description of the psychoanalytic perspective?
> • that each individual is unique
> • that there are factors outside of a person's awareness (unconscious thoughts) which influence his or her thoughts, feelings and actions

- that the past shapes the present

Perhaps this very broad description is all that we can hope for.

It seems that so much of the difficulty that we have in dealing with each other, whether it is in regard to different theories, or modified theories, or different approaches, has to do with the experience that we, as individuals, are therefore not being acknowledged and accepted for our own needs. That is, we are not having our selfobject needs reflected by the responsiveness of our colleagues. We need the reaction and response of others to maintain our sense of self. Some of us are particularly sensitive to these selfobject failures whereas many can maintain the cohesiveness of the sense of self as the "center of independent initiative" in spite of a lack of outside affirmation.

But let us get to the problem of the angry, combative, splitting and demonizing that has gone on in psychoanalysis all these years. To offer a contrary view, could these adversarial conflicts have a positive way of allowing for a synthesis which is actually an advance? Let us look at another view. Can we say, as many have, that all organizations suffer from this type of difficulty, namely, different points of view, argument, and division? Or can we also say that at least psychoanalysts are supposed to be aware of some of the issues within themselves that might lead to difficulties and adversarial points of view?

Perhaps analysis of individuals who go into our field does not necessarily lead to an analysand's sense of self becoming an independent center of initiative. In other words, a training analysis may become a way in which the analysand conforms and remains close to the analyst's thinking as a way of maintaining his or her sense of self, and thus any new ideas are experienced as a threat. Recall Kohut's remark that it is not the trying of the new that is the problem, but the giving up of the old. In contrast, in some instances the training analysis allows some analysands to realize more fully their inner organization and convictions, their sense of a cohesive self that is an independent center of initiative. These analysands may not be as disturbed about conflicts over theory and new ideas. Certainly Kohut was one of those people. He had a wonderful career in mainstream psychoanalysis, as we all know, but he put himself in the position of being ridiculed, and being disagreed with; for some, his status was depreciated by virtue of his new ideas.

Several of the central ideas of self psychology are very relevant to the concerns I am discussing. We are constantly dealing with a very difficult area of our own subjective experience and trying to understand the subjective experience of another person and the meanings of our interactions with that person. We do not have a "hard" science to help us find "the truth." We have gone into this peculiar work of trying to understand others and ourselves, an endeavor with many questions, many models, many theories that many of us would say are much more of an art than a science. We teach the art or the science to one another, and we go on from there to try to help others. What does that do in terms of our own sense of self? We become committed to a point of view. Many may become disillusioned, and it would be very interesting to study how many people who have had psychoanalytic training have left the field because they have not found it very valuable for themselves or for working with others. Some analysts have been able to search further, to find new and different ways to understand what they are doing. At some point, we have to commit ourselves to a point of view, but we always need to remain open to and to consider new ideas. To paraphrase Kohut, we cannot know *the* truth, but we may analogize approximations and describe what we see from various points of view to explain it as best we can in a variety of ways.

If we have become connected to a point of view and a theory, or even an idealization of an individual, then that is a part of our own sense of self. When someone differs from that point of view, they might precipitate a failed selfobject experience. When the sense of self is therefore threatened, our anxieties, our frustration, and our aggression are mobilized. Then come the rivalries, the difficulties, the splits, and the rancor in our field. David Terman (1972) says that this is what is so disturbing to the older analyst when the younger analyst is different and does not go along with the older analyst's point of view. The younger analyst is not maintaining the self experience of the older analyst by agreeing with him or her. It is not an affirmation of the other.

Psychoanalysis 50 years ago was an adventure. An adventure that was, in good part, unknown. Many of us felt like pioneers exploring the best we could. We did have therapeutic zeal, even though we were cautioned against it in our training. Better to be a distant surgeon–observer, we were taught, than to be too interested in our patients getting better. But it was an exciting time. And seminars were exciting at first. However, in my experience, our seminars overall were rather dull. They were the major disappointment in my training, and if it were not for certain colleagues with whom I went through seminars and with whom I could debate and argue, that learning experience would have been poor. Psychoanalysts were not professional teachers. Many of them were pedantic people who read Freud line by line, and that is what and how we studied. There were exceptions. I believe that today's seminars are much better taught than they were many years ago.

However, we all went to meetings. It was a full house every time there was a Society meeting and presentation, which was at least monthly. Our seminars were in the evening, sometimes as often as three nights a week. By the way, that Veterans Administration Hospital, which had 2200 beds in 1950, now has about 300 beds. After a few other wars, the large number of people under arms in World War II has never been repeated.

And now I will revisit my dream from my first analysis. There was a ship that was at the dock, sort of wedged in. My analyst said that the ship represented my mother, and I tried hard to believe. I had completely forgotten the dream. Forty-five years later I was reading James Fosshage's "The Organizing Functions of Dream Mentation" (1997) when I suddenly recalled the dream, and I believe I understood it. In the dream I was stuck in place, and so I was in the analysis. A self-state dream.

CONCLUSION

My historical review suggests to me that the sometimes adversarial nature of our psychoanalytic community leads to syntheses that might be useful. In self psychology we now have many different points of view. I suspect that most all of us who are influenced by self psychology have some feelings of connection to Kohut's work in one way or another and to some of the major ideas that have developed from that point of view. Stolorow, Brandchaft, and Atwood (1987, p. 15) have suggested that there are three significant changes that have occurred with self psychology. They are: The primacy of the empathic introspective stance of listening and of data gathering; the concept of selfobject and selfobject transferences; and the primacy of motivation of self experience rather than instincts and drives.

In addition there are many other ways of discussing self psychology, and we should welcome them all. Perhaps it is a strain to have to change and see something differently, but I think we should all make the effort. We have to be constantly letting go and modifying our views. Ivan McGuire (1960, personal communication) said we should always be a little bit ashamed of the way we were five years ago. This applies generally to our lives and also to our development as psychoanalysts. To me this means that, looking back, we could have dealt with some of our patients, and our own understanding, in a somewhat different way five years ago, that we have learned more and gained more understanding and experience.

Well, where does this leave us? I think it leaves us in a very exciting developing field in which we are all trying to understand and learn more. I think we also have to be as courageous as we can to give up or modify some ideas and try new ones. I do not think this is easy, for me or anyone else, but I think it is necessary for progress. And progress has been made over many years, and we have many new, different, enlightening ideas. We continue to hear many different points of view, and they all deserve respect and recognition and thought. Hopefully, these different points of view will not be experienced as threats to our sense of self, but as gifts to enhance our own understanding and capacities as psychoanalysts. Although we may say we are influenced by self psychology, we have to remember that self psychology is not a final theoretical answer, but hopefully it can continue to be a path to further modifications, new developments, and enhancement in our own field.

I will close with my favorite quotation from Kohut (1977):

All worthwhile theorizing is tentative, probing, provisional—contains an element of playfulness.

I am using the word playfulness advisedly to contrast the basic attitude of creative science from that of dogmatic religion. The world of dogmatic religion, i.e., the world of absolute values, is serious; and those who live in it are serious because their joyful search has ended—they have become defenders of the truth. The world of creative science, however, is inhabited by playful people who understand that the reality that surrounds them is essentially unknowable. Realizing that they can never get at "the" truth, only at analogizing approximations, they are satisfied to describe what they see from various points of view and to explain it as best they can in a variety of ways [pp. 206–207].

REFERENCES

Fosshage, J. (1997), The ongoing functions of dream mentation. *Contemp. Psychoanal.*, 33:429–458.

Greenberg, J. & Mitchell, S. (1983), *Object Relations in Psychoanalytic Theory.* Cambridge, MA: Harvard University Press.

Hoffman, L. (2001), E-mail open line statement. *Amer. Psychoanal. Assn.* Available: www.apsa.org.

Kirsner, D. (2000), *Unfree Associations: Inside Psychoanalytic Institutes.* London: Process Press.

Kohut, H. (1959), Introspection, empathy and psychoanalysis: Examination of the relationship between mode of observation and theory. *J. Amer. Psychoanal. Assn.*, 7:459–483.

——— (1966), Forms and transformations of narcissism, *J. Amer. Psychoanal. Assn.*, 14:243–272.

——— (1968), The psychoanalytic treatment of narcissistic personality disorders: Outline of a systematic approach. *The Psychoanalytic Study of the Child,* 23: 86–113. New York: International Universities Press.

——— (1971), *The Analysis of the Self.* New York: International Universities Press.

——— (1972), Thoughts on narcissism and narcissistic rage. *The Psychoanalytic Study of the Child,* 27:360–400. New Haven, CT: Yale University Press.

——— (1977), *Restoration of the Self.* New York: International Universities Press.

——— (1979), The two analyses of Mr. Z. *Internat. J. Psychoanal.* 60:3–27.

Malin, A. (1993), A self-psychological approach to the analysis of resistance: A case report. *Internat. J. Psychoanal.*, 74:505–518.

Richards, A. (2001), E-mail open line statement. *Amer. Psychoanal. Assn.* Available: www.apsa.org.

Stolorow, R., Brandchaft, B. & Atwood, G. (1987), Reflections on self psychology. In: *Psychoanalytic Treatment: An Intersubjective Approach.* Hillsdale, NJ: The Analytic Press.

Terman, D. (1972), Dependency and autonomy in the student situation: Summary of the candidates' pre-congress conference, Vienna, 1971. *Internat. J. Psychoanal.*, 53:47–48.

Part Seven

BOOK REVIEWS

INTRODUCTION

JOYE WEISEL-BARTH

*W*elcome to the new Book Review Section of *Progress in Self Psychology*. This 2004 issue inaugurates the book review as another way to respond to the important expansions, shifts, and changes occurring in contemporary psychoanalytic thought. Why do we need a book review section? What are some specific reasons for this addition? Our premise is that a book review essay generally has a wider lens than that of a particular journal article. It can take a broader look at thematic changes within the field, can survey the development of a particular individual's thought over time, and can trace the elaboration of ideas that may have first appeared in more condensed form on these very pages. It is, thus, a place to compare and contrast the developed ideas of our colleagues and to measure their theoretical and clinical implications.

This year we offer two pieces in the Review Section, an interview with Robert Stolorow on the occasion of the publication of *Worlds of Experience* and a description and discussion of Frank Lachmann's three latest psychoanalytic contributions. Coincidentally, both men identify similar themes in their lives and work: the importance of collaborations; the importance of contexts and relationships in the unfolding of their thinking; and the unpredictable, nonlinear, constructivist nature of their respective life trajectories.

Read on and enjoy!

Twenty

THE WIDE-RANGING WORLDS
OF FRANK LACHMANN

JOYE WEISEL-BARTH

IMPRESSIONS AND MUSINGS

rank Lachmann—I have a Santa Claus transference to him that may bias this review. It started several years ago at my first Self Psychology Conference when, as a new student at the Institute of Contemporary Psychoanalysis, alone and shy, I took a seat at the first plenary session. To mask self-consciousness and to take the temperature of this new community, I began to people watch. Several rows ahead of me a man and woman stood engaged in conversation. The man's body leaned easily into the conversation as he listened with twinkling eyes and merry intensity. "That woman must be very smart," I thought, "What must she be saying to magnetize such rapt and buoyant attention?" Evidently, it must have been something very funny, for suddenly the man exploded in laughter. He threw back his head and shoulders so that his back and chest arched in pleasure. Had his belly been larger, I thought, it would have "shook when he laughed like a bowlful of jelly." I smiled as I watched him and felt myself relax. "Santa!" How I wanted in on that conversation! I said to myself that with members like this man, so present and so spirited, this self psychology group must be okay. Later I learned the man was Frank Lachmann. So began my Santa Claus transference.

In the spirit of Santa Claus, Frank Lachmann has recently gifted us with practically a sleighful of books: *Infant Research and Adult Treatment: Co-constructing Interactions*, *A Spirit of Inquiry: Communication in Psychoanalysis*, and *Transforming Aggression: Psychotherapy with the Difficult-to-Treat Patient*. This is a veritable publishing "*Blitzen.*" The first two books represent his important collaborations: first, with Beatrice Beebe in infant–parent research and then with Joseph Lichtenberg and James Fosshage in an expansion of their ideas about exploration and communication in human development and analytic work. The third book, my favorite, is Lachmann's personal statement—in his own lively voice—about the contributions of self-psychology, developmental theory, motivational theory, communication theory, and dynamic systems theory to his understanding of the human condition and of the analytic process.

Before turning to the books, I would like briefly to address two issues: Lachmann's collaborations and his empirical and aesthetic curiosities. Surveying the field of contemporary psychoanalysis, I am struck by the number of collaborations that have generated new theoretical and clinical ideas. The Ornsteins; the Tolpins; the Shanes; Stolorow, Atwood, Brandchaft, and Orange; the Process of Change Study Group in Boston; the New York relational study groups in their various configurations; Lachmann and Stolorow; Lachmann and Beebe; and Lachmann, Lichtenberg, and Fosshage—these dyads, triads, and more are the collaborative engines driving new ways of thinking about psychoanalysis. As collaborations, they exemplify one of Lachmann's major ideas—indeed, probably the defining idea of contemporary psychoanalysis—that human relatedness and human minds develop, expand, and transform in complex interaction with other minds.

Lachmann was lucky in his teachers, peers, and students. Or perhaps he made excellent choices from the array of people he encountered. As he tells his life story, he emphasizes his collaborations and the openness and curiosity of his associates. Lloyd Silverman was an early close friend, of whom Lachmann says, "[H]e was a devout Freudian, but a curious, not doctrinaire one." Of studying for seven years with Martin Bergmann, he says, "This experience was probably the most direct influence in shaping my professional life. He is a truly inspired teacher with a very questioning mind, also not doctrinaire." Of a seminar he taught in which Bob Stolorow participated, Lachmann says, "It was probably the back-and-forth of that seminar that was another major influence in my thinking." And of his supervisee Beatrice Beebe, Lachmann relates how their supervisory dialogue led to their major joint clinical papers as well as to a reversal in their relationship when she became his teacher of infant research. These collaborations and others underline the importance of the dialogic process, of contexts and relationships, in Lachmann's intellectual and professional life. To expand on Tronick's dynamic systems idea, they exemplify the concept of dyadic/triadic/quadratic expansions of consciousness.

My second observation about Lachmann is that he is at heart an empiricist with an aesthetic sensibility. While he clearly has the gifts of a theorist, his impulses and temperament are those of a scientist and humanist. He was educated at the Bronx High School of Science and in a primarily research-oriented psychology program at Northwestern University. Therefore, his theoretical ideas—although clearly filtered through his own intuition and affective responses— reflect careful observation and analysis of data. This scientific bent explains the ease with which Lachmann can discard old ideas and clumsy linguistic terms that no longer accord with his empirically based conclusions.

For example, he has substituted the empirical infant of Daniel Stern and Beatrice Beebe for the Freudian one whose psychological growth depended on fixed theoretical stages of development. In contrast to Freud's infant, the development of the contemporary empirical infant is contextual and co-constructed. That is, it occurs in the give-and-take context of the infant–caretaker relationship. Lachmann concludes that it is lived experience that determines the emergent patterns and transformations in a child's development. Such experience includes the myriad meetings and leave-takings; the moments of confirmed expectations and congruence; the instances of misattunement and disappointment; and the countless disruptions, repairs, and heightened affective moments in the self-regulatory and interactive regulatory processes between a parent and child and later between a child and his relational environment. One important and optimistic implication of this conclusion is that change may continue throughout life as relational contexts change and expand. Lachmann, for example, is impressed that later events in a person's life may play important roles not only in producing psychological difficulties, but also in discovering psychological resources and creating healthy life strategies. A corollary to this idea is that change can occur at any time in the context of a rich analytic relationship.

Beyond the empirical impulse, Lachmann has a wide-ranging curiosity about cultural things—about music, literature, and theater. This curiosity insinuates its way into his work. For example, in his book on aggression he treats characters from Shakespeare, Ibsen, and Melville with the same familiarity and seriousness with which he treats the patients in his case studies. Similarly, I imagine that Lachmann's love of music influences his analytic thinking. In his discussion of the nonverbal, implicit relational system, he describes it as functioning out of awareness and separately from the linguistic or explicit relational system. Yet, he argues, the implicit system is nonetheless as important as the explicit system in human relations. Might not this idea derive as much from Lachmann's sensitivity to the rhythms, tones, and affective power of music as from frame-by-frame analysis of mother–infant interactions?

Lachmann's cultural interests also breathe pleasant fresh air into his essays. His breadth of knowledge and imagination and his love of fun and humor enlarge the meanings of his observations and keep his writing vibrant and relatively jargon-free. Recently, his case presentations have emphasized the nonverbal, the gestural, the improvisational, and the spontaneous in describing self- and interactive regulatory processes in psychoanalysis. The case studies of David, Karen, and Clara, for example, all have an animated and literary quality to them, concerned as they are with the nonverbal subtleties and nuances of interpersonal encounters. These studies stand in contrast to traditional and static one-person case descriptions, which usually consist of a history and dynamic formulation of the patient, followed by the analyst's explicit interpretative strategies. It is no exaggeration to say that Lachmann's cases represent a new model for examining the clinical process.

THE BOOKS

Infant Research and Adult Treatment: Co-constructing Interactions is the product of Frank Lachmann's 30-year collaboration with Beatrice Beebe. It is an updated collection of their major papers on infant research with a new final chapter; and in its breadth of scholarship, it provides a good general survey of the infant research field. This work is part of the revolution in psychoanalysis during the last 30 years, a revolution that recognizes the contextual and constructivist nature of human mind, relationship, and the analytic process.

The purpose of the book is "to explicate the value of infant research and a systems view for psychoanalysis." Yet, as Lachmann writes, "The value of the research . . . goes beyond its application to adult treatment and an interactive model of mind. It provides a systematic view of the origins of the processes of relatedness itself" (Beebe and Lachmann, 2002, p. 232).

Beebe and Lachmann have a complicated, threefold aim in this book. First, they offer a coherent design for the architecture of mind, of self, and of human relatedness as organized in infant–caretaker interactions. Then, they layer their descriptions of the origins of self with a dynamic systems view of development. Finally, they apply their model to change processes in the psychoanalytic treatment of adults. Fancy footwork, indeed; and in my view they pull if off with only a few stubbed toes.

From Beebe's microsecond observations of infants and mothers, the authors suggest that, babies are born with "an ongoing capacity for self-organization in the context of the interactive field" (p. 84). This organization unfolds from birth in infant–mother interaction; and by the end of the first year, a child has established both expectations about relationships and his own self-regulatory style. These develop through mutually regulated nonverbal exchanges, which Beebe and Lachmann place in the foreground as they explore dimensions of the developing self. These include rhythm matching of body and voice, modulation of vocal contour and pace, pauses, postural matching, and gaze regulation. The authors also attend to contingency patterns in the infant–parent dyad and to what they term principles of salience—the ongoing regulation, disruption, repair, and heightened affective moments in relationship. Music may serve as a metaphor for these nonverbal processes, with moments of easy harmony, deep feeling, sometimes minor sometimes searing dissonance, and resolution.

In Beebe and Lachmann's view three important implications issue from a view of self- and interactive regulation as the primary determinants of psychological development. First, internal processes and relational processes are inextricably coordinated and organized concurrently. Therefore, there is no inner self that is separate from interactive experience. Simply put, a person's expectations for relationship—how he registers dyadic modes of regulation—constitute what we have formerly called internal organization or representation.

Second, Beebe and Lachmann take a systems view of representation. As we have just seen, they conceive of representation as a reflection of an individual's history of self- and interactive regulations. While provisionally patterned in the first year of life— they say that "a trajectory" is established—representations are open to change. Using the process model of dynamic systems and perturbation theory, the authors argue that representations are relational patterns that soft-assemble but are inherently dynamic and changeable. Hence, the concept of representation—or "organizing principle"—shifts toward a continuously reorganizing process. Only in trauma or severe pathology does the capacity for change and transformation become severely limited.

And, finally, nonverbal, presymbolic processes persist alongside verbal or symbolic processes throughout the lifespan. Therefore, they necessarily become an important focus in analytic work. Often in psychoanalytic treatment implicit and explicit levels of experience are integrated seamlessly. The analyst balances attention to regulatory process and enactments, on one hand, with traditional dynamic interpretation, on the other. However,

> [w]ith "difficult-to-reach" patients in particular, the interaction between analyst and patient requires close, continuous attention. . . . These are the treatments in which attention to the system, the unfissionable unit (Kohut, 1984), and the moment-to-moment process carry the therapeutic leverage [Beebe and Lachmann, 2002, p. 218].

In keeping with the themes in the book, the case examples in *Infant Research and Adult Treatment* trace and emphasize the nonverbal dimensions of analytic treatment. For example, in discussing his patient Karen, Lachmann describes his difficulty in damping down his own natural energy levels and voice pitch and rhythm in order to meet and match the woman in the "midrange" of response (pp. 47–62). For me the original and creative case presentations are the highlight of the book. Yet, in praising their efforts, I wish Beebe and Lachmann had said more about the ways in which their analytic partners had affected and changed them. Because their research puts the bidirectional nature of regulation and influence center stage and because it emphasizes an interactional foundation for the construction of experience, I would like to hear more about the analysts' personal transformations. This minor caveat holds for the case material in the other two books as well.

A *Spirit of Inquiry: Communication in Psychoanalysis* (2002) exemplifies the dynamic systems notion that living ideas do not remain fixed and static but are subject to continuous updating and remapping. Here Lichtenberg, Lachmann, and Fosshage reexamine the exploration dimension of their motivational systems theory. They update it, elevating and broadening its importance. According to the authors, exploration, or the spirit of inquiry, pervades the other motivational dimensions as well as all affective communication in the analytic relationship. As Lachmann proposes, "A spirit of inquiry in the form of exploration or inquisitiveness is an ever-present dimension of communication in psychoanalytic therapy" (p. 54).

In the book Lachmann and Fosshage each contribute one chapter to Lichtenberg's six. Yet, in tribute to their common theoretical convictions and their trust in each other as collaborators, the men share equal authorship. They draw from the same theoretical material as the Beebe and Lachmann book in order to describe the origins of nonverbal communication. They then add a chapter that reviews the development of symbolic processes. This chapter not only contains attachment ideas about the relationship between coherent affective narrative and healthy psychological growth, but it also cites research describing the enormous cognitive leaps that occur with the advent of speech.

In chapter 3, which is Lachmann's essay, attention shifts to clinical material. Here Lachmann focuses on two interesting clinical issues: first, the therapeutic necessity of perturbing the analytic system; and then the complex and changing factors involved in an analyst's therapeutic choices. Given his goal of opening and broadening dyadic communication, Lachmann uses his patient Nick to describe the bases for many discriminations and choices he makes in the ongoing treatment.

> Our view that the analyst-patient dialogue is coconstructed includes affect, empathy, and transference in the

communications by both analyst and patient. We recognize
that in the service of communication with the patient, an
analyst utilizes a variety of approaches. These include
silence, neutral mirroring, refraining or participating in a
transference enactment, explaining, questioning, advice-
giving, and reveries and various forms of personal disclosures
[Lichtenberg, Lachmann, and Fosshage, 2002, pp. 58–59].

The patient Nick, a 36-year-old homosexual, is fearful and
rageful, alternating in his life between impulsive, self-destructive
outbursts and affective withdrawal. As a result of experience in his
first family, he expects Lachmann's to be a voice of disapproval and
criticism. Thus, the analytic task is to find strategies for opening and
deepening the therapeutic dialogue without confirming Nick's
pathogenic expectations. Lachmann believes that a too-rigid
adherence to the traditional analytic model—"patient talks, analyst
listens and interprets"—runs the risk of deadening the analysis,
"repeating the original trauma," or seeming to be "an unresponsive or
uncaring caretaker." Therefore, "a modicum of enactments is crucial
for the analysis to be alive and to capture relevant childhood
experiences" (p. 73). Lachmann often chooses to avoid verbal
interpretations with Nick while participating, instead, in verbal and
behavioral enactments. In this dyad, he finds that humor provides a
channel for the deepening of emotional connection and the
establishing of a safe "play space." Lachmann states, "Humor, irony,
and playful exaggeration characterized our unique personal
communication and our connection" (p. 65). He clearly enjoys the
back-and-forth banter with Nick and sees their humorous verbal
interactions as perturbing Nick's existing affective and relational
organizations.

Perhaps with an eye to relational psychoanalysis, Lachmann
describes for us his personal responses to Nick, his moment-to-moment
feelings and dynamic formulations. Afterwards, he mostly chooses not
to disclose those feelings or make those interpretations to Nick. The
question here—for him and for us—is "when to hold and when to
fold"; that is, when to interpret and when to refrain. Unfortunately,
the answer to this question resides as much in the realm of art and
uncanny human understanding as it does in a text on analytic
technique. In fact, such delicate discriminations may be impossible to

teach. Exquisite sensitivity and intuition guide Lachmann in deciding what interventions will likely facilitate and what will arrest the analytic process.

Yet Lachmann does offer some teaching guidelines. For example, if opening new avenues for analytic inquiry is the goal, the analyst must be alert to irrelevant personal disclosures, authoritarian power tactics, and humiliating or shaming interventions that may impede the goal. He states:

> [Avoid interpretations or] inquiries with an agenda or an authoritarian edge. They are not conducted in the spirit of further understanding, rather they impart an opinion and criticism without so stating. But, most important, they delineate a gulf between therapist and patient [p. 66].

He also cautions against trailing edge interventions that may be shaming. For example, Nick dreams about entering his uncle's house through a back door, and Lachmann associates the image of the back door to a wish for anal intercourse. Because he does not believe that Nick is ready to deal with sexual shame or that this interpretation will yield new material, he inquires instead, with good success, about the meaning of Nick's having easy access to his uncle's home. However, Lachmann comments that at another time the sexual interpretation might be quite apt and facilitative. Timing, context, ripeness are all!

Santa takes the gloves off in *Transforming Aggression: Psychotherapy with the Difficult-to-Treat Patient* (Lachmann, 2000). Loud and clear, he acknowledges the dark, angry depths of human experience and behavior, and he admits to a curiosity about evil. From the old Christmas song—the one that terrified us as children—we know that Santa Claus understands darkness: "He knows if you've been bad or good/So be good for goodness sake!" Nevertheless, we are surprised and a bit delighted at the ferocity of Frank Lachmann's revenge fantasy toward critics of self psychology.

Transforming Aggression is an answer to those critics who claim that self psychologists are naïve about aggression and, therefore, incapable of conducting serious, deep analyses. In the book, Lachmann explores aggression in its most extreme forms, which he terms "eruptive aggression." In this explosive form, aggression appears biologically based or internally driven, an observation consistent with the views of many classical, object relational, and Kleinian analysts. Yet Lachmann, as a contemporary self psychologist, is committed to viewing aggression not as a primary drive but as a reactive response to a number of complex external factors. These include frustration from trauma, neglect, separation, and insecure attachment as they interact with such influences as parental, social, and cultural models and possible neurological anomalies.

So how does Lachmann explain eruptive aggression? Essentially, what he does is take the conditions that foster self-organization, self-stabilization, and self-righting and imagine their absence in a child's development. He comes up with five conditions that may result in eruptive aggression or violence:

(1) An early history of noncontingent, abusive, deceptive, neglectful treatment in important relationships.

(2) Persistent misregulation in the early parent–child dyad, misregulation that interferes with the development of self-cohesion and increases fragmentation.

(3) Sexualization of experience as a drastic attempt to fulfill numerous nonsexual functions; sexualization used for self-repair of states of deadness and fragmentation.

(4) Neurological abnormalities such as those depicted in PET scan patterns.

(5) Experiences of humiliation and shame, disrespect and ridicule.

Imagine a child whose parents and caretakers—and, perhaps, whose culture—have failed to respond to the child's basic needs, failed to provide soothing for her pain or regulation for her physical and emotional arousal. At the same time, imagine that these same caretakers have prevented "the organization of the other [motivational systems] such as attachment, exploration, and sensual and sexual pleasure." The child who receives such treatment dies psychologically. Lachmann notes that common to all serial killers is "some variant of deadness," lifelessness, and lack of affectivity. Here he introduces a paradoxical way to think about violence. On the one hand, we are accustomed to think of violence as an expression of self-fragmentation. On the other hand, violence for some extremely aggressive people may serve an arousing and enlivening function, an antidote to existential nothingness. For them "the need to react aversively joins or recruits the other motivations" (p. 146).

Lachmann (2000) is persuasive in imagining the origins of much eruptive rage. Nevertheless there remains a dimension of evil beyond his imaginings, a depth of depravity that simply stumps him. He struggles with a number of possibilities, for example, "perversions of aversiveness" and neurological glitches—until he finally concludes:

> At the far end of this continuum [of evil] stands Iago. Whether we can extend our empathy to include his level of destructiveness is questionable. But beyond Iago, off this continuum, live the serial killers. We are hard pressed to find a context for their aggression that we can understand [p. 144].

The ways in which Lachmann thinks about treatment in *Transforming Aggression* are complex and masterful, particularly with his patient, Clara. For Lachmann, the goal of analysis is to create new relational experiences, ones that perturb the patient's old relational organizations and create new opportunities for self-transformation. Finding interventions that create such perturbation is especially difficult with aggressive patients like Clara. In his description of her case, we relive with him the struggle to establish a footing with her, a working analytic relationship, and to find effective interventions. For example, he demonstrates the slipperiness of the leading edge/trailing edge idea, the difficulty of choosing one or both of these edges at any given point.

Angry and contemptuous, Clara clings to murderous rage because it provides for her a sense of self-cohesion, vitality, and integrity. A model scene from Clara's childhood serves as a template for the themes that organize her adult relationships. When Clara was eight years old, she neglected her horse, neglect which resulted first in its illness and, then, in its death. On the day the horse was to be put down, Clara agreed to go on a picnic with her parents. For her the picnic not only represents complicity with her parents in denying her responsibility for the animal's death, it represents a corrupting act of self-betrayal. To avoid further self-betrayal, she has come to resist any relationship based on empathy or generosity. With Lachmann she insists that he accept her as a murderer because her destructiveness is intrinsic to her self-definition. Lachmann's leading edge formulations and his efforts to put her childhood experience in a broad and compassionate context enrage Clara. She feels that he is unable to accept her as bad and angry and rails against his naive "niceness." Only when he "joins" her, when he recognizes and accepts her as a killer, can she begin to establish a sustaining selfobject transference to him and can they begin together to create the conditions for change and transformation.

In the complexity of this case presentation—and of many others in the three books under review—Lachmann illuminates for us the limitations and elusiveness of theoretical models and clinical rules and techniques. Instead, this mature thinker and clinician leaves us with several vivid impressions about the analytic enterprise. We remember that each analytic relationship has a unique configuration; that behavior, arousal patterns, and subjective awareness are organized interactively; that each relationship undergoes continuous refashioning and recreation; and that the efficacy of every analytic choice and intervention depends on relational history, timing, and context.

REFERENCES

Beebe, B. & Lachmann, F. M. (2002), *Infant Research and Adult Treatment: Co-constructing Interactions*. Hillsdale, NJ: The Analytic Press.

Lachmann, F. M. (2000), *Transforming Aggression: Psychotherapy with the Difficult-to-Treat Patient*. Northvale, NJ: Aronson.

Lichtenburg, J., Lachmann, F. M. & Fossage, J. (2002), *A Spirit of Inquiry: Communication in Psychoanalysis*. Hillsdale, NJ: The Analytic Press.

Twenty-One

WORLDS OF EXPERIENCE
AN INTERVIEW WITH ROBERT D. STOLOROW

PETER BUIRSKI

Peter: The first question I wanted to ask is for readers who might not be familiar with your previous work. Would you describe what led you to write *Worlds of Experience* with George Atwood and Donna Orange and how it builds on your previous work.

Bob: Well, we've been developing a perspective in psychoanalysis that we now call intersubjective systems theory, for nearly three decades. The first article in which we use the phrase "intersubjective perspective" was written in 1976 and published in 1978. First, we've been developing the intersubjective perspective as a clinical theory, looking at all the basic clinical phenomena that occur in psychoanalytic treatment as occurring at the interface of the interacting experiential worlds of patient and analyst. Second, we have been rethinking some of the basic theoretical pillars of psychoanalytic theory. The present book was primarily directed at looking at the philosophical foundations of our perspective. We contrast those with the philosophical foundations of traditional psychoanalytic theory and practice and then try to demonstrate that the differing philosophical foundations make a huge clinical difference. That was the basic idea. To elaborate a little more, we came to the conclusion that traditional psychoanalytic theory and practice along with some contemporary approaches like self psychology and relational psychoanalysis have very powerful roots in Descartes's philosophy of the isolated mind. One way of looking at the philosophical foundations of our intersubjective perspective is that it's an attempt to ground intersubjective systems theory and practice in a post-Cartesian, or maybe more accurately, a non-Cartesian philosophy of mind, which we refer to with various terms, such as intersubjective systems theory or more broadly as a kind of psychoanalytic contextualism. The basic idea is that personal experience always takes form in a context of interrelatedness.

Peter: It seems like a way of thinking that lends itself to working collaboratively with colleagues in writing a book.

Bob: Absolutely. As a matter of fact it was George's idea, long ago, that the collaboration among all of us is sort of a metalog for the basic theoretical principle, which is that all psychological products take form within formative intersubjective contexts. The process of developing intersubjective systems theory is a sort of metaphor or a metalog for the basic concept of the theory.

Peter: Can you say something about the process of the three of you working together developing these ideas and then something about how you write together.

Bob: Well, we had a vision of this book several years ago. As is usually our way, we didn't sit down and try to write a book. We usually decide on various individual articles that we want to write, with an eye toward later pulling them together into a book. That's what we definitely did with virtually all of the chapters in this book. They were originally written as articles. There are a couple exceptions: part of the introductory chapter and the chapter on perspectival realism. Other than that they were written as individual articles but definitely with an eye toward a larger book. We wrote the individual articles with the guiding idea that I mentioned before about looking to the philosophical foundations of both traditional psychoanalysis and our psychoanalytic perspective and their profound clinical implications. So that's how we went about it. We would take an individual article, which would then become a chapter, and, it may be that all three of us would be interested in that particular topic or two of us or one of us or whatever the case may be, and if more than one of us were interested in that particular topic, then we would divide up that topic between the coauthors, and then we would edit each others' work. All of us would edit what each of us individually would write.

Peter: Living in different parts of the country, do you actually get together, do you dialogue together by phone, or do you to do it by sending the articles back and forth?

Bob: Well, both: we would send them back and forth and we would usually get together two or three times a year or we'd speak over the phone. I'm actually beginning to overcome my computer fear and use e-mail.

Peter: I'm really curious about how the ideas develop and whether they develop out of dialogue. Are the three of you sitting in a coffee shop talking about this, or on the phone?

Bob: They absolutely developed in a dialogue. And it's been going on between George Atwood and me since we first met each other in 1972. Very quickly after we met at Rutgers University, we discovered that a kind of magic would take place every time he and I would sit down and start to talk about ideas. Ideas would just kind of tumble into our discussion in ways that just don't happen in other contexts. Each of us might be having a dry spell for a long period of time, and so as we begin talking about something—sitting down, over the phone. All of a sudden ideas start appearing like magic, and Donna joined the club around 1995, and something kind of similar happens with Donna also. It doesn't have as long a history. There's something about the way that George's and my experiential worlds play off one another and later Donna's with both of ours. It's just kind of magical.

Peter: I wonder if you would apply your approach from *Faces in a Cloud* (Atwood and Stolorow, 1993), of exploring personal subjective origins of theories, to your own work.

Bob: Absolutely. I don't want to speak for Donna and George but, speaking for myself, you know there are two basic pillars of intersubjective systems theory that have profound personal, emotional sources in my life history. One is the idea of a level epistemological playing field—what Donna Orange later came to call perspective realism. There is a chapter in our new book about that. It holds that any act of knowing or perceiving is always going to be partial because it's going be particularized and delimited by the personal perspective that the knower or the perceiver brings to that act. To use the words of the philosopher Gadamer, every act of knowing and perceiving is prejudiced. It is always delimited by the horizons of one's own history and organizing principles—these are more my words— so that means that nobody's personal reality is more true inherently than anyone else's. We've applied this principle to the psychoanalytic situation very specifically, but that goes back to my history of growing up with a father who had a God's-eye view of the truth and my own reaction against that kind of epistemological arrogance.

Peter: You're describing a know-it-all kind of stance.

Bob: Yeah. I've had a very strong emotional reaction to those kinds of know-it-all posturing that one frequently encounters with more traditional psychoanalysts. The second aspect of intersubjective systems theory that has a profound root in my own history is the focus on the psychology of affect. That again probably derives from my father because his own very powerfully expressed affectivity kind of dominated family life when I was growing up. It particularly dominated my mother's emotional existence, which had two consequences: I often had the experience of kind of disappearing, and my mother, as a result of subjugating her own emotional life to his for a prolonged period of time, was prone to rather severe wooden depressions. The idea of recapturing her affective aliveness along with my own became an important source of the focus on affectivity and the expansion of emotional horizons, which is a central focus of our psychoanalytic perspective.

Peter: What was your personal experience with your analyst and analytic training? Did you have a traditional know-it-all analyst?

Bob: No, I had a very interesting analyst, Alexander Wolfe. You knew him, didn't you?

Peter: Yes.

Bob: Well, he was a very interesting guy because he paid lip service to classical theory but he was not at all a know-it-all analyst and in particular he was wonderful at attuning to my emotional states. And when I began to experience that, I thought I'd died and gone to heaven. It was very mutative for me, his ability to stay with my affective life in a very attuned way, and because of that I could forgive him a lot of his Freudian interpretations.

Peter: The institute, Postgraduate Center for Mental Health, was ego psychology oriented. I guess I'm just struck with how hard it must have been to break away from the profound influence that the training experience carries.

Bob: I have two reactions to that. One is that it usually is not too hard for me to break away from things. I've always been kind of a maverick. In fact, whenever I start feeling that my ideas are getting too close to the mainstream, I get very uneasy. That's one reaction. Always kind of looking for ways to be subversive, and I think that was true even back then. A very important influence though was Frank Lachmann, whom I took a course from and who became by far my best supervisor. Frank had become interested in the early writings of Kohut, his 1966 and 1968 papers on narcissism and the treatment of narcissistic personality disorder. Frank was very instrumental in expanding my horizons theoretically in that way. And then some fellow subversives, a guy named Peter Buirski was one them, put together a private study group on contemporary views of narcissism and hired Frank to be our leader. That study group was a great adjunctive source of ideas and inspirations well beyond what I was learning at the institute.

Peter: In your new book, *Worlds of Experience*, you discuss the case that you originally wrote up for graduation from the Institute and then revisited it from the new perspective. In reading it, I think it seems like a very beautiful illustration of the different ways that clinical material can be understood. What made you go back to that case?

Bob: Well, because it just seemed like a wonderful example of an alternative to the Freudian theory of repression. It was for the chapter called "World Horizons," and it just seemed to be a case that beautifully demonstrates the ways in which what can be allowed into consciousness and what must be prevented from coming into being consciously are determined within particular intersubjective contexts, both developmentally and in the therapeutic situation. I believed that I had known that intuitively when I was doing the analytic work, with Frank as my supervisor of the case, but that intuitive understanding was not yet really articulated by me and didn't find a place in the original case report for my graduation paper from Postgraduate Center, nor did it find its way into a published article that Frank and I did together later. But it still kind of remained with me in kind of an unarticulated way until I was able to articulate it when I took another look at it from the standpoint of intersubjective systems theory.

Peter: In this new book, *Worlds of Experience*, you introduce the notion of world horizons. Would you say more about that?

Bob: Well the concept of horizons of experience is a concept that comes from continental philosophy. It's a concept that I believe may have originated with Husserl but was also used by Heidegger and very powerfully by Gadamer. The idea of a horizon beyond which one cannot experience or perceive seemed to me to be a beautiful metaphor for the problem of unconsciousness in psychoanalysis. The beauty of it, the way we conceptualize the horizons of experience or horizons of awareness, is that they are always an emergent feature of ongoing intersubjective systems rather than being fixed properties of isolated minds. So in a certain way the concept of intersubjectively embedded worlds of experience or intersubjectively formed horizons of emotional experience is a beautiful example of a post-Cartesian rather than a Cartesian view of the problem of unconsciousness.

Peter: You seem not to be using the phrase "organization of experience" much in the book. You talk more in terms of "worlds of experience." Is there a shift that's taken place for you?

Bob: Well, there may be a subtle shift. The concept of organizations of experiences is still extremely important to us. We still use the concept of organizing principles but the concept of worlds is a more powerful metaphor for capturing the relentlessly contextual quality of personal experiencing. One of the ways it's put in the book—and actually it was Donna who came up with this marvelously poetic statement—is that we inhabit our experiential worlds even as they inhabit us. To me that's a beautiful statement of a post-Cartesian or a non-Cartesian way of understanding human experience. We inhabit our experiential worlds even as they inhabit us. There's no trace of an isolated mind in that statement, nor is there any trace of the Cartesian split between subject and object or between inside and outside. All of those dichotomies are deconstructed within a post-Cartesian framework. So the three of us came to the idea that the concept of worlds of experience is a metaphor that captures the post-Cartesian or a non-Cartesian outlook more powerfully than the idea of organizations of experience, although that continues to be an important idea for us also.

Peter: In prior writings you refer to intersubjective systems theory as a "metatheory." What do you mean by that?

Bob: Well, it's a little confusing because actually I think there are probably two meanings of the phrase intersubjective systems theory. As a metatheory, we mean that it's a framework or really a sensibility, as Donna Orange also was the first to say, a sensibility that constantly emphasizes context. And by emphasizing context it always emphasizes perspective also, context and perspective. And as a sensibility with that emphasis, it can be employed by people who still have an allegiance to other clinical theories: Freudian, object-relational, and so on. So, in a sense it can be a metaframework that can guide people using various other theoretical perspectives. It can also be a theory of theory because it contains within it, going back to *Faces in a Cloud* (Atwood and Stolorow, 1993), an idea about the contextual aspect of theory formation itself. So that's one meaning of the term *intersubjective systems theory*. But then another meaning of it is that there has also been a rather specific clinical framework that has developed among us, among all of the collaborators. In the context of elaborating the more general metatheory, this more specific clinical theory includes things like unconscious organizing principles, a view of transference as unconscious organizing activity, the idea of two basic aspects or dimensions of transference—the repetitive/ conflictual/resistive dimension and the developmental dimension—and particular theoretical ideas about the formation of different states of mind such as so-called borderline states and psychotic states. So there's a rather elaborate and specific clinical theory that also goes by the name intersubjective systems theory. That's not what we're talking about when we say that we are offering a metatheory. Then we're talking about that first more general sensibility that I was describing before.

Peter: Pam Haglund and I just finished a paper on the incompatibility of isolated mind and contextualist positions. Our feeling is that, I'm sure you agree, the two are not reconcilable. So, as a metatheory, I don't see how an isolated mind theorist can also be a contextualist.

Bob: Well, it provides a framework for deabsolutizing, deuniversalizing, and contextualizing basic ideas from other theories.

Peter: Which radically transforms the other theories.

Bob: Of course it does.

Peter: Yeah. (*laughter*)

Bob: That's our secret, actually, so that some of the clinical contributions of the other theories can be retained but they are radically contextualized. (*laughter*)

Peter: Yeah. (*laughter*)

Bob: You found me out. (*laughter*)

Peter: You thought you could sneak it by. (*laughter*)

Bob: You can keep this in. (*laughter*)

Peter: You see, you believe that nobody is listening. (*laughter*)

Bob: Not carefully, huh? (*laughter*)

Peter: I think it's very hard for someone with a different sensibility to take in an intersubjective systems sensibility. It's a bit like coming from a different culture and trying to make sense of a whole unfamiliar way of looking at things.

Bob: Yeah. Well, I think it goes deeper than that. It's a problem of trying to understand things from different linguistic systems. I think that much of traditional theory harks back to Descartes's philosophy of the isolated mind. Descartes's philosophy was also guided by the quest for certainty, for clear and distinct ideas, for knowledge that was so unassailably true that it could never be doubted. And so isolated-mind philosophy is very much tied up with the quest for certainty, or what I sometimes refer to as the longing for bedrock. To give up that philosophy and the corresponding illusions of certainty and clarity and bedrock, to give up absolutes and universals, to give up the illusions of objectivity, all of those things that are legacies of Descartes's philosophy, to give them up exposes one to tremendous anxiety, what the philosopher Richard Bernstein refers to as the Cartesian anxiety and what George Atwood and Bernie Brandchaft and I refer to as the dread of structureless chaos. So to embrace the basic principles of intersubjective systems theory which, on a theoretical level includes the idea of radical contextualism and on the epistemological level includes a kind of radical perspectivalism, means living without bedrock, living without absolutes and universals, living without objectivity, living without certainty. That can mean, getting back to our basic theme of affect, tolerating a lot of anxiety. People find that very difficult in a field such as ours, which often leaves us swimming in a sea of uncertainty. That's by the way why I think you find these fads coming in where nowadays people are jumping, for example, on the bandwagon of attachment research. Here we seek more certainty, hard research, bedrock. Or neurobiology—now there we've really got something to stand on. We've got the brain to stand on.

Peter: Yeah. Although, I just read Beatrice (Beebe) and Frank's (Lachmann) new book, and it felt reassuring to be able to say that intersubjective systems theory isn't just experience-near but research-near too. It seems to be so compatible with some of the infant research.

Bob: Yes, well I'm in favor of any research that confirms my perspective. (*laughter*)

Peter: Yes. (*laughter*) Now here's a question that I've been pondering as I've been studying your work and the radical contextualist position, and that is that traditional personality is defined as an enduring set of traits. So how is the view of personality changed by a contextualist perspective?

Bob: Well, you would have to look at the issue of themes that seem to persist across different sectors of a person's life. You would have to look at the persistence of those themes in terms of the relational or intersubjective systems that recurrently get created and recreated. You could not see those themes as properties of isolated minds or isolated personalities. So you'd have to rethink them in terms of recurring patterns of intersubjective relatedness.

Peter: That can vary according to the contexts in which people find themselves.

Bob: Well, if you're looking for that contextual variance, I think you'll find it. I'm a little rusty on my personality research, but I think a lot of the studies that speak to the issue of enduring personality traits were designed to eliminate contextual variance, but I don't know if you should quote me on that since it's been 40 years since I've read them.

Peter: Well, but there is sort of the understanding in more traditional perspectives that if you show borderline traits with John you'll show them with Mary.

Bob: Well, that's just plain wrong. That was one of the clinical findings that got us started. Maybe it would be good for me to review this a little bit. This might be fun for people to read about.

Peter: Yes.

Bob: At the Second Annual Self Psychology Conference in Los Angeles in 1979, Bernie Brandchaft gave an amazingly courageous paper on negative therapeutic reactions, which up until then had been largely seen as properties of isolated, deranged minds. And Bernie gave some of his own case material to show that the so-called negative therapeutic reactions came about as a result of the intersection of the patient's difficulties with the analyst's insistence on a certain interpretive stance that was retraumatizing the patient. The analyst being Bernie. I had written some similar things and happened to have the page proofs with me, which I showed to Bernie, and we immediately felt an intellectual kinship. He invited me to speak at a conference on borderline states at UCLA in 1980. I said I would do it if he would write the paper collaboratively with me. He agreed, and in the course of our discussions, we discovered that, despite the fact that we were very different people with very different backgrounds—Bernie, nearly 30 years older than I am and a medical practitioner before becoming a psychiatrist and a psychoanalyst, he was from the West coast while I was on the East coast at the time and came from an academic psychology background, nonmedical and analytic training—we had made almost identical observations about so-called borderline states. Namely that if you take a very vulnerable, archaically-organized patient and try to treat that patient according to the theoretical ideas and technical suggestions, probably more like commandments offered by Kernberg, very soon that patient would start to show all the features that Kernberg described as the borderline personality organization. The pages of Kernberg's books will come alive right before your eyes. On the other hand, if you take that same vulnerable, archaically organized patient and treat him or her according to the therapeutic recommendations offered by Kohut, very soon that patient will start looking like a severe narcissistic personality disorder. And the pages of Kohut's books will start to come alive right before your eyes.

Peter: Yeah.

Bob: Until there's a major disruption in the transference and then the patient will start to look more like one of Kernberg's patients. And so on. And so that led Bernie and me to write a paper with the title, "The Borderline Concept: Pathological Character or Iatrogenic Myth?" (Brandchaft and Stolorow, 1984). And it would totally debunk the idea of enduring so-called borderline personality traits as well as the idea that you articulated a moment ago, that a patient will look borderline no matter whom the patient is with. It is just not true. Context makes a huge difference. We formulated in that paper the idea that borderline states take form within an intersubjective field co-determined by the patient's psychological organization and the way that organization is understood and responded to by the therapist.

Peter: You've also taken on quite eloquently the notion of projective identification.

Bob: Yeah.

Peter: In Worlds of Experience, you have a chapter in which you talk about the relational school of thought and the way that projective identification is accepted even though it is permeated with isolated-mind thinking.

Bob: Yeah.

Peter: So why do you think it's been so hard for the relationalists to come to terms with the intersubjective systems perspective?

Bob: I think probably the largest barrier has been the differences in clinical sensibility among many of us and many of them. Even though on a kind of metatheory level, there are a lot of similarities between the New York University relational people and us, there are some very important differences in clinical sensibility and I think that has been primarily due to the fact that there is a strong Kleinian influence among the relationalists, as shown by their use of projective identification. In contrast, our clinical sensibility was very strongly influenced by Kohut. And unfortunately there's a tendency among some of the relational people, not all but some, to disparage Kohutian ideas. To the extent that they have associated us with self psychology, there has been a similar kind of distancing from, or even devaluing of, us among some relational analysts.

Peter: When you read Mitchell, Aron, and other relationalists, there are so many points of commonality in theory but when you get to the clinical material, the Kleinian influence seems to creep in.

Bob: Yeah, the Kleinian influence is there even in Lew Aron's work. If you want to think of Freud as a Cartesian, Klein was a Cartesian to the second power. Virtually everything was to be explained through the workings of an innate destructive instinct, from deep within the interior of the isolated mind.

Peter: How are you feeling about the way your work is being accepted and heard today?

Bob: I'm feeling pretty good about it. Because I tend to write in a way that is designed to be provocative, sometimes both my colleagues and I evoke strong negative reactions in people. But the way I'm organized, that's okay. (*laughter*) At least I know I'm getting somebody's attention.

Peter: If I recall correctly, I heard that Steve Mitchell was asked by the American Psychoanalytic Association to be an honorary member. I gather they didn't extend that same invitation to you.

Bob: No they haven't, but so far they're also refraining from trying to have me locked up in prison and having my head chopped off. (*laughter*) They haven't extended that invitation to me yet. Somehow I think that may not be in the cards.

Peter: Yeah. (*laughter*) Well, it's interesting that there seems to be the sense that Mitchell's relational ideas are more palatable.

Bob: I think Steve was quite radical in his own way. This is just a speculation—I think that Steve might be more acceptable to the American despite the radical nature of his ideas because his clinical writing does dip back into Kleinian theory, in some respects. Correspondingly, our group might be less acceptable to the American because our clinical stuff really dips more into Kohut's contributions in self psychology. I think there's probably more resentment toward self psychology among the traditional people than toward the relational ideas. That would be my guess.

Peter: Charles Brenner just published an article in which he discards structural theory. What he retains is compromise formation and conflict, but he believes that structural theory is no longer a good description of how the mind works.

Bob: I've never had a problem with focusing on conflict and compromise; I think that was one of Freud's really good ideas that has stood the test of time. In my view, conflict is always about affect rather than drive. It always was. In Freudian theory, the dual instinct theory was really a dual affect theory. Hostility and lust. And those are very important affects. The problem is that, besides lust and hostility, there are many other important affects that can become sources of conflict. Once you make affect rather than drive the focus of conflict then you automatically contextualize it because affect is a relational-systems phenomenon. Affect is always something that both originates and is regulated or misregulated within intersubjective systems. So if you put affect at the center of psychological conflict, then you automatically put conflict within intersubjective contexts.

Peter: Because the affect is the experience. And the experience occurs in relationship?

Bob: It occurs in a relational context. A quick definition of affect for me would be subjective emotional experience.

Peter: Within a context.

Bob: It's always within a context.

Peter: So then the conflict is between the experience of the affect and the capacity of the surround to tolerate that affect?

Bob: Yeah, exactly, or at least the perceived capacity. So between one's own authentic affective experience, on the one hand, and some perceived relational danger of having that experience or expressing that experience on the other.

Peter: What about guilt?

Bob: A couple of decades ago a very prominent self psychologist,
        whom I won't name, said that he no longer experiences guilt
        in his consulting room, that he only experiences shame. I still
        experience plenty of guilt in my consulting room (*laughter*) on
        both sides of the intersubjective field. Guilt is an affect state
        and it can be implicated in psychological conflict just like any
        other affect state can be. I think one important origin of guilt
        has to do with the child's perception of what parents require
        of the child for the parents' own emotional well-being, whereby
        any deviations from those requirements are perceived to injure
        or damage the parents and thereby produce guilty feelings. I
        don't see any reason to either privilege or devalue any affect
        state. I think they're all important. One area that my late wife
        Dede and I focused on was that of depressive affect—sadness—
        and how normal depressive affect, sadness, can become a source
        of intense emotional conflict. There was hardly anything in
        the psychoanalytic literature about that when we began writing
        about it.

Peter: Is there anything else you want to talk about that *Worlds of
        Experience* covers?

Bob: Well, if I had to pick one theme that the book is trying to drive
        home, it's that one's underlying philosophical assumptions can
        make a huge difference in one's clinical work. That is probably
        the central thing that we are trying to drive home in that book.

Peter: And you include some good examples of that.

Bob: Especially in the chapter on the treatment of psychotic states,
        which was primarily written by George. It's sort of George's
        "magnum opus." It took a lot of blood, sweat, and tears from
        him. Another thing I might say about the book in terms of the
        collaboration is that I think the book probably combines the
        best of the three of us.

Peter: Well, say more about that.

Bob: Well, I think I have a gift for theoretical clarity, and for
        rethinking various aspects of psychoanalytic theory from an
        intersubjective perspective. So my contribution in a certain
        way is a culmination of three decades of trying to do that. I
        think George has a particular gift for clinical phenomenology,
        particularly in being able to capture in a highly evocative way

the phenomenology of extreme states of mind, such as experiences of personal annihilation. And Donna brings a gift for understanding and being able to articulate philosophical foundations and philosophical assumptions because of her background in philosophy. So I think when you put the three of us together, you get a pretty powerful combination.

Peter: When you're writing, and you meet with points of disagreement, how do you resolve those? Maybe it doesn't happen much.

Bob: It never happens. I mean, there may be an apparent point of disagreement, but as we dialogue about it, it transforms into an agreement. We usually reach an agreement on things. I can't think of any significant disagreements that remained disagreements after dialogue. That illustrates one of the philosophical ideas that is very important to us. It has to do with dialogue and how dialogue between people who have different perspectives enlarges the perspective of each. And that certainly has happened with all of us. And it's one way of describing the changes that take place within an analytic dialogue. There's an enlargement of the perspective of both patient and analyst.

Peter: Bob, I've really enjoyed this. I really have struggled with these ideas and I'm glad that you've been able to clarify them.

Bob: Well thanks, Peter. I think it's kind of cool that this takes us back really to the beginnings of both of our psychoanalytic education when we were fellow candidates.

End of Interview

Donna Orange and George Atwood were invited to share some thoughts about the interview. Donna offered the following comments:

Donna: First, I think we do have small differences in perspective, as one would expect from three troublemakers, but that they are so minor as to seem to disappear in the context of our massive commonalities of thought and sensibility. George and I, for example, who had weekly breakfast meetings for more than ten years, argue from time to time about the possibility of, and importance of, dialogue with those with whom we disagree.

Bob and I differ in our feeling about the term *affect*, which he loves and which I almost never use. For him, it denotes "subjective emotional experiencing." For me, it sounds like reductionist jargon reminiscent of psychiatric case conferences, where reified (as it seemed to me) "affects" were ascribed to patients by God's-eye-view clinicians, without any reference to relational contexts, or to the participation or bias of the clinician. I speak, instead, of emotionality (emotional memory, emotional availability, emotional communication) and consider emotion an emergent property of relational experience (according to processes well-described by Beebe and Lachmann). The Italian language captures this well using "to emotion" (*emozionare, emozionarsi*) as a verb, both active and reflexive. But surely you can see that these differences have more to do with ways of expressing ourselves than with anything substantial. I mention these instances to convey some of the quality of our dialogues and trialogues.

My second thought concerns the Faces-in-a-Cloud question. My mother's nicknames for me, "worthless" and "good-for-nothing," reinforced by a reign of terror organized by both parents, led to a lifelong sense that I have no value at all, either in myself, or to anyone else. The only possible, and only temporary, escape from this emotional conviction (my term for an organizing principle) has been to be useful as a caregiver and protector, beginning with my nine younger siblings. Finding myself recognized as a valuable collaborator by Bob and George in the past 10 to 15 years has at least allowed me occasionally to call this conviction into question. Working with them has convinced me experientially that personal experience is formed and maintained, and can be at least partially transformed, in specific relational contexts.

Peter: Would you respond to the question I've often heard asked of what it is that patients and analysts bring to the meeting from their own unique lives.

Donna: It seems to me that when I bring my organization of experience to a relational situation, what I bring is a range of expectancies, emotional convictions, and ways I am prepared to respond or react. This range may be narrower or wider, depending on my whole life history in relational contexts, and on what possibilities of therapeutic transformation have been available to me so far. Then this specific situation evokes particular aspects of my organized experience with more or less intensity, again depending on many particular aspects of the intersubjective situation. What I bring is just an enduring set of possibilities and leanings, nothing actual until I meet you. Whatever I experience in the situation with you is not something inside of me, but rather, it is my participation in the world we inhabit together.

REFERENCES

Atwood, G. E. & Stolorow, R. D. (1993), *Faces in a Cloud: Intersubjectivity in Personality Theory*. Northvale, NJ: Aronson.

Brandchaft, B. & Stolorow, R. D. (1984), The borderline concept: Pathological character or iatrogenic myth? In: *Empathy II*, ed. J. Lichtenberg, M. Bornstein & D. Silver. Hillsdale, NJ: The Analytic Press, pp. 333–357.

Stolorow, R. D., Atwood, G. E. & Orange, D. M. (2002), *Worlds of Experience: Interweaving Philosophical and Clinical Dimensions in Psychoanalysis*. New York: Basic Books.

———— ———— & Ross, J. (1978), The representational world in psychoanalytic therapy. *Internat. Rev. Psycho-Anal.*, 5:247–256.

Part Eight

ADDENDUM

ADDENDUM

Twenty-Two

THE ROLE OF EMPATHY AND INTERPRETATION IN THE THERAPEUTIC PROCESS
COMMENTARY ON DISCUSSIONS OF SALEE JENKINS'S CLINICAL CASE*

JAMES L. FOSSHAGE

*I*n addressing Marian Tolpin's and Daniel Kriegman's interesting and radically different discussions of Salee Jenkins's fine clinical presentation, I highlight, discuss, and evaluate, as I see it, the essential points of each discussant. I close by adding a few ideas of my own to the discussion of empathy and interpretation.

I agree with Tolpin (2002) that "self psychology has set in motion a change in total attitude to the psychic work for patient and analyst" (p. 113). In her close tracking of Jenkins's (2002) clinical work, Tolpin contributes to and illustrates this change of attitude, anchored in her framework for interpretation that includes both "trailing" and "forward edge" transferences. Trailing edge transferences are revivals and repetitions of the decisive "childhood self-disorder and its genetic context origins now with the analyst . . . that exerts a compulsive unconscious influence on the self-organization and a powerful pull back to the most pathogenesis constellations and solutions of the past" (p. 114). . . . [The] "forward edge" transferences "are, at first, barely noticeable tendrils of stunted, thwarted, almost crushed self strivings,

---

* This paper was inadvertently omitted from *Postmodern Self Psychology: Progress in Self Psychology, Vol. 18* (Goldberg, 2002). It is a commentary on Marian Tolpin's (2002) and Daniel Kriegman's (2002) discussions of Salee Jenkins's (2002) clinical case. The editor is pleased to include it at this time.

all the harder to recognize because they are invariably intertwined with . . . the self disorder" (p. 114). In presenting us her theory of therapeutic action, Tolpin states that when these tendrils are recognized, understood, interpreted, and their origins and interruptions in their growth are reconstructed, they "grow into *bona fide* transferences—resurgence of the most powerful motive forces [Freud] of the nuclear self" (p. 114). The nuclear self refers to the inchoate capacities of the individual, including a primary motivational thrust to grow or develop. It is the resurgence of the original developmental strivings and hopes for selfobject experiences that, in Tolpin's words, provide "the impetus for renewed development, working through, and therapeutic action," which for her are "one and the same" (p. 115).

These two classes of transference emerge in the writings of a number of self-psychological/intersubjective authors. What Stolorow, Brandchaft, and Atwood (1987) call the selfobject dimension and what my coauthors and I (Lichtenberg, Lachmann, and Fosshage, 1996) call the selfobject experience-seeking dimension of the transference is central to self-psychological theory. Tolpin's most significant contribution, however, is her unyielding emphasis on, appreciation of, and sensitive attunement to, the developmental strivings and, in her words, to the tendrils of the "nuclear self." Indeed, while Jenkins and Tolpin recognize both repetitive and selfobject transferences, Tolpin is recommending an even more consistent interpretive *accent* on the patient's attempts to grow. She has provided us with a number of cogent illustrations from the clinical material in which her emphasis on "the growth edge" would most likely highlight, support, and encourage the patient's developmental efforts. I heartily agree with Tolpin. I wish to emphasize, however, that the focus on trailing and forward edges requires a very subtle and, at times, tricky balance. Focusing too exclusively on the trailing or repetitive edge— traditionally a central problem in psychoanalysis—can easily undermine, as Tolpin makes clear, the patient's strivings toward growth. Yet, accenting the forward edge too exclusively creates a potential danger of insufficiently highlighting the repetitive problematic organizations, a necessary task that gradually promotes freedom from their dominance.

Tolpin argues for placing the growing edge as well as the trailing edge under the rubric of transference. For her, both transferences are "real," "[reviving] the unconscious depths of childhood psychic reality"

(p. 115). An alternative formulation of new relational experience with a "new object," in her view, undermines the transferential power inherent in the forward edge transference. One problem in this strategy, as I see it, is that the term *transference,* apart from Freud's unobjectionable positive transference and Kohut's selfobject transference, carries with it terminological baggage with connotations of inappropriate, unrealistic, or unreal (Fosshage, 1994). These connotations can easily undermine the "realness" and power of the new selfobject experience or new relational experience that occurs within the analytic relationship and is central to therapeutic action. The use of the terms *expectations, percepts, images, attitudes, organizing patterns,* and *repetitive* and *new relational experience,* in my view, more satisfactorily captures those central experiences that we have been calling transference.

Tolpin uses the empathic listening stance consistently in focusing her inquiry and does not utilize or refer to any other listening perspective. In keeping with Kohut's conclusion that, even more than the empathic stance, self psychology theory has extended the empathic grasp of patients, Tolpin emphasizes the importance of her framework for interpretation. As she makes clear, our models of development, transference, and therapeutic action shape what and how we interpret.

Tolpin presents a remarkably expanded view of interpretation. Interpretations are no longer simply words, content, and meaning. Interpretations are complex cross-modal communications both verbal and nonverbal, the words proper and the music of language and intonation (see Knoblauch's, 2000, *The Musical Edge of Therapeutic Dialogue*), body language, and the range of affective communication. While interpretations convey an understanding and explanation from an empathic vantage point, her emphasis, like Kohut's, is not as much on insight as on interpretations as carriers of the analyst's selfobject functions. Thus, interpretations anchored within an empathic vantage point can, in providing selfobject functions, include responses ranging from understanding and explanation to spontaneous guiding advice to coaching to willingness to be available for a spontaneous phone call from a patient on a plane, all of which are part of Jenkins's clinical work with Laura. Accordingly, Tolpin here does not differentiate between interpretation and other forms of intervention or other relational experiences, for the concept of interpretation is expanded to cover the wide range of responses that occur in the analytic encounter.

I am heartened by Tolpin's expansion of the term *interpretation* to include a wide range of interventions that are increasingly viewed as part of the analytic encounter within self psychology and within psychoanalysis at large. Yet her expansion of the term not only may stretch the term well beyond recognition and its original meaning, but it may also tend to obfuscate rather than highlight the variability of responses required in the analytic encounter. Conceptually it may detract from the specificity of responses (Bacal, 1998), a specificity required for a more detailed understanding of analytic interaction. To put it another way, I am in full agreement with Tolpin's music, but I am questioning her words. Interestingly, Tolpin, too, may find the term interpretation to be too confining, for she does not include it when she states: "What is the therapeutic action of the analyst's [being in empathic touch with, understanding, and responding to her patient's] reaching for the idealized goal of mothering and being mothered?" (p. 119). Tolpin is an active responder, a far cry from the position taken within self psychology in the 1970s and 1980s illustrated by, among many, Goldberg's (1978) statement: "this is the essence of analytic treatment: interpretation without gratification per se. . . . The analyst does not actively mirror; he interprets the need for confirming responses" (pp. 447–448). At that time Goldberg was aware that the analyst's presence, talking, and understanding could all have self-confirming effects on the patient and he responded by saying, "and they are so interpreted" (p. 448).

Kriegman (2002) feels, as did Tolpin, that Jenkins functioned as a very good analyst for Laura. Kriegman believes that Jenkins was "reaching into her own reservoir of innate wisdom and using it to make essential modifications to . . . [a] basically self psychological model" (p. 87). By a reservoir of innate wisdom, he means that we have certain knowledge pre-wired or biologically built into our system about the biologically based structure of relationships. Kriegman's interpretive framework is organized principally around the thesis that "fundamental and extremely problematic interpersonal conflicts of interest . . . pervade all human relationships" (p. 92). While he does not discount "overlapping interests . . . [that is] mutual aims to have a sense of shared, productive closeness and understanding" (p. 106), the guiding principle in his interpretive framework concerns the fundamental conflicts of interest between patient and analyst and how these are negotiated in the analytic arena.

In his view, the empathic stance serves as a crucially important antidote to the fundamental conflict of interests between patient and analyst. Kriegman states, "If the analyst's and patient's needs are in profound, problematic conflict, then *only* by emphasizing *the patient's* experience can the patient's interests be protected from analysts' conscious and unconscious pursuit of their own agendas, often at their patients' expense" (p. 93). While using the empathic stance, which for Kriegman variably denotes a mode of listening as well as a mode of response, may protect a patient from an analyst's imposition of his or her agenda, it, of course, does not eliminate the fundamental conflicts of interest between patient and analyst.

In etching out what is fundamental to human nature, Kohut (1982) sought to replace Freud's use of the oedipal myth, which features intergenerational conflict and strife, with the Odysseus myth, which highlights the primacy of intergenerational support. Slavin and Kriegman (1992) posit from an evolutionary perspective that conflicts of interest are fundamental to human beings and are inadequately addressed in self-psychological theory. From Kriegman's perspective, there is "an inherent conflict of interest between the identity of the analyst and the psychological needs of the patient" (p. 89). Patients intuitively know that there are conflicts of interests and frequently attempt to address them. Clinically it is the analyst's open acknowledgment of the conflicts of interests that validates the patient's experience and, thereby, gradually creates trust and facilitates the necessary mourning and subsequent internalization of the analyst's selfobject functions. This is, in Daniel's view, how change takes place. Not recognizing these conflicts of interests positions the analyst to invalidate the patient's experience of the conflicts and either to blame the patient for "distorting" or, I suspect, to blame oneself for insufficiently responding.

I believe that Kriegman and Slavin are importantly noting, on the basis of their reading of evolutionary theory, that fundamental conflicts of interests are a part of human relationships, including the analytic relationship. Recognition of this has important clinical implications that need to be added to self psychology models. I disagree with Kriegman, however, and with some of the arguments he sets forth to support his thesis regarding the extent to which conflicts of interests are fundamental to being human and, perhaps most important, the degree of such conflicts within the psychoanalytic situation.

I have time to address only a few examples of Kriegman's argument and emphases. Turning to the clinical material, Laura's mother needed to have Laura join her in the denial of a most trouble-ridden reality to maintain her self-cohesion. Kriegman uses this pathological scenario as an example of the universality of fundamental conflicts of interests. Without a doubt the mother's marked self pathology took precedence over her maternal caring and created a serious conflict of interests between mother and child—a type of pathology carefully etched out by Brandchaft (1994) as pathological accommodation. Even if this source of pathology is common, however, it does not make it fundamental to human nature. As you may recall, when Kohut (1984) was asked why pathological oedipal conflict was so common if it was not fundamental to human nature, Kohut cogently argued by using the analogy that the frequency of cancer or tooth decay does not make these common conditions normal or fundamental to human nature.

A second example involved Laura's need for mirroring and her objection to Sallee's use of the pronoun "us," which, based on past experience, Laura fearfully experienced as obliterating her. Kriegman suggests that Laura's need for mirroring fundamentally conflicted with Jenkins's need to maintain her analytic identity through sharing her "wisdom and interpretive understanding." He also notes, as did Kohut, that a mirror transference can be trying for an analyst. While this conflict emerged, it is not, in my view, evidence of fundamental and inevitable conflict of interests, but was a conflict specifically shaped in part (and momentarily I might add) by Jenkins's definition of her analytic identity, which emphasized interpretative activity—a definition that I hope self psychologists will help us to reject. To the extent that our conception of analytic activity is expanded to include more than exploration and interpretation, Jenkins's analytic identity can easily be maintained when shifting out of a verbal interpretive mode. In this clinical situation Jenkins did, in fact, shift out of the confines of an interpretive role and, as Kriegman points out, interacted with Laura in a way that conveyed profound understanding to her patient. Moreover, I believe that an analyst can (and I believe Jenkins did) implicitly affirm and maintain her analytic identity through understanding and negotiating the mirror transference. Shifting motivational priorities and self-states easily create conflicts of interests in human relationships that, as Kriegman is telling us, importantly need to be recognized and openly acknowledged by the analyst, particularly when patients are attempting to address them. In my view, the danger with making conflicts of interests fundamental to being human, however, is that its wholesale application tends to obfuscate and, thereby, blunt our analytic pursuit of understanding the particularities of past and present relational experience in which these conflicts of interests arose. Its emphasis also tends to underplay experiences in which mutuality of interests reign and are vitalizing for both parties.

In contrast to Tolpin, Kriegman differentiates between interpretive and noninterpretive interventions. He notes that, in making an interpretation, Jenkins "was, in fact, *intruding* in an attempt to *alter* Laura's experience by introducing her *own* analytic reality" (p. 88). Interpretive activity was Jenkins's contribution to Laura's experience of intrusion; Laura's contribution was her proneness to experience intrusion. As Kriegman delineates, Jenkins was shaped by this repetitive transference that rendered interpretive efforts problematic. Jenkins's subsequent noninterpretive action, in turn, conveyed an understanding of Laura's experience that (and I agree with Kriegman here) enabled their relationship to proceed.

In Kriegman's view of transference, I experience him as retaining terminology associated with the classical or displacement model of transference that is wedded to positivistic science while simultaneously attempting to integrate and redefine on the basis of the constructivist (Hoffman, 1991, 1998) or organization (Fosshage, 1994) model of transference anchored in relativistic science. Substantive philosophical issues and considerable empirical research emerging in cognitive psychology are at stake in the shift from the classical to the constructivist or organization model of transference that have profound implications for us analysts. The main problem, clinically, in speaking of "distortion of reality" is that it invalidates the cues, however small they may be, and the experience or "reality" of the perceiver. It is quite clear that Kriegman aims to understand the experience of the perceiver. Perhaps he will have an opportunity to clarify why he wishes to maintain the old language.

While Tolpin has expanded the definition of interpretation, Kriegman has made a case for noninterpretive interventions that are not only facilitative, but often convey understanding better than interpretation. Both discussants are making clear that psychoanalytic theory must go beyond interpretation (in the traditional sense of the word) to embrace a wide range of responses that are facilitative in creating "moments of meeting," using Stern et al.'s (1998) term and in enhancing development and deepening the analytic process.

In conclusion, it is most important, in my view, to differentiate between selfobject relatedness—that is, when the patient's selfobject needs for mirroring and idealization are in the foreground—and intersubjective relatedness—that is, when the patient is more interested in the subjectivity of the other and in the "we-ness" between them (Fosshage, 1997, 2003). (Shane, Shane, and Gales, 1997, refer to these forms of intimacy as "self with self-transforming other" and "self with interpersonal-sharing other.") The empathic stance is at its quintessential best when selfobject relatedness is in the foreground, while what I (1995, 1997) call the other-centered listening/experiencing stance is required in order to respond in a facilitative manner when intersubjective relatedness is in the foreground. The other-centered listening/experiencing stance refers to the experience of what it feels like to be the other in a relationship with the patient. For example, if a patient inquires about the therapist's reactions to the patient, the therapist must be attuned to his or her experience as the other in a relationship with the patient to be able to respond effectively.

For Laura, mirroring and idealizing selfobject needs were in the forefront of her experience. Even within the area of selfobject relatedness, however, Laura varied as to how much of the analyst's subjectivity she wished to encounter. Based upon her experience of mother as intrusive and dominating, Laura initially experienced the analyst's subjectivity in the form of interpretations as intrusive and obliterating. As analysis proceeded and self-consolidation increased, Laura desired to experience the analyst as a person more fully. Laura stated, "I really like it when you talk to me and give me advice. You changed our lives when you said, 'Why don't you just put Emily down?' . . . I know this is supposed to be analysis but the things that matter to me . . . well, the dream about you giving me a lift . . . maybe that had to do with you saying, 'Park at the Hyatt when there's a convention.' I loved it. I love the elevator talks. You seem so human then. I guess I want more of your self here. It gives me a lift" (Jenkins, 2002, p. 84). With our changing understanding of the required range of responses and authentic engagement within the analytic encounter, hopefully all of us as analysts and patients are increasingly feeling less constricted and less guilty for those healing, disciplined, spontaneous "moments of meeting."

REFERENCES

Bacal, H. (1998), Optimal responsiveness and the therapeutic process. In: *Optimal Responsiveness: How Therapists Heal Their Patients,* ed. H. Bacal. Northvale, NJ: Aronson.

Brandchaft, B. (1994), To free the spirit from its cell. In: *The Widening Scope of Self Psychology: Progress in Self Psychology,* Vol. 9, ed. A. Goldberg. Hillsdale, NJ: The Analytic Press, pp. 209–230.

Fosshage, J. (1994), Toward reconceptualizing transference: Theoretical and clinical considerations. *Internat. J. Psychoanal.,* 75:265–328.

———— (1995), Countertransference as the analyst's experience of the analysand: Influence of listening perspectives. *Psychoanal. Psychol.,* 12:375–391.

———— (1997), Listening/experiencing perspectives and the quest for a facilitative responsiveness. *Conversations in Self Psychology: Progress in Self Psychology,* Vol. 13, ed. A. Goldberg. Hillsdale, NJ: The Analytic Press, pp. 33–55.

———— (2003), Conceptualizing self psychology and relational psychoanalysis: Bidirectional influence and proposed syntheses. *Contemp. Psychoanal.,* 39:411–448.

Goldberg, A., ed. (1978), *The Psychology of the Self: A Casebook.* New York: International Universities Press.

———— (2002), *Postmodern Self Psychology: Progress in Self Psychology,* Vol. 18, ed. A. Goldberg. Hillsdale, NJ: The Analytic Press.

Hoffman, I. Z. (1991), Discussion: Toward a social-constructivist view of the psychoanalytic situation. *Psychoanal. Dial.,* 1:74–105.

———— (1998), *Ritual and Spontaneity in the Psychoanalytic Process: A Dialectical-Constructivist View.* Hillsdale, NJ: The Analytic Press.

Jenkins, S. (2002), The interpretive process with a phobic young woman. In: *Postmodern Self Psychology: Progress in Self Psychology,* Vol. 18, ed. A. Goldberg. Hillsdale, NJ: The Analytic Press, pp. 77–86.

Knoblauch, S. (2000), *The Musical Edge of Therapeutic Dialogue.* Hillsdale, NJ: The Analytic Press.

Kohut, H. (1982), Introspection, empathy and the semicircle of mental health. *Internat. J. Psychoanal.,* 63:395–408.

———— (1984), *How Does Analysis Cure?* ed. A. Goldberg & P. Stepansky. Chicago: University of Chicago Press.

Kriegman, D. (2002), Interpreting and negotiating conflicts of interests in the analytic relationship: A discussion of Salee Jenkins's clinical case. In: *Postmodern Self Psychology: Progress in Self Psychology,* Vol. 18, ed. A. Goldberg. Hillsdale, NJ: The Analytic Press, pp. 87–112.

Lichtenberg, J., Lachmann, F. & Fosshage, J. (1996), *The Clinical Exchange: Techniques Derived from Self and Motivational Systems.* Hillsdale, NJ: The Analytic Press.

Shane, M., Shane, E. & Gales, M. (1997), *Intimate Attachments: Toward a New Self Psychology.* New York: Guilford Press.

Slavin, M. & Kriegman, D. (1992), *The Adaptive Design of the Human Psyche*. New York: Guilford Press.

Stern, D., Sander, L., Nahum, J., Harrison, A., Lyons-Ruth, K., Morgan, A., Bruschweiler-Stern, N. & Tronick, E. (1998), Non-interpretive mechanisms in psychoanalytic therapy: The "something more" than interpretation. *Internat. J. Psycho-Anal.*, 79:903–921.

Stolorow, R., Brandchaft, B. & Atwood, G. (1987), *Psychoanalytic Treatment: An Intersubjective Approach*. Hillsdale, NJ: The Analytic Press.

Tolpin, M. (2002), The role of empathy and interpretation in the therapeutic process: Discussion of Salee Jenkins's clinical case. In: *Postmodern Self Psychology: Progress in Self Psychology, Vol. 18*, ed. A. Goldberg. Hillsdale, NJ: The Analytic Press, pp. 113–125.

Author Index

E

Ehrenberg, D. B., 9, *19*
Elkin, G., 101n, *108*

F

Falicov, C. J., 127, *147*
Ferenczi, S., 97, *108*, 257, *258*
Fonagy, P., 66, *77*, 154, 155, *164*, 224,
   228, *230*, 253–255, *258*
Fosshage, J. L., 5, 6, 8n, *19*, 21–27,
   35n, 42, *45*, 46, 79, 81, 83,
   84, 86, 89, *91*, 151, *164*, *165*,
   242, *251*, 256, *258*, 286, 288,
   299–300, 304, 326, 327, 331,
   332, *333*
Frankenberg, R., 129, *147*
Frawley, M. G., 5, 7, *19*, 95, 96, *108*

G

Gabbard, G. O., 257, *258*, 260, *263*
Gabbard, K., 257, *258*
Gadamer, H.-G., 130, *147*, 155, *164*
Gales, M., 23, *46*, 151, *165*, 332, *333*
Gehrie, M., 7, *19*
Gergely, G., 154, 155, *164*, 253, *258*
Ghent, E., 65, 70, *77*
Gill, M. M., 25, *45*, 71, *77*
Giordano, J., 135, *148*
Goldberg, A., xvi, *xvi*, 7, *19*, 328, *333*
Goldman, D., 68, *77*
Gorkin, M., 137, *147*
Grand, S., 179, *187*
Greenberg, J. R., 283, *288*

H

Hainer, M., 171
Hardy, K. V., 134, *147*
Harris, A., 67, *77*, 224, *230*
Harrison, A., 35n, *46*, 84, 92, 256, *258*,
   332, *334*
Hedges, L., 37n, 40, *45*

Herman, J. L., 95, *108*
Hirsch, I., 7, *19*
Ho, M. K., 127, 128, 134, *147*
Hoffman, I. Z., 6, 9, *19*, 35n, 46, 79,
   91, 196, 198, 205, 331, *333*
Hoffman, L., 283–284, *288*
Hong, Y., 131, *147*
Howard, G. S., 129–130, *147*
Hsu, J., 127, *147*

I

Ibrahim, F., 127, *147*

J

Jacobs, T. J., 170, *187*
Jaffe, J., 24, *45*
Jenkins, J. H., 129, *147*
Jenkins, S., 325, 332, *333*
Jurist, E. L., 154, 155, *164*, 253, *258*

K

Kashima, Y., 129, *147*
Kirsner, D., 276, *288*
Kitayama, S., 130, *147*
Knoblauch, S., 327, *333*
Kohut, H., xii, *xvi*, 23, 32, 43, *46*, 51,
   53, 54, 83, *91*, 95n, 96, *108*,
   132, 137, *147*, 151, *165*, 174,
   187, 197, 199, 205, 227, *230*,
   235, *251*, 261, 264, 279, 280,
   287–288, *288*, 298, 329, 330,
   333
Kriegman, D., 40, *46*, 75, *77*, 328, 329,
   333, *334*

L

Lachmann, F. M., 5, 6, 10, 14, 18, 21–
   24, 26, 27, 30, 34n, 35, 35n,
   42, *45*–46, 79, 83, *91*, 95,
   108, 151, 153, 155, *164*, *165*,
   172, 176, *187*, 195, 205, 242,

SUBJECT INDEX

A

affect
conceptions of, 320
vs. drive, as source of conflict,
317
psychology of, 308
affect mirroring, 253–254
aggression, 301–304. *See also*
aversiveness
causes, 302
relationalists *vs.* self psychologists
on, 194–196
"aggressive-submissive" enactments,
81–82
American Psychoanalytic Association
(APsaA)
Board on Professional Standards
(BOPS), 269, 275
certification process, 274–275, 281
lawsuit against, 273, 276
membership qualifications, 269,
273–275
self psychology, the fate of new
ideas, and, 278–286
analyst(s)
dissociation between cognitive and
affective states, 170–172,
174–177
emotional openness, 176
failure. *See* shame, of analyst
narcissistic vulnerability, 176, 181

revealing their experience, 172–173,
175, 186–187
analytic authority, 190, 196–198, 204–
205
analytic relationship, 176, 181. *See also*
relating, forms of; *specific
topics*
asymmetry, 198–199
real relationship, provision, and
"extraordinary measures," 73–
75
attachment needs, 23, 44–45
attachment systems, 164. *See also*
cases, Tyler and Ben
attachment theory, 11n
Atwood, George E., 318
on Stolorow interview, 320
authority, 160, 196–198, 204–205
aversiveness, extreme, 22, 85. *See also*
cases, Jack

B

bilingual individuals, 130–131
biracial couples. *See* cases, Tyler and
Ben; intercultural couples
blame, 192–196. *See also* cases, Carol;
shame
boundary crossings, 37, 52, 74–75, 80–
81, 88–91. *See also* cases, Jack
Brenner, Charles, 317
"brief vignettes," 172–173